Beyond ISIS:
History and Future of Religious Minorities in Iraq

Publication of this book is partially funded by

"I can confidently recommend this up-to-date, fascinating collection of articles authored mainly by new Kurdish and European scholars on Iraq's post-ISIS, religious minorities including Christians, Jews, Yazidis, Shabaks, Kakais, Bahais, and Zoroastrians, as well as labor migrant Hindus and Buddhists, among others."
- Michael M. Gunter, Professor of Political Sciences, Tennessee Technological University, United States.

Beyond ISIS:
History and Future of Religious Minorities in Iraq

Edited by
Bayar Mustafa Sevdeen
Thomas Schmidinger

TRANSNATIONAL PRESS LONDON
2019

Beyond ISIS: History and Future of Religious Minorities in Iraq
Edited by Bayar Mustafa Sevdeen and Thomas Schmidinger

Copyright © 2019 by Transnational Press London

All rights reserved. This book or any portion thereof may not be reproduced or used in any manner whatsoever without the express written permission of the publisher except for the use of brief quotations in a book review or scholarly journal.

First Published in 2019 by TRANSNATIONAL PRESS LONDON in the United Kingdom, 12 Ridgeway Gardens, London, N6 5XR, UK.
www.tplondon.com

 Transnational Press London® and the logo and its affiliated brands are registered trademarks.

Requests for permission to reproduce material from this work should be sent to: sales@tplondon.com

Paperback
ISBN: 978-1-912997-15-2

Cover Design: Gizem Çakır

www.tplondon.com

Publication of this book is partially funded by

ABOUT THE AUTHORS

Birgit Ammann is Professor of Political Science at the University of Applied Sciences Potsdam and Research associate at the Berlin Society for the Advancement of Kurdish Studies – European Center for Kurdish Studies.

Lana Askari has a PhD in Social Anthropology with Visual Media from the Department of Anthropology at the University of Manchester. She is also a movie director. Her background from a Haqqa family gave her close access to research material about the Haqqa movement.

Ghazwan Youssef Baho is a Chaldean priest and a professor at Babel College for Philosophy & Theology in Ain Kawa (Erbil, Iraq). His research on the Christian religion in Kurdistan, published recently in the book entitled Religions in Kurdistan, Misbar Publishing House, Dubai 2018.

Matthew Travis Barber is a PhD student in the Department of Near Eastern Languages and Civilizations at the University of Chicago, studying Islamic thought and modern Middle Eastern history. He has worked extensively with minorities in Iraq, in particular with the Yazidis as a proponent of the humanitarian and advocacy response to the Yazidi Genocide. He served for one year as the first executive director in Iraq of Yazda, a multi-national Yazidi organization, developing humanitarian, advocacy, and social outreach programs.

Seyedehbehnaz Hosseini completed her doctoral research in the Department of Oriental Studies at the University of Vienna where she focused on migration and minorities in Iran and Iraq especially Yārsāani. As a research fellow with the Department of Sociology, University of Alberta, Canada, she currently researches Iraqi minorities and forced migration of women.

Seda D. Ohanian was born in Basra, Iraq. She is a researcher at Armenia's National Academy of Sciences, Division of Armenology and Social Sciences at the Institute of History. She has published extensively on the Armenians in Iraq.

Saad Salloum is Assistant Professor at the faculty of Political Sciences at the University of Mustansiriyah, Baghdad and an expert on religious diversity in Iraq. He co-founded the Iraqi Council for Interfaith Dialogue and the National Center for Countering Hatred in Iraq, and is General Coordinator for MASARAT Foundation for Cultural and Media Development (MCMD). He has 15 publications on Diversity in Iraq and the Middle East, including *Minorities in Iraq: Memory, Identity & Challenges* (2013), *Christians in Iraq: Comprehensive History and Current Challenges* (2014), and *The End of Diversity in Iraq* (2019). In 2018, he won three awards: The Stefanus International Prize (Stefanus Alliance International) in Oslo/Norway, Kamil Shiyaa's Award for Enlightenment in Baghdad and the Chaldean Patriarchate Award.

Thomas Schmidinger is Lecturer for Political Science at the University of Vienna and for Social Work at the University of Applied Sciences Upper Austria. He is secretary general of the Austrian Association for Kurdish Studies and Co-editor of the Vienna Kurdish Studies Yearbook. His recent books are about Rojava, Afrin and the Genocide against the Yazidis in Sinjar. Foreign Policy advisor on Kurdish issues, minority questions, Middle East for S&D Vice President Josef Weidenholzer in the EU parliament.

Bayar Mustafa Sevdeen is Assistant Professor and researcher at the College of International Studies at the American University of Kurdistan (AUK), he is also AHDA fellow at the Institute of the Study of Human Rights at Columbia University. He served as a diplomat in the Turkey Division at the Iraqi Ministry of Foreign Affairs from 2010 to 2013. Currently, he is a principal investigator in ongoing projects focusing Yazidi and other religious groups in the Middle East, in cooperation with LSC and UCF. He is also working on his latest book entitled Contemporary Politics of Kurds and Kurdistan.

Maria Six-Hohenbalken is a social anthropologist and researcher at the Austrian Academy of Science. She is president of the Austrian Association for Kurdish Studies and co-editor of the Vienna Kurdish Studies Yearbook.

Michiel Leezenberg is an associate professor at the University of Amsterdam in the Department of Philosophy. He coordinates the Research Masters in Philosophy, and the B.A. honours program in philosophy and participates in the M.A. program Islam in the Modern World. Leezenberg is also a well-known specialist on Kurdish Studies and particularly the Shabak.

Areshpreet Wedech was born in 1993 in Dasuya (India). At the University of Vienna, Austria, she obtained a BA in German Philology and Languages and Cultures of South Asian and Tibet. Subsequently, she completed an MA in Culture and Society of Modern South Asia at the University of Vienna, where her master thesis focussed on the first translation of the holy scripture of the Sikhs. Driven by an interest in the Sikh diaspora, she has started at the University of Vienna doctoral studies on the traditions of the Sikh community in Austria.

Arzu Yilmaz was Chair of Department of International Relations at the American University of Kurdistan based in Duhok and IPC-Mercator Fellow at the German think tank SWP. She obtained her PhD in International Relations from Ankara University in Turkey, where she wrote her dissertation on Kurdish refugees and the political identity of the refugee agent.

Archimandrite Emanuel Youkhana is a priest (Archimandrite) of the Assyrian Church of the East and president of CAPNI (Christian Aid Program Northern Iraq) based in Duhok.

CONTENT

About Authors i

Content 1

PREFACE
    Josef Weidenholzer 3

INTRODUCTION
    Bayar Mustafa Sevdeen and Thomas Schmidinger 5

CHAPTER 1

Minorities in Iraq: National Legal Framework, Political Participation, and the Future of Citizenship Given the Current Changes
    Saad Salloum 11

CHAPTER 2

The Jews of Iraq
    Birgit Ammann 33

CHAPTER 3

The Lost Readers of the Scripture: Some notes on the Karaite community of Hīt
    Thomas Schmidinger 57

CHAPTER 4

John the Baptist's Water: Extinction of a Millennial Culture
    Saad Salloum 71

CHAPTER 5

The Gurdwara of Baghdad and the Forgotten History of Sikhs in Iraq
    Areshpreet Wedech 99

CHAPTER 6

Christians in Iraq
    Thomas Schmidinger 113

CHAPTER 7

Fleeing ISIS: Aramaic-speaking Christians in the Niniveh Plains after ISIS
    Archimandrite Emanuel Youkhana 125

CHAPTER 8

Armenians of Iraq
  Seda D. Ohanian 151

CHAPTER 9

The Yazidis: Religion, Society and Resentments
  Thomas Schmidinger..165

CHAPTER 10

The Yazidi Quest for Protection in Sinjar in the Post-ISIS Iraq
  Arzu Yılmaz and Bayar Mustafa Sevdeeen 175

CHAPTER 11

Kakai Internal Displacement in Kirkuk and the Fear of Violence from the So-called Islamic State in Iraq (ISIS)
  Seyedehbehnaz Hosseini..189

CHAPTER 12

The Shabak: Between secular nationalisms and sectarian violence
  Michiel Leezenberg..197

CHAPTER 13

The Haqqa Movement: from Heterodox Sufism, to Socio-Political Struggle and Back
  Lana Askari...207

CHAPTER 14

Bahaism and the Bahai Community in Iraq: A Fateful Past and Fragile Present
  Maria Six-Hohenbalken..221

CHAPTER 15

Kurdish Zoroastrians: An Emerging Minority in Iraq
  Matthew Travis Barber...229

CHAPTER 16

Migrant Religions in Iraq: Hindus and Buddhists
  Ghazwan Yousif Baho 237

PREFACE

Josef Weidenholzer

Member of the European Parliament and Vice President of the S&D group in the European Parliament

We have to pay attention to the situation of the people in Iraq. Iraq heavily suffered under the aggression of the so-called Islamic state (ISIS) and the war with these jihadi terrorists. In this very area, the worn-out and often misused term 'free world' suddenly gains a new elementary meaning, because it is the place where our freedom is vindicated. The henchmen of the ISIS set back Mosul by centuries. As if there had never been a declaration of human rights, a Hague convention, or an abolition of slavery. A group made up of ideologically deluded extremists gone mad disregards every human accomplishment in terms of civilisation.

The people in this area - Yezidis, Christians, Shabaks, Shiites and Sunnis - who refused to give in to this jihadi interpretation of Islam, had to endure barely imaginable suffering within a year: murder, abduction, slavery, flight and expulsion. Especially, the uncertainty whether one will ever be able to return. In their delusion, the ISIS troops destroyed cultural monuments in cities and the countryside alike, simply everything, which countered their simplistic worldview. The Christian communities native to this area are being banished and purged. Many Christians fear that their two-thousand-year-old historical presence in the region will end.

Consequently, more than two million refugees have joined the five million inhabitants of Kurdistan. Others fled to Baghdad and the south of Iraq. The governments of Iraq and the Autonomous Region of Kurdistan steadily become unable to deal with the infrastructural challenges posed by the wave of refugees. However, different segments of the Iraqi population have demonstrated compelling solidarity. Without their generous support, it would be impossible to master these challenges. This is why we need to help the people in regions threatened by the so-called 'Islamic State'.

Religious minorities were the most vulnerable targets of the extreme violence of the so-called 'Islamic State'. Therefore, we decided to focus on the situation of religious minorities in a conference organized together with the American University of Kurdistan in Duhok. However, these religious minorities were not the only victims of ISIS. Also, Shiite and Sunni Muslims were targeted by the extreme forms of violence committed by the so-called

'Islamic State'.

People in all parts of Iraq now require our attention, solidarity, and assistance. We need to support the autonomous region of Kurdistan, the government of Iraq and the different communities of Iraq in their attempt to reconstruct. We should not forget that there were also European citizens involved in the violence committed against Iraqi citizens. Young people from countries like France, Germany, Belgium, Britain, Denmark or Austria joined the ranks of the criminals who committed mass murder, rape and other forms of violence in Iraq. Thus, we Europeans have some responsibility for the future of the survivors of these atrocities. The European Union must ensure that sufficient resources are being provided for the reconstruction of the region; specifically, financial projects should be directed towards reconstruction as well as sending funding and investments directly to the administration. Europe shall support the people in their efforts to reconstruct their region. Only through joint efforts and coordination will we truly be able to achieve peace in the region.

INTRODUCTION

Bayar Mustafa Sevdeen and Thomas Schmidinger

The issue of existential threats against the remaining religious minorities in Iraq became dramatically important in June 2014. The so-called 'Islamic State' (ISIS) occupied one-third of the territory of present-day Iraq and advanced towards the Kurdistan region through the province of Mosul, the base of most religious minorities. The ISIS undertook systematic ethno-religious cleansing of this borderland between the Kurdistan region and the central government in Baghdad. The area was mainly populated by Christians and Yazidis and had been the last resort for most religious minorities in the country. The United States government and United Nations agencies reported the murders of about 9,000 people, the abduction of 6800 (one-third of them still missing in January 2019), and about 400,000 displaced in the Kurdistan region. Prior to 2005, about 700,000 Yezidis lived in Iraq; after August 2014, less than 500,000 Yezidis remained. In January 2019, most still live in refugee camps. Since 2005, the number of Christians has decreased from an estimated 1.4 million to less than 300,000 in 2017, mostly in refugee camps in the provinces of Kurdistan. Besides the Christians, also Shabak and Kaka'i, also called Yarsan or Ahl-e Haqq, were displaced by the occupation of the Nineveh Plains by the ISIS.

Then Iraqi prime minister Haider al-Abadi at a mass rally in Mosul on 10 July 2017 proclaimed the final victory over the ISIS, calling on the displaced people to return to their cities and homes. The US Embassy in Baghdad and other Western diplomats supported him. Later events proved those official statements were not realistic, but were – intentionally or unintentionally – an attempt to create confidence and a misunderstanding of the general concerns of displaced people and the particular issues important to ethno-religious minorities. The real implications of wars defending the minorities starkly appeared after the end of the battle against ISIS; more dangerously, Iraq's central government became more entrenched and smarter in dealing with the consequences of ethnic cleansing led by ISIS against minorities. For example, in the city of Sinjar, which was liberated in March 2015, less than 10% of its inhabitants were able to return to their original villages and towns. The villages in the south of the Sinjar region are still uninhabited. In the Christian town of Batnaya, 10% of the population may be returned; the situation is not better in the town of Tel Keppe (Telkif).

As for the political participation of minorities, the general parliamentary elections in May 2018 almost directly reflect the deplorable reality on the ground. Only one Yazidi was seated in the new parliament; the Yazidis had seven representatives in the parliament of 2013. In addition, the Christian minority accused religious parties and militias of seizing Christian quotas during the last election.

However, the so-called 'Islamic State' was not the only existential threat for religious minorities in Iraq. The management of diversity and particularly religious diversity has been a very difficult task of the modern Iraqi state. One year after Iraq's independence, the new Iraqi army was deployed against Assyrian survivors of the Ottoman genocide of 1915. In August 1933, the armed forces of the Kingdom of Iraq led by Bakr Sidqi systematically targeted the Assyrians of northern Iraq. This campaign led to the destruction and looting of dozens of Assyrian-Christian villages around Duhok and Mosul. The town of Simele became the last refuge for Assyrians from the looted villages, where they were massacred on 11 August 1933 by Iraqi soldiers.

In 1941, the Jewish population of Baghdad was targeted by Nazi sympathizers. In the power vacuum following the British victory in the Anglo-Iraqi War, more than 180 Jews were killed and 1,000 were injured between 1 and 2 June 1941. This pogrom, called 'Farhud' set in motion the increasing anti-Semitism that resulted in the Jewish exodus from Iraq following the establishment of Israel in the early 1950s.

Both cases, the Simele massacre against the Christians and the Farhud pogrom against Iraq's Jews, also show the link between internal Iraqi politics and European politics and colonialism. The problems between Assyrian Christians and Iraqi Muslims, were aggravated by the British use of Assyrian fighters for their colonial rule during the mandate period. Kurdish-Assyrian tensions were also shaped by Assyrian fighters joining the Russian Cossacks under Nikolai Baratov to massacre the Kurdish population of Rawandiz during World War I. The British applied a divide and rule strategy after World War I; this included the use of Christian minorities to control a predominantly Muslim land. The resulting resentment also added to the precarious status of Iraq's Assyrian Christians. Finally, Britain did not protect their former allies when Iraq gained its independence. Moreover, the British watched the massacre as a kind of test for the new Iraqi army.

The Farhud pogrom is unthinkable without the global political context of World War II. Modern antisemitism in Iraq was mainly imported through Arab nationalist circles who sympathized with Nazi Germany because they thought that they could get rid of British dominance with the help of its main enemy, the Germans. People like Rashid Ali al-Gaylani or Mohammed (Haj) Amin al-Husseini, who spread hatred against Iraqi Jews, were strongly inspired by Nazi ideology and fled to Germany after their failed attempt to switch Iraq towards the Axis during World War II.

This international context of the atrocities against Iraq's religious minorities, of course, does not exculpate the Iraqi perpetrators. However, it would be irresponsible to neglect the interactions between Iraqi and international politics and the atrocities against Iraqi minorities. These local acts resulted from a fatal combination of colonialism and misled anticolonial inspirations of Arab nationalists. This unfortunate marriage of Arab nationalism and anti-colonialism found its continuation in the Arab Socialist Ba'ath Party and after 2003 in its cooperation with jihadist groups that led to the establishment of the so-called 'Islamic State'.

Saddam Hussein and his Ba'ath Party mainly targeted non-Arabic religious minorities, such as the Kurdish-speaking Yazidis, Shabak, and Kaka'i and the Aramaic-speaking Christians who did not accept the doctrine of Arab nationalism and fought alongside the Kurdish resistance movements against the regime. However, Saddam Hussein focused most attention on the religious majority rather than the religious minority. For him, the Shiites of Iraq were seen as the fifth column of Iran and, along with the Kurds and Communists, an archenemy.

Finally, the confessionalisation of Iraqi politics after the end of the Baath regime in 2003 also led to a violent marginalisation of religious minorities when jihadist terrorist groups started to target religious minorities. As we know, large parts of the old security apparatus of Saddam Hussein's regime finally ended up as part of the so-called 'Islamic State'. Genocidal methods of the Ba'athist regime influenced the genocide committed by ISIS in 2014.

After the emigration of nearly the entire Jewish population of Iraq, the Mandeans are today the religious minority who might be the closest to extinction in Iraq. In the early 1990s, about 60,000 Mandeans lived in Iraq; only about 5,000 remain today. Most others found new homes in Europe, Australia, and the USA.

In general, along with senior leaders and politicians proclaiming victory over ISIS, there have been many activities, conferences, analyses, books, and even initiatives. They seem to have been confined to security and military issues. The long and medium-term repercussions have been neglected, especially in their demographic and social aspects. Little consideration has been given to the important issue of justice for victims such as compensation, legal accountability, and a suitable environment to rebuild victims' lives again in their villages and towns. Iraqi authorities have not done much; the liberated cities do not even have official government statistics on the victims and properties seized by ISIS.

This book shares papers from a conference taking a deeper look at the victims of ISIS and beyond that all religious minorities of Iraq. This is the first book that considers all the religious minorities that existed in modern Iraq, including both historic communities and new groups that recently came

Introduction

with labour migration, especially to the Autonomous Region of Kurdistan.

The book resulted from a conference in 2018 organized exactly at the site of the Simele Massacre in 1933. The campus of the American University of Kurdistan is located on the site of the first big massacre against a religious minority in Iraq. The conference entitled 'Beyond ISIS: Minorities and Religious Diversity in Iraq and the Future of Êzîdî, Christians, Shabak, Yarsan, Mandeans and other Religious Minorities in the Middle East' brought together Iraqi and international scholars, activists, and religious and community representatives. This book contains papers presented at the conference that included contributions on Iraq's religious diversity and the historical and contemporary consequences of genocide and persecution on the religious minorities of Iraq.

The conference was a joint effort by scholars and activists and co-hosted by The American University of Kurdistan (AUK) and Joseph Weidenholzer, a Member of the European Parliament and Vice-President Group of the Progressive Alliance of Socialists and Democrats in the European Parliament. We want to thank Joseph Weidenholzer and the AUK President & Provost, Ambassador John K Menzies, Prof. Nazar Numan for their financial, organisational, and intellectual support. Additionally, we also want to thank Rebecca Kampl and Michael Goldbeck from the office of MEP Weidenholzer and Bina Mustafa, Ajin Saadi from the American University for their organisational support.

Our initiative was divided into three phases. The first phase provided an 'open platform' for the leaders and representatives of minorities to freely express their fears, perceived threats, and their expectations for the future by organising a 'private dialogue table' on 12 October 2018. The second part included over 20 international academics and minority specialists who were invited to the American University on 13 October 2018 to present research papers on ethno-religious minorities endangered with extinction in Iraq. Their vision and strategies to prevent the end of minorities were also shared with government representatives and deputies of the parliaments in Iraq and Kurdistan region. You are now reading the third part: an international publication of research papers to find its place in libraries in order to make these topics available to concerned decisionmakers and political activists. These contributions – extremely varied in scholarly style and depth – have not been subject to academic peer review but simply share the research and views of scholars and activists sympathetic to the very diverse and endangered religious minorities in Iraq.

Instead of using 'thematic units', we have decided to make each article a separate chapter. This very diverse group of articles and contributors have tried their best to achieve some complementarity and consistency between its topics and discussions contained in each part, so that this work can emerge as a unified entity. Therefore, chapters providing an overview of Christianity in Iraq and the Yazidi religion were added.

The book follows a kind of chronology of disappearance. After a general introduction on the legal and political situation for religious minorities in Iraq by Baghdad-based political scientist Saad Salloum, it starts with religious communities who were present in Iraq but are now largely or completely displaced from Iraqi soil. It ends with new religious communities; new for Iraq, because they were brought in by recent labour migration.

The political scientist Birgit Ammann starts the book with her work on the history of Iraqi Jews, followed by Thomas Schmidinger's paper on the Karaite community that has disappeared from Iraq. Both communities, the rabbinical Jews and the Karaite Jews, now mainly live in Israel and cannot visit their old homeland. Areshpreet Wedech, a young Austrian Sikh, offers interesting insights on the historic Gurudwara of Baghdad and the forgotten history of Sikhs in Iraq. Saad Salloum from Baghdad's Mustansiriya University provides a detailed account of the Mandeans, who lost more than 90% of their adherents since the end of the twentieth century in Iraq. Although the Mandeans still have a community in Baghdad, in some of the southern Iraqi cities and, thanks to internal migration, also a new one in Erbil, many more Iraqi Mandeans now live in Australia, Europe and the US than in their old homeland.

After Thomas Schmidinger presents a short introduction on Christianity in Iraq, the Archimandrite Emanuel Youkhana, a priest-activist who established one of the most important Christian NGOs in Iraq, provides an overview of the Aramaic-speaking Christians in Iraq after their displacement by ISIS in 2014. His paper is followed by a text of Seda D. Ohanian from the Armenian Academy of Science in Yerevan about Iraq's Armenians.

An introduction to the Yazidi religion and a detailed paper by Arzu Yılmaz and Bayar Mustafa Sevdeeen from the American University of Kurdistan in Duhok describes the situation of the Yazidis from Sinjar after the genocide of 2014. Although the Christian and Yazidi communities of Iraq are still larger than the remaining Mandean communities, they have also lost many members due to migration.

Michiel Leezenberg from Amsterdam University wrote a chapter about the Shabak. Seyedehbehnaz Hosseini from the University of Alberta wrote about the Kaka'i, also called Yarsan or Ahl-e Haqq. Maria Six-Hohenbalken from the Austrian Academy of Sciences wrote about the Bahai of Iraq, who had their traditional centre in Baghdad but partially moved to Iraqi Kurdistan recently. Matthew Travis Barber gives a brief introduction to Iraqi Kurds who converted to Zoroastrianism and thus bring back a new form of an old religion that existed in Iraq as the official religion of the Sasanian Empire but completely disappeared, even as a minority religion, during the Ottoman Empire. Finally, Ghazwan Youssif Baho, from Babel College based in Ain

Introduction

Kawa, describes the religions, like Buddhism and Hinduism, brought by labour migrants in recent years,. Although these religions are not yet institutionalised and legalised in Iraq, adherents practice these religions in their homes. The examples of Gulf States like the United Arab Emirates, Qatar, or Bahrain show that labour immigrants from South Asia will soon establish their temples. Hindu temples, Sikh Gurudwaras, and Buddhist shrines are today an integral part of the religious landscape of the Gulf Region. Iraq will likely see such a development because of the growing number of labour immigrants from India, Nepal, and Sri Lanka to Iraq and particularly to Iraqi Kurdistan.

Thus, despite the danger to some of Iraq's oldest cultures and religions, religious diversity is unlikely to just disappear. One of the most important issues for Iraqi society and politics will be how to deal with religious diversity and how power relations between majorities and minorities will be structured. After all, religious freedom in not only a universal human right, but also a foundation for any pluralistic and democratic society.

This book's different texts vary in length and style as much as their authors do. These contributions were written by international and Iraqi scholars, but also by activists and community members, by established and experienced academics and some promising young scholars. This book is not a final standard reference for the history of religious pluralism in Iraq. However, we hope that it offers some impulses for future discussions as well as help to re-establish links with diaspora communities and Iraq and to contribute to a peaceful coexistence of all components of Iraqi society.

CHAPTER 1

MINORITIES IN IRAQ: NATIONAL LEGAL FRAMEWORK, POLITICAL PARTICIPATION, AND THE FUTURE OF CITIZENSHIP GIVEN THE CURRENT CHANGES

Saad Salloum

Minorities have been one of the main targets of the violence that has swept through Iraq after the American occupation in 2003. This violence reached a pivotal turning point when the so-called 'Islamic State' (ISIS) invaded Nineveh governorate, including Mosul, the second largest city in Iraq, and extended their control over other areas in the Anbar and Saladin governorates.

In the areas under ISIS control, the world has witnessed unprecedented levels of violent extremism including horrific images of public executions, violations of freedom of religion and belief by forcing non-Muslim minorities to convert to Islam and kidnapping, torture, rape, sexual trafficking, looting, and destruction of private property belonging to individuals and religious sects. This tragedy has resulted in the disappearance of diversity in Iraqi society and the decline of minorities' demographic presence, because they must flee or be killed. This threatens some minorities with extinction and has changed the diverse demographic composition of the whole society and particularly in some mixed areas.[1]

These developments culminated a decade of chaos and rampant violence after the American occupation in 2003 and placed Iraq and the other countries of this region on the threshold of a post-nation-state environment. These nation-states were formed directly after the area's liberation from colonial rule based on the model (state/nation) founded on a single, shared identity. This conception of identity, however, did not respond to the diversity prevalent in societies throughout the Middle East and satisfy the

---

[1] Saad Salloum, *End of Diversity in Iraq, History under the Sword: Tracking Cultural Heritage Destruction, Human Migration, and the Dynamic Nature of Conflict in Iraq.*' Exploratory Seminar at the Radcliffe Institute for Advanced Study, Thursday and Friday, July 9-10, 2015.

ambitions of the members of these societies to achieve equality, or provide a sense of citizenship.

Semantic Struggles in Describing Communities and Its Link to the Socio-Cultural Context

The choice of the term 'elements,' instead of the terms 'majority' and 'minority,' and its continual use in political and media discourse in Iraq after 2003 reflected a desire to impose some kind of formal equality between the majority and minority groups. Political and religious representatives of minority communities would constantly defend themselves against being called 'minorities' in internal rhetoric in Iraq. This was a response to the downsides to the blind quantitative perspective that relegates individuals to second-class citizenship and places their communities lower on the hierarchy. However, in their rhetoric to the international community, they armed themselves with the legal protection offered by the term 'minority'.

Therefore, these groups realised that they had been branded by the negatively charged designation, 'minority' that frequently led to a bifurcated approach. The Iraqi Constitution of 2005 cautiously uses the alternative word, 'elements,' both as a response to demands by minority representatives and as an escapist attempt to solve linguistically the discrimination present in the Iraqi reality. This can be seen in Article 2.2 and Article 125 of the Constitution.

Those who want to end the power and influence of the 'majority identities' characteristically renounce the Iraqi state policies from 1921 to 2003 of non-recognition, forced integration, and assimilation. Redefining the community as an independent ethnic identity also represents the desire to stay out of the conflict between the majority communities (Shias, Sunnis, Kurds). The Yazidis, Kakais, Shabaks, and Turkmen tend to recognise their identities as 'independent,' having no relation to any major group and thus freeing themselves from the power struggle between the majority groups and avoiding be a bargaining chip in the Kurdish-Arab or Sunni-Shia conflicts. This is like saying: 'We are not a part of your struggle. We only want respect for our special culture and do not want to play the game of majorities versus minorities. We cannot pay the price of being added to the group that you want to appear as a majority.'

A Map of National, Religious and Linguistic Diversity in Iraq

Compared to the awareness of the majority groups' struggle for power and wealth, the international actors have had an almost total ignorance of Iraq's national, religious and linguistic diversity and this has had a major impact on international response to minority issues. As a result, when dealing with Iraq, some international actors take a shortcut and only consider the views of the three majority groups (Sunnis, Shias and Kurds). Because minority identities have intersecting ethnic characteristics, some minority groups have been considered as a part of majority groups (Yazidis, Shabaks, and Kakais as part of the Kurds; Turkmen, Shabak Shias, and Feyli Kurds as Shias). This matter has become even more complicated when a group can be classified within more than one majority group (Feyli Kurds are both Kurdish and Shia).

Therefore, a map of this diversity must depart from the framework of classifying Iraq's diversity into three majority groups. This must be done so that the international community can determine an appropriate approach to deal with Iraq's rich social structure and depart from the mould that has left a negative impact on these groups' former sense of equality and citizenship. Briefly, the map of national, religious and linguistic diversity can be drawn as follows.[2]

- Christians (Chaldeans, Syriacs, and Assyrians):

Iraqi Christians do not have a unified or homogeneous identity (there are 14 officially recognised Christian cults, 12 political parties and 7 armed units). Therefore, Christian have difficulty agreeing on many current issues such as the future of disputed areas, the nature of their representation in parliament, and the limits of their right to freedom of belief.[3] However, the identity of the Christians of Iraq can be determined on diverse ethnic and sectarian grounds: the Armenians, Chaldeans, Syriac and Assyrians ethnicities have Orthodox Christians, Catholics and Protestant denominations. Although they are scattered in different parts of Iraq, most Christians live in Baghdad, Erbil (Ainkawa region), Mosul, and the Nineveh Plains in Nineveh province.

The most prominent demands of Christians are to increase their political representation in parliament, the federal government and the Kurdistan region, according to their demographic size (from 5 to 15 seats in the parliament), to protect their disputed areas between Arabs and Kurds (Nineveh Plains), and finally to turn the Nineveh Plains into a province administered by Christians or in association with the Shabak (the second largest minority in the Nineveh Plains).

- Yazidis *(*Ezidis*)*:

They live in the north, northwest of Iraq in the area surrounding the Sinjar mountain west of Mosul, and in Shikhan, some villages and districts of Tel Kef district, the Baashiqa district, Zakho and Simele districts of Dhuk

---

[2] For more information on minorities in Iraq, see the following issues from the Masarat Institute for Cultural and Media Development: *Masarat Magazine* 2 (2005) on the Yazidis; Issue 8 (2006) on the Mandeans; Issue 13 (2009) on the Jews of Iraq; Issue 14 (2010) on the Christians of Iraq and other minorities. See also: Saad Salloum, *Minorities in Iraq: Memory, Identity, Challenges*. (Baghdad/Beirut: Masarat Institute for Cultural and Media Development, 2013). Saad Salloum, *100 Delusions about Minorities in Iraq*. (Baghdad/ Beirut: Masarat Institute for Cultural and Media Development, 2015), 24-45.

[3] Saad Salloum, Armed disputes reveal Iraqi Christians' discord, *Al-Monitor*, (published 15 August 2017). https://www.al-monitor.com/pulse/originals/2017/08/christians-armed-factions-iraq-minority.html.

governorate. Yazidis are among the oldest ethnic and religious groups in Iraq with religion roots going back thousands of years in Mesopotamia. Some common stereotypes about this religious minority, such as that they worship Satan, has caused their persecution. In their history, they have suffered 73 genocides with the recent genocide by ISIS in 2014 considered as number 74.

Due to the lack of official statistics, special estimates must be made of the size of their population in Iraq. The Religious Endowments Directorate in the Kurdistan region states that there are around 500,000 Yazidis. That has decreased after ISIS invaded their areas and committed genocidal atrocities. (The statistics of the Yazidi Endowment in Kurdistan region estimates 100,000 Yazidis emigrated after the genocide).[4]

The Yazidis' most important demands include improving their political participation by giving them a seat in the Kurdistan regional parliament in Erbil and increasing their seats in the federal parliament in Baghdad from one to five;[5] protecting their disputed areas between Arabs and Kurds (Sinjar); combating discrimination based on faith and hate speech by some Muslim clerics; and finally the return of ISIS-abducted women (estimated in thousands) and Yazidi children (estimated in hundreds).

- **Jews:**

Iraq was home to one of the largest Jewish communities in the Middle East, and today very few Jews, not more than six people, live in Baghdad. They represent the latest evidence of the erosion of the Jewish presence that has lasted more than 2,500 years in Iraq until almost the entire population migrated to the newly established state of Israel.[6] The Jews of Iraq spoke with an ancient Arabic accent that evolved in the days of the Caliph Harun al-Rasheed, known as the Arabic-Jewish, close to the dialect of the people of Tikrit and the dialect of the people of Mosul. Their language is full of Biblical Hebrew vocabulary, Biblical symbols, a mixture of Persian, Turkish, and Aramaic words, and then added after the British occupation some English terms and words, and a few European terms.

After the founding of the Iraqi state of 1921, the Jewish community established an independent social life headed by a great rabbi, who supervised the educational system of the community and the religious court, and the tax on Kosher meat. They had fully merged into the political, social and

---

[4] Private interview with Khairy Bouzani, Director of Endowments Department, Ministry of Endowments and Religious Affairs, Kurdistan Region, 9 August 2018.

[5] Private interview with Hassou Hormi, President of the Yazidi Foundation in the Netherlands, Erbil on 10 August 2018, and Murad Ismail, Executive Director of the Yazda Foundation in Baghdad on 2 August 2018.

[6] The assessment was confirmed by the researcher in his meeting with the Vice-President of the European Jewish Congress, 'Edwin Shuker,' of Iraqi origin, where Mr. Shuker himself was the sixth person as well as the five Jews living in Baghdad, a private interview of the researcher in London, on 20 July 2018.

economic context and were fully Arabised with social traditions indistinguishable from their Arab peers.[7]

The demands of the Iraqi Jews now revolve around the restoration of Iraqi nationality, which was legally severed under the law on the deprivation of citizenship for Jews who leave Iraq for Israel. They also seek restitution of property confiscated by force or sold at low prices by the Iraqi government, while some in the third generation of Iraqi Jews living in exile still dream of connecting with their Iraqi legacy, in the context of the awakening of an Arab identity for the eastern Jews (the Mizrahim) in Israel and some western countries. Iraq still has many sacred shrines for Jews, most notably: the tomb of the Prophet Ezekiel in Babel province, the tomb of Ezra Hasofer (al-'zer) in Maysan province, the tomb of prophet Daniel in Kirkuk province[8], the tomb of prophet Jonah in Mosul (destroyed by ISIS), and finally the tomb of prophet Nahum.

- Sabean Mandaeans

The followers of 'John the Baptist' live in Baghdad and southern Iraq (Maysan province) and form a culture resisting the challenges, empires and religions that have been on the land of Mesopotamia for more than 20 centuries and since the expulsion of the Jews are now the oldest representatives of monotheistic religions in Iraq.

Historically, the Sabean lived by the rivers in southern Iraq, and the Ahwaz areas of Persia (Iran). The most famous of the cities they inhabited are Basra, the city of Al-Tayeb in Maysan, the city of Amarah, al-Kahla, and Al- Majar Al -Alkabir, Al-Mashrah, Nasiriyah, and Suq al-Shuyukh, as well as the city of Mendi and Wasit. From these cities, some moved to the capital city of Baghdad in the early twentieth century. When the leadership of the Mandaean community shifted in the late 1950s to Baghdad, the Sabeans became most concentrated in the capital. Others moved for economic reasons to new areas, such as Diwaniyah, Anbar and Kirkuk. In the chaos that swept Iraq after 2003, the insecurity, the spread of crime and the targeting of minorities forced some Mandaeans to flee to the Kurdistan region of Iraq and to settle in the city of Sulaimaniyah and Erbil.

The Mandaeans believe that their culture is in real danger and that they are threatened with extinction, so they demand unification in one country rather than dispersal in exile. Because their ritual language is restricted to clerics and a few researchers, it risks dying out. Their non-proselytising

---

[7] Saad Salloum, 'Minorities in Iraq - Memory, Identity, Challenges' *Masarat Magazine* 13 (2014). Further Issue No. 13 (2019), on the Jews of Iraq. On Kurdistan Jews, see Erich Brauer, *The Jews of Kurdistan*. Translated by Shetkhwan Kirkukli and Abdul Razzaq Botani. (Erbil: Dar Earas for Printing and Publishing, 2002). Orit Bashkin *New Babylonians, New Babylonians: A History of Jews in Modern Iraq.* (Palo Alto: Stanford University Press, 2012). is considered the most important publication recently issued about the Jews of Iraq in English.

[8] The Tomb of the Prophet Daniel (near the castle of Kirkuk).

religion does not allow for marriage outside the community. They apparently have a bleak future in the country of their oldest presence.

- Kakais:

One of the religious minorities spread around northern Iraq, the Kakai originally lived in villages southeast of Kirkuk. Now, Kirkuk is their main home and the banks of the large Zab river in the Iraqi-Iranian border Area. They are also scattered in Khanaqin, Mandali, Jwalla, Erbil, Sulaimaniyah and Horaman. Those living in Shirin, Sahnah, Kermanshah and Sarbil Zahab (in Iran) are called 'Ahl al-Haq' or People of Truth, and have a noticeable presence in the Nineveh Plains (al-Hamdania district of Nineveh province). No accurate official data confirm their numbers, but the 2011 report of the International Minority Rights Group, estimates they have about 200,000 followers.

The Kakai have no representatives in the Ministry of Endowment and Religious Affairs in the Kurdistan region, mainly due to the conflict between two Kakai parties: one declares Kakai as a religious minority independent of Islam, while the second claims they are Muslims. Because there is no quota for Kakai representation, no official Kakai delegate serves in the federal parliament, the Kurdish territory's parliament, the federal government and the territorial government. However, Law No. 5 of 2015 (protection of the rights of the components in Kurdistan-Iraq) mentions Kakai as one of the religious and sectarian groups in the Kurdistan region of Iraq.

- Zoroastrians

At a time when Middle Eastern countries, particularly Syria and Iraq, risk losing their religious diversity, the circumstances – created by the newly emergent ISIS's threat to religious diversity – have facilitated the return of a religion missing for fifteen centuries since the entry of Islam into Iraq.[9] The public appearance of Zoroastrians in the Kurdistan region in 2015 was accompanied by the revival of their festivals, the demand for the construction of temples for religious rituals, the attempt to revive some abandoned temples, their return to public life and the demand for their formal recognition. Ms. Awat Hussam Aldeen Tayib serves as their official representative in the territory's Ministry of Endowments[10] and they are recognised in the law on the protection of minorities in the Kurdistan region of Iraq.

The recognition of the Zoroastrian religion, as one of the religious beliefs in the Kurdistan region,[11] encouraged Zoroastrians to officially start

---

[9] Saad Salloum, 'So Zoroaster spoke in Kurdistan' *Al-Mada newspaper* 3546 (published 13 January 2016).

[10] Private interview with Mrs. Oat Hossam El-Din, representative of the Zardashtin in the Ministry of Endowments and Religious Affairs in the Kurdistan Region, on 16 August 2018.

[11] Available in the Kurdistan Parliament website at the following link:

returning to Sulaimaniyah to open the headquarters of the Zoroastrians after an absence over the past centuries and to choose a representative for the Zoroastrians in the Ministry of Endowments and Religious Affairs.

- Turkmen:

The Turkmen, the third largest ethnic group after the Arabs and the Kurds, live in northern Iraq in an arc stretching from Tal Afar, west of Mosul, through Mosul, Erbil, Altun Kupri, Kirkuk, Tuz Khormato, Kifri and Khanaqin. Most are Sunni or Shia Muslims, while some are Roman Catholic Christians.

- Shabaks:

The Shabaks have lived in northern Iraq for nearly five centuries. Most are Shia Muslims, while some are Sunnis. Their language differs from both Arabic and Kurdish. They live among other minority groups, like Christians, Yazidis and Kakais in the Nineveh Plains in the Mosul Governorate.

- Feyli Kurds:

The Feyli Kurds are spread along the border with Iran in the Zagros Mountains and in areas of Baghdad. They have a complex identity with multiple elements. Despite the ethnic characteristics that group them with the Kurds, they differ in the sense that they belong to the Shia sect (most Kurds are Sunnis of the Shafi'i school) as well as having a language (Feyli Kurdish and Bakhtiari) that differs from the rest of the Kurdish dialects (Sorani, Bahdiani and Zazaki).

- Baha'is:

The Baha'is are one of the smaller religious minorities, having one of the newest religions in the contemporary world. They are dispersed throughout different regions of Iraq. Since they conceal their identities and are afraid to publicly proclaim their religion, no accurate estimates exist of their number. However, their community estimates they have several hundred (less than a thousand) people throughout Iraq.

- Iraqis of African Descent:

The Iraqis of African descent are an ethnic minority descended from multiple African origins. Their ancestors were brought to Iraq during different periods of Islamic history and they settled in different areas of southern Iraq. Some are Nubian (from Nubia) and Zanzibari (from the island of Zanzibar), from which the Arabic word for 'negro' [*zinjiyy*] is derived. It was used to describe the blacks during their uprising known as the Zanj Rebellion. Others are from Ghana and from Abyssinia (now Ethiopia).[12]

---

http://www.perleman.org/Default.aspx?page=byyear&c=LDD-Yasa&id=2015

[12] Saad Salloum, 'Will Iraqi Blacks Win Justice?' *The New York Times*, (published 22 July 2014)

They are concentrated in the Basra governorate and other cities in southern Iraq.

-Chechens, Dagestanis and Circassians

The Iraqi Caucasus tribes (Chechens, Dagestanis and Circassians) suffered forced displacement carried by Tsarist Russia in 1864. They were displaced from the North Caucasus to the territory of present-day Turkey. The Ottoman administration, in turn, settled them in Jordan, Syria and Iraq.

In Iraq, these minorities have become forgotten because they are few in number and their families integrated into Arab, Kurdish, and Turkmen societies. Although the Dagestani minority are scattered throughout Iraq and do not live in concentrated areas, Iraqis, however, became aware of this minority through the presence of some prominent Dagestani symbols and personalities. Moreover, people are more familiar with the Dagestani name compared to other minorities, such as the Circassians. For this reason, the Circassians started to call themselves Dagestanis because they are closely related to Dagestanis. According to Ahmad Kato, one of the prominent representatives of the Circassians in Iraq, they are not recognised as a distinct component in Iraq with special representatives in the existing political parties or with their own parties.

An Analysis of the Iraqi Constitution and Rights of Groups and Individuals

oth before and after the writing of the new Iraqi constitution, many minority groups feared that the process would marginalise them. The constitution-drafting committee had three seats for the Turkmen, only one for the Chaldo-Assyrians and none for the Mandeans. Minorities like the Chaldo-Assyrians, Turkmen and Arabs of Kirkuk feared being marginalised in the federal regions of Iraq Kurdistan. Religious minorities, facing escalating violence, voiced their concern about Islamic influence on the constitution and the dangers this could create for their religious freedoms and ways of life.[13] However, when ratified in 2005, the Iraqi Constitution listed a broad range of rights and ensured a system for recognizing groups by specifically mentioning them.

Nevertheless, such rights and the recognition of particular groups cannot guarantee equality and non-discrimination among citizens if the official structures and institutions do not protect the constitutionally guaranteed rights. Furthermore, declaring Islam as the state's official religion increases risks to the nation's pluralistic identity. Islamic political parties may dominate and hamper the creation of a civil state based on a pluralism guaranteeing a

---

http://is.gd/Rb0fpy.

[13] Faleh A. Jabar, *The Constitution of Iraq: Religious and Ethnic Relations* (London: Minority Rights Group International, 2005), 3.

balance between the rights of individuals (citizenship) and the rights of different groups. Furthermore, some doubted that a judicial framework could effectively deal with the grim reality of the country's de facto loss of pluralism because of ongoing violence, ethnic cleansing, and migration.

The Legal Framework for the Rights of Citizenship and Minorities

The Iraqi Constitution includes a wide range of civil, political, economic, social, and cultural rights. Article 14 provides for the right to equality and non-discrimination. Under Article 16, the state guarantees equal opportunities for all Iraqis and shall undertake effective measures to ensure this. Article 7, with the desire to break away from the legacy of discrimination states: 'First: No entity or program, under any name, may adopt racism, terrorism, the calling of others infidels, ethnic cleansing, or incite, facilitate, glorify, promote, or justify thereto, especially the Saddamist Baath in Iraq and its symbols, regardless of the name that it adopts. This may not be part of the political pluralism in Iraq. This will be organised by law.'

The constitution also provides for the right of political participation and the enjoyment of all political rights in Article 20, which states: 'The citizens, men and women, have the right to participate in public affairs and to enjoy political rights including the right to vote, to elect and to nominate.' It recognises the right to freedom of religion and belief in Article 42, which stipulates, 'Each individual has freedom of thought, conscience and belief.' Article 41 states that all Iraqis are free to organise their personal lives according to their religions, sects, beliefs or choices. Article 43 further guarantees the freedom of belief and the state's protection of this right, stating:

> First: The followers of all religions and sects are free in the: practice of religious rites, including the Husseini ceremonies [Shia religious ceremonies] and management of the endowments, its affairs and its religious institutions. The law shall regulate this.

> Second: The state guarantees freedom of worship and the protection of the places of worship.

These articles enjoy support from Article 2(c), which stipulates that no law can be enacted that contradicts the rights guaranteed in the Constitution. In accordance with the Iraqi Constitution and international commitments, the Iraqi legislature must enact laws that ensure the implementation of and respect for these provisions.

The Constitutional System for Official Recognition of Pluralism

In the constitution, the system of official recognition includes religious, national, and sectarian pluralism. Article 3 of the constitution indicates, 'Iraq is a country of many nationalities, religions and sects.' In its official recognition of minorities, the constitution adopted a compound approach that distinguishes between religious and national minorities. Article 2.2 indicates the rights of religious minorities in saying, 'This constitution guarantees the Islamic identity of the majority of the Iraqi people and guarantees the full religious rights of all individuals to freedom of religious belief and practice such as Christians, Yazidis, and Mandean Sabeans.'

Article 125 addresses the rights of national minorities, saying, 'This constitution shall guarantee the administrative, political, cultural and educational rights for the various nationalities, such as Turkmen, Chaldeans, Assyrians and all other components. This will be organised by law.' The final part of this constitutional article that refers to 'all other components' indicates that the names of those minorities that appear in the constitution is not an exclusive list of groups that should be offered protection. It states, rather, that all citizens enjoy protection whether they are religious or ethnic minorities. However, some minorities not mentioned in the constitution seek constitutional amendments that mention their names. The Shabaks[14] in particular are doing so, but also other minorities, such as the Baha'is, the Kakais, the Feyli Kurds, and Iraqis of African descent.

Though the federal government and the Kurdistan Regional Government have made some progress in protecting minorities and other groups, they have not adopted the legal or practical mechanisms needed to implement an effective framework for protection. Furthermore, the state has not made any significant progress in reforming potentially discriminatory Iraqi laws. Nor has the state adequately provided for the use of the courts, compensation or any alternative arrangements to treat the former and ongoing persecution and discrimination experienced by vulnerable groups within the population.[15]

Recognition of Minorities in the Iraqi Kurdistan Region

The Kurdistan Region apparently has a more comprehensive recognition of religious minorities both mentioning them each by name in the constitution and mentioning them in the law (No. 5 of 2015) regarding the 'protection of the rights of citizens of the Iraqi Kurdistan Region.' In Article 1 paragraph 2, this law recognises religious and ethnic/sectarian groups (such as Christians, Yazidis, Mandaeans, Kakais, Shabaks, Faylis and Zoroastrians) as citizens of Iraqi Kurdistan.[16] The regional law more comprehensively

---

[14] The Shabak representative in Parliament, Dr. Hanin al-Qadu, believes that the lack of mention of the Shabak people in the constitution resulted from a Kurdish-Shia deal during the writing of the constitution. The Shabak people would not be mentioned in the constitution so their identity could benefit a larger Shia or Kurdish identity. Personal interview with the researcher, 14 May 2014.

[15] Institute for International Law and Human Rights, *Iraq's Minorities and Other Vulnerable Groups: Legal Framework, Documentation and Human Rights*. Report. (Washington, D.C/Baghdad.: IILHR, 2013), 12.

[16] Law No. 5 of 2015 (protection of the rights of components in the Iraqi Kurdistan), issued by a decision taken by Law No. 5 the presidency of the Iraqi Kurdistan Region, No. 9 of 2015.

appoints minority representatives at the Ministry of Endowment and allocates directorates for Christians, Yazidis, Baha'is, Mandaeans, Zoroastrians, and Jews.

Recognition in the constitution: The draft constitution now recognises all 'religious, national, and ethnic' components of the region. In addition, representatives of the Christians, Yazidis, Baha'is, Mandaeans, Zoroastrians, and Jews have been appointed to the Endowment Ministry of the region's government and directorates for them have been established. They also participate in the ministry's official events and have budgets for their own activities. However, some question the recognition of the Kakais because of the lack of a clear perception of how to deal with them despite the regional governments support of Kakai cultural centres. The lack of agreement between the Kakais as to whether they have their own religion or are Muslims complicate their status as a minority.

Recognition at the level of legislation: Law No. 5 of 2015 recognises the rights and necessary guarantees of the protection and development of cultural, religious, linguistic, and identity rights of all citizens in the Iraqi Kurdistan Region. This law expanded rights and explicitly named all minorities. The law also stresses four important areas for the development and protection of rights: freedom of belief and the practice of this freedom; preservation of identity, language, and culture; prevention of all types of discrimination with a guarantee of political participation and development; and the prevention of demographic changes.

The Nature of the Relationship between Religion and the State and Its Effect on the Rights of Minorities and Citizenship

The 2005 Iraqi Constitution recognised multilingualism and the nature of religious, national and sectarian diversity within Iraqi society. More than one article grants rights to religious and national minorities. At the same time, though, the constitution recognised Islam as the state's official religion and adopted the approach of having a relationship between religion and the state. This casts a shadow over the guarantee of pluralism in Iraqi society. The Iraqi Constitution stipulates that, according to the constitution, Islam is the official state religion and a fundamental source of legislation.[17]

We see this, for example, in Article 2.1 (a) which states that no law may be enacted that contradicts the established provisions of Islam. An article such as this one makes the rights guaranteed to minorities merely as an exception to the rule and opens these rights up to the possibility of being restricted or being stripped of their substance. For example, the enactment of a law that protects minorities and stipulates equality for and non-discrimination against religious minorities could be seen to conflict with the

---

[17] Article 2.1: 'Islam is the official religion of the State and it is a fundamental source of legislation'

fundamentals of Islam. This is because 'the centrality of Islam may adversely affect a range of rights of non-Muslim minorities and other vulnerable groups, including, for example, rights of religion, expression, equality before the law, the right to participate in government affairs, the right to participate in work of one's own choosing, family rights, and women's rights.'[18]

One can also raise the possible issue of some religious minorities' rites and beliefs or the individual's right to embrace any intellectual or religious doctrine as contradicting the principles of the Islamic religion. Thus, a conflict arises with the provisions of Article 43 of the constitution that guarantees freedom of belief for the followers of all religions and doctrines as well as with Article 42 which guarantees freedom of thought, conscience and belief to all.

Article 2 of the constitution does not mention a system of ethics and morals shared by Islam and other religions. For this reason, some recommend amending this article so it reflects the shared values of all religions in Iraq. Thus, Article 2(1)(A), 'which currently disallows any law that contradicts the established provisions of Islam, would be changed to include the commonly held practices or tenets of all heavenly religions, rather than just Islam.'[19]

The Nature of Minorities' Participation in Public Life

After 2003, minority groups in Iraq tried to ensure their political presence. This took many forms, including delegations who visited the major political blocs and coordination with the United Nations and other organisation to increase their political participation. Even minority groups whose beliefs prohibit political action (such as the Baha'is, Mandeans and Yazidis) participated in these efforts in order to establish their existence and to demand all of their rights. This was in line with the acceleration of the pace of events on the ground, especially after the majority groups (Shias, Sunnis and Kurds) confirmed the power of ethnicity in the results of the elections that brought their elites to power.

The quota system failed to boost minorities' political participation. Minority representatives faced struggles between the majority groups that controlled the political scene as well as internal conflicts within the minority groups themselves. Therefore, an increasing trend is to create more flexible and universal institutional frameworks that could strengthen minority participation and provide them with more effective representation.

The small number of Mandeans, their dispersal throughout most of Iraq's governorates, and the fact that they did not join in any political party or

---

[18] Institute for International Law and Human Rights, *Minorities and the Law in Iraq*. (Washington, D.C./Baghdad: IILRH, 2011), 35.
[19] Ibid.

alliance in an official capacity meant they were not represented in the Council of Representatives during its first session from 2006 to 2010. This motivated them to demand increased participation. Thus, they gained a single seat in the quota system both in the Baghdad Provincial Council and in the Federal Parliament. Mandeans could increase their participation in local governments by obtaining a quota seat in the district of Al-Rusafa within the Baghdad governorate and in the central Amarah district in the Maysan governorate. They still attempt to obtain a quota seat in the Basra Provincial Council and to increase the number of seats allotted to them in the Council of Representatives from one to two.[20]

To increase their political representation, some minorities resorted to the courts. The Yazidis, for example, demanded increased political participation. On behalf of the Yazidi independent list, Mirza Dinnayi filed an official suit in the federal court on the proportion of Yazidis in the quota system. He won a judgement that considered the proportion of the Yazidis in the general population and then granted the Yazidis two representatives in accordance with the quota system.

For their part, the Mandeans also tried to appeal to the courts to improve the electoral mechanisms so they could increase their political participation. A suit was filed before the Federal Supreme Court on behalf of the leader of the Mandean community in Iraq and the wider world, Sattar Jabbar al-Hulu, against the speaker of the Council of Representatives. The court issued a verdict considering the seats allocated for the Mandeans in the quota system to be all within one electoral constituency, as is the case with the Christians.[21]

Through these actions, we conclude that the 'quota system' is relatively unimportant, although it was sometimes the only way for minority political representatives to get into Parliament. In effect, it merely offers compensatory quotas to address discrimination against minority representation. It should not be a ceiling for the participation of minorities, nor should it impede efforts by minorities to achieve more balanced representation.

Political representation for minorities has been, in the best cases, symbolic or ineffective, amid the struggle between the larger blocks. Minority representatives were appointed to build bridges with one of the larger blocks, especially the two largest (Shias and Kurds). As a result, minority representatives (except for a few exceptions) followed the political positions of a larger block rather than advocating issues important to the minorities.

The large political parties sometimes deliberately tried to exclude minority representatives from the Council of Representatives, despite the election law

---

[20] Researcher's personal interview with the Baghdad Provincial Council member for Mandeans, Raad Jabbar Saleh, 1 June 2014.
[21] The Republic of Iraq, decision of the Federal Supreme Court, 7 - Federal, 2010.

allocating seats for minorities. For example, in the 2010 elections for Federal Parliament, the Kurdistan Democratic Party gained control of three of the seven seats allocated for minorities (one from the Shabaks and two from the Christians). They did so by pushing some of their members to compete for these seats, depriving the independent representatives for these minorities from reaching the Council of Representatives. This happened because of different attitudes towards the (disputed areas) and other sensitive issues.[22]

Due to the continuing lack of recognition for the participation of some minorities, activists for Iraqis of African descent in Basra founded the Movement of Free Iraqis. Because of their weak chances of getting into the governorate council, they demanded to be included in the quota system, like all other minorities. They want to be represented in the parliament and governorate councils and to increase their participation in public affairs.[23] On 27 April 2013, someone assassinated Jalal Dhiyab, an activist who had led the Supporters of Human Freedom Association, a civil association working particularly in Basra, for the betterment of people with brown skin (Iraqis of African descent). It helped found the Movement of Free Iraqis, a liberally oriented political movement to raise black awareness of their political rights and increase their political participation. This unsolved murder weakened the movement to defend the rights of Iraqis of African descent. Furthermore, the investigation into his assassination did nothing to identify the perpetrators and portrayed it as only a criminal event. This revealed the extent of the structural imbalances in Iraq's justice system victimising minorities and weakening minority individuals' sense of equality and citizenship.[24]

Some minorities had religious beliefs discouraging political participation. For example, the Baha'is' beliefs prohibit political activism. Also, the Kakais have no clear political voice and cannot express their identity outside of a Kurdish framework[25].

Some minority groups have divisions that further weaken their effectiveness and ability to obtain effective political representation. The Feyli Kurds, for example, have multiple parties, movements, or associations that did not come together in one representative body. They tend to vote according to ethnic determinants among the Kurdish parties or sectarian

---

[22] Personal interview by the researcher with Amin Farhan Jejo, a member of the Iraqi Council of Representatives and President of the Yazidi Movement for Reform and Progress 23 March 2014 and a personal interview by the researcher with Muhammad al-Shabaki, Secretary of the Iraqi Minorities Council 15 May 2014.
[23] Personal interview with the activist in defending the rights of blacks, Jalal Dhiyab, president of the Supporters of Human Freedom Association and Secretary-General of the Movement of Free Iraqis, Basra, 24 December 2012.
[24] Saad Salloum, 'From the Zanj Revolution to the Birth of the Supporters of Human Freedom Movement,' *Al Mada Newspaper* 3346, (published 25 April 2015).
[25] Interview with Recep Assi, director of the Yarstan Institute in Kirkuk, and interviews with Kaka'i activist in Erbil and Sulaymaniyah on different dates.

loyalty among Shia parties.²⁶ Also, the Turkmen found that following a centralised authority and allying themselves with the Shia majority was the best way to achieve recognition as a constitutive element beyond their minority position. This allows powerful resistance to the Kurd's intractable ambitions in the disputed areas (especially Kirkuk).²⁷

The political parties representing the various Christian denominations have been politically off-balance amidst the struggles among the majority groups and the lack of a unified political movement for the Christian populace within the political process. For this reason, the widest attempt to unite Iraqi minorities was the Chaldean Syriac Assyrian Popular Council, an attempt, under a fanciful label, to bring together the ethnically diverse Chaldeans, Assyrians, and Syriacs and the ideologically diverse Catholics, Orthodox, and Protestants.²⁸

The previous information reveals the incomplete representation for those ethnic and religious minorities not mentioned in the constitution, such as for the Baha'is, Kakais and Blacks, whose state protection was weak and symbolic. Therefore, minorities have tried to create institutional frameworks to raise their effectiveness and participation in public life in the following ways.

The Creation of Alternative and Flexible Institutional Frameworks

Because of the poor representation of minorities and to overcome the fragmentation of identity, there was a movement to create universal institutional frameworks, such as the Chaldean League along the lines of the Maronite, Syriac, and Armenian leagues.²⁹ Also, the Council of the Heads of Christian Sects was developed in order to form a unified body for the Christian presence in Iraq. The Christian clergy attempted to provide representation that protects the identity of Christians in Iraq, as opposed to the fragmented identity provided by political representation through the various political parties and movements that represent different Christian sects. They also tried to unify attitudes towards the increasingly high emigration of Iraq's Christians, which destroys the Christian community and threatens the future of the Christian presence in Iraq.³⁰ The founding of the Yazidi Supreme Council was also an attempt to not limit the most important

---

[26] Saad Salloum, *Different and Equal: A Plan to Strengthen the Rights of Minorities in Iraq*. (Beirut: United Nations Development Program, 2013).

[27] For more information, see Saad Salloum et al., *At a Crossroad: Iraq's Minorities after the ISIS*. Report on Violations of the Rights of Minorities 1 (Brussels: Masarat Institute for Cultural and Media Development 2015), 87-89.

[28] Interviews with members of the Chaldean Democratic Platform (Adel Bakkal and Kemal Yaldo), Michigan, United States, 18 August 2015.

[29] Saad Salloum, 'Christmas 2015: Signs of the Demise or the Rebirth of the Church of Iraq?' *Al-Mada newspaper* 3247, (published 24 December 2014).

[30] Personal interview with Avak Asadourian, Secretary of the Council of the Heads of Christian Sects, Armenian Orthodox diocese, Baghdad, 23 April 2015.

representation for the Yazidis to the sect's religious council and to broaden the base of participation in public affairs to all classes and segments of the Yazidi community.

The Turkmen Rescue Foundation was founded on a similar principle: to confront the marginalisation of the Turkmen's rights and to lift them out of oppression and injustice. This was especially important because, for the past ten years, the Turkmen political elites had failed to increase Turkmen political participation and to realistically represent the Turkman presence and interests.[31]

Additionally, some groups have been absent or marginalised for various reasons during the past years and could not restore their dispersed communities. The ISIS occupation resulted in a crushing blow to the social fabric caused ethnic and religious cleansing of minorities in pluralistic areas, as in the Nineveh Plains or Sinjar. In this context, a Supreme Sufi Council was founded in Iraq to fight the challenge of *takfirism* discourse and to revive a moderate, centrist position[32].

Furthermore, new institutional frameworks were announced for religions to declare themselves publicly for the first time in present-day Iraq. For example, in Erbil, the Supreme Council of Zoroastrians could establish itself in the Iraqi Kurdistan region[33]. Such frameworks do not attempt to entrench sectarianism or to challenge a universal Iraqi identity. Instead, they want to strengthen the various Iraqi groups' participation in public life, to stop further fragmentation by establishing more effective universal frameworks, and to not limit minorities' representation to purely political frameworks. If successful, these frameworks will have a positive impact on minority individuals' sense of citizenship through effective participation in shaping public affairs and through strengthening their presence in public life.

Disparity in the Representation of Minorities in the Kurdistan Region and the Federal Government

The Kurdistan Parliament has 111 seats distributed among the various factions: 100 seats for the Kurds, 5 for the Turkmen, 5 for the Chaldo Syriac Assyrians, and 1 for the Armenians. The Federal Parliament has 328 seats: 320 seats for the Muslims, 5 for the Christians, 1 for the Mandaeans, 1 for the Yazidis and 1 for the Shabaks. The political representatives of Christians believe that, when compared to the Federal Parliament's representation of Christians, the Kurdish Parliament fairly represents Christians, given the

---

[31] Personal interview with Ali Akram Al-Bayati, head of the Turkmen Rescue Foundation, Baghdad, 25 June 2015.
[32] Founding statement of the Supreme Sufi Council in Iraq, 11 May 2015. From a copy in the possession of the researcher who received it by email.
[33] 'Zoroastrian Council in Kurdistan: We Strive to Build Zoroastrian Temples and to Spread Its Concepts in the Region' *Alsumaria News*, (published 21. April 2015). http://is.gd/xwNRFp.

number of Christians living in the Kurdistan Region.³⁴ Out of 111 seats, Christians have 6 seats, one of which is allocated for Armenians. In comparison, the Christians have one ministerial position in the Kurdistan government. However, the Kurdish leadership often chooses the person for this position from among those who are close to this leadership or from among Christian parties close to influential parties in the region. Chaldean political activists complain that the person chosen for this ministerial position has always been a member of the Assyrian parties rather than the Chaldean parties. Nevertheless, most observers admit that the Kurdistan region offers better conditions and protection of rights of Christians than the federal government. In general, Christians enjoy good respect.

The Orthodox Armenians offer unique example of religious and ethnic crisis. Although, classified as Christian minority group, they distanced themselves from the political Christian wing, due to their dissatisfaction with the Christian personalities and their weak representation of Armenian interests. They preferred to emerge as an independent national Armenian ethnicity demanding a quota in the Federal Parliament (outside of the quota designated for the Christians). Armenians currently have one deputy in the Kurdistan Region and one seat in the Dohuk provincial council but are not represented in the Iraqi Parliament. Some Armenians serve as general managers and executives in the federal government, but they don't have any ministers representing them. Armenians demand greater political representation in the form of a ministerial position in the Kurdistan regional government and a seat in the Federal Parliament.³⁵

Malkoun Melkonian, head of the administrative committee of the Armenian Orthodox church in Baghdad, Iraq, believes that the Armenians have the right to demand a designated seat in the federal parliament and in provincial councils, municipalities, districts, and villages, where there are Armenians. Specifically, this includes Baghdad (the center), al-Basra (the center), Kirkuk (the center), Erbil (the center and Ain Kawa), Dohuk (the center, Zakho, Avzork, and Howerisk), and the Ninewa province.³⁶

Economic Deprivation and the Challenges of Equality and Citizenship

Many factors can worsen the poverty experienced by minorities, including economic deterioration, ethnic tensions, and growing discrimination. In many countries, minorities cannot fully exercising their social rights because of economic inequality and poor infrastructure in areas where minorities live.

---

³⁴ Interview with Ablahad Afram, Secretary General of the Chaldean Democratic Union Party, Michigan, and an interview with Anwar Matti Hadaya, Chairman of the Independent Syriac Assembly Movement (ISAM) and the representative of the Christian quota in the Ninewa provincial council.

³⁵ Interview with Ervant Aminaan, representative of the Armenian quota in the Kurdistan Parliament, Erbil.

³⁶ Interview with Malkoun Melkonian, head of the administrative committee of the Armenian Orthodox Church in Iraq, Baghdad.

In this context, economic exclusion places minority groups in the lowest ranks of citizens. This constitutes both a cause and a consequence of discrimination. Members of minority groups in Iraq often face discrimination when seeking a job, even in the civil service.

Moreover, the minorities reside in some of the poorest regions or some of the most remote, that provide only limited opportunities for economic growth. This includes the Yazidis in the Sinjar district in the Nineveh governorate as well as Christians, Yazidis and Shabaks, among other minority groups, in the Nineveh Plains, located outside of the capital of the governorate in Mosul. This poverty can be found in the regions in southern Iraq, for example, the Az Zubayr region in the Basra governorate, stronghold of the Iraqis of African descent, the Mandean areas on the outskirts of the Maysan governorate and, in the north of Iraq, the villages inhabited by the Kakais on the outskirts of the Kirkuk governorate.

Property disputes dating back to the era of the Baath regime also affect Iraq's minorities. Many of these lawsuits and the associated claims have remained unresolved because of massive displacement of minorities[37] as well as individuals taking control over minorities' property. Politicians from the executive branch and members of the judiciary have been embroiled in these property-rights issues, according to research by minority-rights organisations.[38] The chaotic atmosphere, the weak rule of law, and impunity throughout the country have had a particularly negative economic impact on minorities.

Many minority groups have noted discrimination in access to public services. Often this happens because they live in areas disputed by the Arabs and Kurds. Both the Nineveh Plains and Sinja fall administratively within the budget for the Nineveh governorate; however, they have only received token amounts of budget allocations. The city of Qaraqosh (Al-Hamdaniya), for example, received only 40 per cent of its budget, thus leading to suspension of its infrastructure projects. Meanwhile, other funds in the budget were allocated for non-existent projects. The Sinjar areas have relied on Kurdistan to assume responsibility for its security situation, although it is administered by the Nineveh governate.[39]

Minority groups also reported discrimination in access to jobs related to security and civil service. A study by the Iraqi Minorities Council in 2011 noted that 38 per cent of those surveyed reported discrimination in access to government jobs.[40] After the ISIS invasion and displacement of minorities

---

[37] Researcher's interview with the retired judge, Hadi Aziz Ali, Baghdad, 8 October 2015.
[38] Saad Salloum et al., *At a Crossroad: Iraq's Minorities after the ISIS*. Report on Violations of the Rights of Minorities 1 (Brussels: Masarat Institute for Cultural and Media Development, 2015), 53-55.
[39] Preti Taneja, *Iraq's Minorities: Participation in Public Life*, Minority Rights Group International. Report. (London, Minority Right Group International, 2011), 17.
[40] Ibid., 17-18.

from the Nineveh governorate, the lack of job opportunities and the lack of sources of income results in most displaced minority groups now living below the poverty line. For this reason, emigration has become a better option than waiting for an uncertain future while enduring poverty and economic discrimination.

Economic discrimination mixes with other manifestations of discrimination. Majid Hassan, a Yazidi researcher, noted a large-scale movement to allocate government lands to build mosques in Kurdistan. Because of this, the three current governorates of Kurdistan have more than 5,200 mosques. At the same time, the government has completely neglected the building or reconstruction of Yazidi temples. For more than five years, although the government has claimed to allocate more than a million dollars from the government's budget to rebuild the Lalish temple (holy to the Yazidis), not a single dollar has been spent thus far.[41]

Throughout 2014 and 2015, some people have targeted Yazidis who own liquor stores in Baghdad. Most victims migrated to the Kurdistan region. The Yazidis see this targeting as giving few choices to members of minority groups because it deprives them of their sources of income and places restrictions on their jobs and trades not performed by the Muslim majority.[42]

The social exclusion and deprivation from education results in despair and the loss of all hope to climb the social ladder. The hopelessness of the situation increases tensions and directly causes emigration without plans to return.

Promoting Social Diversity and Individual Equality

To promote pluralism and regain social diversity, to maintain the fabric of society, and to restore the lost confidence, so as to promote a sense of citizenship, the following points should be addressed:

The Disputed Areas: The process must begin, under international supervision, to resolve the disputed internal borders that form the regions rich with diversity and that have been subjected to Arab-Kurdish conflict. This ongoing conflict could push the country into an internal war. The constitution's Article 125 must be turned into legislation that ensures the self-administration of minorities over the disputed areas where they live; thus, they can avoid the conflicts between the majority groups. Their right to self-administration does not entail support for seceding. The proposed self-administration would be below the governorate level and includes guaranteeing minorities the independent management of their affairs. In this context, the international coalition against ISIS, the United Nations, and the

---

[41] Researcher's communications with Majid Hassan, an academic at the University of Bamberg in Germany and specialist on Iraq's religious minorities.
[42] Interview with Saib Khadr, advisor to the Yazidi Spiritual Council, Baghdad, 7 October 2015.

European Union should be pushed to launch negotiations to guarantee the rights of minorities in their historic regions.

Societal Dialogue from the Bottom Up: Drawing a roadmap to address the current challenges undoubtedly requires a comprehensive societal dialogue and not just bargaining between the political elites that only maintain their mutual elite interests. This is especially necessary because of the loss of political trust and the extremism promulgated by some clerics, thereby reinforcing a loss of societal trust. For this reason, launching a bottom-up dialogue would effectively address the rifts in the social fabric. This means supporting projects that build bridges between young people or promoting dialogue between Sunni and Shia clerics and between Muslim and non-Muslim religious elements in order to stop extremist ideologies.

National Reconciliation Project: A comprehensive societal dialogue will facilitate the mobilisation of civil forces to support a national reconciliation project. Without that dialogue, you cannot delegitimise extremist ideologies nor can you encourage the government to begin a package of reforms necessary to achieve reconciliation. Some of these reforms include fighting corruption, the release of arbitrary detainees, conducting immediate investigations into human rights violations, and abolishing legislation that discriminates against or oppresses minorities. Furthermore, the government must join the Rome Statute of the International Criminal Court and accept its jurisdiction during the current conflict, recognize minorities not mentioned in the constitution, and abolish all legislation left over from the Baath era that conflicts with the rights contained in the constitution.

Legislation to Ensure Equality and the Protection of Diversity: Diversity's importance in maintaining the unity of Middle Eastern countries has become obvious and so has the fact that the emigration of minorities leads to the destruction of entire communities, creating ethnically pure groups that cannot be a foundation on which to transform 'groups' into a 'society'. Therefore, legislation must be passed that maintains diversity, promotes the preservation of minorities' identities and cultures and protects the pluralistic identity of society, without which it would become easy to divide Iraq into regions based on ethno-sectarian geography. This legislation must also address discrimination and promote equality, because legislation is a critical mechanism for accelerating change and guiding the society's culture towards fighting all forms of discrimination and social, political, and economic exclusion.

Equality of Opportunity and the Impartiality of the State: We cannot address discrimination, exclusion, and the widespread violence that affects members of all different groups except by affirming the impartiality of state organs and by building a state of institutions. The effect of the institutionalisation of the state also extends to its impartiality, as state impartiality is a fundamental basis for a sense of loyalty to the state and a sense of belonging to its universal, national identity. All state organs must be neutral. In particular, the security services should be based on professional considerations and not on narrow sectarian loyalties, in order to boost all citizens' senses of security.[43]

The Balance between Collective and Individual Rights: The approach that included recognition of pluralism in the Iraqi Constitution only resulted in a formal recognition that had no value on the ground. This is because administrative structures and state institutions remained subject to discrimination through the quota policy. This quota policy institutionalises discrimination at the state level. Therefore, diversity should be recognised on the basis of the rights of citizenship and to adopt a comprehensive approach on the subject. The individual bears fundamental rights and rebuilding social trust can only occur through strengthening the sense of citizenship.

School Curricula: Appropriate curricula should be constructed for an ethnically, and religiously diverse society. Developing curricula that promote knowledge of the other can save future generations whose imaginations are at risk of developing in a culture of polarisation and disregard of the other. This will prepare the necessary climate to disseminate policies of tolerance and to promote acceptance of the other. Thereby, the victory of strengthening the acceptance of values of pluralism and citizenship can be achieved in the hearts and minds of the people.[44]

Conclusion: Founding a Model of a State Based on Citizenship

The post-2003 philosophy of 'the state made up of various elements' stripped the rights contained in the 2005 constitution of any practical value. The individual, as the bearer of fundamental rights, has had these rights confiscated under the banner of the rights of 'the element.' Elites used this fiction to pursue their interests through sectarianism that mobilised against others who are different. The state model of various elements resulted in a deal for the tripartite sharing of power between the three majority groups (Shias, Sunnis and Kurds) with symbolic representation for minorities. Consequently, the model did not result in a real recognition of diversity and failed to establish a system to manage diversity.

Therefore, the necessary goal must be an alternative model that recognises diversity on the basis of the rights of citizenship. The individual bears fundamental rights and rebuilding social trust can only occur by strengthening the sense of citizenship. However different we are as groups, we must be equal as individuals in the end.

---

[43] Saad Salloum, *Christians in Iraq: Comprehensive History and Current Challenges*. (Baghdad/Beirut: Masarat Institute for Cultural and Media Development, 2014), 815.

[44] Saad Salloum, *Creative Diversity: Roadmap to Enhance Pluralism in Iraq* (Baghdad: Masarat Institute for Cultural and Media Development, 2015) 25-27.

Minorities in Iraq

State models without any recognition of diversity tend to end like that: Mosul after ISIS 2018. (Picture: Thomas Schmidinger)

CHAPTER 2

THE JEWS OF IRAQ

Birgit Ammann

Describing the Jewish communities in the multi-religious history of Iraq can only take place from a historical perspective, simply because they no longer exist. Apart from a few individuals, there is no future perspective at this point in time.

The history of the Jews in what today is Iraq, goes back before the establishment of the Kingdom and later the Republic of Iraq, the Ottoman Empire, the Abbasi Caliphate during the Middle Ages and into the Assyrian and Babylonian periods. Beginning with the ninth century before the Common Era means a timeframe of almost 2800 years for Jewish history. There are two entirely different stories: the story of the Arab Jews and the story of the Kurdish Jews.

There have been two different major waves of deportation. At the relevant time, there were two adjoining Jewish Kingdoms: the Kingdom of Israel (Jerusalem) and the Kingdom of Judah (Samaria – today's Nablus). The ancestors of Kurdish Jews had been exiled from ancient Israel to Assyria around 724 BCE and the ones usually referred to as Iraqi or Baghdadi Jews have been deported more than 100 years later from ancient Judah to Babylon.[1]

The Old Testament from a Christian perspective has several references to these major deportations. The Old Testament refers to the Assyrian Captivity: 'In the ninth year of Hoshea, the king of Assyria captured Samaria, and deported the Israelites away to Assyria. He settled them in Halah in Gozan, on the Habor River and in the towns of the Medes'.[2] Hoshea has been king of ancient Israel in 724 BCE; the king of Assyria has been Shalmaneser. The ancient city of Samaria had been located near today's Palestinian Nablus on the West Bank. Halah might have been today's Çele (Kurdish) Çukurca (Turkish) in Turkey.[3] Gozan had been an Aramaean city-

---

[1] Among all the mono-dimensional designations, this contribution for practical reasons does not use Babylonian and Assyrian Jews but the terms Arab and Kurdish (Jews).
[2] 2 Kings 17:6.
[3] Birgit Ammann, 'The Kurdish Jewish Communities – Lost Forever' In *Religious Minorities in Kurdistan:*

state in the tenth century BCE, near the archaeological site Tell Halaff in Al-Hasakah Governorate, Syria. The Habor River, of course, corresponds to the modern Khabur River and finally the towns of the Medes were to be found in the Zagros Mountains, today's north-western Iran and northern Iraq. In the described area, Kurds have been the dominant ethnic group since they entered the historical record in the seventh century CE, trying to withstand the Muslim armies.[4]

About the Babylonian Captivity more than a hundred years later, the Old Testament notes: 'So, Judah went into captivity, away from her land. This is the number of the people Nebuchadnezzar, carried into exile: in the seventh year 3,023 Jews; in Nebuchadnezzar's eighteenth year, 832 people from Jerusalem; in his twenty-third year, 745 Jews taken into exile by Nebuzaradan the commander of the imperial guard. There were 4,600 people in all.'[5] Nebuchadnezzar II had been king of Babylon from 605–562 BCE and there is a common understanding that the Arab part of Iraq claims the geographical heritage of Babylon.

While most Jews in Babylon returned to Israel after around 70 years, there is no mention of a collective return of Jews from Assyria. Therefore, the myth of the ten lost tribes developed. Even though they have been there all the time with their existence quite well documented, the Kurdish Jews are still not officially acknowledged as these lost tribes. As will be pointed out later, the Kurdish Jewish community had enormous cultural, language and class differences with the Baghdadi or, in general, the urban Arab Jewish community.

Arab Jews on their way to Israel 1951

Most Arab Jews lived in an urban environment, they were usually well educated, influential in many respects and many were very wealthy. In this picture, taken in a transit camp a few hours after arrival in Israel, clothes, hairstyle and looks express a modern life style as compared to the Kurdish men in the following picture.

Kurdish Jews have mostly been living in a rural environment. They had very little or no formal education, often depended on tribal leaders with a low social status and most were very poor. Families in a series of pictures in the Israeli National Photo Collection look massively overwhelmed and intimidated.

Beyond the Mainstream, Edited by Khanna Omarkhali (Wiesbaden: Harrasowitz, 2014), 271-300, 274.
[4] David McDowell, *A modern history of the Kurds*. (London: Tauris, 1997), 21.
[5] Jeremia 52: 28-30

Photo: Brauner Teddy, 1951. Copyright © 2019 National Photo Collection.

In this picture taken in a transit camp a few hours after arrival in Israel, clothes, hairstyle and looks express a modern life style as compared to the Kurdish men in the following picture.

Photo: Brauner Teddy, 1951. Copyright © 2019 National Photo Collection.

The intimidated facial expression and the fact that the man holds to his teakettle as part of his probably very meagre possessions indicates being very poor as well as being very religious by trying to keep the kettle kosher.

The two Jewish communities were hardly bound together by a nation state. The Kurdish-Jewish community had been part of a supranational ethno-cultural entity reaching out to parts of Turkey and Syria.[6] (Connections between the two communities have not been studied systematically. Historical origins can never be proven because hypotheses develop from oral history related to early travellers, researchers or politicians through times. For instance, the once entirely Jewish village of Betanure had oral traditions that they would be descendants of the Babylonian – as opposed to the Assyrian – exiles,[7] even though the village is in the heart of the Kurdish regions.

Naturally, religion offered a possible collective identity based on both groups making collective pilgrimages to holy places such as the tombs of various prophets scattered over the country. They were clearly connected through trading relations and occasional intermarriage. Places with mixed populations like Mosul, Kirkuk, and al-Qosh provided a regional connection and it is not clear whether the division between Kurdish and Arab has been prevalent or another overall Jewish identity had been built there.

Another connection was Kurdish Jews working in Jewish households in the Bagdad and Basra communities as housekeepers, gardeners and the like or were engaged in other physical work.[8]

In 1920, the entire Jewish population in Iraq was estimated at about 88,000, out of a total population of 2.8 million.[9] Around 80 per cent had been living in an Arab setting, Baghdad, Basra[10], Amara, Anah[11] and other cities. At the beginning of the twentieth century, around 40,000-50,000 Jews lived in Bagdad.[12] In the mid-twentieth century, Jews numbered around 137,000 with 80,000 in the city of Baghdad alone.[13] Jewish educational institutions in Baghdad enrolled 13,476 students in 1950. Also, two hospitals were managed by Jews (Jewish Virtual Library).

The Babylonian Jews in the region of today's Iraq became especially famous for compiling the Talmud, the most important source of Jewish theology. Their predominant language was a particular form of Judeo-Arabic

---

[6] Birgit Ammann, 'The Kurdish Jewish Communities – Lost Forever' In *Religious Minorities in Kurdistan: Beyond the Mainstream*. Edited by Khanna Omarkhali (Wiesbaden: Harrasowitz, 2014), 271-300, 271ff.

[7] Hezy Mutzafi, *The Jewish Neo-Aramaic Dialect of Betanure (Province of Dihok)*. (Wiesbaden: Harrasowitz, 2008), 4.

[8] Mordechai Zaken, Jewish Subjects and their Tribal Chieftains in Kurdistan. A Study in Survival. (Leiden: Brill, 2007), 132. Tamar Morad / Dennis Shasha / Robert Shasha (eds.), Iraq's Last Jews. Stories of Daily Life, Upheaval, and Escape from Modern Babylon. (New York: Palgrave Macmillan, 2008), 70.

[9] Moshe Gat, 'The Immigration of Iraqi Jewry to Israel as Reflected in Literature' *Revue Européenne des Migrations Internationales* 14/3 (1998), 45-60, 46.

[10] For a historical in-depth description on the Basra community, see Sassoon 1929

[11] Mordechai Ben-Porat, *To Baghdad and Back: The Miraculous 2000 Year Homecoming of the Iraqi Jews*. (Jerusalem: Gefen Publishing House, 1998), 33, 192.

[12] Moshe Gat, 'The Immigration of Iraqi Jewry to Israel as Reflected in Literature.' *Revue Européenne des Migrations Internationales* 14/3 (1998), 45-60, 46.

[13] Tamar Morad / Dennis Shasha / Robert Shasha (eds.) *Iraq's Last Jews. Stories of Daily Life, Upheaval, and Escape from Modern Babylon*. (New York: Palgrave Macmillan, 2008), 4, 95.

partly using Hebrew characters.[14]

Even though Iraqi Jewry was the largest and most affluent Jewish historical community in the Middle East and most Arab Jews lived in an urban setting, they did not all belong to the rich, cosmopolitan upper class. Gat states: 'This is not to say that the majority of the Jewish community engaged in trade and banking, but only a small minority. Most of the Jews earned their livelihood as small tradesmen and peddlers.'[15] Morad et al. notes that Baghdad had many quarters well known as Jewish areas while also being the poorest in the city.[16]

In a tragic way, this alleged overall wealth shows some parallels to Germany with one per cent Jewish population, most of which had not been rich. Among other forms of antisemitism, Jews also faced economic discrimination that developed extremely fast and climaxed in genocide.

However, it is true that well-educated Iraqi Jews played an important role in civic life and that the 'icons of Iraqi society were its Jews'.[17] The first Minister of Finance during the monarchy (1921 – 1958) was Jewish. Jews controlled trade, money changing, and various banking activities. Jews founded the first banks in Iraq. The first Iraqi government-owned bank was founded in 1936 with most employees being Jewish.[18] Jews were important in developing the judicial and postal systems. Records from the Baghdad Chamber of Commerce show that 10 out of its 19 members in 1947 were Jews.

At the time of the monarchy, Jews played an enormously important artistic role; for example, most professional musicians in Bagdad were Jewish.[19] Many Jews held significant positions in the bureaucracy. The first Iraqi parliament had six seats reserved for Jews.[20] While living a traditional religious life with an estimated sixty synagogues in Bagdad alone, Jews were fully integrated into Iraqi society. They felt that they were Jews by religion

---

[14] Ibid, 1.
[15] Moshe Gat, 'The Immigration of Iraqi Jewry to Israel as Reflected in Literature' *Revue Européenne des Migrations Internationales* 14/3 (1998), 45-60, 46
[16] Tamar Morad / Dennis Shasha / Robert Shasha (eds.) *Iraq's Last Jews. Stories of Daily Life, Upheaval, and Escape from Modern Babylon.* (New York: Palgrave Macmillan, 2008), 243.
[17] Ibid., 243.
[18] Moshe Gat, 'The Immigration of Iraqi Jewry to Israel as Reflected in Literature' *Revue Européenne des Migrations Internationales* 14/3 (1998), 45-60, 46.
[19] Tamar Morad / Dennis Shasha / Robert Shasha (eds.) *Iraq's Last Jews. Stories of Daily Life, Upheaval, and Escape from Modern Babylon.* (New York: Palgrave Macmillan, 2008), 22ff. Morad et al has a section on music written by the son of one two of the most famous Iraqi musicians at the time: the Kuwaity Brothers. Dudu Tassa, Israeli grandson of one of the brothers, very successfully reinterprets their music (see https://www.the-kuwaitis.com/).
[20] Mordechai Ben-Porat, *To Baghdad and Back: The Miraculous 2000 Year Homecoming of the Iraqi Jews.* (Jerusalem: Gefen Publishing House, 1998), 283.

and Arabs by nationality[21] and strongly identified with the country.[22] The overall atmosphere was one of coexistence, friendship, and partnership. They were part of the elite and found themselves at the centre of its political and intellectual life. They viewed themselves as helping to shape the character of Iraqi society and state.[23]

The political views among the Jews had three perspectives.[24] The wealthy establishment believed that the future for the Jews was to be in Iraq and the tragic problems should be solved within the country. Zionism and emigration to them was not an alternative. They saw Zionist activities as a grave risk for the entire community.[25]

A second political perspective came from the small Zionist movement in Iraq[26]. Its activities had started around the end of WW I and had been 'flourishing' by the end of the 1920s.[27] Brauer states that Kurdistan also had Zionist activists.[28] The chief aim of Zionism was to protect the lives of the Jews in the event of a recurrence of Muslim violence. They maintained that a future in Iraq was not secure, and the solution should be the return to the Jewish homeland.[29]

The third political perspective was from Jews active in the Communist Party and opposed to the Zionist movement. The Communists strove for the end of class and religious differences in Iraqi society, for equality and mutual respect. They considered Zionism yet another form of imperialism.[30]

Even though integrationists and the Communists strongly opposed each other, both felt very patriotic and shared opposition to the British colonial status. In particular, they felt the British-controlled Iraq Petroleum Company 'pumped out the country's wealth'.[31]

The following description gives an impression of the situation and the

---

[21] This individual and immediate state of emotion is well illustrated in a documentary from 2003, which shows how much an 87-year-old man from Bagdad who immigrated to Israel as one of the last Jews living in Bagdad emotionally relates to Muslim Arabs – let aside all political implications. https://www.youtube.com/watch?v=LTZ4jwQclyQ

[22] Moshe Gat, 'The Immigration of Iraqi Jewry to Israel as Reflected in Literature' *Revue Européenne des Migrations Internationales* 14/3 (1998), 45-60, 47.

[23] Ibid., 47.

[24] Ibid., 49.

Tamar Morad / Dennis Shasha / Robert Shasha (eds.), *Iraq's Last Jews. Stories of Daily Life, Upheaval, and Escape from Modern Babylon.* (New York: Palgrave Macmillan, 2008), 7.

[25] Moshe Gat, 'The Immigration of Iraqi Jewry to Israel as Reflected in Literature' *Revue Européenne des Migrations Internationales* 14/3 (1998), 45-60, 49.

[26] For an in-depth account on the Zionist movement in Iraq, see Alexander 2011.

[27] Shlomo Hillel, *Operation Babylon. Jewish Clandestine Activity in the Middle East.* (London: Fontana, 1989), 21f.

[28] Erich Brauer, *The Jews of Kurdistan.* (Detroit: Wayne State University Press, 1993), 48.

[29] Moshe Gat, 'The Immigration of Iraqi Jewry to Israel as Reflected in Literature' *Revue Européenne des Migrations Internationales* 14/3 (1998), 45-60, 49.

[30] Ibid., 49.

[31] Shlomo Hillel, *Operation Babylon. Jewish Clandestine Activity in the Middle East.* (London: Fontana, 1989), 145.

climate in Bagdad in the 1930s when the situation began to become tense and dangerous:

> Here and there Jews (...) found themselves under physical attack – an extension, so to speak, of the anti-Jewish ferment in Palestine. A demonstration might get out of hand, and before you knew it, Jewish shops were the target of wanton destruction and plunder. The best defense in the circumstances was to hole up at home and wait for the storm to pass. A day or two later, life would resume as usual, though a hint of menace lingered beneath the surface.[32]

In 1932, Iraq achieved full independence after the British mandate ended. In 1933, the Nazis came to power in Germany, and their influence was soon to become strong in Iraq. The new King Ghazi was a fervent admirer of the Nazi ideology.[33] Iraqi nationalists viewed Nazi ideology as coinciding with their anti-British and anti-Jewish views.[34] At the same time, the British meant a certain protection for the Jews. The German ambassador Fritz Grobba was a highly popular figure in governmental circles at the time. He had Hitler's, *Mein Kampf* translated into Arabic and serialised in a newspaper. His antisemitic propaganda has partly been responsible for the Farhud pogrom.[35]

In October 1939, just after the outbreak of World War II, the Mufti of Jerusalem, a violent anti-Semite, made Baghdad his new base. He thereby escaped his arrest after an Arab revolt against the British Mandate in Palestine. He played an active part in a venomous and unrelenting campaign against Iraq's Jewry community and closely collaborated with the Nazi regime.[36] (Jewish Virtual Library). In June 1941, over a period of two days, the Rashid Ali regime carried out Nazi-inspired pogroms in Baghdad that murdered 180 Jews and involved other terrible acts of violence. It was to become part of a traumatised collective memory of Iraqi Jewry. After an attempted coup d'etat against the British, a security vacuum emerged that allowed the pogrom involving random murders of Jews on the streets.[37]

The massiveness of the Farhud pogrom had been unpredicted and came as a total shock, not only to the Jews. From today's perspective, a 1933 massacre against Assyrian Christians in the town of Semile in northern Iraq

---

[32] Ibid., 22.
[33] Ibid., 199.
[34] Moshe Gat, 'The Immigration of Iraqi Jewry to Israel as Reflected in Literature.' *Revue Européenne des Migrations Internationales* 14/3 (1998), 45-60, 47.
[35] Norman A. Steillman, *The Jews of Arab Lands in Modern Times.* (Philadelphia: The Jewish Publication Society, 1991), 117ff.
[36] He was to live in Berlin between 1941 and 1945.
[37] Tamar Morad / Dennis Shasha / Robert Shasha (eds.), *Iraq's Last Jews. Stories of Daily Life, Upheaval, and Escape from Modern Babylon.* (New York: Palgrave Macmillan, 2008), 7.
Mordechai Ben-Porat, *To Baghdad and Back: The Miraculous 2000 Year Homecoming of the Iraqi Jews.* (Jerusalem: Gefen Publishing House, 1998), 41.

as well as the 1938 November Pogroms in Germany could have been an advanced warning[38] and indeed did alarm some Jews.[39] The Farhud pogrom changed everything, discrimination turned into systematic persecution. The traditional, quite natural and comfortable, coexistence came to an end, even though most Jews continued to believe in Iraq as their homeland.[40]

Conditions once more terribly deteriorated with the declaration of independence of Israel in May 1948 when the Jews became collective scapegoats for the Iraqi defeats in the war over Palestine.[41] Personal letters between families in Iraq and Palestine – interpreted as 'maintaining ties with the enemies' most irresponsibly turned over by the British led to yet another wave of mass arrests.[42] In September of the same year, Shafiq Ades, 'an assimilated Jew par excellence'[43] from Basra was executed on grounds that are not worth mentioning. The message meant, if a man as well connected and powerful as Ades could be eliminated by the state, other Jews would not be protected any longer.[44] It had also been a special warning to the Basra community. By that time, Iraqi economy had declined since more than 40 per cent of the national budget was spent on the battle against Israel.[45] From the viewpoint of the regime, distraction from these ills became obviously necessary by inciting outrage against their Jewish countrymen.

While a vast amount of academic as well as other literature, high-quality journalism, and documentaries analyse the Iraqi-Arab Jews, few academic works consider the Kurdish Jews and very little fiction[46] is available. Very little knowledge of the Kurdish Jews circulates in general. Publications on the Jews of Iraq[47] subsume the Kurdish Jews under the overall Jewish population and hardly ever mention them by name. Kurdishness, the region, the language, living conditions or other features do not appear except in allusions. Assessments of the size of their community are quite speculative since no official records seem to document the Jewish Kurds. The British estimated 16,856, the Iraqis counted 11,798 Jews living

---

[38] Tamar Morad / Dennis Shasha / Robert Shasha (eds.), *Iraq's Last Jews. Stories of Daily Life, Upheaval, and Escape from Modern Babylon*. (New York: Palgrave Macmillan, 2008), 126.

[39] Shlomo Hillel, *Operation Babylon. Jewish Clandestine Activity in the Middle East*. (London: Fontana, 1989), 19ff.

[40] Orit Bashkin, *New Babylonians: A History of Jews in Modern Iraq*. (Stanford: Stanford University Press, 2012), 138.

[41] Shlomo Hillel, *Operation Babylon. Jewish Clandestine Activity in the Middle East*. (London: Fontana, 1989), 283f.

[42] Ibid., 152. Joseph B. Schechtman, 'The Repatriation of Iraq Jewry' Jewish Social Studies 15/2 (1953), 151-72, 163.

[43] Shlomo Hillel, *Operation Babylon. Jewish Clandestine Activity in the Middle East*. (London: Fontana, 1989), 153.

[44] Orit Bashkin, *New Babylonians: A History of Jews in Modern Iraq*. (Stanford: Stanford University Press, 2012), 90.

[45] Shlomo Hillel, *Operation Babylon. Jewish Clandestine Activity in the Middle East*. (London: Fontana, 1989), 219.

[46] To the authors knowledge, Baruch 2016, Neurink 2018 and Sabar 2008 have written the only scholarly works. All three claim convincingly that most of their work is based on serious research.

[47] Hillel 1989, Ben Porat 1998, Gat 1998, Morad et al. 2008, Rejvan 2010, Bashkin 2012.

in the Mosul vilayet.[48] As mentioned previously, not all Jews in the vilayet have necessarily been Kurdish.

Morad et al.[49] estimate around 20,000 Kurdish Jews lived in north Iraq until the early 1950s. Zaken[50] presents most exact numbers, partly based on Iraqi statistics: in 1947, almost 23,000 Jews lived in the north of Iraq; 3,109 in Erbil province, 4,042 in Kirkuk, 10,345 in Mosul, 2,271 in Suleimania and 2,851 in Diyala. Both numbers make sense since not all Jews in Mosul are to be characterised as Kurdish. Apart from a few exclusively Jewish settlements like Sandur[51] and Betanure,[52] Kurdish Jews lived in ethnically mixed towns and villages in their separate quarters, as was common for all the different ethnic communities.[53]

In an ethnic sense, with all the political implications, their loyalty was to their Kurdish setting and not to the Arab or Turkish culture. Apart from religious rites and rules, their material culture has been identical to that of Muslims and Christians.[54] Vastly outnumbered by Islamic Kurds and to a lesser degree Aramaic- and Armenian-speaking Christians, Yezidis, and other groups, Jews have held, for centuries, a clearly underprivileged position as dependents in a tribal and feudal society. The dominant, privileged majority had been Sunni Kurds. Whereas most of them and some of the Christians were tribal people, the Jews were not. In reference to their status as *dhimmi*[55] they more or less all depended on the protection of tribal chiefs, whereas other groups did so only in part. Dependents were subject to their landlords' jurisdiction and, were, in the nature of feudalism, arbitrarily granted patronage. However, Jews played a special and important economic role as craftsmen, especially as weavers and silversmiths.[56]

Among the leading urban Jewish families were Zakho, Aqra, Amadiya, Dohuk, Erbil, Koy Sanjaq and Sulaimaniya; some served as representatives in the municipal councils.[57] Jews lived in separate urban neighbourhoods just

---

[48] Liam Anderson / Gareth Stansfield, *Crisis in Kirkuk: The Ethnopolitics of Conflict and Compromise*. (Philadelphia: University of Pennsylvania Press, 2009), 25.

[49] Tamar Morad / Dennis Shasha / Robert Shasha (eds.), *Iraq's Last Jews. Stories of Daily Life, Upheaval, and Escape from Modern Babylon*. (New York: Palgrave Macmillan, 2008), 8.

[50] Mordechai Zaken, 'The Jewish communities in Kurdistan within the tribal Kurdish Society' In *The Routledge Handbook on the Kurds*. Edited by Michael M. Gunter (New York: Routledge, 2018), 181 – 201, 181.

[51] Henry Aaron Stern, 'Journal of the Reverend H. A. Stern' Jewish Missionary Intelligence 14 (1848), 112 – 120, 113. Walter Joseph Fischel, 'The Jews of Kurdistan. A First-Hand Report on a Near Eastern Mountain Community' Commentary 8/6 (1949), 554 -559, 557.

[52] Hezy Mutzafi, *The Jewish Neo-Aramaic Dialect of Betanure (Province of Dihok)*. (Wiesbaden: Harrasowitz, 2008).

[53] For a listing of some places including historical settlements in Turkey, Iran, and Syria see Ammann 2014, 278-286 and Zaken 2007, 372f.

[54] Birgit Ammann, 'The Kurdish Jewish Communities – Lost Forever' In *Religious Minorities in Kurdistan: Beyond the Mainstream*. Edited by Khanna Omarkhali (Wiesbaden: Harrasowitz, 2014), 295f.

[55] Non-Muslim groups in Islamic states; restricted but protected in return for levies.

[56] Ibid., 287.

[57] Mordechai Zaken, *Jewish Subjects and their Tribal Chieftains in Kurdistan. A Study in Survival*. (Leiden: Brill, 2007), 26.

as Christians did; in Kurmanji-Kurdish, the Jewish quarters have been called *mahalle jîya* and in Sorani-Kurdish, *mahalle jewlakan*.[58] Urban and rural life had closely knit connections. Urban Jews often travelled in rural areas where they were subjects to tribal rules. At the same time, part of the urban population was composed of migrants from rural villages.[59]

Unlike the Arab part of Iraq, the Kurdish area had almost no modern infrastructure supporting the supply of electricity, water supply, medical supply and transportation.[60] Nomadic, semi-nomadic, or settled tribes surrounded the handful of cities and towns. They controlled the country's communication system and held nine-tenths of its land. In 1933, a year after independence of the new Iraqi State, tribesmen had approximately 100,000 rifles whereas government forces held only 15,000.[61] That situation reflects what has been the case for centuries. To tribal individuals, as well as the non-tribal Jews, the authority of the hereditary tribal leadership, represented by the *agha* and his family, was much more powerful than the government officials.[62] In other words, the central power of the young republic had little influence on the archaic social structures, especially in the mountainous regions. When the central state powers seriously asserted control, the Jews had already left.

The Kurdish Jews' first and native language has been Aramaic with different regional vernaculars and very slight differences from the version spoken by the Christian population with whom communication in Aramaic has been possible. The Jewish variant used Hebrew characters if written; their second language was Kurdish.[63]

According to studies around the time of their emigrating in the 1950s, small communities of the Jews in Kurdistan had little social or religious organisation and almost no communal institutions.[64] The few existing synagogues served their purpose, usually offered activities on Sabbath and religious holidays. In the mid-1950s, they were described as mostly old wooden structures, devoid of any ornamental or decorative attraction and in a state of utter neglect and decay.[65]

---

[58] Birgit Ammann, 'The Kurdish Jewish Communities – Lost Forever' In *Religious Minorities in Kurdistan: Beyond the Mainstream*. Edited by Khanna Omarkhali (Wiesbaden: Harrasowitz, 2014), 271 – 300, 287.

[59] Mordechai Zaken, *Jewish Subjects and their Tribal Chieftains in Kurdistan. A Study in Survival*. (Leiden: Brill, 2007), 21.

[60] Ibid., 9.

[61] Ibid., 22.

[62] Ibid., 23.

[63] Yona Sabar, *The Folk Literature of the Kurdistani Jews: An Anthology*. (New Haven: Yale University Press, 1982), xxxiv. Erich Brauer, *The Jews of Kurdistan*. (Detroit: Wayne State University Press, 1993), 241f.

[64] Walter Joseph Fischel, 'The Jews of Kurdistan. A First-Hand Report on a Near Eastern Mountain Community.' Commentary 8/6 (1949), 554 -559, 558. Mordechai Zaken, Jewish Subjects and their Tribal Chieftains in Kurdistan. A Study in Survival. (Leiden: Brill, 2007), 28.

[65] Walter Joseph Fischel, 'The Jews of Kurdistan. A First-Hand Report on a Near Eastern Mountain Community.' *Commentary* 8/6 (1949), 554-559, 558.

Kurdish Jews had very low religious and general education. Unlike other Jewish communities, illiteracy was not unusual. Despite their shallow religious knowledge, their traditionally religious life strictly followed the relevant dietary laws and holidays.[66]

For both Jews and their neighbours, the rural economy centred on agriculture and was largely self-sufficient. Most were farmers and herdsmen. Also, some Jews were artisans,[67] peddlers, boatmen, or other physical workers[68] with a very small number of medical doctors or lawyers.[69]

Through the centuries, Kurdish Jews had a generally undisturbed coexistence with non-Jews, but due to the nature of feudalism, certainly not based on equal rights. The Jews in Kurdistan lived in relative peace and security even though there had been some harassment and anti-Semitism, but not comparable to the Farhud pogroms and other atrocities in Bagdad and other Arab cities.[70] The descendants of the Kurdish Jews in Israel have a generally positive collective memory relating to the Kurdish areas.[71]

From 1951 to 1952, most members of both Jewish communities – 110,618 to be exact[72] – were airlifted on 950 flights to Israel in the so-called Operation Ezra and Nehemiah.[73] About ten per cent of the total Jewish population had already left for Palestine, later Israel, before the airlift,[74]

---

[66] Erich Brauer, *The Jews of Kurdistan*. (Detroit: Wayne State University Press, 1993), 96f.

[67] Ora Shwartz-Be'eri, 'Jewish Weaving in Kurdistan' *Journal of Jewish Art* 3/4, (1977), 74–89. Ora Shwartz-Be'eri, 'Kurdish Jewish Silvercraft.' *The Israel Museum Journal* 1 (1988), 75–86. Rudolf Berliner / Paul Borchhardt, *Silberschmiedearbeiten aus Kurdistan*. (Berlin: Dietrich Reimer Verlag, 1922), 8. Walter Joseph Fischel, 'The Jews of Kurdistan. A First-Hand Report on a Near Eastern Mountain Community' *Commentary* 8/6 (1949), 554 -559, 556.

[68] Mordechai Zaken, *Jewish Subjects and their Tribal Chieftains in Kurdistan. A Study in Survival*. (Leiden: Brill, 2007), 156.

[69] Joyce Blau, 'Les Juifs au Kurdistan' *Mélanges Linguistiques offerts à Maxime Rodinson* Supplement 12. (Paris: Protocolles de la Groupe Linguistique d'études chamito-sémitiques, 1985), 123–132, 125.

[70] Birgit Ammann, 'The Kurdish Jewish Communities – Lost Forever' In *Religious Minorities in Kurdistan: Beyond the Mainstream*. Edited by Khanna Omarkhali (Wiesbaden: Harrasowitz, 2014), 271 – 300, 296. Isaac Ben-Zvi, 'Lost and Regained: They That Were Lost in the Land of Assyria' *Phylon* 16/1 (1955), 57-63, 59.

[71] Birgit Ammann, 'The Kurdish Jewish Communities – Lost Forever' In *Religious Minorities in Kurdistan: Beyond the Mainstream*. Edited by Khanna Omarkhali (Wiesbaden: Harrasowitz, 2014), 271 – 300, 290. Lauren S. Marcus, 'The Kurdish immigrants who built Israel' *Forward* (published 15 October 2017). https://forward.com/life/faith/385209/the-kurdish-immigrants-who-built-israel/ (accessed 11 November 2018). Daniela Segenreich, 'Kurdistan und Israel – eine ungewöhnliche Freundschaft.' *NZZ* (published 19 October 2017) https://www.nzz.ch/feuilleton/kurdistan-und-israel-eine-ungewoehnliche-freundschaft-ld.1322350 (accessed 11 September 2018).

[72] Mordechai Ben-Porat, *To Baghdad and Back: The Miraculous 2000 Year Homecoming of the Iraqi Jews*. (Jerusalem: Gefen Publishing House, 1998), 283.

[73] Ezra and Nehemia were both leading figures in the Biblical account of remigration from the Babylonian Exile. The airlift operation has popularly also been called 'Operation Ali Baba'. Ben-Porats book calls it 'Operation Babylon'.

[74] Mordechai Ben-Porat, *To Baghdad and Back: The Miraculous 2000 Year Homecoming of the Iraqi Jews*. (Jerusalem: Gefen Publishing House, 1998), 183f. Tamar Morad / Dennis Shasha / Robert Shasha (eds.), *Iraq's Last Jews. Stories of Daily Life, Upheaval, and Escape from Modern Babylon*. (New York: Palgrave Macmillan, 2008), 95.

among them at least 8,000 Kurdish Jews.[75]

Iraq, as well as Israel, had completely underestimated the number of people willing to leave. Iraq had hoped to be rid of maybe 7-10,000 Jews.[76] Both countries were not prepared for the self-dynamic snowballing effect. After the Revocation of Citizenship bill ratified on 3 March 1950,[77] people quickly registered for emigration by the thousands.[78] Between having their citizenship revoked after registering for emigration and actually leaving with the airlift operation, the backlog of denationalised Jews attempted to survive without support.[79] Tens of thousands of stateless Jews, many in panic over steadily rising harassment, including several bombings of places associated with Jews, lingered around the emigration centres in Bagdad without food and other supplies.[80] In the Kurdish town of Zakho, more than half of the Jewish population had registered for emigration and found themselves in a desperate situation.[81] In Mosul, a small-scale revolt took place and people forced their way into one of the centres.[82] In Basra, the affected described their situation in a telegram:

> We, the Jewish citizens of Basra, Kal'at Salh and El-Azar, are putting our plea before you just as Moshe asked mercy from God, and hereby approach you to ask for your sympathy as Arabs to save us from our distress and suffering. Five months passed since we left our homes and our situation is very sad. We and our children are facing disaster. The planes are continuing from Baghdad but we cannot understand the reason for refusing flights from Basra. Please, look upon us with sympathy and generosity. Save us from hunger and misery, in fact from death. Our lives rest in your generous hands. Rescue us from this injustice. We are putting all our faith in you.[83]

---

[75] Isaac Ben-Zvi, 'Lost and Regained: They That Were Lost in the Land of Assyria' *Phylon* 16/1 (1955), 57-63, 59.

[76] Richard Stretton, 'Ezra & Nehemia: Operation Ali Baba' *Yesterdays Airlines* (published 25 August 2017) https://www.yesterdaysairlines.com/airline-history-blog/ezra-nehemia-operation-ali-baba (accessed 18 November 2018).

[77] Mordechai Ben-Porat, *To Baghdad and Back: The Miraculous 2000 Year Homecoming of the Iraqi Jews*. (Jerusalem: Gefen Publishing House, 1998), 148.

[78] Shlomo Hillel, *Operation Babylon. Jewish Clandestine Activity in the Middle East*. (London: Fontana, 1989), 304, 308.

[79] Joseph B. Schechtman, 'The Repatriation of Iraq Jewry' *Jewish Social Studies* 15/2 (1953): 151-172, 162.

[80] Shlomo Hillel, *Operation Babylon. Jewish Clandestine Activity in the Middle East*. (London: Fontana, 1989), 304, 350ff. Mordechai Ben-Porat, *To Baghdad and Back: The Miraculous 2000 Year Homecoming of the Iraqi Jews*. (Jerusalem: Gefen Publishing House, 1998), 152f.

[81] Ariel Sabar, *My Father's Paradise. A Son's Search for his Jewish Past in Kurdish Iraq*. (Chapel Hill: Algonquin Books of Chapel Hill, 2008), 97f.

[82] Mordechai Ben-Porat, *To Baghdad and Back: The Miraculous 2000 Year Homecoming of the Iraqi Jews*. (Jerusalem: Gefen Publishing House, 1998), 152.

[83] Ibid., 166f.

Israel, however, began to realise that it was becoming overburdened with the immigrants. Initial conditions were bad and disappointing to many of the new immigrants, who were thrust into a completely new reality.[84] In 1949, a third of Baghdad's companies were Jewish while Jewish firms handled 45 per cent of the nation's exports and nearly 75 per cent of the imports; therefore, Iraq profited enormously from the mass emigration by confiscating property and freezing assets.[85] The Iraqi Prime Minister was on the board of the airline operating the airlift. Israel benefitted by having its financial authorities demand a 20 per cent commission for incoming bank transfers.[86]

An ongoing, widespread debate exists in both Israel and Iraq about several bombings quite randomly targeting Jewish institutions, companies and individuals while the airlift operation was going on. Some claim that Zionist agents executed the attacks in order to accelerate the emigration of the Jewish population. Several Iraqi-Jewish men, members of the Zionist underground, were arrested in Iraq and interrogated under torture, two were sentenced to death. Ben-Porat explains the circumstances of the bombings in Baghdad and Basra from the point of view of a person affected by the allegations. Two consecutive inquiry commissions in Israel proves the allegations wrong.[87] Additional later findings make it clear, however, that the last assaults had probably been done by another Iraqi member of the Zionist underground.[88] Overall, there is no clear evidence of who were the perpetrators of which attack. True or not, the persistence of the debate reflects a certain retrospective scepticism towards Israel's motives and especially the hard times the emigres went through upon arrival as well as their negative experience as Mizrahi.

As already mentioned, in comparison to the Arab Jews, little general information exists concerning the life of the Kurdish Jews and the circumstances of their emigration.[89] Everything along the mountainous border to Turkey seemed terra incognito. Contemporary witnesses and central agents in the airlift, Hillel[90] and Ben-Porat do not mention the

---

[84] Shlomo Hillel, *Operation Babylon. Jewish Clandestine Activity in the Middle East*. (London: Fontana, 1989), 379ff. Mordechai Ben-Porat, *To Baghdad and Back: The Miraculous 2000 Year Homecoming of the Iraqi Jews*. (Jerusalem: Gefen Publishing House, 1998), 174.

[85] Confiscating Jewish Property Bill ratified on 22 March 1951 (Ben-Porat 1998: 185).

[86] Mordechai Ben-Porat, *To Baghdad and Back: The Miraculous 2000 Year Homecoming of the Iraqi Jews*. (Jerusalem: Gefen Publishing House, 1998), 274.

[87] Ibid., 176-188.

[88] Yehouda Shenhav, 'The Jews of Iraq, Zionist Ideology, and the Property of the Palestinian Refugees of 1948: An Anomaly of National Accounting' *International Journal of Middle East Studies* 31/4 (1999), 605-630. Tom Segev, 'Now It Can Be Told: Yehuda Tager, an Israeli agent who operated in Baghdad, sheds new light on a 55-year-old mystery: Who carried out the bombing of the Masuda Shemtov synagogue' *Haaretz*, (published April 6, 2006) https://www.haaretz.com/1.4900019 (accessed 11.9.2018).

[89] No systematic historical research has been undertaken or at least published to the author's knowledge.

[90] Hillel (1989: 192) had no idea of Aramaic being the spoken language of the Kurdish Jews. This becomes obvious when he is with Assyrians describing his astonishment about their active use of the Aramaic language. His book (1989: 196f) provides details about Christian-Assyrians, but not the history of the neighbouring Jews.

Kurdish Jews in their memoirs. It seems as if they did not even know about the enormous cultural differences between the two groups.[91] However, the situation of the Kurdish Jews has been far less traumatic than that of the Arab Jews in the years before the airlift. Nevertheless, they had reason to leave. For example, in 1941 and in 1942, the headman of the village of Sandur expressed the ardent wish for the 50 families to leave the village and asked for permission to immigrate to Palestine.[92]

The special dynamics and general circumstances of their emigration needs to be explored in more detail. Probably a mass panic broke out, the Kurdish Jews had heard of the Farhud pogrom and other atrocities in the Arab parts of the country. Rumours of the Shoah in Europe had most certainly reached them just like the Arab Jews. As in the general difficulty of assessing the proportion of push and pull factors that caused migration, the Kurdish Jews were instrumentalised by both sides within the Jewish-Arab conflict when transferred to the newly founded state of Israel. Due to their society's patriarchal and tribal structure, the common villagers did not take part in the decision to leave their homeland. Zaken describes the Kurdish Jews as 'generally submissive',[93] which seems to fit the following quote of a flight attendant who accompanied many of the flights to Israel: '…in many cases they didn't really know why they were going except that it was what everyone was doing.'[94] As Schmidinger points out in this volume[95], the collective memory – even though mostly positive – is influenced by the Zionist narrative that every Israeli child learns in school. Real memories or parents' oral history might mingle with the view that it had always and everywhere been a natural thing for Jews to long for and migrate to Israel.

There is very little written of how people, especially the thousand in remote rural areas, were collected and how they got to Bagdad. Zaken [96] mentions that three bus convoys of Jews left Zakho and how a friendly Muslim protector escorted them. Since there had been a train connection between Mosul and Bagdad since 1940, they very likely all took that route at least in the context of the official airlift in 1951/52. The villagers of Sandur left for Israel via Bagdad.[97] It is also documented that the entire population

---

[91] This is also reflected in the most important organisation of the Jews from Iraq, the Babylonian Jewry Heritage Center in Or Yehuda founded by Mordechai Ben-Porat and Shlomo Hillel.
[92] Mordechai Zaken, *Jewish Subjects and their Tribal Chieftains in Kurdistan. A Study in Survival*. (Leiden: Brill, 2007), 132.
[93] Mordechai Zaken, 'The Jewish communities in Kurdistan within the tribal Kurdish Society.' In *The Routledge Handbook on the Kurds*, edited by Michael M. Gunter (New York: Routledge, 2018), 181 – 201, 181.
[94] Tamar Morad / Dennis Shasha / Robert Shasha (eds.) *Iraq's Last Jews. Stories of Daily Life, Upheaval, and Escape from Modern Babylon*. (New York: Palgrave Macmillan, 2008), 120.
[95] Thomas Schmidinger: The Lost Readers of the Scripture: Some notes on the Karaite community of Hīt in this book.
[96] Mordechai Zaken, 'The Jewish communities in Kurdistan within the tribal Kurdish Society' In *The Routledge Handbook on the Kurds*. Edited by Michael M. Gunter (New York: Routledge, 2018), 181-201, 192.
[97] Personal conversation with emigrants in Afula November 1987.

of another exclusively Jewish villages, Betanure, left for Israel in 1951,[98] probably on the same route.

After the airlift operation in 1951/52, only around 9,000 Jews, mostly Arab, stayed behind.[99] All Jewish institutions were henceforth seen as instruments of Zionism and the Iraqi government completely turned against everything Jewish. Those who had stayed behind hid their identity and suffered from severe anti-Semitism and persecution especially under the rule of the Baathists. At least 4,000 more Jews have left Iraq via Iran since the airlift before 1997.[100]

In the early nineties, after the Saddam regime had put down a Kurdish uprising, Israel took in some 1,000 refugees in two secret airlifts. These Kurds claimed to be of Jewish descent and/or expressed interest in actively converting to Judaism. Most left Israel after things calmed down.[101]

On the sidelines of the Kurdish-Israeli relations, a somewhat peculiar discourse has arisen about defining Jewishness and the question whether secret Kurdish Jews are still living in the Kurdish Region. There have been longstanding, originally secret, political relations between the Kurds in Iraq and Israel[102] (Bengio 2014). Following the motto of the uniting power of a common enemy, both sides had good reasons to cooperate. However, it had been risky especially for the Kurds to ally openly. Visits of Mustafa Barzani and two of his sons to Israel in the 1960s and the military aid that Israel had offered the Kurds in the 1970s constituted a very strong taboo even in the Iraqi-Kurdish diaspora until the 1990s. Since the official establishment of the Kurdistan Region in Iraq in 1992, relations have intensified and are not secret anymore. In 2015, so-called Law of Minorities allowed Jews to return to the Kurdish region. Both sides openly and regularly refer to their friendship. The general taboo on ties between Israelis and Iraqis has also been cracking after 2003 within the Arab-speaking part of Iraq.

The Iraqi Kurdistan Ministry of Religious Affairs had appointed a Jewish representative along with six other minority representatives. He soon stated that a Jewish community of about 430 families existed in the Kurdish part of

---

[98] Hezy Mutzafi, *The Jewish Neo-Aramaic Dialect of Betanure (Province of Dihok)*. (Wiesbaden: Harrasowitz, 2008), xiii, 8.

[99] Mordechai Ben-Porat, *To Baghdad and Back: The Miraculous 2000 Year Homecoming of the Iraqi Jews*. (Jerusalem: Gefen Publishing House, 1998), 283.

[100] Ibid., 289.

[101] Ariel Ben Solomon 'Publicity seeking Kurdish official brings back memories of Jewish Kurd aliya fiasco' *Jerusalem Post*, (published 7 December 2015). https://www.jpost.com/Middle-East/Use-of-Jewish-issue-by-KRG-official-may-cause-confusion-and-damage-436499. Ziv Genesove, 'Stranded in Iraq, some Jews say Israel abandoned them.' *Times of Israel* (published 5 January 2018). https://www.timesofisrael.com/stranded-in-iraq-some-jews-say-israel-abandoned-them/ (accessed 11 August 2018). Judit Neurink, 'Jews of Kurdistan want more recognition' *Deutsche Welle*, (published 15 July 2016) https://p.dw.com/p/1Iy7U (accessed 1.11.2018).

[102] Ofra Bengio, 'Surprising Ties between Israel and the Kurds' *Middle East Quarterly* 21/3 (2014), 1-12. www.meforum.org/articles/2014/surprising-ties-between-israel-and-the-kurds. (accessed 26.10.18).

Iraq. Soon after reaching international attention, the ministry dismissed the report.[103] The idea of a kind of crypto-Judaism with thousands of individuals outwardly professing Islam but having secretly practiced Judaism for decades had not been heard of and caused astonishment and in some cases annoyance.[104]

Jews are an ethno-religious group, with strong interrelationships between their ethnicity and religion. Theoretically, if one follows religious Jewish law, the female lineage transfers the Jewish identity. Anyone with a Jewish mother, grandmother and great-grandmother could theoretically be considered Jewish, although in practice rabbinic authority would have to be consulted. The Israeli Law of Return is not intended for male Jewish lineage and causes some trouble for potential immigrants to Israel.[105] Knowingly, or unknowingly, many Kurds descended from Jews who converted to Islam. Many of these ancestors were young girls who had married Muslim men voluntarily or by force. Their grandchildren or greatgrandchildren begin to address the subject and often acknowledge their Jewish ancestors with a certain pride.

The former Jewish representative on the question of Jewish identification described himself as a member of the community: 'Yes, my father is Muslim, but my mother is a *Benjew*. Of course, if you ask her, she will not admit it after 70 years fearing for her life because she is Jewish.'[106] The term *Benjew* is a neologism that corresponds with the term *Benfalah*, which in the region is used for the descendants of Christians, who were abducted as children and adopted by Kurdish Muslims.[107] It goes back to a somewhat racialist concept that defines Jews strictly according to bloodline and not on the grounds of self-positioning. Being of Jewish ancestry has been a very strong taboo in Kurdish, as well as Arab society, in both Saddam and post-Saddam Iraq.

It is very speculative to claim that several hundred Jews live today in the Kurdish Region.[108] The weak argument that people would deny their Jewishness out of fear blocks any possibility of verification. To mix those with a few hundreds of Kurds with Israeli passports or identity cards in Kurdistan, learning the Hebrew language[109] is a different story altogether.

---

[103] The ministry has indirectly confirmed the dismissal, but denied reports that the dismissal had been aimed at appeasing Baghdad. The ministry has not answered an inquiry per Email as of October 31, 2018.

[104] Ariel Ben Solomon 'Publicity seeking Kurdish official brings back memories of Jewish Kurd aliya fiasco' *Jerusalem Post*, (published 7 December 2015) https://www.jpost.com/Middle-East/Use-of-Jewish-issue-by-KRG-official-may-cause-confusion-and-damage-436499.

[105] Judit Neurink, 'Jews of Kurdistan want more recognition' *Deutsche Welle*, (published 15 July 2016) https://p.dw.com/p/1Iy7U (accessed 1 November 2018).

[106] Judit Neurink, *The Jewish Bride: Iraq's lost past 2018.* (Independently published, 2018).

[107] In the neighbouring Kurdish district of Hakkari in Turkey the term *Juleï* is used.

[108] Apart from Israeli-Kurdish relations, claiming a Jewish identity might be part of an upcoming tendency to find ways out of a rigid Islamic social morals. Unconventional and new non-Muslim identity-shaping might support socially legitimate ways to escape strong norms and find more personal freedom and, in some cases, pursue individual careers.

[109] Ariel Ben Solomon, 'Publicity seeking Kurdish official brings back memories of Jewish Kurd aliya

The present Kurdish Jewish narrative is on shaky grounds if no political and cross-cultural/cross-religious study considers former Kurdish residents in Israeli, the identity of the descendants of Jewish individuals as well as the circumstances of their ancestors' conversion to Islam and their understanding and engagement with religious life. Especially problematic is using pictures of religious objects and clothing to transmit the impression of religious Jewish life in Kurdistan. To outsiders unfamiliar with conditions and historical facts in Iraq's Kurdistan, the idea of the sudden reappearance of a lost world might seem exotic and fascinating; in an international political context, it is not helpful.

Israel was the only state that openly supported the failed Kurdish independence referendum in 2017.[110] It remains unclear what role the claiming of Jewish descent plays in the context of a possible emigration to Israel. There is no systematic research on the numbers of Kurds interested in emigrating to Israel; possibly, they see their Jewish ancestors as an opportunity to emigrate to Israel or elsewhere.

In any case, the Iraqi Jews, having once constituted about three per cent of the overall population, have virtually vanished with only a handful living in miserable circumstances in Baghdad today.[111] Most Jewish institutions once reinforcing religious identity have been destroyed all over Iraq, including the large synagogues and cemeteries. Only some ruins and leftovers like the cemetery at Sadr City in Baghdad are to be found with effort. Some former Jewish pilgrim destinations still exist, mostly tombs attributed to different prophets and holy men.[112] These tombs include those for Ezekiel in Kifl,[113] Ezra in Uzair near Basra,[114] Yona and Daniel in Mosul, both destroyed by ISIS in 2014,[115] and finally the comparatively well maintained

---

fiasco' *Jerusalem Post*, (published 7 December 2015) https://www.jpost.com/Middle-East/Use-of-Jewish-issue-by-KRG-official-may-cause-confusion-and-damage-436499. Ziv Genesove, 'Stranded in Iraq, some Jews say Israel abandoned them' *Times of Israel*, (published 5 January 2018). https://www.timesofisrael.com/stranded-in-iraq-some-jews-say-israel-abandoned-them/ (accessed 8 November 2018).

[110] Daniela Segenreich, 'Kurdistan und Israel – eine ungewöhnliche Freundschaft.' *NZZ*, (published 19.October 2017) https://www.nzz.ch/feuilleton/kurdistan-und-israel-eine-ungewoehnliche-freundschaft-ld.1322352 (accessed 11 September 2018).

[111] After the Six Day War in 1967, only about 3,350 Jews remained in Iraq (Morad et al. 2008: 9). In 1973, the number had gone down to 250 (Morad et al. 2008: 210). In 1997, only 60 were left (Ben-Porat 1998: 289). In 2008, the number had dwindled down to less than 12 people (Morad et al. 2008: 10); while in 2018 there is only a handful remaining Jews (personal conversation with Thomas Schmidinger October 2018).

[112] Various locations are named for the different sites. Discussions on which one are most accepted is beyond the scope of this paper.

[113] Steven Lee Myers, 'Crossroads of Antiquity Can't Decide on New Path' *New York Times*, (published 19 October 2010) https://www.nytimes.com/2010/10/20/world/middleeast/20ezekiel.html (accessed 11 August 2018).

[114] Abu Zeed, Adnan, 'Jewish shrine reminds Iraqis of religious coexistence.' *al-Monitor*, (published 14 February 2016). https://www.al-monitor.com/pulse/en/originals/2016/02/iraq-tomb-jewish-prohet-ezra-turned-islamic.html (accessed 10 March 2018).

[115] Sigal Samuel, 'ISIS Destroyed Jonah's Tomb, but Not Its Message. Iraqis of Armenian, Arab, Assyrian, and Jewish descent recall what the shrine symbolised on the third anniversary of its destruction' *The Atlantic*, (published 24 July 2017) https://www.theatlantic.com/international/archive/

tomb of Nahum in al-Kosh near Mosul.[116] Some of these sites were also revered in Christian and Muslim traditions.[117] In the Kurdish parts, Jewish buildings have mostly just been abandoned until falling apart; the rubble was then used as material for new houses. Former Jewish quarters in towns are still recognisable but gradually disappearing. Synagogues in Zakho and Betanure are in ruins.

While Kurdish Jews almost exclusively have settled in Palestine, later Israel Arab Jews from Iraq had established communities in many parts of the world. As early as 1750, the cities of Singapore, Manila, Taipei, Harbin, Shanghai, Rangoon, and Surabaya were home to Jewish communities due to trading relations.[118] At the beginning of the twentieth century, virtually every wealthy Jewish merchant had business relations in Asia.[119] In addition to the seven cities mentioned above, there were synagogues listed in Bombay, Calcutta, Poona, and Hong Kong between 1884 and 1932.[120] Before World War II and until today communities exist in Manchester, London, New York City, Los Angeles, and Sydney.[121] Other communities exist in North America,[122] Holland, and elsewhere.[123]

Israel today has around 600,000 out of a population of some 8.8 million who can claim some Iraqi ancestry.[124] The first generation had a very difficult time in Israel. It is hard to tell whether the shock upon arrival has been harder for the Kurds or the Arabs for various reasons concerning class, culture, language and education. Many new immigrants describe the deep humiliation of being sprayed by DDT when entering Israel.[125] In Israel, both groups identified with the Mizrahi community, descendants of Jews from the Middle East, Central Asia, and North Africa, as opposed to the Ashkenazi Jews of

---

2017/07/tomb-of-jonah-mosul-isis/534414/ (accessed 26 October 2018).

[116] Henry Aaron Stern, 'Journal of the Reverend H. A. Stern' *Jewish Missionary Intelligence* 14 (1848), 112-120. Judit Neurink, 'Jews of Kurdistan want more recognition' *Deutsche Welle*, (published 15 July 2016) https://p.dw.com/p/1Iy7U (accessed 11.1.2018).

[117] Mordechai Ben-Porat, *To Baghdad and Back: The Miraculous 2000 Year Homecoming of the Iraqi Jews*. (Jerusalem: Gefen Publishing House, 1998), 290.

[118] Jonathan Goldstein, *Jewish Identities in East and Southeast Asia. Singapore, Manila, Taipei, Harbin, Shanghai, Rangoon, and Surabaya*. (Munich: de Gruyter Oldenbourg, 1998), 17ff.

[119] Moshe Gat, 'The Immigration of Iraqi Jewry to Israel as Reflected in Literature' *Revue Européenne des Migrations Internationales* 14/3 (1998), 46.

[120] Joan Roland, 'The Baghdadi Jews of India'*My Jewish Learning* (without date) https://www.myjewishlearning.com/article/the-jews-of-india/ (accessed 23 November 2018).

[121] Moshe Gat, 'The Immigration of Iraqi Jewry to Israel as Reflected in Literature' *Revue Européenne des Migrations Internationales* 14/3 (1998), 46.

[122] For detailed information on the US and Canada see http://www.iraqijews.org/usa.html and https://ijao.ca/category/canada/

[123] Mordechai Ben-Porat, *To Baghdad and Back: The Miraculous 2000 Year Homecoming of the Iraqi Jews*. (Jerusalem: Gefen Publishing House, 1998), 289.

[124] Chmaytelli, Maher 'With Jews largely gone from Iraq, memories survive in Israel' *Reuters*, (published 18 April 2018) https://www.reuters.com/article/us-israel-independence-iraq-jews/with-jews-largely-gone-from-iraq-memories-survive-in-israel-idUSKBN1HP1ID (accessed 1November 2018).

[125] Interesting testimonies from second-generation immigrants from Iraqi Kurdistan can be found at https://www.zochrot.org/en, especially concerning the former Arab village of Lifta. See also Marcus 2017 and Sabar 2008: 109ff.

European descent. Mizrahi constitute one of the largest ethnic divisions on Israel, making up roughly half of its Jewish population.[126] From the beginning, there have been severe problems with discrimination against Mizrahi or part-Mizrahi Jews.[127] Unlike other immigrants, most Mizrahi immigrants were first sent to shantytown transit camps. They were marginalised by the European leaders of the founding Labour Party. The European-descended elite dominated government, military and business institutions and had much better networks as the founders of the country.[128]

Immigrants to Israel were registered by state of origin only,[129] but the division among the Iraqi Jews nevertheless very clearly continued. They settled in different areas and continued to speak their own languages. Research with regard to their history, way of living and language as well as publications, visibility, general awareness focuses almost exclusively on the Arab Jews of Iraq; Kurdish Jews were again subsumed into a larger group and not acknowledged.[130] Arab and Kurdish Jews from Iraq and their descendants again live in distinct areas and are almost exclusively surrounded by folks sharing their ethnic identity.[131]

In Israel, any talk of the 'Iraqi Jews' relates to the Arab Jews from Iraq. In many respects, they have succeeded in society, tend to live in urban areas, and quickly made their way into the educated middle classes of the country. Their exceptional presence on the book market especially singles them out.[132] Many novels have helped rediscover the extinct Arab-Iraqi communities and their immigration to Israel. Since the beginning of the century, Israeli writers such as Eli Amir, Sami Michael, and Shimon Ballas have been reflecting on their own past and have reached an international audience.[133]

What singles out the Kurdish Jews is the history of heavy discrimination

---

[126] The extent of stigmatisation expressed itself among other phenomena in the so-called 'boureka films' – called after borek pies – of the 60s and 70s. These low-level, but very popular, films depicted new immigrants from Arab countries in a most pejorative way.

[127] Lauren S. Marcus, 'The Kurdish immigrants who built Israel.' *Forward*, (published 15 October 2017) https://forward.com/life/faith/385209/the-kurdish-immigrants-who-built-israel/ (accessed 22 November 2018). Tamar Morad / Dennis Shasha / Robert Shasha (eds.), *Iraq's Last Jews. Stories of Daily Life, Upheaval, and Escape from Modern Babylon*. (New York: Palgrave Macmillan, 2008), 236.

[128] Alexander Fulbright, 'Netanyahu apologizes for 'Mizrahi gene' remark' *Times of Israel*, (published 17.03.2017) https://www.timesofisrael.com/netanyahu-apologizes-for-mizrahi-gene-remark/ (accessed 23.11.2018). Dalia Gavriely-Nuri, 'Why Have Transit Camps for Mizrahi Jews Been Written Out of Israeli History?' *Iraqi Jewish Association Of Ontario*, (published 3.9.2018) https://ijao.ca/why-have-transit-camps-for-mizrahi-jews-been-written-out-of-israeli-history/ (accessed 23.11.2018).

[129] Ora Shwartz-Be'eri, *The Jews of Kurdistan. Daily Life, Customs, Arts and Crafts*. (Jerusalem: The Israel Museum, 2000), 19.

[130] Originally ethnologists did not even bother to catalogue Kurdish historical documents, photographs, ritual objects according to their origins (Shwartz-Beeri 2000: 19).

[131] Tamar Morad / Dennis Shasha / Robert Shasha (eds.), *Iraq's Last Jews. Stories of Daily Life, Upheaval, and Escape from Modern Babylon*. (New York: Palgrave Macmillan, 2008), 146.

[132] Zvi Ben-Dor, 'Invisible Exile: Iraqi Jews in Israel.' *Journal of the Interdisciplinary Crossroads* 3/1 (2006), 135-162, 137.

[133] Moshe Gat, 'The Immigration of Iraqi Jewry to Israel as Reflected in Literature' *Revue Européenne des Migrations Internationales* 14/3 (1998), 45-60.

against them. They were – and sometimes still are – a favourite subject of ethnic jokes:

> The phrase 'Ana Kurdi' which literally means,' I am a Kurd' symbolised them. It implies that the Kurd speaks in a straight forward manner, without hesitation. It also signifies someone who is simple minded and ignorant. The term 'Kurd' in Israel has a negative connotation. This stereotype prevailed mainly during the 1950s and 1960s. Nevertheless, many people are still stereotype oriented. A young professional told me that once, during a job interview she could not answer a question addressed to her. She simply replied: 'Ana Kurdi ' only to find out that the interviewer was of all things Kurdish. She did not use this phrase out of racial prejudice but, rather due to intercultural conditioning. Itzhak Rabin, a former Israeli Prime Minister, was once asked in a cabinet meeting (in 1974) whether Israel was interested in Kurdish pressure on Iraq and whether the United States prevented such pressure. 'I don't know' he replied. One of the cabinet members, Dr. Yoseph Burg, added immediately the phrase 'Ana Kurdi ', to indicate the ignorance which such an answer reflected.[134] (Zaken 1994: 2).

The native language of the rapidly dwindling first generation of Kurdish migrants is Aramaic, which resembles modern Hebrew and by mistake is quite often called *Kurdi*. The elder generation still strongly identifies with Kurdistan; their non-religious cultural traits like language, traditions and values closely resemble the corresponding generations of their former compatriots. For years, groups have organised cultural heritage tours, travelling first to the Kurdish parts of Turkey and since the 1990s to the Kurdish parts of Iraq.[135] Israel has Kurdish neighbourhoods and Kurdish synagogues.[136] Many Kurdish Jews went into the construction business, especially road construction.[137] Since the 1970s, the Kurdish festival *Saharane* has become popular and a strong factor in expressing and stabilizing ethnic identity.[138]

---

[134] Mordechai Zaken, 'The Kurdish Jews in Transition: From Kurdistan to Israel' *Mamostayê Kurd* 22 (1994), 59-68. Originally published in Kurdish. English version uploaded by the author on academia.edu.

[135] Birgit Ammann, 'The Kurdish Jewish Communities – Lost Forever' In *Religious Minorities in Kurdistan: Beyond the Mainstream*. Edited by Khanna Omarkhali (Wiesbaden: Harrasowitz, 2014), 271-300, 296.

[136] Mordechai Zaken, 'The Kurdish Jews in Transition: From Kurdistan to Israel' *Mamostayê Kurd* 22 (1994): 59-68. Originally published in Kurdish. English version uploaded by the author on academia.edu. Lauren S. Marcus, 'The Kurdish immigrants who built Israel' *Forward*, (Published 15.10.2017) www.forward.com/life/faith/385209/the-kurdish-immigrants-who-built-israel/ (accessed 22.11.2018).

[137] Mordechai Zaken, 'The Kurdish Jews in Transition: From Kurdistan to Israel' *Mamostayê Kurd* 22 (1994): 59-68.

[138] Ammann, Birgit. 'Die Kurdischen Juden in Israel.' [The Kurdish Jews in Israel] In *Jahrbuch für Vergleichende Sozialforschung 1987-1988*. Edited by Jochen Blaschke, 241 -258. (Berlin: Berliner Institut für

The Jews of Iraq

The number of '200,000 Kurdish Jews'[139] or even more[140] somehow implying that Kurds would not intermarry with other Israeli groups is frequently stated without valid documentation and ignores the findings of contemporary research on ethnicity. When Iraq's Kurdistan Region issued its Law of Minorities in 2015 that allowed Jews to return to the region, the number of '200,000 Kurdish Jews' encouraged modern anti-Semites in Turkey and Iran. In somewhat identical press campaigns,[141] they warned of and protested against 'Kurdistan' as a 'second Israel' in the region.

The enormous sympathy that many Israelis of Kurdish descent show for Iraq's semi-autonomous northern Kurdish region seems to reflect their discontent with their long-time position in Israel as marginalised Mizrahi and simultaneously a hidden part of the Jewry of Iraqi descent.

While some descendants of Jews and non-Jews all over Iraq tend to distort–in the Kurdish regions even romanticise–aspects of the past, both countries, in the three societies historically most affected, have an increasingly critical debate on the subject. The past cannot be changed, and it should not be edited, but acknowledging historical outcomes could be a good basis for wiser and more mindful perceptions and actions.

Vergleichende Sozialforschung, 1989), 255ff. Moshe Gat, 'The Immigration of Iraqi Jewry to Israel as Reflected in Literature' *Revue Européenne des Migrations Internationales* 14/3 (1998), 45-60, 57. Gabriele Shenar / Sarah Yona Zweig. 'Sehnsucht nach der anderen Heimat. Kurden in Israel' *ARD Studio Tel Aviv*, (Published 5 November 2016) https://www.ard-telaviv.de/saharane/ (accessed 26 October 2018).

[139] Vera Kelly-Eccarius, 'Israel' In *The Kurds: An Encyclopedia of Life, Culture, and Society*. Edited by Sebastian Maisel, (Santa Barbara: ABC Clio, 2018), 256-260, 259.

[140] Daniela Segenreich, 'Kurdistan und Israel – eine ungewöhnliche Freundschaft.' *NZZ* (published 19 October 2017) https://www.nzz.ch/feuilleton/kurdistan-und-israel-eine-ungewoehnliche-freundschaft-ld.1322352 (accessed 11 September 2018).

[141] See AP, 'Iraq vice president warns against 'second Israel' in Kurdistan' *The Times of Israel*, (published 17 September 2017) https://www.timesofisrael.com/iraq-vice-president-warns-against-second-israel-in-kurdistan/ and Sue Surkes, 'Turkish nationalists protest against creation of 'second Israel' in Kurdistan' The Times of Israel, (published 17 September 2017). https://www.timesofisrael.com/turkish-nationalists-protest-creation-of-second-israel-in-kurdistan/.

Meir Taweig Synagogue is the last remaining Synagogue in Baghdad. (Picture: Thomas Schmidinger)

With these books Jewish children were taught Hebrew in Iraq in the 1950s and 1960s. (Picture: Thomas Schmidinger)

Synagogue in al-Qosh with the Shrine of Prophet Nahum. (Picture: Thomas Schmidinger)

Synagogue in al-Qosh with the Shrine of Prophet Nahum. (Picture: Thomas Schmidinger)

CHAPTER 3

THE LOST READERS OF THE SCRIPTURE: SOME NOTES ON THE KARAITE COMMUNITY OF HĪT

Thomas Schmidinger

The Karaites are one of the religious communities erased from the memory of Iraq. Today hardly anybody in Iraq remembers this centuries-old religious community rooted in the Abrahamic faith of Islam, Christianity and mainstream Judaism. Multiple marginalisations resulted in nobody ever telling the story of the last Karaites in Iraq. The isolated and rural community in the town of Hīt in Anbar did not have any intellectuals to document their history. Later, Karaite Jews became a minority among the rabbinic Jews in Israel and the Iraqi Karaites were even a tiny minority within the minority of the Karaites of Israel. Without anyone interested in their history, even the second generation in Israel did not think that the stories of their parents and grandparents would be worth recording and telling.

It would go far beyond the scope of this article to tell a history that ends with the last Karaites who still remember Iraq, but at least it is an attempt to record some kind of memories of this ancient Iraqi community that became a victim of the political developments of the Middle East in the twentieth century.

What is Karaism?
Karaites believe in a specific form of early Judaism that emerged in the eighth and ninth centuries in present-day Iraq and spread all over the Middle East, to Crimea, Lithuania, Poland[1] and Galicia.[2] The term Karaite come from the Hebrew word for read (*qara*) because they are regarded as readers of the holy scriptures. Unlike rabbinic Judaism, Karaites do not accept the Talmud and only focus on the Torah. Karaite Judaism has a historical connection to Ananites, a sect founded by Anan ben David who failed to

---

[1] Mikhail Kizilov, *The Sons of the Scripture. The Karaites in Poland and Lithuania in the Twentieth Century*. (Berlin/Munich/Boston: De Gruyter, 2015).

[2] Mikhail Kizilov, *The Karaites of Galicia. An Ethnoreligious Minority among the Ashkenazim, the Turks and the Slavs 1772-1945*. (Leiden/Boston: Brill, 2009).

become the Exilarch in Baghdad and led to a split in the Jewish community. Although the exact historical developments around this split and the relationship between the Ananites and the Karaits are still disputed, it is clear that under the rule of al-Maʿmūn (*CE* 813–33, *AH* 170-280), the Muslim authorities accepted the Karaites as a distinctive religious community no longer under the rule of the Exilarch.[3] This means that at least since the ninth century the Muslim empire accepted them as a different religious community.

However, Karaites still considered themselves as Jews. It is unclear when rabbinic Jewish and Karaite communities started to consider each other as adherents of different religions and stopped intermarrying. This could have also been a gradual process and could have differed according to regions where Karaites lived. We do know that by the time of the modern state of Iraq in the twentieth century, the two communities had different rituals and had not intermarried for centuries.

Faith and philosophy of the Karaites were not only developed in interaction with rabbinic Judaism, but also engaged in an intellectual debate with the dominant religion in the Middle East: Islam. Yoram Erder, from the Department of Jewish History at Tel Aviv University, sees Karaism as a result of the 'cultural encounter between Judaism and Islam'.[4] However, it is hard to tell which religious tradition influenced the other. I strongly doubt that the intellectual and religious discussions during the Abbasid Caliphate had an impact on only one side. As much as Islamic philosophy and religion influenced Karaism, also Karaite scholars influenced Islamic thinking in Abbasid Baghdad and finally both were also influenced by ancient Greek philosophy and Christianity. It might be hard to exactly trace these influences, but it can be easily observed that there are certain similarities between Karaism and Islam.[5]

Karaites focused intensely on the oneness of god and called that oneness of god in Arabic *tawhid*, the same terminology used by Muslims to focus on absolute monotheism. And it seems that early Karaism was also strongly influenced by the rationalism of the Islamic school of the Muʿtazila. Karaite and Muslim philosophers did interact with each other in Baghdad and influenced each other. Already in the first Muslim source about the Karaites, the book Kitab at-Tanbih wa-l-ʿIshraf ('The Book of Notification and Verification'), written by Abu ʾl-Ḥasan ʿAlī b. al-Ḥusain al-Masʿūdī (896–956), it is mentioned that the Karaites are among those 'who profess (God´s)

---

[3] Moshe Gil, 'The Origins of the Karaites' In *Karaite Judaism. A guide to its history and literary sources*. Edited by Meira Polliack. (Leiden: Brill, 2003), 73-118.

[4] Yoram Erder, 'Early Karaite Conceptions about Commandments Given before the Revelation of the Torah' *Proceedings of the American Academy for Jewish Research* 60 (1994), 101-140, 102.

[5] Daniel J. Lasker, 'Islamic Influences on Karaite origins' *Studies in Islamic and Judaic Traditions* 2 (1989), 23-47.
Meira Polliack, 'Rethinking Karaism: Between Judaism and Islam' *AJS Review* 30/1 (2006), 67-93.

justice and absolute unity'.[6] This shows that al-Mas'ūdī and most probably also his contemporaries saw the Karaites as 'the Jewish equivalent of the Islamic Mu'tazila',[7] a connection that was also drawn by the twelfth-century scholar Muhammad ash-Shahrastānī.

Besides intellectual influences from Islam in general and the Mu'tazila in particular, there are also ritual and cultic influences between Islam and Karaism. Karaites take off their shoes when they enter their synagogue like Muslims when they enter a mosque and their prayers are very physical and evoke the Muslim *salāt*. They have differences with mainstream Judaism regarding ritual purification and ritual slaughter.

Unlike rabbinic Jews, Karaites eat milk and meat together. Karaites read the prohibition not to cook a young goat or lamb in its mother's milk[8] literally—as they do with many other religious laws. Therefore, for them, it is not forbidden to eat milk products and meat at the same time only to cook a goat or lamb in its mother's milk.

Karaites also follow a different version of the Jewish calendar than rabbinic Jews. Like Muslims they do not have a pre-calculated calendar, but a lunar calendar where each month can have either 29 or 30 days, depending on the visibility of the moon. Karaites believe this is the original Biblical calendar. However, it can be also influenced by the Islamic calendar. Nevertheless, it is also easy to imagine that this way to determine the start of a new month might have been originally used by both the ancient Arabs and Israelites to calculate the start of the new month.

Karaites also reject many traditions seen as Jewish today but that might be innovations of the time after the split between Karaites and rabbinic Jews. They do not affix a mezuzah on their doors, neither do they wear tefillin. And Karaites only keep holidays already mentioned in the Torah. They celebrate Passover, Purim, Yom Kippur, and Yom Teruah (Rosh Hashanah) or Shavuot, but they celebrate these holidays differently. For example, they do not blow the shofar on Yom Teruah, nor do they light candles for Purim. Jewish holidays who are not part of the Torah, like Hanukkah, are not celebrated by the Karaites.

Karaites follow a patrilineal descent and not a matrilineal descent like rabbinic Jews. Belonging to Karaite Judaism depends on the father's identity and not by the mother. However, that does not mean that women have a less important position than in mainstream Judaism. Of course, Karaites are part of the Middle Eastern patriarchal tradition; but from their religious doctrine,

---

[6] Abu al-Hasan Ali b. al-Husayn al-Mas'ūdī, *Kitāb al-Tanbīh wa l-ishrāf*. Edited by Michael Jan de Goeje. (Leiden: Brill, 1894), 113.

[7] Michael G. Wechsler, *The Arabic Translation and Commentary of Yefet ben 'Eli the Karaite on the Book of Esther* (Leiden/Boston: Brill, 2008), 41.

[8] Ex 23:19, 34:26 and Deut 14:21.

women must observe the same religious duties as men. Women have the same obligation to keep the commandments and study the Torah as men; some women have become noted religious scholars in Karaite history.

After all, both Karaites and Rabbinites consider themselves as adherents of the original Jewish religion and consider the other as a splinter group of 'real Judaism'. Thus, we must speak about two different religious who have a lot of common history and beliefs but Karaites are not just a form of Judaism, like Reform Judaism, Conservative Judaism, Reconstructionists, or Orthodox Judaism. Rabbinic Jewish authorities ask Karaites to convert, if they want to marry a rabbinic Jew. Thus, the relationship between Karaites and mainstream Judaism could be compared with Samaritans and Jews. Both have many common religious traditions and share the same (or, in the case of the Samaritans, at least a very similar) Torah. However, this is something we can also say about Christians.

Because Karaites and Rabbinic Jews do not consider each other as varieties of the same religion and did not intermarry, we must consider both versions of Judaism as independent forms of the Abrahamic religion that share more than they share with Islam and Christianity, but are nevertheless religious communities that developed into different directions for the last 1,200 years.

Karaites in Iraq

Present Iraq was the centre of early Karaism after it emerged in the eighth and ninth centuries and before many of the Karaite scholars went to Jerusalem because they thought that it would be a religious duty to return to their holy land. Iraq lost its significance for the development of Karaism from the ninth century onwards. However, from the eighth century until 1950, Karaite communities had a continuous presence in Iraq. We do not know when the last Karaites from Baghdad and other major Iraqi towns left for Israel or became part of mainstream Judaism. The decline of small religious communities did not get much attention. Its last community, in the central Iraqi town of Hīt existed until the end of 1950, when the last Karaites left for Israel along with most of Iraq's rabbinic Jews.

The history of this last Karaite community of Iraq is largely untold. With the loss of an intellectual class, Karaites of Iraq did not write their own history unlike Karaites in Cairo, Istanbul or in the Ukraine. The small, very rural, community that survived in the small town of Hīt had little access to urban intellectuals and the centres of power and learning in Iraq. With time, the remaining Karaite Community in Hīt continued shrinking. In 1869, only 20 Karaite families were left in Hīt. By 1951, only 13 families remained.[9]

---

[9] E. Goldschmidt / K. Fried / A.G. Steinberg / T. Cohen, 'The Karaite community of Iraq in Israel: a genetic study'. *The American Journal of Human Genetics* 28/3 (1976), 243-252, 243.

In 1951, these Karaites were resettled like the rabbinic Jews with the Operation Ezra and Nehemiah to Israel. According to the authors of a genetic study performed in 1970 only 14 members of the community stayed in Hīt. When I did my interviews in 2017, adherents of the community told me that 'two or three' wanted to stay behind and that they never heard any more about the remaining people. Interestingly, they told me that they heard that these 'two or three' were 'hiding'[10] so they could stay. This notion of people hiding so that they could stay does not speak for a voluntary migration to Israel. The migration from Baghdad, Basra, and Mosul is well known, but no scholars have documented how the migration of the Iraqi Jews from smaller communities was organised. Speaking with old Iraqis from Kifri and some villages in the Duhok region, I heard similar stories of some Jews hiding when the transports came to take them to Baghdad. From such a perspective, the migration of Jews from some smaller Iraqi towns and villages looks like an organised and involuntary deportation rather than a voluntary migration. Keeping in mind the highly disputed circumstances of the migration from Baghdad, especially the series of bombings of Jewish targets in Baghdad between April 1950 and June 1951, one must acknowledge that both the Israeli and the Iraqi government at that time wanted the Iraqi Jews to leave to Israel. Therefore, it is not unlikely that this migration from some parts of Iraq was more a forced deportation rather than a voluntary migration.

Because I could not talk to any witnesses, the questions must stay open as to how this migration was organised and if the migrants voluntarily left their homes. The narrative of the next generation, that it was the most normal thing to move to Israel after its establishment, nevertheless has to be questioned. Why did the Karaites – like other Jews of Iraq – not move to Israel in 1948 then? It is possible, that they did not have the opportunity to do so and the Iraqi regime did not allow them. But was this the only reason? Especially if some people even tried to 'hide' to stay behind.

However small the group that stayed behind, most likely these people converted to Islam and became part of the Sunni Muslim majority population of Hīt. Given the anti-Semitic attitude of the Baath-regime of Saddam Hussein, it is very unlikely that anybody adhering to Karaite religious practices survived in Hīt. Nevertheless, surely people of Karaite descent still live in Hīt; perhaps an elderly person still lives in Iraq who was born as Karaite and could still share some memories about a time when the Karaite community still existed. The political circumstances and the treatment of religious minorities in Iraq prevented these people from sharing their stories and consequently deprived Iraq of part of its history.

From today's perspective, we still do not know exactly how and why the

---

[10] Interview with David Barham (Abraham) in Beersheba, August 18, 2017, Beersheba.

Karaites from Hīt migrated to Israel. The Karaites in Israel believe today that their families in Iraq were persecuted and had the religious obligation to move to the modern state of Israel as soon as it was established. However, this perspective may be shaped by the Zionist narrative that these second-generation Karaites learned in school; they may have a limited knowledge of their family history in Iraq. One informant told me that his grandfather was killed in a pogrom in Hīt. However, he could not really tell me the year that happened, but supposed that this was when Israel was established sometime in 1947 or 1948. There are memories of a pogrom and persecution by Muslim Iraqis, but these memories are very uncertain and could very well also be blended with the history of the al-Farhūd pogrom against the Jews of Baghdad in June 1941.

The first-generation Karaites from Iraq, the last who still can directly remember Iraq, must have more precise memories. However, they never told them to family; when I finally found them in 2017, they were not willing to tell their memories anymore. In Israel, the Karaites from Hīt were resettled in the southern city of Beersheba and became part of the local Karaite community, mainly dominated by Karaites of Egyptian origin. In 2017, only three persons in their 80s and 90s could still remember Iraq. I travelled to the Karaite community in Beersheba hoping to talk to them. Moshe Firrouz, the local rabbi of the Karaite community had asked the families and two agreed to talk to me. However, when I arrived, they told Rabbi Firrouz that they were no longer willing to meet me. I did not meet any Karaite born in Iraq. Only one elderly woman told her grandson that she would talk to me, if I would bring her back to Iraq, because she would prefer to die in Hīt than in Israel.

Of course, I could not fulfil this wish. However, these message brought to me through her grandson gave me both a small glimpse of her sadness and longing for home, a home that was still Iraq after more than 67 years in Israel and also the impression that there would have been many more stories of exile and migration with much more ambiguities than the official history.

The community in Hīt was relatively isolated for centuries. Although Karaites had more communities in Iraq during the medieval era, in recent centuries most Karaites lived in Jerusalem, Cairo, and Istanbul. Thus, the Karaite community in Hīt did not have much interaction with others. This interested geneticists who surveyed them in 1970. They concluded that 'In Iraq this group maintained a highly inbred existence but married Karaites from Egypt after their immigration to Israel in 1951. Observation of several unique gene frequencies for blood group and isoenzyme markers, not described among other Jewish groups, are explicable by isolation and genetic drift in a very small community.'[11]

---

[11] E. Goldschmidt / K. Fried / A.G. Steinberg / T. Cohen, 'The Karaite community of Iraq in Israel:

Like the Iraqi Jews, the Karaites spoke Arabic. A dialect study about the Arabic of the Iraqi Karaites in Israel conducted by Semitist Geoffrey Khan found some features of the dialect 'spoken in the old urban settlement of Hīt.'[12] However, there must have been interactions with Bedouins as well: 'Although the Karaite community is a direct descendant of the medieval urban settlement, their dialect has been extensively bedouinised.'[13]

Both the bedouinised dialect and the genetic particularities point towards a long isolation from other Karaites and Iraqi Jews. This isolation of the Karaites from Hīt led also to an interesting religious conservatism. The small community of Iraqi Karaites kept religious laws that other communities had abandoned, but they may also have taken over practices of other religious traditions in Iraq. Already adhering to a very literal form of Judaism that refused many modernisations of mainstream rabbinical Judaism, the Karaits from Hīt were the most conservative of the conservative.

The Karaites of Hīt practiced a very rigorous tradition of purification by running water that might remind us of the Iraqi Mandaeans use of baptism until today. Until they left for Israel, the Iraqi Karaites 'used to immerse themselves in the Euphrates twice a day before their morning and evening prayers.'[14]

An example of preserving old forms of religious laws is lighting Sabbath candles. While rabbinical Jewry traditionally light candles in the evening at the start of the Sabbath, Karaites believed for centuries that this is forbidden by the verse from the Torah 'You shall cause no fire to burn throughout your habitations on the Sabbath day.'[15]

However, in the fifteenth century, Menahem Ben-Yosif Bashyachi, who served as Dayan (judge) for the Karaites of Istanbul, permitted the lighting of candles on Sabbath, which caused a split in the community. 'For example, Avraham Ben Ya'aqov Bali of Adrianople in 1505 wrote a tract entitled, *Igret Isur Ner Shel Shabbat*, which denounced the admission of this rabbinic practice. Ultimately, carrying on his father´s legacy of promoting rabbinic practices in Karaism, Eliyahu Bashyachi, through his immense popularity, was able to remove much resistance to candle lighting on Shabbat in Turkey, the Crimea, and Europe. While this practice was prevalent in Europe, it was rejected in Egypt, as mentioned by Mordehai Ben-Nisan […]. It was not adopted there until the nineteenth century, after the influence of Crimean

---

a genetic study'.
The American Journal of Human Genetics 28/3 (1976), 243-252, 251.
[12] Geoffrey Khan, 'The Arabic Dialect of the Karaite Jews of Hit' *Zeitschrift für Arabische Linguistik* 34 (1997), 53-102, 94.
[13] Ibid.
[14] Mikhail Kizilov, *The Karaites of Galicia. An Ethnoreligious Minority among the Azhkenazim, the Turks and the Slavs 1772-1945.* (Leiden/Boston: Brill, 2009), 149.
[15] Ex, 35:3.

practices was more heavily felt there.'[16]

While the Egyptian Karaites took over that rabbinical tradition in the nineteenth century, the even more isolated small community in Iraq stayed with their original Karaite tradition and refused the lighting of candles on Sabbath until they left Hīt in the mid of the twentieth century and learned about these new habits when they met other Karaites in Israel in 1951. Although these differences with the religiously less conservative Karaites from Egypt, Turkey, or the Soviet Union, were not strong enough to keep the small Iraqi community separated from other Karaites, it must have been a challenging experience for the Karaites from Hīt to be confronted with much larger Karaite communities from Egyptian, Turkish, or Eastern European traditions whose Karaism differed in some ways from their own traditions.

There is not much written evidence for the history of the poor Karaite community in Hīt isolated from the centres of Karaite scholarship. We know about a letter in the Cairo Genizah, a collection of about 300,000 Jewish manuscript fragments that were found in the storeroom of the Ben Ezra Synagogue in Fustat, Cairo, where the head of the Karaite Community in Istanbul tries to answer some questions of the Karaite Community from Hīt about the evaluations of the new moon and we have the information the famous Karaite scholar Abraham Firkovich (1786–1874), who wanted to travel to Hīt during his second journey to the Middle East. He finally could not travel to Hīt, but could speak in Jerusalem with a representative of the Karaites from Hīt. The representative told Firkovich about the hardship of the community in Iraq and that the sheer distress of the community leads them to seek for their fortune in Jerusalem, but they would not even have enough money to move to Jerusalem. According to Firkovich, he himself was willing to help pay to relocate a part of the community to Jerusalem.[17]

Some years later, the Bavarian traveller Jacob Obermeyer (1843-1935) wrote about his visit to Hīt in 1868. Obermeyer reported about 20 Karaite families in Hīt and that other Karaite families abroad send money for the poor community. Obermeyer interprets the financial support by other Karaite communities as an attempt to preserve the last community in of the old 'Babylonian mother settlement'.[18]

In 1947 some members of the 'Young Men´s Israelite Karaite Association' in Cairo formed a committee to establish a relationship with Karaite communities abroad. According to Mourad el-Kodsi, they received

---

[16] Yoseif Yaron / Avraham Qanaï et al., *An Introduction to Karaite Judaism: History, Theology, Practice, and Culture.* (New York: Al-Qirqisani Center, 2003), 164.

[17] Hannelore Müller, *Religionswissenschaftliche Minoritätenforschung. Zur religionshistorischen Dynamik der Karäer im Osten Europas.* (Wiesbaden: Harrassowitz Verlag, 2010), 43.

[18] Jacob Obermeyer, *Die Landschaft Babylonien im Zeitalter des Talmuds und des Gaonats: Geographie und Geschichte nach talmudischen, arabischen und andern Quellen.* (Frankfurt am Main: J. Kauffmann Verlag, 1929), 68.

answers from Istanbul, Jerusalem, Lausanne, Paris, and Hīt.[19]

This might have been the last contact the small community from Iraq had with Karaite communities abroad. In the same year the United Nations Partition Plan for Palestine was proposed and on 14 May 1948 the state of Israel declared its independence. Not only rabbinical Jews in Arab lands, but also Karaites were subsequently caught in the crossfire of the Arab-Israeli conflict.

Iraqi Karaites in Israel

When the Karaits from Hīt were brought to Israel in 1951, they were first dusted with DDT on arriving at Lod Airport, just like the rabbinical Jews from Iraq. Israel at that time considered the Arab Jews as a health risk that might be full of parasites and other health dangers.

Like the rabbinical Jews from Iraq, the Karaites from Hīt had to live in tents when they arrived in Israel. From the perspective of a Karaite from Hīt, Israel must have been a disappointment. The shock for a rich Jew from Baghdad may have been greater, but still, the Karaites from Hīt left their houses and small workshops to move to a tent in a refugee camp.

When the Karaites from Iraq and the much larger group from Egypt arrived in Israel, the chief rabbinate opposed their immigration. Even the head of the Jewish Agency Immigration Department, Yitzhak Raphael tried 'to keep them out'.[20]

The secular Zionist establishment of that time included the Karaites into what they considered the Jewish nation. Yitzhak Ben-Tzvi, the second president of Israel who was personally and scholarly interested in the Karaites, was the driving power behind the decision 'to treat the Karaites as Jews' and subject 'them to compulsory military service, the most significant marker of Jewish identity in Israel'.[21] However, the religious establishment still has not recognised them as Jewish.

Later, they were settled in the rural, agricultural village of Meshek Ezer, a few kilometres outside the town of Beersheba. The Karaites from Hīt – now in Meshek Ezer – had little contact with other Karaites. In the centre of Beersheba, an active Karaite Community was made up by Karaites from Egypt. The Iraqi Karaites from Meshek Ezer originally did not become part of the Egyptian dominated community. While the Karaites of Egyptian origin in the city prayed in a small provisional synagogue, the first generation of Iraqi Karaites maintained a separate community in Meshek Ezer and

---

[19] Murad Al-Qudsi, *The Karaite Jews of Egypt 1882-1986*. (n.p., 2006), 44.
[20] Michael R. Fischbach, *Jewish Property Claims Against Arab Countries*. (New York: Columbia University Press, 2008), 42.
[21] Joel Beinin, *The Dispersion of Egyptian Jewry. Culture, Politics and the Formation of a Modern Diaspora*. (Berkeley, University of California Press, 1998), 183.

prayed in a provisional prayer room inside one of the private houses

However, Meshek Ezer became gradually integrated into the growing city of Beersheba during the 1970s, when the first Karaites born in Israel came to the age of marriage, this also helped to establish a contact between the two communities. When the Karaite communty of Beerhsheba decided to erect a proper synagogue in 1980, the Karaites from Meshek Ezer also joined and a unified Karaite community was established. The prayer room in Meshek Ezer was closed and the Karaites who wanted to join religious services travelled to downtown Beersheba to visit the new synagogue with its rabbi of Egyptian descent. However, the synagogue was built in a poor quarter of the city centre of Beersheba, where most Karaites from Kairo lived. For the Karaites from Iraq, now living in Meshek Ezer, the synagogue was relatively far away, especially if they had to reach it for the early morning prayers at sunrise. On the Sabbath, when driving a car is not permissible for religious Karaites, they would have to walk about an hour to reach the synagogue.

This was the time when the community from Iraq started their final disintegration. Many of the younger generation married either Karaits of Egyptian origin or rabbinical Jews. Because Israel still does not have civil marriage and because it was easier for a rabbinical Jew to become Karaite than the other way around, many rabbinical Jews ended up as Karaites. However, mixed families moved out of Meshek Ezer and raised their children in Hebrew, not in Arabic. Because there was not even a common prayer room anymore, the community disintegrated into the larger Karaite community of Israel, whose historical memory was mainly from Egypt. Many descendants of the Iraqi Karaits have only one Iraqi grandmother or one Iraqi grandfather anymore and the stories of the Iraqi side of their families fade away.

Many Karaites of Iraqi origin no longer participate in the religious live of the Karaite community in Israel. A well-known Karaite Hakham (religious scholar), Rabbi Moshe ben Yoseph Firrouz, who also serves as rabbi of the Karaite community of Beersheba and spiritual leader of the Karaite Jewish Committee of Israel, told me in 2017 that the Iraqi Karaites actively participated in the religious life of the synagogue after it was erected in 1980. However, today only very few find their way from Meshek Ezer to the city centre, where the synagogue is located. According to his observation, most Karaites from Iraq either adopted a secular lifestyle or integrated into rabbinical Jewish communities closer to their home. Firrouz: 'Our synagogue is just too far away from their home.'[22]

When I visited the morning prayers of the Beersheba Karaite synagogue, only one of the believers who participated in the prayers had two

---

[22] Interview with Rabbi Moshe ben Yoseph Firrouz, August, 18, 2017, Beersheba.

grandparents from Hīt, while his other two grandparents were from Egypt. He was the only participant in the prayers who came all the way from Meshek Ezer to the synagogue. According to Rabbi Firrouz, the participation of Iraqi Karaites on Sabbath prayers and high holidays is not much higher either.

Apparently, Karaites from Hīt never felt the need to write their own history. While there are many written records of Iraqi Jews from Baghdad, but also from smaller towns, no memories of any Karaite from Iraq are known. A son of a Karaite family of mixed Iraqi and Egyptian family told me, that the community continued to be very isolated in Israel and that the first generation was scared all their life. When I asked him why, he mentioned that it might have been of 'what happened in Iraq'.[23]

However, exactly that – 'what happened in Iraq' – is still very vague. The younger generation of Iraqi Karaites seem to share a narrative of oppression and pogroms in Iraq. However, they do not have any precise memory when and where these pogroms happened and the history of the pogrom against the Jews of Baghdad in 1941. The Iraqi pogroms in Israeli history books could very well be blended with vague memories of discrimination of Karaites in Hīt. This history might be forgotten forever.

Neglected history and marginalisation

Finally, I would like to discuss the question why this history is forgotten, even by the descendants of Iraqi Karaites. Why did nobody write (or at least publish) any memories? Why was nobody of the three last Karaites from Hīt willing to share their story with me? Honestly, we can only speculate about that, but some ideas came into my mind while trying to assemble the small pieces of information I could find about the Iraqi Karaites.

Iraqi Karaites were a multiple marginalised community already in Iraq. They lived isolated in a small town in Anbar, were not part of a larger group and they were poor and poorly educated. The Karaites from Hīt did not have successful entrepreneurs, intellectuals or artists, like the Baghdadi Jews. They were simple people in a rural small town with very limited access to information and urban life.

When brought to Israel, they were again at the margin of the society. They were settled in a rural place in the suburbs of Israel's poorest city in the middle of the arid Negev landscape. The religious establishment did not see them as proper Jews and they were different from most Karaites, who were of Egyptian origin. This multiple marginality could have triggered earlier experiences of marginalisation in Iraq.

Without any intellectual leadership and without any emancipatory movement, the Iraqi Karaites might have tried to get rid of their stigma of

---

[23] Interview with David Barham (Abraham) in Beersheba, August, 18, 2017, Beersheba.

marginalisation by disappearing. There are similar experiences of other marginal groups who had the chance to disappear or assimilate into a larger society. For example, many of the so-called Yenish people in Austria and Germany, after what happened to them under the Nazis, tried to disappear by becoming proper Germans and Austrians and hiding their Yenish identity. In the United States, I met Native Americans who tried to become Latinos and hide their native identity. All of these people shared a common experience of a long history of multiple marginalisations and a lack of an intellectual leadership that could form a counter-narrative for themselves.

These are just fragmented considerations about the puzzle of why no Iraqi Karaites wrote their own history and why they were not willing to tell it. Their grandchildren told me that their grandparents always were suspicious and lived in fear. They could not understand why anybody without bad intentions wanted to know about their history. That could be the reason why they will take their history to their graves.

Iraqi Karaites in Israel in the 1960s. (Picture: Barham Family collection)

Street in Meshek Ezer where the Karaites from Iraq settled in Israel. (Picture: Thomas Schmidinger)

Wedding of Iraqi Karaites in the 1950s in Israel. (Picture: Barham Family collection)

The Lost Readers of the Scripture: Some notes on the Karaite community of Hīt

Synagogue of the Karaites in Beersheva. (Picture: Thomas Schmidinger)

Synagogue of the Karaites in Beersheva. (Picture: Thomas Schmidinger)

CHAPTER 4

JOHN THE BAPTIST'S WATER: EXTINCTION OF A MILLENNIAL CULTURE

Saad Salloum

At the end of filming a documentary, I sat with the Reesh Umma[1] Sattar Jabbar Al Hilou, head of the Mandaean sect, in his religious headquarter in Qadisiya locality on the banks of the Tigris River in Baghdad. The man stood like an old angel descending from the sky with his white beard and his clothes, made up of pure white cloth, which the Mandaeans call Al Resta. He was awaiting the baptism of two new clerics.

'It's an occasion that happens every ten years,' he said, shifting his gaze to the other side of the river, as if he were contemplating the members of his sect dispersed around the globe. Then he added, 'We now have less than 45 Mandaean clerics around the world and they are the last ones speaking this language. It is a ritual language we no longer use in everyday life.' As if he were a delicate version of the good magician 'Gandalf' in the film *Lord of the Rings*, leaning on 'Al Markana' stick made of the olive tree that symbolises peace, he went down to the river bank and stretched out his hands inside the water. While we were discussing the importance of UNESCO's inclusion of the Mandaean language in 2006 in its annual *Atlas of the Endangered Languages*,[2] I asked him about the numbers of the remaining community members. He shook his head and refused to answer. It is not difficult to explain his silence. Of the 50,000 Mandaeans in Iraq before the US invasion, only 3,000 remain; their bags are ready for traveling as soon as there is a chance for asylum in any foreign country.

The Mandaean language reveals a 'story of another extinction' resulting from religions ruled by teeth and claws, and the blind modernisation that crushes ancient cultures so a previous age's dominant language becomes confined to the theological circles and used only in religious rituals or by a few international specialists. Of the 45 Mandaean remaining clerics, we do

---

[1] A Mandaean title meaning head of the nation or the sect, or the king priest, which is the highest religious rank in the hierarchy of the Mandaean clerical ranks.
[2] See: Christopher Moseley, *Atlas of the World's Languages in Danger*. (Paris: UNESCO Publishing, 2010). http://www.unesco.org/languages-atlas/.

not know for sure who completely masters this language. Less than 150 years ago, in 1875, the French Consul in Baghdad, Nicola Sioufi, wrote the first modern study of the Mandaeans. His informant, a Mandaean called Adam, had converted to Catholicism and spoke only Mandaean, his mother tongue. He was 'completely ignorant of the Arabic language, which he could barely spell and knew just what some people in the countryside need.'[3] Within a few decades, modernisation related to building the nation-state had a strong impact on a culture that has maintained its purity through ecological isolation and keeping away from the city centres.

The Mandaean language today receives the least attention by the state and Iraqi universities. During the decades of nation-state building, it has not been officially recognised as one of the circulated spoken languages or recognised for the minorities. This contrasts with the preservation of the Syriac language for the Christians, the Turkmen language for the Turkmens, or Kurdish for the Kurds. The Official Languages Text of 2014 Law mentioned the Mandaean language without referring to its status as an extremely ancient language threatened with extinction.

The Mandaeans and Building the Nation-State in Iraq

The cleric Nizam Kreidi greeted me with opened arms during my arrival at the baptism rituals at the bank of Tigris River in Mendi (the worshipping home) in Maysan,[4] regarded as the capital of the Mandaeans in southern Iraq. However, we exchanged a symbolic hug as it was not appropriate for us to touch during the performance of the rituals. More than 90 years ago, his ancestors welcomed the British anthropologist, Lady E.S. Drower, with the same wonderful spirit. Drower sat amid a millennial culture, contemplating a spiritual miracle that lasted for more than twenty centuries. Although she wrote about the Yazidis in Iraq,[5] the Mandaean world seized her imagination. She wrote a wonderful anthropological work and a dictionary of an ancient language on the brink of extinction.[6] Her most renown book, which was translated into Arabic, was *Along the Banks of the Tigris and Euphrates*. It represents her views on the diversity of Iraq and includes a chapter about the Mandaeans.[7] She also had an important book, *The Mandaean Sabaeans in Iraq and Iran*[8]. She has other related books, such as *The Secret of Adam*.[9]

In his memoirs, the Mandaean educator Ghadban Al Rumi mentions

---

[3] Nicola Sioufi, *The Sabaeans: Their Beliefs and Traditions*. Translated by Aref Abu Yussef, (Damascus: Dar Al Takween, 2010), 17.

[4] It is called *miyya siana*, meaning the clay land in Mandaean.

[5] E. S. Drower, *Peacock Angel*, (London: J. Murray, 1941).

[6] Rudolf Macúch et al., *A Mandaean Dictionary*. (London: Clarendon Press, 1963).

[7] E.S. Drower, *On the Banks of the Tigris and the Euphrates*. Translated by Fouad Jamil, (n.p.: Dar Al Warraq, 2008).

[8] E.S. Drower, *The Mandaeans of Iraq and Iran: Their Cults, Customs, Magic, Legends and Folklore*. (Oxford: Clarendon Press, 1937).

[9] E.S. Drower, *The Secret Adam: A Study of the Nasoraean Gnosis*. (Oxford: Clarendon Press, 1960). http://khazarzar.skeptik.net/books/mandaean/adam.pdf.

Drower's wish, beyond her curiosity, to help take care of the community that had drawn her interest. In 1930, during her visit to Qal'it Saleh area in Amara, in an encounter with thirty leaders and honourables of the Mandaean community, she urged them to contact the League of Nations, which at that time, guaranteed the rights of religious minorities. This would be similar to the Assyrians, who struggled for special status with letters to the League. The Baha'is also presented petitions over the seizure of Bahá'u'lláh's House in Baghdad. Drower told the Mandaeans, 'You know that Iraq is about to enter the League of Nations and the Sabaeans must have clear and fixed rights and their name to be mentioned in the constitution, but This happens only when the Sabaeans present a petition of that to the League of Nations. I have brought the petition and you just have to sign it.[10]

Al Rumi mentions that the Mandaeans did not respond to this call. This is perfectly consistent with their non-confrontational and isolated history over the last centuries and their policy of avoiding any provocation of an uncalculated reactions of the Muslim majority around them. Their reluctance to interfere in political affairs has remained an inherited character since the Islamic Middle Ages. An example of their typical cautious behaviour preceded Drower's call by more than sixty years, when they rejected the proposal of the British Consul Henry Layard in Basra in 1865 to build the Mendi temple for the Mandaeans in Amara province. They objected to a British agreement with one of the Mandaean clerics to provide financial support to the community in exchange for support of British policy in Iraq.[11] As a result, the Mandaeans avoided involvement in political conflicts such as the sad fate of the Assyrians in the 1933 massacre or the Yazidis in Sinjar, who were divided between the French, British and Turkish influence in 1935. They did not suffer the tragic destiny of the Jews in the Farhud pogrom of 1941 following the political conflict between the two fronts of Germany and Britain supporters and their forced displacement in 1950 and 1951 after the founding of Israel.

A Symbolic Border for Recognition

Consequently, the Mandaeans remain cautiously open. The British needed to designate a head of the community or a spiritual council through which to shape the relationship between the community and the invader. The military ruler in Iraq, Colonel N. Wilson, appointed the cleric Dakhil Sheikh Idan president of the Mandaean sect together with his assistant clerics Sheikh Zuhron and Sheikh Abd on 6 June 1919.[12] In the Mandaean's view, the British Mandate government's official acknowledgement of the sect might substitute for the traditional medieval recognition through the Islamic Law

---

[10] Ghadban Al Roumi, *Mandaean Memoirs*. (Damascus: Dar Al Mada, 2007), 63.
[11] Nizar Yasser Sakr Al Haidar, *The Decree of Queen Victoria for the Protection of the Mandaean Sabaeans*. See ankawa website http://www.ankawa.com/forum/index.php?topic=55714.0.
[12] See: *The Mandaean Afaq Journal* 13 (2000).

(Shari'a). After the coronation of Faisal I as King of Iraq in 1921, Dakhil Sheikh Idan tried to obtain Iraqi state ratification of his presidency of the Mandaeans by sending his congratulation to the King and asking him to 'issue an order to ratify his presidency.'[13] But recognition of the Mandaeans did not go beyond this symbolic limit. After launching the nation-state project, the Official Holidays Act No. 72 of 1931, legislation regulating religious communities did not specifically consider the Mandaeans or mention the Mandaean feasts. Also, the other legislations issued in 1931 to regulate some Christian sects, such as the Armenian Orthodox Community Law No. 70 and the Israeli Community (Musawi) Law No. 77 ignored the Mandaeans. This deprived them of control over the personal status affairs of their community members and of autonomy in administering their internal religious affairs. Similar to the Yazidis, the Mandaeans remained subject to Islamic law and the Hanafi doctrine of inheritance, marriage, and divorce. Their cases were settled according to the jurisprudence of the Muslim judiciary, far from the provisions of their own law.

The Local Languages Act of 1931 granted importance to only three languages: Arabic (language of the Muslim majority), Turkish (language of the old occupier) and Kurdish (language of the largest ethnic group). It regulated the use of languages locally according to the ethnic population concentration in line with the importance of Arabic in the national project of building a nation-state and use of Kurdish and Turkish in the courts in areas that include dense Kurdish or Turkmen population.[14] The law did not mention the Syriac, Armenian or Mandaean language. To justify this language policy, Iraq's 1936 Directory stated that Iraq has 'several languages: Arabic, Kurdish, Chaldean, Hebrew, Turkish, and Armenian, but Arabic is the mother tongue of all and the children of all the elements learn it as major language of the homeland, as well as the language of science, politics, and commerce.' Despite this, the Kurdish and Turkmen languages are respected in the northern regions as official languages in the courts and schools while the rest of the Iraqi languages are common in small communities, temples and some non-official schools.'[15] Recognition of the Mandaean language as one of the languages used in Iraq took more than eighty years. The text of the Official Languages Act of 2014 stated that it sought to 'support and develop the Arabic and Kurdish languages and the other Iraqi languages such as the Turkmen, Syriac, and Mandaean Sabaean.'[16]

Symbolic Demands

When the nation-state emerged, the Mandaean had minimal demands that

---

[13] Ibid.

[14] Article 2 of the Local Languages Law No. 74 of 1931, *The Iraqi Chronicles* 989, (published 1 June 1931)

[15] The official directory of Iraq for 1936, 'Directory of the Kingdom' (Baghdad: Denkor for Printing and Publishing, 1936), 722.

[16] 'The Official Languages Law No. 7 of 2014' *The Iraqi Chronicles* 4311, (published 24 February 2014).

did not differ from the Baha'is and Yazidis. A hierarchy inherited from the medieval Islamic theological realm had two categories of recognition: The first category of religions (Islam, Christianity and Judaism) represents the first class of the heavenly or Abrahamic religions, and the second category of beliefs were considered to be of a lower class (Yazidism, Mandaeism and Baha'ism).

On the political level, this hierarchy resulted in Mandaeans not demanding representation, similar to the Jews and Christian, in the Senate. The head of the Mandaean royal family, Anisi Fayadh, was close to obtaining this Senate membership, but was prevented by the community head, Dakhil Sheikh Idan. This may have been due to the clergy and secularists competing over the positions of power in the community.[17] In all cases, the policy of caution deprived the Mandaeans from parliamentary representation as well as legislation to regulate their personal status, similar to the Christian and Jewish (Musawi) communities.

In the early 1930s, the Mandaeans did not receive an official response when they sought recognition of their feasts. The educator Ghadban Al Rumi first attempted as an individual with a 1930 petition to the then Minister of Education Abdel Hussein Al Chalabi. He defended the right of the Mandaeans, especially state employed teachers, to obtain holidays for their feasts.[18]

The courageous attempt of a secular Mandaean stirred the stagnant water. The Mandaean elites approved of the individual's effort and tried to expand the demands to involve exemption of the clerics from military service. On 1 February 1932, the leaders and dignitaries of the community in Al Msayaida (Kahla-Amara) area petitioned Prime Minister Nuri Al Saiid for exemption of spiritual leaders from the compulsory military service and to recognise some Mandaean feasts: Al Banja feast (five days) Yahya Prophet birthday (one day), the Big Feast and the New Year's Day (four days). On those days, Mandaean retreat to their home for 36 hours, when no one should see him or name him except his family members. The document reveals that the community had 15,000 individuals 'deprived of rights and privileges which facilitate practicing their religious rituals as the other communities do.' The community also complained of the recently enacted Compulsory Recruitment Law, which obliges them to join the army without considering the sect though the law 'took into consideration the rights of all the sects, but because the Mandaean community is far from participating in the government structure and positions, no one paid attention to it.' However, admitting Mandaean members into state jobs requires recognition of the community 'by having the rights and commitments that others do.' More

---

[17] Sadeq Shahid Al Tai, *The Magic of Silver The Water Secret: An Anthropological Study of the Sabaean Community in Iraq*. (Cairo: The Supreme Council of Culture, 2010), 218.
[18] A Written Letter sent by Mr. Ghadban Al Roumi to the Minister of Education on 14 March 1930.

specifically, the petition first noted that the special traditions of the unique class of Mandaean clerics must be considered since 'our clerics have their own religious duties, and their own way of living and managing their own affairs so that they cannot engage in the army. Also, our clerics are not allowed in any way to cut their hair or eat food cooked by other than themselves, and whoever violates that is a rogue in his religion.' The petition also stressed the need for equality with non-Muslim communities since 'all the heads of other communities have been exempted from recruitment in the army, it was necessary to exempt us similar to others as the right and law require.' Another point in the petition indicates that some feasts, like Al Banja feast, require special rituals in which 'each Sabaean must abstain from food, drink and doing any work, and must swim in the running water when he eats and drinks. So how could the Sabaean do that while he is recruited in the army?' The petition's third point differed from the traditional calm of the Mandaeans and threatened immigration if the demands were not met.' Freedom of religion is enshrined in all international laws and treaties as well as it is stipulated in our Iraqi constitution so that not allowing us to practice our religious affairs freely makes us forced and obliged to leave this country…'[19] The holidays were first confirmed in 1936, six years after Al Rumi's letter during the reign of Hikmat Suleiman, and four years after community dignitaries submitted demands to Prime Minister Nuri al-Saiid. However, without justifications, the recognition was soon revoked in 1946 during the government of Arshad Al Omari.

Contradictory Narratives in the context of Nation-State Building

Early on 14 November 2014, I was drinking tea with the cleric Alaa Aziz Taresh, the deputy Head of the Mandaean community, before he performed the religious rituals at his residence in Al Qadisiya Mendi in Baghdad. His eyes glowed when mentioning Lady Drower. The Mandaeans have a gratitude tantamount to reification for the colonialist Christian scholar. 'She wrote justly about the Mandaeans, learned our language and lived among us. Her study involved field data and she would have embraced our religion had it been a proselytising one,' the cleric told me and added, 'while the study of our Muslim citizen Abdel Razzaq al-Hassani was void of these data and high reverence.' I felt his words warned me to not to follow al-Hassani's easy path, but to follow Drower's steep path.

Al-Hassani and Drower symbolise the contemporary history of the Mandaeans, who lived in a small world and could meet in such a sacred place and drink tea and talk about the miracle of the 'living fossils' present for centuries in the marshes (al-Ahwar) of southern Iraq. Al-Hassani and Drower lived in Mesopotamia during the same period, but they presented two different narratives about its people's culture and ancient beliefs. When

---

[19] A Letter sent by the leaders of the Mandaean community in Iraq to the Iraqi Prime Minister on 1 February 1932.

we remember them today as being responsible for the contemporary interest in the Mandaeans, the state historian Abdel Razzaq al-Hassani is remembered as promoting the medieval narrative about the Mandaeans and a reproducer of the legends that led to a judicial conflict with them. The British anthropologist, Lady Drower presented a different narrative that became a source of pride for the Mandaeans in their culture, language and beliefs unlike a medieval narrative that degraded them to the level of worshippers of the stars and planets.

During the twentieth century, the Mandaeans' journey was fraught with difficulties after their compatriot Abdel Razzaq al-Hassani defamed them through his book, which resulted in a famous court case.[20] The Mandaeans spiritual leader, Dakhil Sheikh Idan (1888-1964) presented a complaint to the Ministry of Justice, the Court of Cassation,[21] and won a verdict condemning the author and forcing him to withdraw the book and apologise. In the book's subsequent editions, Al Hassani denies the Mandaeans' won the case, 'We received the Sabaeans' noise and objection that dragged us into lengthy trials, but they ended in the plaintiffs' failure for lack of a fault in what we wrote and published.'[22] However, in the following editions, he added on the cover, 'Extensive study based on personal observations and accurate follow-ups, and a revised and edited edition, added to it information not found in the first and second editions,' in an attempt to add a fieldwork character to his study, and a reference to the judicial requirement that he amend and revise his book.

Sheikh Dakhil's arguments in the trial are considered the first public defence of the essence of their faith in contemporary Iraqi history. Sheikh Dakhil began by reviewing the history of the Mandaeans, their beliefs and relationships with other religions, and explaining the religious rituals and beliefs, and the role of the Mandaeans in the Renaissance of the Islamic Civilisation. He referred to Lady Drower's study, which contradicts that of al-Hassani. Then he dealt with the Holy Book *Gnza Rba* and started to read specifically in the first book *Praise of Monotheism*, which confirms their monotheism to refute al-Hassani's thesis. Father Anastas al-Karmeli translated from Aramaic into Arabic after the court assigned him to conduct the translation.[23] The ruling in favor of the Mandaeans was a temporary victory for them. Although the book was reprinted in many subsequent editions and contained new revisions and additions, it still carried many

---

[20] Abdel Razzaq Al Hasani, *The Sabaeans, Past and Present.* Presented by: Ahmad Zaki Pasha (Cairo: Al Khanji Library, 1931). This edition entails terrible inaccuracies, the Mandaeans filed a legal suit against the author.

[21] Lami'a Abbas Amara, 'Personality of the Edition: Sheikh Dakheel' *The Mandaean Magazine* 0 (1990).

[22] Abdel Razzaq Al Hasani, *The Sabaeans in Their Present and their Past.* (Sidon: Al Irfan Press, 1963), 7.

[23] Details of the case and the debate between Sheikh Dakheel, the spiritual leader of the Mandaean Sabaean community and the Iraqi historian Abdel Razzaq Al Hasani, including the article by Abdel Hamid Al Sheikh Dakheel, 'The Encyclopedia of Springs of Knowledge' *Mandean Network*, (n.d.). http://mandaeannetwork.com/Mandaean/sabians_mandaean_past_and_recently_al_hassani.html.

inaccuracies not accepted by the Mandaeans.[24]

The Political Revolution of the Educated Elite

The policy of caution followed by the Mandaean sect for centuries did not assure that religious leaders could control the educated elite, who soon joined political parties struggling for social justice. With its transnational ideology, the Communist Party attracted the elites of the religious minorities of Judaism, Christians, and Mandaeans. Their affiliation to a party transcending religions provided a vision of a possible alternative system that through political revolution can achieve de facto, not only legal equality.

Among the most prominent Mandaeans belonging to the Communist Party was Aziz Sabahi. As the party's historian, he wrote a huge book about the history of the Iraqi Communist Party[25]. The book is considered the best contemporary documentation of the history of the party, thanks to the documents and testimonies given to the researcher due to his participation in the Communist Party for nearly six decades as a member, a political prisoner, and a cultural figure.[26] The book is also considered the most mature attempt by the Communists to document their history in a way distinct from the great classical work of Hanna Batato about *The Old Social Classes and the Revolutionary Movements in Iraq,* which was also translated into Arabic, in three parts[27] covering two consecutive decades of Batato's history of the party until the mid-1970s. Sabahi explains the desire of the Mandaeans to belong to the Communist Party by the fact that they faced 'a kind of oppression, sometimes hidden and sometimes exposed, by the society and the government, which is the result of this society that produces an insidious, ideological and materialistic oppression which does not admit their equality (...) so it was logical that the youth go specifically to the Iraqi Communist Party (...) since it is open to the people, without placing for them any restrictions or conditions, be they national, religious, or tribal.'[28]

One of the most controversial Mandaean figures was Malek Saif, who joined the Communist Party in 1942 under the pseudonym Kamal, rapidly rose to leadership before betraying the party.[29] He was appointed secretary of the local committee of the party in Maysan province in 1943. Then, in

---

[24] See an assessment of Al Hasani written by the Iraqi historian Rashid Al Khayoun, 'The Iraqi Historian Abdel Razzaq Al Hasani 1903-1997, Brilliance in Political History and Confusion in the History of Religions and Beliefs' *Al Hayat Newspaper*12797 (published 17 March 1998).

[25] Aziz Sabahi, *Decades of the History of the Iraqi Communist Party*. (Damascus: New Culture Publications, 1999).

[26] Hanna Batato, *Iraq – the Social Classes and Revolutionary Movements from the Ottoman Era until the Establishment of the Republic*. Translated by Afif Al Razzaq. (Beirut: Arab Research Foundation, 2003).

[27] Interview with Aziz Sabahi, conducted by Musa Al Khamisi, Interview with Aziz Sabahi, conducted by Musa Al Khamisi, *Masarat Magazine* Special Issue 9 (2007) 54.

[28] Hanna Batato, 'The Second Book (The Communist Party)' *Masarat Magazine* Special Issue Supplement 3-9 (2007), 176-177.

[29] Malek Saif, *History has a Tongue. Memories and Issues Related to the Iraqi Communist Party Since its Founding until Present*. (Baghdad: Freedom House for Printing, 1983), 3.

1946, he was transferred to Basra to take charge of organising the party's local committee. He began to direct the Iraqi Communist Party after the arrest of Fahd, the party's Secretary General on 18 January 1947.[30] Malek's betrayal of the party resulted in the execution of Fahd Yusuf Salman—the charismatic Syriac personality who founded the Iraqi Communist Party in the thirties—although he had asked Malek to come to Baghdad to take over the responsibility because Malek had 'sufficient political maturity and other qualities that qualify him to lead the movement in such circumstances,'[31] according to the letter sent by Fahd from prison to Yehuda Siddiq. Accordingly, the Christian Fahd, born in Bartala / Nineveh Plains, commissioned the party's secretariat to the Mandaean Malek Saif and withdrew it from the Jewish Yehud Siddiq, member of the Anti-Zionist Committee of the Iraqi Communist Party. Malek became the party's main official after Fahd's arrest at the end of June 1947.[32] Malek Saif's confessions, which led to the execution of the Communist Party leaders (Fahd, Sarem, Hazem), were published in the secret encyclopaedia of the Communist Party, issued by the Iraqi Government in 1949, leaving a suspicious impression of a figure who died in the mid-1980s after writing books defaming the Communist Party, such as *The Truth of Communism,* 1952; *My Experience in the Communist Party*, 1974; *History has a Tongue*, 1983.

Other notable names include Naiim Badawi and the physicist Abdel Jabbar Abdallah (1911-1969) who was considered an icon of the Mandaeans. He studied at the American University of Beirut in 1930. He formed a cultural association with Abdel Fattah Ibrahim (a pioneer of sociology and founder of the Democratic Union Party) and Mohammad Hadid (one of the founders of the National Democratic Party and father of the famous architect Zuha Hadid). He then travelled to the United States and received his doctorate in natural science (physics) from Massachusetts Institute of Technology MIT in 1944. After his return, he worked with Dr. Matti Akrawi on founding Baghdad University and he was its second president (after Akrawi) between 5 October 1957 and 1 August 1958. Abdel Jabbar Abdallah competed for the presidency of the university against the national historian Abdel Aziz Al Duri. The scientific and cultural circles had a heated debate over the two candidates. Najib al-Rubaie, chairman of the council of sovereignty, objected to Abdel Jabbar Abdallah for his being a Mandaean. So, the Interior Minister Ali Ahmad Mohieddin answered him, 'We want an Imam for the university, not an Imam for a mosque for worshipers.'

---

[30] The Government Press, *Fahed's Letter to Yehuda Freim Siddiq*, (dated 17 May 1948), published in the Public Police, Division of Criminal Investigation Directorate, *A Secret Encyclopedia of the Iraqi Communist Party* (Baghdad: Government Press, 1949) ///c1, 227.

[31] The Government Press, *A Secret Encyclopedia of the Iraqi Communist Party*. (Baghdad: Government Press, 1949) 21, 53.

[32] See what the historian Al Musalli Sayyar Al Jamil wrote about the story of the choice: Abdel Jabbar Abdallah (2/2): *From the Secretariat and Reverence to Insult and Imprisonment*, Elaf website, (published 20 December 2010) http://elaph.com/Web/opinion/2010/12/617659.html

President Abdel Karim Qassem ended the debate by supporting Abdel Jabbar's appointment with the logic that the revolution does not discriminate between Iraqis on religious grounds and that it places every Iraqi in the suitable position.[33] The choice may reflect General Qassim's national Iraqi policy in contrast to the supranational Arab policy to rival General Abdel Salam Aref. However, the story may be just a myth reflecting a Communist nostalgia for the period of General Qassim; perhaps the Mandaean Communists exaggerated the issue. General Qassim choice was not for the famous Mandaean scholar with the communist roots as much as against Abdel Aziz al-Duri, who had undesirable political views in the new revolutionary era.[34]

The Mandaean spring was short. With their 1963 coup d'état, the Baathists formed militias to liquidate their Communist opponents. Al-Jabbar was arrested, tortured, and dismissed from the University of Baghdad. He was forced to immigrate to the United States, where he died. Also, the Mandaean educator, Ghadban al-Rumi, was forced to retire although he was not interested in politics. Among other Mandaean elites, the educator Najia al-Marani was also forced to retire and that motivated her to obtain a Bachelor of English Literature degree from the University of Hikma, Baghdad, 1969. Then she joined the American University of Beirut in 1970 for a master's and then doctorate in English literature. The Lebanese civil war forced her to interrupt her study and return to Iraq.

The West approved and perhaps directly supported the 1963 coup d'état and the policy to contain the Communist Party during the 1970s. However, in less than two decades this led to the gradual deprivation of the religious minorities of political alternatives other than the ruling party, as well as weakening the secular opposition. Due to complicated and cumulative circumstances, the weakening of the opposition allowed the Islamists to become the strongest opposition to the oppressive secular government of the leading ruling party. These outcomes became clear after the US invasion of Iraq in 2003. But after having been stripped of political alternatives, these educated and secular elites revolted in a different manner through forming a defensive narrative of the Mandaeans against the subversive, degrading medieval narrative of the first generation. The second generation that inherited the defensive narrative, pressed to modernise the Mandaean religion. They led an internal revolution to reform and democratise the community from within by separating the religious power from the temporal one. This took place over many years, before reaching its peak in the mid-to-late 1990s.

---

[33] Abdel Aziz Al Duri – An Intellectual and a Historian, a scientific symposium held by the Department of Historical Studies, House of Wisdom, Baghdad, 2011. 10.

[34] Basem Abdel Hamid Hamoudi, 'Ghadban Al Roumi, a Researcher and Educator' *Al Mada Newspaper* 1295 (published 12 August 2008).

Formation of a Defensive Mandaean Narrative in the 1970s

In the 1970s, the *Popular Heritage* magazine provided a platform for the religious minority elites. Their first scholarly publishing about Mandaeism was by the pioneering educator Ghadban al-Rumi (1905-1989), who learned the Mandaean language from clerics in 1918. He became the most prominent educator in al-Amara by inaugurating al-Kahla School in 1923 and establishing a teachers' association in 1926. Al Rumi was the first Mandaean employee and teacher to be appointed by the government. He moved in various teaching positions until he settled down as a teacher of English in Baghdad, 1950, when he was commissioned by Munir al-Qadi, Secretary of the Council of Ministers and later the Minister of Education, to prepare an introductory book about the Mandaeans. Together with his colleague Naiim Badawi, Al Rumi co-authored a booklet entitled *The Sabaeans in Iraq*, published in 1955. Under the supervision of the scholar Abdel Jabbar Abdallah, he wrote a book with his colleague Badawi, but the book was lost during the arrest of Badawi on charges of communism in the early days of the Baathist coup d'etat in 1963.[35] Al-Rumi wrote in *The Popular Heritage* magazine a controversial article entitled *If the Sabaean Boy Died*[36] in which he responded to al-Hassani's article published in the same magazine. He expressed his reservations, which left an impression that he was accusing al-Hassani of sheer ignorance. Among the reservations was 'he does not know a word from the Mandaean Aramaic language, and that he lives in a place far from the centres of the Sabaean presence and the centres of their temples and religious scholars. So how could al-Hassani write about their traditions, beliefs, myths and rituals?' Al-Rumi pointed out that al-Hassani's book *The Sabaeans in Their Present and Past* reflects a gloomy atmosphere about the people of this community. Despite this, the Mandaeans understood 'his mistakes calmly and solemnly and judged him for what he has issued.'[37] The article's impact equalled the critique the Yazidi researcher Khodr Suleiman addressed to the state historian al-Hassani in a series of articles published in the *Popular Heritage* magazine. The best response to al-Hassani and his state narrative was for al-Rumi and Naiim Badawi to translate the anthropologist Drower's book about the Mandaeans. The translated book was issued in two parts, the first in 1969, while the second, related to the legends and popular stories, was issued in 1973.

Al-Rumi wrote other books alone; the most prominent was commissioned in 1983 by Abdel Razzaq Muhiuddin, President of the Iraqi Academy of Sciences, and placed the Mandaean religion in the context of the first monotheistic religion. The book contained bold views on the origin of Prophet Abraham and proposed that he was Mandaean and that his brother

---

[35] Ghadban Al Roumi, 'If the Sabaean Boy Dies' *The Iraqi Popular Heritage Magazine* 12 (1974).
[36] Ghadban Roumi Akla Al Nashi, *The Sabaeans: A Historical Sociological and Religious Research about the Sabaeans*. (Baghdad: Ummah Press, 1983), 100-104.
[37] Ghadban Al Rumi, 'If the Sabaean Boy Died' *The Popular Heritage Magazine* 12 (1974).

was even Rish Amma. According to the Mandaean books, Abraham was plagued with a disease that necessitated cutting off part of his sexual organ (considered circumcision in the Mandaeans' doctrine). This prevented him from practising baptism, slaughtering, or becoming a cleric (Mandaeism does not allow the disfigured and those with deficient organs to become a cleric). Therefore, Abraham departed and settled in the desert, where Mandaeans with deficient organs (they are called *Basrana ed sereh*, disfigured by the moon) followed him; their descendants are not pure except after seven generations. With the proliferation of Abraham's followers of the destitute and the disfigured by the moon, his group became powerful. This caused a split with the other Mandaeans (the pure ones) so that the rivalry led Abraham to attempt to force the pure ones to follow him. With the development of the dispute, he crossed the Euphrates River with his followers; they were called 'transients.'[38] The book included an Arabic translation of Mandaean holy texts from the holy book *Ginza Rba*, including a whole chapter on the rule of the prophet Yahya 'John the Baptist.'[39] And in line with the community's official policy of non-confrontation, these bold views and translation of the sacred texts prompted the Mandaean community's Supreme Spiritual Council to seal the book with the warning that Al Rumi has nothing to do with this book, and he does not bear responsibility for its content. The Council disagreed with the author in many points mentioned in the book.

During the same year, 1974, when Al Rumi was publishing his books, Najia al-Marani, who was specialised in English literature, began publishing about Mandaeism in the same magazine (The Popular Heritage). Her first study had a modest title *Lights about the Mandaean Sabaeans*.[40] Following that book, al-Marani published a very important study about the Mandaean language. Then she published in 1976 an article entitled *Is Mandaeism a Dialect from Arabic?*[41] She returned to collect her previous studies in an expanded book entitled *Mandaean Sabaean Concepts* printed in Baghdad in 1981. The book contained an Arabic translation of Mandaean texts from the *Ginza Rba*, the Mandaean holy book.

In 1972, another Mandaean writer, Abdel Fattah al-Zouhairi, began to be interested in writing about the Mandaeans, trying to defend a Mandaean narrative of an ancient, authentically monotheistic religion. After more than a decade, his efforts culminated in the publication of a huge book entitled *Briefing in the History of the Demise of the Arab-Mandaean Sabaeans* which was published in 1983, the same year Ghadban al-Rumi's book was published. The book describes the Mandaeans as 'the demise Arabs' coinciding with the ideological line of the ruling regime in Iraq at the time. We also note that on

---

[38] Ibid.,148-163.
[39] Abdel Fattah Al Zuhairi, *A Summary in the History of the Mandaean Sabaeans*. (Bagdhad: Al Arab Al Ba ida, 1983) 5.
[40] Najia al-Marani, 'Lights about the Mandaean Sabaeans' *Popular Heritage* 8 and 9 (1974).
[41] Najia al-Marani, 'Is Mandaeism a Dialect from Arabic?' *Popular Heritage* 2 and 3(1976), 21-46.

his book's front pages, the author placed three Quranic verses mentioning the Mandaeans, confirming that they were 'a distinct religious group in the era of Prophet Mohammad.'[42] Due to his pride in the Mandaean medieval scholars, the researcher presented them as part of the Arab nation. The back cover has, written in Arabic and Mandaean, an appeal for official acceptance 'The Arab nation has been proud of its scholars since ancient times, and if you follow this book, you find among them quite a good number of Aramaic Mandaean Sabaeans.' Despite this, the author succeeded in passing his message by 'tackling the right aspects of the Mandaean religion' that oppose the medieval narrative.[43]

In the mid-seventies, Sabih al-Suhairi completed his thesis on the Mandaeans as the first to be written by a Mandaean researcher specialising in the German language. In 1969, he studied at the University of Hamburg. In 1972, his teacher asked him to change his major from German to Oriental studies and to specialise in studying Mandaeism. After that, he came back to Iraq under critical circumstances as the theological dispute was at its height about baptising in al-Isala water in an artificial basin of running water instead of doing that in a river's running river water. The clerics in Basra and Baghdad were divided between pro-modernisation of the rituals and those who see in that an exit from the millennial rituals. Al-Suhairi went around among the regions to study the contemporary conditions of his community and presented the outcomes of his work as a doctoral dissertation in German about *The Mandaeans in Iraq Nowadays* in 1975.

Upon his return, al-Suhairi could not pass on his experience about his religious doctrine to the new generation of university students in what might be considered 'an ethnic or theological issue' that infuriates the government. During the next two decades, he moved between Baghdad and Basra universities before he finally succeeded in 1993 in moving to the Faculty of Languages in Baghdad University to teach the Mandaean language. It was the first faculty to teach this language among the Semitic languages in the Middle East. With that, the academic opportunity for the new Mandaean generation to specialise in their culture and language became available so that during the nineties, two dissertations by al-Suhairi students: *The Mandaean Ihraz Tools in the Iraqi Museum* by Ferial Zuhron Ni'man 1996, and *The Mandaean Scholars' Names in Ginza Rba* by Majid Saiid al-Sabahi in 1997. During that period, Al Suhairi translated Kort Rudolf's book *Development and Creation in the Mandaean Religion* in 1993. His most important work has been participating with his colleague professor Yusuf Quzi in translating *Ginza Rba*, literally preserving the historical and religious content while resisting the linguistic formulation

---

[42] Abdel Fattah Al Zuhairi, *A Summary in the History of the Mandaean Sabaeans*. (Bagdhad: Al Arab Al Ba ida, 1983), 13.
[43] About the history of this jurisprudential dispute, see the article by Al Tarmiza Khaldoun Al Naseh, 'Yardna - The Running Water' *The Mandean Associations Union* (n.d.). http://www.mandaeanunion.org/en/culture/item/1157-2014-03-29-15-10-46

(Arabisation) done by the poet Abdel Razzaq Abdel Wahed.

The Sect Moved to Baghdad

The Mandaeans migrated from their geographical locations in Amara, Basra and southern Iraq to Baghdad for economic purposes and studying because the universities and important schools were concentrated in the capital. The mass Jewish emigration of 1950 and 1951 left an economic and commercial vacuum that could offer new and easy opportunities for the other religious minorities. That encouraged the Christians to migrate from the villages of Mosul to Baghdad for the same reason. Therefore, the minorities migrated from two directions: Christians from the north and the Mandaeans from the south. In 1959, the head of the Mandean community, Dakhil Sheikh Idan, moved from the province of Dhi Qar (Nasiriyah) to Baghdad. This brought the community presidency to the capital and closer to the centre of decisionmakers. That triggered intensified Mandaean migration to Baghdad so that more than two-thirds of the community has settled in Baghdad by the seventies, according to sources from within the community.

The first Mendi (temple) was built in the Dora area at the end of the 1960s in Baghdad. The Mandaeans built on land overlooking the Tigris River allocated to them by the state in the mid-seventies in al-Qadisiya area. However, it was confiscated because it was located within the land of the Dora power station. A new temple was built in al-Qadisiya area and became the headquarter of the community presidency, the Supreme Spiritual Council and the administrative councils including the House of Commons and the Council of Community Affairs. The Mandaeans started to concentrate in this area next to the temple, especially after building a basin for baptism. That important ritual reform included an advisory of allowing washing before prayer (al-Rashama) with Isala water. The Mandaean clerics were divided about this reform. The advisory was considered a kind of modernisation compatible with the life of the big cities and adapted to its rhythm, especially that the Mandaean individual has difficulty reaching the river water three times a day to wash before prayer and to perform the prayer 'al-Brakha'.[44] According to the testimony of the Iraqi anthropologist, Sadeq al-Ta'i, the idea was born in Basra in the seventies in the temple of the community, which is located on the river Ashar, whose water, over time and as a result of neglect, became impure and baptism rituals could not be performed in it. Consequently, a basin was built to hold the baptism rituals. In Basra, Genza Bira Abdallah al-Sheikh Najm asked the head of the community in Baghdad, Sheikh Abdallah al-Sheikh Sam, for permission for this modernisation, but the latter rejected it as a 'heresy'. When Abdallah al-Sheikh Najm assumed the presidency of the sect in the early 1980s and moved to Baghdad, the

---

[44] Sadeq Shahid Al Tai *The Magic of Silver The Water Secret: An Anthropological Study of the Sabaean Community in Iraq.* (Cairo: The Supreme Council of Culture, 2010), 222-223.

Mandaeans' request to establish a baptismal basin was approved so that curious people would not watch the baptism of their women in the river.[45]

The Mandaeans' request came after the temple of the sect, built in al-Qadisiya area and overlooking the Tigris River, lost its religious function related to its position on a running river since al-Khar River, next to the temple site, became dry and eventually turned into an administrative centre that includes the community councils. The community then demanded a piece of land on the Tigris River (under the Jadriya bridge) to practice the baptismal rituals (it was called then the land of baptism) and simple temples were arranged for resting and eating the ritual meals and going down into the river water for baptism. The area became a place where the Baghdadis had the opportunity to watch the Mandaeans' baptism during the Mandaean feasts, such as the feast of the creation al-Brunaya, but the land has remained leased so far without transferring its ownership to that of the community.

From the Council of Tolerance to the Spiritual Council

The movement of the Mandaeans and their concentration in Baghdad motivated their community's institutionalisation in 1975 through the 'Council of Tolerance' that runs its affairs. The council was formed of the most prominent Mandaean personalities, headed by al-Genz Bara Abdallah al-Sheikh Sam (1890-1981). Later, it was renamed the Spiritual Council of Mandaean Sabaean community to add importance and a religious character to it. The council was officially recognised in 1981, especially after the issuance of the Official Communities' Act in Iraq, a law stating that the Mandaean community is among the officially recognised communities.[46] The council has 19 Mandaean personalities, notably: Al-Genz Bara Abdallah al-Sheikh Sam, Ghadban al-Rumi, poet Abdel Razzaq Abdel Wahed, and others. The Ministry of Endowments and Religious Affairs officially approved the council on 29 March 1984. The Ministry of Endowments began to dominate and practically run the affairs of the religious communities. That meant that the community was stripped of complete independence in administering its religious affairs, but the Mandaeans did not seem to object because, at least, their status has become legally equivalent to the 14 Christian communities and the Jews.

The Era of the Nineties: From the Water of Life to the Land of the Nation-State

Due to the UN sanctions imposed in 1991, many Mandaeans especially the middle-class, were impoverished. In those years, as a student at Baghdad University, I had Mandaean friends living in the neighbourhood of Palestine Street, where most middle-class Baghdadis resided. During a discussion of

---

[45] The Extension System of the System for the Care of Religious Communities (officially recognised religious communities in Iraq No 32 of 1981).
[46] The meeting is available on YouTube at https://www.youtube.com/watch?v=GNEpC4payvw

Claude Lévi-Strauss's book, *The Savage Mind*, a Mandaean friend belonging to the Communist Party and from a once-wealthy family working and trading in gold suddenly revealed his desire to convert to Islam, but for not for obvious religious conviction. I could understand his motives after the tea vendor near his workplace refused to bring tea to him or to his guests because he could not clean the tea cup after a Mandaean drank from it. Such beliefs had shaped behaviour in the countryside, but now had started to sneak into the cities as well. Like my secular Mandaean friend, the whole Mandaean community faced social isolation due to the suspicion of non-monotheism. Consequently, the Mandaeans began to seriously discuss translating their holy book into Arabic to put an end to centuries of accusations of being pagan.

The secular elite movement within the Mandaean community ended because of the Gulf War of 1991. The cultural movement that began in the 1970s to clarify the ambiguity surrounding Mandaeism contributed to mitigating the stereotypical medieval narrative about the Mandaeans, but their discussions did not change much widespread social prejudices against them. The state's curricula were not open to diversity but instead instilled the ideology of the political system and its vision of forced integration. Translating the British anthropologist Drower's book into Arabic, and the writings of the Mandaeans themselves, such as Najia al-Marani and Ghadban al-Rumi since the 1970s, and Aziz Sabahi in the 1990s, did not influence more than a narrow circle of intellectuals.

Islamisation of the State and Return of the Medieval Narrative Impact

Under the influence of the Gulf War and the subsequent thirteen-year economic blockade, the officially secular Baathist regime initiated an official policy of Islamising the state. Adopting 'religion' rather than 'nationalism' as the definitive basis of identity allowed for a strong return to the influences of the negative medieval narrative about the Mandaeans, who then began to face discrimination even in a modern city like Baghdad. These social pressures to Islamise the community threatened the internal cohesion of the group. In face of the religious extremism, the Mandaeans boldly decided to translate their holy book, *Ginza Rba*, into Arabic, ending a cultural tradition that had endured a millennium.

The decision to translate *Ginza Rba* into Arabic culminated a rapid social transformation in the community after its migration to the centres of the cities, especially to the capital Baghdad, during the nation-state building in the twentieth century. A new cycle in radical theological transformations began after issuing an advisory permitting baptism in the Isala water and abandoning baptism in the water of a running river. This was a first attempt to adapt the community's rites to the challenges of a world where, in Marx's phrase, 'All that is solid melts into air, all that is holy is profaned.'

The pressures of official Islamisation raised the suspicion and concern of the religious minorities, such as the Christians, Mandaeans, and Yazidis. Religious discrimination began to push some to emigrate while many others converted to Islam. Though many Mandaeans officially registered their conversion to Islam in the 1990s, many conversions have not been registered at all, such as my secular friend's conversion. Due to the Mandaeans' fragile demographic situation, this minority was more affected than others by the religious conversion processes, especially as a non-proselytising religion that does not welcome new believers, nor does it allow those who leave the Mandaean religion to return again.

The growing rhetoric of hatred and incitement resulted in harassment of the Mandaeans and the non-Muslim minorities seeking economic and educational opportunities. As the weakest among the minorities, Mandaeans became particularly anxious. Some Mandaean families living in extreme poverty were pressured to convert into Islam in return for economic or social benefits. The community noticed with concern the high levels of Mandaeans converting into Islam through marriage of Muslims. Many mass conversions to Islam took place in the poverty belts around Baghdad.

The government ignored those events for many reasons. First, the Mandaeans' conversion to Islam supported the government's position as a guardian of the official state religion. Second, these conversions meant the community was distracted with its internal conflicts and not attacking the government for the great vacuum in their lives and the gloomy and depressing future. Since discussions about the government were forbidden, it was easy (and permissible) for people to focus their anger at each other. The religious minorities were a scapegoat sacrificed by the government to dispel the wrath of the social majority.

The Last Theological Transformation

Together with other members of the young elites who, after 1995, took over leadership of the Mandaean Community Councils, al-Haidar addressed the Mandaean clergy and community and persuade them of the need to translate their holy book regardless of the theological taboos. The secular elite and the former head of the sect fought over the translation project in particular, and the clerical class in general. The clerical class believed that since their religious books have been preserved as manuscripts for thousands of years in the Mandaean language, they must retain their sanctity and their original language. The books should not be translated for fear of distortion, or 'harming it.' The Mandaean clergy's first objection focused on the complicated rituals of writing and reproducing the book, since the Mandaeans believe that *Ginza Rba* has been preserved as a manual manuscript for thousands of years. There is a special way to deal with it to preserve its sanctity. For instance, one should consider the method of manual reproduction, the identity of the reliable Mandaean cleric performing the reproduction; which original should be the source of the reproduction, and who owns it? Even the type of ink to be used in the reproduction should be hand-made, with special characteristics and composition. A special type of paper must be used and covered with white linen cloth because it must not be covered with animal skin due to its sanctity. After considering all these issues, reproduction starts after registering on its first page the codifier's name, year, during which rule, king or state it was codified, and if there was any particular event, disaster, war, or anything unique to be recorded on it. In addition to that, the following should be written on the book: Its religious name, the descendant family of the codifier, and whom the copy will be addressed to. Also, there should be a special introduction with a warning that the text should be strictly observed, without deletion, erasure, or change. After the warning, there are prayers to be said against whoever deliberately abuses, manipulates, or changes the text.

The second objection to the translation project concerns the scarcity of the persons proficient in the Mandaean language. Therefore, the translators may not be fully qualified to understand the texts and convey their meaning from one language to another, given the depth of the texts, their varied philosophical concepts and the sanctity of the Mandaean alphabets of 24 characters. Some considered that the sanctity of the book is embodied in its original language, which will be lost upon its translation. Why translate the holy book when the Mandaean religion is non-proselytising, and the texts of the holy book only concern the Mandaeans? Why inform others of it? Despite that, the contents of the holy book do not contain anything that should prevent translation.

After overcoming the internal objections in 1997, the Council of Community Affairs decided to proceed with translating the Mandaean holy book. A higher committee was formed to supervise translating and printing it. The translator would be the professor Yusuf Mati Quzi, a specialist in the Semitic languages, especially the Aramaic. He teaches the Mandaean language at the Faculty of Languages at the University of Baghdad. It took two years to translate the holy book. The literary formulation of the translated text was done by the famous Mandaean poet Abdel Razzaq Abdel Wahed. The full work took nearly four years between the direct literal translation from Mandaean to Arabic, the literary formulation and editing, intellectual integrity, handwriting, production, design, printing and distribution.

The committee supervising the translation did not succeed in persuading all members of the Mandaean society and its religious leaders inside and outside Iraq of the importance of the decision. As a result, some still objected to translating the holy book as well as others who objected to the decision on baptising in the Isala waters. The Yazidi community and other religious minority communities have a similar struggle between supporters of reform and its opponents across the Middle East. This results from the pressures of globalisation, forced modernisation, the consequences of insane violence, and the forcible integration of their cultures.

In order to attract attention to the unprecedented translation of the *Ginza Rba* at the end of 2000, a huge celebration was planned for the beginning of 2001. The Mandaeans began disseminating the book among the elites who have influence on the perception of the Mandaeans in Iraq and the Arab and Islamic world. They risked sending a copy of the holy book to the Shiite authorities in Qom, Iran. This was important because Mandaeans in Iran are not constitutionally recognised as a religious minority. A copy was offered to the Supreme Leader of Iran, Ali Khamenei. The book apparently influenced Khamenei's advisors to consider the Mandaeans as monotheistic and owners of a heavenly book. Also, a copy was sent to al-Azhar's Grand Sheikh Mohammad Tantawi in Cairo because he represents the Sunni moderates. A copy was sent to Pope John Paul II in the Vatican, where they still stereotype the Mandaeans as 'the Christians of John the Baptist'. For the same reason, copies were sent to the leaders of the Christian communities in Iraq and to various cultural and political figures in the Arab world.

The Holy Book in the Hands of the President

The best strategy for spreading the impact of translating the Mandaean holy book inside Iraq was to send a copy to Saddam Hussein, whose daily presence on television was of interest to the media and television stations. An hour-long interview was arranged between Saddam and a Mandaean delegation. While addressing his speech to Saddam Hussein, the head of the community, Sattar Jabbar Helou, explained the importance of the decision to Arabise the book by saying, 'We have kept it (meaning the Holy Book) in the chests of our mothers and men for many decades and we have preserved it with our lives so that we united with it as well as it united with us, but today, we are pleased to offer you the first Arabic version of it.' And the poet Abdel Razzaq Abdel Wahed read a poem in which Saddam was portrayed similar to the famous leader Salahuddin, who was surrounded and attacked by nations, but he stood courageously to confront them.

During the meeting, Saddam Hussein's speech coincided with his new image as 'Abdellah the Believer' produced by the Gulf War, 'We want Iraqis to be believers, every one according to their religion,' he said. 'We accept neither the Muslims, nor the Christians or the Sabaeans to be non- believers. We want all our children to be believers so that God takes care of Iraq with His generous care and blesses it.' Saddam Hussein did not conceal his pleasure at Arabising the book since that advanced the community's relationship to the project of building a nation-state with an Arab nationalistic content. He warned of the political recruitment of religion within a traditional security approach, 'Iraqis are free in their religions whether they are Muslims, Christians, or Mandaeans, but what we wish for is not to let the foreigner exploit the Iraqis under the guise of religion or sects, by spreading the seed of split or enmity among them and by weakening them in order to dominate.'[47] The meeting was transmitted via the media and retransmitted daily for a week, and its content was published in the newspapers and magazines. Also, the president's declarations and his depicting the Mandaeans as the 'golden community' based on their absolute loyalty to the state had its impact in limiting the abusive campaigns against the Mandaean religion, according to the Mandaeans' opinion. As a result of the meeting, *Ginza Rba* was considered a holy book like the Quran and the Bible, a basic reference for the courts and the judiciary in jurisprudential affairs. Mandean witnesses in the courts could ask for their holy book to swear on it, something he previously had to do on the Quran. Saddam promised the Mandaean delegation to build a temple (Mendi) for the community.

Translating the *Ginza Rba* motivated Abdel Razzaq to Arabise the rest of the other religious books which the Mandaeans retain as manuscripts in their original Mandaean language. That enabled the Mandaeans, research students, scholars, and academics from within and outside the community to read the book. The translation helped to focus more on the Mandaean language and the need to learn it, especially by members of the community. For that purpose, Mandaean schools inside and outside Iraq were established for different age groups. Also, the translation helped to stimulate scientific and academic research about Mandaeism inside Iraq and activated the cultural movement inside the community.

From the point of view of the pro-translation project, it has achieved its primary goal of the non-Mandaeans acceptance of the Mandaean religion and raising the level of respect towards the Mandaeans after having been able to present a solid defensive narrative. Finally, Arabisation of the holy book is symbolically the last step in integrating the Mandaean identity into the culture of the majority. The journey that began with the waters of John the Baptist more than two thousand years ago, ended in the land of the modern nation-state and then crashed on the rocks of the Gulf War and the international

---

[47] Interview with Raad Jabbar Saleh, a member of the Baghdad Provincial Council for Mandaeans, Baghdad, January, 2016.

sanctions.

The Mandaeans under the State of Components

The Mandaeans did not participate in the 2003 Iraqi Governing Council, which was formed by a decision of the Unified Coalition Authority that was granted partial powers in the administration of Iraq affairs. The Unified Coalition Authority had full powers according to the laws of war and military occupation agreed upon at the United Nations. The period of limited powers of the Governing Council extended from 12 July 2003 to 1 June 2004, when the Council was dissolved to be replaced by the Interim Iraqi Government.

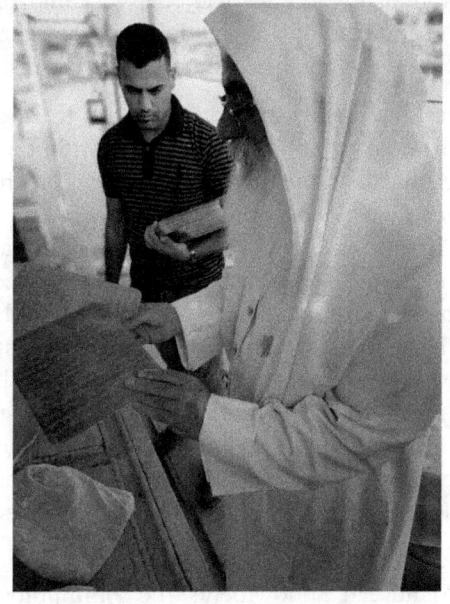

The high priest of the Mandeans shows holy scriptures in the Mandi of Baghdad. (Picture: Thomas Schmidinger)

The US civil administrator, Paul Bremer, had chosen representatives of the various Iraqi factions and sects for membership in this council, but not one Mandaean was among them. However, they were symbolically involved in the 2004 National Assembly. The name of a Mandaean representative was added to the constitutional drafting committees (a sub-committee) without his having any real impact on the general debates concerning drafting the constitution. The few Mandaeans disseminated over most of the provinces and without official affiliation in any of the parties or political alliances resulted in their lack of representation in the parliament in its first session 2006 to 2010. In the second parliamentary session 2010 to 2014, they had a member in the federal parliament and another member in the third parliamentary session 2014 to 2018. This symbolic representation by one out of the 328 seats in parliament makes their political impact of little or no value. In the provincial elections, the Mandaeans were allocated one seat in Baghdad Provincial Council, starting with the second session 2009 to 2013.

The Mandaeans did not, ethnically or religiously, establish any political organisations. After 2003, in order to avoid lacking representation of the Mandaeans, a Higher Political Committee was set up with 9 to 15 members. They sought to extend bridges of cooperation and achieve contact with the decisionmakers, represent the community in political forums and make up for the absence of a Mandaean political party. The head of the Mandean community and the Higher Political Committee had close coordination while allowing the religious head to focus on administering the religious affairs of the community. The head of the Mandaean community influences nominating the parliamentary candidate representing the Mandaeans by recommending his candidacy. However, the Community Public Council makes the final decision on nominations.[48]

The Mandaeans try to control the independence of their representation by holding internal elections (within the community) to sort out their candidate in the Quetta. Therefore, the three councils of the community, the Spiritual Council, the Public Community Council and the Council of Public Affairs, have the right to supervise and nominate any person to senior positions in state institutions through elections within the community in the presence of these three presidencies of the sect. Then the community sends the candidate's name in a letter to the state departments. Accordingly, the Mandaeans tried to block major political movements from employing their representatives, but this did not prevent these movements from dominating the Quetta seats allocated to the Mandaeans by presenting Mandaean candidates loyal to these parties, which the Mandaeans consider stealing their sole seat from them.

On 17 September 2014, Nadia Fadel Mgmas became director of the Mandaean Endowments; the community had never nominated a woman for any important post in the state institutions. In the history of the modern Iraqi state (and perhaps in the Middle East), a woman has never served as a director-general of the endowments of any of the sects whether Islamic, Christian, or Yazidi. Nadia Fadel Mgmas speaks about the difficulties of administering the endowments of a sect that does not own land for a temple on it. It has always been considered a problem to establish these temples along the river banks regarding it as a 'taboo of the river.' Consequently, by accepting their self-imposed ban of construction in these areas, the Mandaeans deprived themselves of owning these lands. They must not build solid and strong worship buildings; instead they must construct mobile installations that are easy to dismantle and lift.

For example, the community leadership tried to acquire the baptism area under al-Jadiriyah bridge because they fear losing it. A Mandaean delegation led by the head of the Mandaean community met with the Prime Minister Haidar Al Abadi on 22 July 2015 to request acquisition of this land. It has become the most sacred landmark for them and has formed the memory of their settling down in Baghdad after the presidency moved to the capital in the 1950s. Besides, this place has become a place where they felt safe to practice their rituals freely. However, the prime minister still has not given a

---

[48] Interview with Nadia Fadel Mghams, Director of the Mandaean Endowments in Baghdad, December 2016

positive response.

The Mandaeans present their objection according to the following logic summarised by Nadia, 'Is it impossible for the Iraqi state to own the only piece of land on which the Mandaeans have held their rituals for decades in the capital while they represent a culture of more than two thousand years old in the country at a time when there are many properties and private real estates owned by influential politicians at symbolical prices, and embassies of countries have been built on the banks of the rivers and under bridges in various taboo areas of Baghdad?'[49]

If the baptism rituals of the Mandaeans are carried out in the running water 'Yardna' and their temples have to be built adjacent to the banks of the rivers, freedom and protection of their belief cannot be guaranteed without taking care of the cleanliness of this water and avoid polluting it. Also, they must be supported in building Mendis or temples for them beside the rivers, where they could practice their rituals without curious stares of strangers. The Mandaeans have become more cautious after extremist religious discourse became a dominant phenomenon when Islamic political parties rose to power following the end of Saddam Hussein's regime. A Shiite cleric in Basra issued an advisory against the Mandaeans involving traditional accusations, such as impurity and the practice of witchcraft while calling on the Muslims to guide them to Islam.[50] However, this advisory was not issued by a cleric representing the leading ayatollahs in Najaf. The cleric followed a populist trend led by the religious leader Muqtada al-Sadr immersed in politics. According to the Mandaeans' testimony, the supreme religious leaders in Najaf did not issue any special advisory against the Mandaeans, which was good, but at the same time, no special advisory has been issued to protect the Mandaeans and to recognise them as a monotheistic scriptural religion and accordingly, forbid harming them. The Mandaean community leader, Sattar Jabbar Helou, has personally requested this statement more than six times from Ayatollah Ali Al Sistani and Ayatollah Mohammad Saiid Al Hakim after his visit to Najaf to recognise them. The advisories that were issued generally encourages fraternity, respect of all Iraqis without distinction and consider the incidents taking place are not directed at a particular religion or sect, but they involve all the Iraqis. These general advisories did not satisfy the Mandaeans as they were under pressure and needed an advisory that mentions them by name. The Mandaeans believe that the narrative inherited about them since the Islamic Middle Ages, has put them at risk of being targeted as non-monotheistic, and the protection provided by having their name mentioned in the Quran is no longer sufficient.

---

[49] Saad Salloum, *Beyond Da'esh, the Minorities of Iraq at a Crossroad*. (Baghdad: Masarat Foundation, 2017), 167.

[50] Interview with Genza Bira Selwan Al Khammas, Head of the Mandaean Community in Sweden, Stockholm, January 2016.

As a result of the reckless and random violence, the Mandaeans faced the risk of emigrating abroad. After the so-called 'Islamic State' (ISIS) took control of large areas of Iraq, approximately 53 Mandaeans were forcibly displaced from areas under the control of the ISIS and other unsafe areas. Despite the formation of a relief committee to provide them with the possible assistance, they had limited assistance from the Red Cross and the Office of the Endowments of the Christian, Yazidi and Mandaean religions. Also, the Mandaeans living in the areas outside the control of ISIS still face pressures that force many to emigrate because of kidnappings and various forms of discrimination that leave psychological and social impact on members of the minority. The Chair of the Mandaean Affairs Council, Khaled Naji, in Qadisiya province tells of Mandaean students facing violence because they belong to this minority. He added, 'Such incidents are not recorded, and we try to solve them by mutual consent by sending complaints to the officials, but in the end, nothing prevents their recurrence.'

Following repeated threats, nearly 90 percent of the Mandaean community have left to settle down in Australia, Sweden, the United States, and other countries. The head of the Mandaean Community Secretary, al-Tarmiza Alaa Aziz Taresh, sent me a letter at the end of 2014 complaining of the Mandaean kidnappings in central and southern Iraq since the Mandaeans have no militias to protect them, and their beliefs prohibit violence of all kinds. Also, no politician helps them because their ballots are barely enough to represent them symbolically in the parliament or local governments. Al-Tarmiza concluded his letter, 'This is the end, and we have no reason to stay in Iraq.' And when I visited him more than once in the Mandaean Sabaeans' Mendi in Baghdad's Qadisiya district, he complained to me about having to stay with his family for many years in the Mendi and tells me despairingly, 'My children left school because of harassment by the rest of the students and they rarely leave the Mendi. I feel afraid they will be kidnapped and I believe that the majority of the Mandaeans carry the same fear for their children, which is what drives them to emigrate in order to ensure the future and security of their families.' Consequently, he applied for an asylum through the refugee agencies and now he settles temporarily with his family in Turkey until he is allowed to move to a safe place. If immigration and requesting an asylum have reached the presidency of the community itself and the most important academic and civil elites, this directs a serious blow to the identity of the group and its presence in a country in which they lived for more than twenty centuries.

Furthermore, the pressure to adapt to exiles might lead to neglecting the ritualistic conditions of the religion by the immigrants who are subjected to a life system that is not compatible with the rhythm of religious beliefs and their complex requirements. For me, it was puzzling to think of performing the baptism rituals in countries where the temperature is below zero centigrade. Despite this, the Mandaeans endure the experience of an alternative homeland completely different from their millennial homeland in Iraq. The head of the Mandaean community in Sweden, Genz Bara Silwan Al Khamis, said that the 9500 Mandaeans are distributed over the Swedish cities and their religion has been recognised so that they have three worshipping halls: The first is in Sandviken province, the second is in Warbarrow, while the third is under construction in Lund.[51]

The Mystery of Water: From Historical Babylon to Current Iraq

The leader of the Mandaean community in Amara, cleric Nizam Creidi, took me through a historical journey that proves, according to his point of view, the extraordinary character of a religious community that has been cared for by God since 'historic Babylon' and even in 'current Iraq.' I confronted him with the concept that John the Baptist's followers had migrated from Palestine, not from Babylon, and that their original homeland was located in the Dead Sea area of Palestine or eastern Jordan, where they practiced the ritual of baptism. A Persian book even considered that these followers were 'the first Palestinian immigrants in the history of the Middle East.'[52] Al Tarmiza's was not curious about the Naja' Hamadi in the early forties or *The Dead Sea Scrolls* in the early fifties that seem to confirm the ancient existence of the Mandaeans in Palestine.

I spoke of the mythology entailed in Diwan *Harran Quetta* (the name of a Mandaean book covering the history of the Mandaeans)[53] about their origins and their emigration from Jerusalem to Mesopotamia, specifically before the end of the Farthy rule, in the first century AD due to the persecution they suffered at the hands of the Jews and their temporal authority in Palestine some 2000 years ago. He moved his hands over his grey beard as though contemplating that march from Palestine to Harran, and from there to the centre and south of Maysan and Khuzestan as if he was adopting an approach emphasizing the extension of their established Mesopotamian existence by pointing out the common rituals between the Mandaeans and the Babylonians. The most common rituals include: Prohibition of shaving beards and the hair, the white religious dress the Mandaeans call Rasta, which was worn by the Babylonian priests while performing their religious tasks, similar to the Mandaean clerics today, and that both the Babylonian and Mandaean religions value water highly as the source of life.

The Mandaeans' deep roots and their cleric's vision of history indicate the Mandaeans' deep wish to link their roots and their future to Mesopotamia's current fate. The community steadfastly remains vital despite all the challenges they have faced through their long history of displacement,

---

[51] Interview with Issam Sabti, Chairman of the Mandaean Community Affairs Council in Baghdad, December, 2015.
[52] Saad Salloum, *Minorities in Iraq: Memory, Identity, Challenges*. (Baghdad: Masarat Foundation, 2013).
[53] Salim Berenji, *The Mandaean Sabaeans - A Study of the History and Beliefs of the Forgotten People*. Translation from Persian: Jaber Ahmad, (Beirut: Al kounouz Literary Dar, no year), 11.

discrimination, physical liquidation, forced conversion of religion, and other forms of persecution. They have been forced to confront threats by hiding underground or in caves; this involved a paradox since the Mandaeans are linked to the running water on the surface of the ground. The archaeologist Burhan Abdel Rida found in the area of Sheikh Saad and north of Al Tayeb, inaccessible caves carved at 8 to 10 meters deep into the rocks adjacent to the Iranian border and in other nearby highlands. The Iraqi archaeologist Abdel Amir Al Hamdani said these caves were most probably formed as refuge for the Mandaeans during the Sassanis' persecution campaigns.

While I was exchanging with Al Hamdani a deep concern about ISIS destroying millennials of religious heritage in Nineveh Province, north of Iraq, he had similar concerns about the extinction of the ancient Mandaean culture in south Iraq. He spoke extensively about the area of Tayeb and its surroundings as a home for the Mandaeans during the Sassanid rule of Iraq (226- 637 AD) and beyond. They were subjected to the Sassanians' persecution and faced murder and violence on several occasions. This forced them to think of temporary solutions to protect and hide themselves through digging tunnels in the rocky areas stretching between Jilat - Bazergan and Al Tayeb up to the east of Sheikh Saad. The permanent solution was to flee to the marshes formed after the collapse of the irrigation system in the two provinces of Kaskar and Maysan during the late Sassanid era, specifically during the rule of King Qabad bin Fairuz (488-531 AD). A relative date of the tunnelling could be dated back to the end of the fifth century AD. Such unwritten stories will be erased from memory and will no longer be possible to restore because of the neglect of these archaeological sites and the possibility of their total destruction in the areas where oil is being explored.

The genocide and ethnic cleansing campaigns the Mandaeans experienced in successive eras, such as the era of the Ottoman occupation and its aftermath, forced them to abandon their places of residence and traditional living in the cities and move in the opposite direction to live in the depths of the swamps. In these villages in the southern marshes of Iraq, they could preserve their precious faith and preserve a seed for the new generations in an intermarried community that embraces a non-proselytising religion. Without that place, the Mandaean rites could not have continued to exist throughout these centuries.

The urbanised Mandaeans have attempted to adapt to a changing Islamic environment so they cannot be differentiated from the rest of the Muslims. You see them participating in the rituals of the Muslim majority, visiting the religious icons and the holy shrines of their Muslim neighbours and friends. Why don't the Mandaeans today use their ancient Aramaic names, and only retain them as religious baptism names? Why do they now have names borrowed from the historical cultural space of the religion of the majority, especially the Shiite names, such as Haidar, Abbas, Fadhel and Ali? Why do the Mandaean clergy prefer the title of Sheikh, which is parallel to the influence of the tribal chiefs (tribal sheikhs) in southern Iraq or their counterparts, the Muslim religious sheikhs, rather than using their religious titles, such as Tarmiza,[54] Genz Bara[55] and Rish Amma[56]? Why has the Mandaean language receded and become a mere language of religious rites? All these questions express the phenomena of response to a different cultural environment as their amazing ability to adapt to the beliefs that prevailed and changed dozens of times around them.

> 'The invaders have gone, and the Mandaeans have remained for twenty centuries.' This attitude eventually allowed them to protect a millennial culture at a time when cultures, religions and empires have disappeared over time. Amin Maalouf says, 'If this last gnostic community could survive to this day, I cannot fail to wonder and feel excited, as this is somewhat similar to the hypothesis of finding today, in southern France, the Cathar sect, which is said to have miraculously survived the holy wars and the ordinary persecutions and continued to practice its rituals in its language, the Occitan language.' Maalouf did not choose this example by coincidence since the origins of the Cathar and 'the other movements, such as the Bogomile sect in Bulgaria and Bosnia, or the Battaran sect in Italy, inspired by Manichaeism that spread in Europe in the 10th and 13th centuries, go back to Mesopotamia in the third century AD, in the palm grove on the banks of the Tigris River, where the doctrine of Mani originated.'[57][58]

As an individual born in a generation disappointed by the projects of building the nation-state, I experienced the outcomes of three wars: 1980, 1991 and 2003, and an economic siege that lasted for 13 years before the moment of change in 2003 and the subsequent sectarian madness of 2006 and 2007. The hope of restoring the well-being of a homeland constantly dropping into an abyss means it is even more essential to consider the Mandaean community's fate. While contemplating the waters of the Tigris River with the Mandaean clergy, I thought about why my country, Iraq, withdrew from the circle of civilization and humanity. This withdrawal was accompanied by the gradual erosion of the symbolic meaning of Mesopotamia and the disappearance of this millennial culture associated with the running water of life, 'from which God made everything living,' as in the

---

[54] Diwan Harran Quota (Harran Interior), translation from Amin Fe'il Khattab, *Mandaeism*. Edited by Luay Zahroun Habib. (Baghdad, n.p. 2003), 7.

[55] It means the student and it is the first religious rank.

[56] It means the one who understands or memorises the holy book (The Treasure). It is a rank to which Al Tarmiza moves after memorising the holy book *Ginza Rba*, its explanation and commentaries, as well as memorising the other religious books.

[57] Head of the nation, a rank reached by Al Canzabra after consecrating seven clerics to the rank of Tarmiza.

[58] Amin Maalouf, *The World's Imbalance, Our Turbulent Civilization*. (Beirut: Dar Al Farabi, 2009), 72-73.

John the Baptist's Water: Extinction of a Millennial Culture

Quranic discourse, or 'the spirit of God passed over it,' as mentioned in the biblical discourse, or life forms formed when the first vapours turned into water, as in the discourse of natural sciences. On my visit to Maysan, I was unhappy to see the Mandaeans' baptism places facing destruction and neglect. The sight of a Mandaean cleric performing his rituals on a river filled with the heavy water debris foreshadows a gloomy future for the guardians of an ancient religious culture. With respect to the Mandaean, to what extent is sabotaging the elements of his initial existence and the history of the religions which stand behind it, considered a violation of the freedom of belief?

I listened to Al Tarmiza Nizam Creidi explain the rituals of baptism called Masabta in the Mandaean language. The Mandaeans must baptise their babies thirty days after their birth, the adults before marriage and a week after their marriage. The woman is baptized a month after giving birth. Baptism should be on a Sunday, on holidays and on religious occasions. Baptism is held in the same way for males and females, but each separately. The Mandaean can get baptized more than once and whenever he wants. Baptism takes place in the running river water while wearing the religious clothing called 'Rasta', made of white cloth as a sign of purity and cleansing of the soul. The process of diving and holding the breath when the person is submerged with water, symbolizes death or extinction. Coming to the surface of the water symbolizes birth, creation, or resurrection. The process of death and resurrection are accompanied by prayers, hymns, and supplications said by the head of the sect and his assistant clerics. The baptised Mandaean reiterates the term *ishkanda*, declaring his repentance and asking for mercy, forgiveness, and guidance from God. Then, a text from the Mandaean Holy Book, *Ginza Rba*, was read: 'Blessing to all the faithful and all the Mandaeans, dyed in the living water, who bear witness to the living and do the righteous works.' While contemplating these rituals, I sensed a deep need to submerge into the running water and to be reborn. I was feeling that my country needs a similar rest, to be immersed in the 'Water of John the Baptist' and come to the surface of the water to be reborn.

CHAPTER 5

THE GURDWARA OF BAGHDAD AND THE FORGOTTEN HISTORY OF SIKHS IN IRAQ

Areshpreet Wedech

Most Iraqis and scholars on Iraq do not know that Baghdad has significant importance for the Sikh religion. Until 2003, Baghdad had a gurdwara (Sikh place of worship); some evidence exists of a historic Sikh community in Iraq. This article explores both the history of the Gurdwara of Baghdad and the Sikhs who lived in Iraq, and also the activities of Sikh humanitarian organizations in contemporary Iraq.

The founder of Sikhism, Guru Nanak, spread his message with travel into the Arabic world. According to the traditional Sikh hagiographies and other Sikh sources, like the 'Vārāṁ' written by Bhai Gurdas, he also visited the holy places and shrines of the Muslims like Mecca and Medina. Before returning to Punjab, Guru Nanak spent some time outside Baghdad where he exchanged ideas on religion with the religious authorities like Pirs. This visit led to the formation of a group of followers who remembered the Guru as 'Baba Nanak'.[1]

After Guru Nanak left Iraq and settled down in Kartarpur (today's Pakistan) in 1522, he only stayed in loose contact with Baghdad. It was not until the First World War that a Sikh regiment discovered Guru Nanak's shrine in Baghdad; they eventually repaired and built a gurdwara there.[2] Following the repair of the shrine, the gurdwara had been of interest of academic research, but not the Sikh community in Iraq. Some scholars, like Manjeet Singh, travelled to Baghdad to see the shrine and the inscriptions and wrote articles about their journeys.[3]

During the Iraq War (2003-2011), the gurdwara was destroyed. The Punjab government and the Shiromani Gurdwara Parbandhak Committee

---

[1] See: Surinder Singh Kohli, *Travels of Guru Nanak*. (Chandigarh: Panjab University, 1997), 143-146.

[2] Sewa Ram Sigh, *The Divine Master. Life and teachings of Guru Nanak*. Edited by. Prithipal Singh Kapur. (Jalandhar: ABS Publications, 1988), 106,

[3] See: Manjeet Singh, 'Past and Present and Guru Nanak's Visit to Baghdad' *The Sikh Review* (October-November 1969)

(SGPC), which is a statutory body and manages the historical gurdwaras, have asked the Iraqi Government to repair it.[4] However, following the rise of the so-called Islamic State (ISIS), many Sikhs had to flee or were imprisoned by ISIS. Additionally, the international NGO 'Khalsa Aid' started many humanitarian projects in Iraq.[5]

Despite the Iraqi Sikh community being one of the oldest worldwide, relatively little is known about this community. Few articles, papers, and research about Sikhism in Iraq have been published. The only architectural evidence of Sikhism in Iraq, the shrine, which was turned into a gurdwara later and housed the inscriptions was destroyed.

This article attempts to close this gap in knowledge and gives an overview about the development of the Sikh community in Iraq. The article's main focus will be on how the community developed and seeks to shed light on the role of the Sikhs in this region.

The first section briefly introduces Sikhism. It summarises the basic teachings of the Sikh-Gurus and their history. The second section examines Guru Nanak's travels, his visit to the Arabic world and Baghdad in specific and the founding of the early Sikh community in Iraq. The next section presents the discovery of Guru Nanak's shrine during the First World War by the British Sikh Regiment. The last section explores the current political situation of Sikhs and Indians in Iraq. It finishes with a look at the humanitarian work of the international Sikh NGO 'Khalsa Aid' and describes their projects in this area. This article presents a review about tradition of Sikhism in Iraq and also covers the recent developments of the new Sikh 'migration'.

What is Sikhism?

Sikhism is one of the youngest religions in the world and was founded in the fifteenth century in South Asia. The word 'sikh' derives from the Sanskrit language and means 'disciple'. Traditionally Sikhism is called *gurmat* (the counsel of the gurus) or *panth* (path). The Sikhs believe in Guru Nanak and the successive Sikh Gurus. The last human form Guru, Gobind Singh, enshrined the Holy Scripture 'Sri Guru Granth Sahib' in year 1708 to Guru. Since that time, the Sikhs regard Sri Guru Granth Sahib as their eternal and living Guru. The Supreme Being *akal purakh* is manifested in the word (*shabad*).[6]

The founder of Sikhism, Guru Nanak, was born in 1469 in Nankana

---

[4] Yudhvir Rana, 'Sikh community to renovate damaged Baghdad gurdwara' *The Times of India* (published 22 May 2011) http://timesofindia.indiatimes.com/articleshow/8510130.cms?utm_source=contentofinterest&utm_medium=text&utm_campaign=cppst.

[5] See: Khalsa Aid, 'Projects.' (no date) https://www.khalsaaid.org/projects (Accessed 23.09.2018)

[6] Othmar Gächter, 'Sikhismus' In *Handbuch Religionswissenschaft. Religionen und ihre zentralen Themen.* Edited by Johann Figl, (Innsbruck/Wien: Tyrolia-Verlag, 2003), 368-383.

Sahib (now Pakistan). He travelled and taught others the message of the Supreme Being. He lived in a political turbulently time and witnessed the invasion of the first Mughal Babur who established the Mughal Empire. Not only did politics go through times of radical change, but also new movements like the Bhakti movement or the Sufism were gaining popularity among people. Guru Nanak was influenced by them and founded a new religious path besides the established religions Hinduism and Islam. With devotion to the Supreme Being the human can get salvation (*mukti*).[7]

He rejected dogmas and rituals as well as castes and gender or social background. Therefore, the Sikhism is a very egalitarian religion with the concept that there are no Hindus or Moslems, there is only the creation of the creator. All human beings have the same pain of separation from the Supreme Being and the desire for the unity with it. The three pillars of Sikhism are: Meditating to God's name (*nām japnā*), work diligently (*kirat karnī*) and sharing with others (*vaṁḍ chaknā*).[8]

Sikhism is a monotheistic religion, the followers believe in one creator, in karma and in incarnation. The human can get out of the cycle of birth and rebirth with the mercy of the Supreme Being and with meditation (*nām simran*). This can only happen in the society; therefore, Sikhism is a householder religion. Sikhs follow a strict code of conduct (*rahit maryādā*) which comprises of hard work, charity, helpfulness, and humanity.[9]

The last human Guru, Gobind Singh founded the 'Khalsa' in 1699. This is a group of initiated Sikhs wearing the 'Five Ks', the five articles of faith.[10] Regardless of caste and gender or social background anyone can be initiated and enter the Khalsa. Guru Gobind Singh also named the Holy scriptures 'Guru Granth Sahib' to the last Guru of the Sikhs. The Guru Granth Sahib is a collection of 6000 shabads and is written in various languages including sant bhasha, Braj Bhasha, Hindui, Punjabi, Sanskrit, Persian.[11] The Guru Granth Sahib was composed not only by the Sikh-Gurus but also by Indian saints from low castes belonging to Hinduism, for example Bhagat Kabir, Bhagat Namdev, Bhagat Ravidas or by Sufis like Sheikh Farid.[12]

The Sikhs see Sikhism as a very practical religion. They strive to implement their doctrines in their daily life. One of these is the free kitchen '*langar*', which had been established by the third Guru, Guru Angad Dev. The

---

[7] See: Jagbir Jhutti-Johal, *Sikhism Today*. (London/New York: Continuum, 2011), 111.
[8] See: Kirpal Singh / Kharak Singh, *History of the Sikhs and their Religion. Volume I. The Guru Period (1469-1708 CE)*. (Amritsar: Shiromani Gurdwara Parbandhak Committee, 2012), 82-83.
[9] See: Othmar Gächter, 'Sikhismus' In *Handbuch Religionswissenschaft. Religionen und ihre zentralen Themen*. Edited by Johann Figl, (Innsbruck/Wien: Tyrolia-Verlag, 2003), 379–381.
[10] In Punjabi each of the five articles begins with 'k': Uncut hair, a wooden comb for the hair, an iron bracelet, undergarment, and an iron dagger.
[11] See: Gurinder Singh Mann, *The Making of Sikh Scripture*. (Oxford: OUP, 2001), 4-5.
[12] See: Surinder Singh Kohli, *Guru Granth Sahib. An Analytical Study. A Critical Study of the Adi Granth*. (Amritsar: Singh Brothers, 1992), 1-5.

purpose was that every person regardless of their social background, religious beliefs, gender, or caste has to eat together as a symbol of equality. This tradition can be seen in every gurdwara.

Today, Sikhism is the fifth largest religion worldwide. Less than two per cent of the Indian population are Sikhs. The approximately 23 million Sikhs worldwide are mostly living in the state of Punjab.[13] Sikhs have migrated to many countries. The biggest Sikh communities outside of India are in Canada (450,000)[14] and the United Kingdom (400,000).[15] There are also Sikhs settled in the Middle East, for example approximately 60 families in Iran.[16] A large Sikh community of 50,000 people live in the United Arab Emirates. In 2012, the largest gurdwara of the Gulf-region 'Guru Nanak Darbar', located in Dubai, was inaugurated. The Vice President and Prime Minister of the UAE Sheikh Mohammed bin Rashid Al Maktoum granted 25,400 square feet of land for the gurdwara. The total cost of the construction was $20 million.[17] Iraq used to have a substantial number of Sikhs, but since the start of the Iraq War the situation changed.

Guru Nanak and his travels
With the emergence of the true Guru Nanak, the mist cleared and the light scattered all around.

As if at the sun rise the stars disappeared and the darkness dispelled. [...]

Wherever Baba put his feet, a religious place was erected and established.[18]

There are two categories of sources to reconstruct Guru Nanak's life and his travels (*Udasis*). The first are hagiographies, which are also called *janamsākhī* (birth story).[19] The second are writings like the Gurū Granth Sāhib or Bhāī Gurdās Jī's *vārāṁ*. Bhai Gurdas Ji was a Sikh historian and philosopher. His *vārāṁ* is a collection of forty ballads ('vārāṁ'), also known as the 'key to the Holy Sikh book'. There are four major hagiographies, which tells us about Guru Nanak's life and his journey. The oldest hagiography is the 'Miharbān Janam- Sākhī', which has been neglected by the Sikhs and has questionable reputation because of the author, Sodhi Miharban. He followed

---

[13] See: Othmar Gächter, 'Sikhismus' In *Handbuch Religionswissenschaft. Religionen und ihre zentralen Themen*, Edited by Johann Figl, (Innsbruck/Wien: Tyrolia-Verlag, 2003), 368-369.
[14] See: Statistics Canada. '2011 National Household Survey: Immigration, place of birth, citizenship, ethnic origin, visible minorities, language and religion' (last modified 9 May 2013) https://www150.statcan.gc.ca/n1/daily-quotidien/130508/dq130508b-eng.htm (accessed 23 September 2018).
[15] cf. Office for National Statistics. 'Religion in England and Wales 2011.' (published 11 December 2012) https://www.ons.gov.uk/peoplepopulationandcommunity/culturalidentity/religion/articles/religioninenglandandwales2011/2012-12-11 (accessed 23 September 2018).
[16] See: Dipanjan Roy Chaudhury, 'Gurdwara in Tehran that thrives on local support.' *Daily Mail*, (published 26 August 2012) https://www.dailymail.co.uk/indiahome/indianews/article-2193713/Gurdwara-Tehran-thrives-local-support.html.
[17] 'About Gurunanak Darbar, Dubai.' *Gurudwara Dubai*, (no date) http://www.gurudwaradubai.com/about-us/ (accessed 23 September 2018).
[18] Bhai Gurdas Ji, Vār 1 Pauri 1
[19] William Hewat McLeod, *Guru Nanak and the Sikh Religion*. (Oxford: Clarendon Press, 1968), 19-20.

the Mina sect, which was hostile towards the Sikhs during that time, resulting in his questionable reputation amongst Sikhs. The other reliable source is the 'Purātan Janam- Sākhīs' also called 'Valāitvalī Janam- Sākhī' or 'Colebrooke Janam- Sākhī'. A similar manuscript has been founded in Hafizabad, thus being referred to as 'Hāfizābād Janam- Sākhī'.[20] These two manuscripts originated in the first half of the seventeenth century,[21] The most famous and supposed to be the eldest hagiography is the 'Bāle Wālī Janam Sakhī'; however, Sikh scholars do not accept this tradition as authentic nor Guru Nanak's excessive miracles written in that hagiography.[22] The last source is the Bhāī Manī Singh - Janam- Sakhī written by Bhai Mani Singh, who was a very prominent Sikh during the time of the last human Sikh-Guru, Guru Gobind Singh.[23] His intention was to rewrite Bhai Gurdas Jis vāraṁ in a simple language. Nevertheless, the influence of the Purātan Janam- Sākhī and Bhāī Bāle Wālī- Janam- Sakhī is visible.[24]

Whereas the visit to Baghdad is missing in the Bāle Wālī Janam Sakhī as well as in the Purātan Janam- Sākhī, the Miharbān Janam- Sākhī' mentions it and Bhai Gurdas Ji's Vāraṁ and Bhāī Manī Singh - Janam- Sakhī explore Guru Nanak's travel in Baghdad.[25]

According to another historical document 'Makke-di-Ghost', which is a collection of Guru Nanak's dialogs in Mecca and Medina, Guru Nanak and his Muslim companion Bhai Mardana went to Dvaraka (state Gujrat, India) and took the shortest route to Mecca via ship. Bhai Mardana accompanied Guru Nanak on his travels and was used to play the Rabab, when Guru Nanak sang Gurbani.[26]

Guru Nanak landed with Bhai Mardana and other Muslim pilgrims in the port of Jeddah and from there set off to travel to Mecca on land. Outside the Kaabaa was a mosque where the pilgrims could sleep, and Guru Nanak slept with his feet towards the Kaaba. The keeper of the mosque, Mulla Jiwan, saw this and mistook Guru Nanak for a kafir. This disrespect enraged the keeper and he woke Guru Nanak up, kicked him and asked him if he does not know how to behave. Then he turned Guru Nanak's feet in another direction. He was shocked when he saw that Kaaba turned in the same direction as he turned Guru Nanak's feet. Guru Nanak explained to him: 'Unto Allah

---

[20] Sukhbir Singh Kapoor / Mohinder Kaur Kapoor, *Janam Saakhi Prampara*. (Amritsar: Singh Brothers, 2005), 10-11.

[21] See: Kirpal Singh / Kharak Singh, *History of the Sikhs and their Religion. Volume I. The Guru Period (1469-1708 CE)*, (Amritsar: Shiromani Gurdwara Parbandhak Committee, 2012).

[22] See: William Hewat McLeod, 'The Hagiography of the Sikhs.' In *According to tradition. Hagiographical writing in India*. Edited by W. M. Callewaert / R. Snell. (Wiesbaden: Harrassowitz, 1994), 15-42, 21.

[23] William Hewat McLeod, Guru Nanak and the Sikh Religion. (Oxford: Clarendon Pr, 1968), 37-38.

[24] William Hewat McLeod, 'The Hagiography of the Sikhs.' In *According to tradition. Hagiographical writing in India*. Edited by W. M. Callewaert / R. Snell. (Wiesbaden: Harrassowitz, 1994), 15-42, 24-25.

[25] See: Fauja Singh / Kirpal Singh, *Atlas, travels of Guru Nanak. Aitalasa-Gurū Nānaka Deva Jī de saphara*. (Patiala: Punjabi Universit, 1976), 35.

[26] Manjeet Singh, 'Past and Present and Guru Nanak's Visit to Baghdad' *The Sikh Review* (October-November 1969).

belong the East and West, and whichsoever direction you turn there is Allah's countenance.'[27] 'In every direction is the House of God. Turn my feet in the direction it is not.'[28]

The other pilgrims were impressed. Mulla Jiwan realised that this was a miracle and this pilgrim was not an ordinary person and he apologised for his harsh behaviour. 'Just as Buddhists see Guru Nanak as an avatara of Buddha, the Hindus call him avatara of Janaka, these pious Muslims considered Nanak as an apostle of Islam. This only shows that Nanak was considered apostle of Truth by all higher religions.'[29]

Guru Nanak also had discussions with Qadis, pilgrims, and other people in Medina. Trilochan Singh mentions that in the Arab world many tribes like the Sabian tribes and Abid fakirs acknowledge Guru Nanak as their prophet and they keep their hair and beard long and live according to a code of conduct which is close to the Sikhism.[30] Guru Nanak took the shorter route from Medina to Baghdad via Faid. This was not only the route which travellers returning to India preferred but also the best-known route. This route was more common than the longer Palestine-Syria route.[31]

Baghdad was at the time of Guru Nanak's visit 'a very old town of historical importance as a centre at once of trade, government and religion, [...]'.[32] Baghdad at the time was ruled by a member of the Safavi dynasty of Iran. Bhai Gurdas and Bhai Mani Singh mentioned this in their accounts.[33] Bhai Gurdas Ji writes in the 35th Pauri (stanza), named 'Going to Baghdad' (of the 1st var, that Guru Nanak; Bhai Gurdas called him 'Baba' that means 'father' or 'elder') stayed outside of the city Baghdad with his companion Bhai Mardana.

In the morning, when it was time for the morning prayer, Guru Nanak gave a shrill call and the whole city woke up hearing Guru Nanak's wonderful voice. According to the Janam-Sakhi the people wanted to know if the voice was human or from an angel and so they began to search for the person who woke them. Not only the ordinary people, but also the Pir of Badghad came. He went to find the person who woke him up with their shrill voice and found Guru Nanak and his companion Bhai Mardana. He saw in Guru Nanak a faquir and wanted to know more about this faquir and enquired about him Bhai Mardana gave him the following answer:

---

[27] Quran 2: 115.
[28] Ibid.
[29] Ibid.
[30] Ibid.
[31] Fauja Singh / Kirpal Singh, *Atlas, travels of Guru Nanak. Aitalasa-Gurū Nānaka Deva Jī de saphara.* (Patiala: Punjabi Universit, 1976), 35.
[32] Ibid.
[33] Ibid.

Observing minutely, he found (in the form of Baba Nanak) an exhilarated faquir.

Pir Dastegir asked him, which category of faquir you belong to and what is your parentage.

(Mardana told) He is Nanak, who has come into kaliyug, and, he recognises God and His faquirs as one.

He is known in all the directions besides earth and sky.[34]

The 36th pauri of the 1st var named 'Manifest power' continues the narrative of Guru Nanak's visit in Baghdad. According to Trilochan Sinh, Pir Dastegir and another well-reputed Sufi Pir called Pir Bahlol Dana discussed religious issues with Guru Nanak on a daily basis. However, two anachronisms can be found. Firstly, old Sikh studies assumed 'Dastegir Pir' to be the same person as Abdul Qadir of Gilan, a saint, who lived from 1077-1166, more than 300 years before Guru Nanak. The currently accepted opinion is that 'Dastegir Pir' refers to the custodian of the shrine, Piran Pir Hazrat Dastgir Abdul Qadir Jilan. Secondly, Pir Bahlol Dana is never mentioned in any stanza. Three Pir Bahlols are known to us; however, all of them lived centuries before Guru Nanak. He is supposed to be one of his successors.[35]

Guru Nanak sang about the glory of God and his creation and 'talked about myriads of netherworlds and skies' (Bhai Gurdas, Var 1, Pauri 36). Bhai Gurdas refers to the Japji Sahib, also written by Guru Nanak. In the 22th Pauri of the Japji Sahib Guru Nanak says: 'There are nether worlds beneath nether worlds, and hundreds of thousands of heavenly worlds above.'[36]

As reported by the Janam Sakhis, Pir Dastagir and Guru Nanak debated about it, because the Pir could not believe that because both were Muslims and accepted the Quran as authority. The Quran says, that there are seven firmaments and fourteen regions. Guru Nanak showed a miracle not only to prove that he is saying the truth, but also to show Pir Dastagir the reality behind the things. Bhai Gurdas Ji describes Guru Nanak's miracle in Baghdad in that way:

Pir Dastegir asked (the Baba) to show him whatever he had seen.

Guru Nanak Dev taking along with him the son of the pir, melted into thin air.

And in a wink of eye visualised him the upper and lower worlds.

From the nether world he brought a bowl full of sacred food and handed it over to

---

[34] Bhai Gurdas, Var 1 Pauri 35
[35] See: Chahal, Devinder Singh, 'Did Guru Nanak meet Pir Dastgir and Pir Bahlol Dana?' *Understanding Sikhism* 1/2 (Janu 2010), 49-52, 50-52. http://www.iuscanada.com/journal/archives/2010/j1212p49.pdf.
[36] Guru Granth Sahib, 5.

pir.

This manifest power (of the Guru) cannot be made to hide.[37]

Following this incident, the pir was convinced and accepted Guru Nanak as his prophet. According to Bhai Kahn Singh the successors of Pir Bahlol and Pir Dastagir became Guru Nanak's followers.[38] Guru Nanak was given a robe (*chola*) when he left Baghdad as a sign of respect and honour. Other sources say that the Queen of Iran had no children and a son was born. Therefore, she made a robe by herself and presented it to Guru Nanak as a sign of gratitude.[39]

This *chola* still exists and is kept at 'Gurdwara Sri Chola Sahib' in the city Dera Baba Nanak (India). The description of the *chola* on the website of the gurdwara provides us with details:

> *The chola, bearing some Qura'nic verses and Arabic numerals, arranged in the form of charms embroidered on it, was procured from Baghdad by Baba Kabali Mall, a descendant of Guru Nanak, it is said. It was brought to Dera Baba Nanak on 20 Phagun 1884 Bk / 1 March 1828. A special shrine was constructed where the Chola Sahib was kept and where it was put on display at the time of a fair held from 21 to 23 Phagun, early March, every year.*[40]

It is unknown how many times or how long Guru Nanak visited Baghdad and the Middle East. There are only very few evidences for Guru Nanak's visit. One of them is the fact that Guru Nanak was in Saidpur on his way back from the Middle East at the same time of Babur's invasion in the year 1521 CE. Guru Nanak was also taken captive by Babur.[41]

Another evidence is a Turkish-inscription, which was translated into English as follows:

Gör ki murad eyledi Hazret-i Rabbı Mecid	Allah the Almighty willed that this monument or building of humble Baba Nanak will be a new benevolent foundation of dissemination of wisdom. Seven saints came to help to erect this building on Hijri 917. [42]
Baba Nanak fakir ola ta ki imaret-i cedid	
Yediler imdad edip geldi ki tarihine	
Yaydı tevvab-ı icrayına inni müridun said	

---

[37] Bhai Gurdas, Var 1 Pauri 36
[38] See: Chahal, Devinder Singh. 'Did Guru Nanak meet Pir Dastgir and Pir Bahlol Dana?' *Understanding Sikhism* 1/2 (2010): 49-52, 51. http://www.iuscanada.com/journal/archives/2010/j1212p49.pdf
[39] Malkit Singh Saini, 'Nanak in Baghdad' *Tribune India*, (published 25 July 2003). https://www.tribuneindia.com/2003/20030725/mailbag.htm
[40] Dera Baba Nanak
[41] See: Chahal, Devinder Singh, 'How long was Guru Nanak's travel towards Middle East?' *Understanding Sikhism* 2 (2007), 34-37, 36-37. http://iuscanada.com/journal/archives/2007/j0902p34.pdf
[42] Ibid.

Hicri – 917

There are two other different translations of the same inscription. None of them seem to be correct.

Sewaram Singh	Manjit Singh
Murad saw the demolished building of Hazrat Rab-i-Majit, Baba Nanak, Fakir Aulila, and rebuilt it with his own hands, so that historical memorial may continue from generation to generation, and His murid-i-s'eed (the blessed discipline) may obtain heavely bless. Year 917 H.	Behold! How a wish has been fulfilled by Holy and High Providence. That the building of Baba Nanak has been newly built with the help of seven autat (great valis). That the happy murad of God (Baba Nanak) has started a fountain of grace issuing new water in the land. 917 Hijri

One miracle is based on the last translation: People of Baghdad were dependent on the water of the Tigris due to the poor water quality in the city. They came to Guru Nanak and complained about the lack of drinking water. Therefore, 'Guru Nanak got a well dug in the southeast corner and it produced sweet water'[43]

This stone-inscription was written in the year hijri 917 (1511 CE.). Some historians dated it to hijri 927, however, it is generally accepted that the inscription is dated to 1511 CE. Hence, Guru Nanak had been in Baghdad around 1511 CE and was captured by Babur's army in Saidpur in 1521 CE. Therefore, Guru Nanak spent at least 11 years in the Middle East (1511-1521).[44] During that time, he must have travelled to the Shrine of Maulana Jalalal ud-din Rumi in Konya and Istanbul in Turkey, because there are also inscriptions on monuments that were discovered in the last few years.[45] The 'Institute for Understanding Sikhism' started a research project to study the history of these monuments and obtain more reliable information about Guru Nanak's travels in the Middle East.[46] (ibid, 5-6).

Sikh Community in Iraq

It is difficult to determine if a continuous community had also existed in Iraq. Reliable sources on the history of the Sikh community in Iraq are sparse.

The only evidence was a shrine of Guru Nanak and at least two inscriptions. One inscription was recorded by Swami Anand Acharya, who was a wandering Hindu-poet, during his travels in the early twentieth century. The inscription was in a shrine outside the city of Baghdad, written in Arabic and was dated hijri 912 (1506 CE.)[47] He was fascinated and wrote a poem

---

[43] Manjeet Singh, 'Past and Present and Guru Nanak's Visit to Baghdad' *The Sikh Review* (1969).
[44] See: Chahal, Devinder Singh, 'How long was Guru Nanak's travel towards Middle East?' *Understanding Sikhism* 2 (2007): 34-37, 36. http://iuscanada.com/journal/archives/2007/j0902p34.pdf
[45] Devinder Singh Chahal, 'Monument of Guru Nanak in Istanbul, Turkey. A new discovery' *Understanding Sikhism*. (2006), 1-6, 3-4. http://www.iuscanada.com/journal/articles/monument2006.pdf
[46] Ibid, 5-6.
[47] See: Harish Dhillon, *Guru Nanak. Spiritual Masters*. (Mumbai: Indus Source Books, 2005), 142-143.

about Guru Nanak's glory:

Upon this simple slab of granite didst
thou sit, discoursing of fraternal
love and holy light, O Guru Nanak,
Prince among India's holy sons!

What song from the source of the
Seven Waters thou didst sing to
charm the soul of Iran!

What peace from Himalaya's lonely
caves and forests thou didst carry
to the vine groves and rose gardens
of Baghdad!
What light from Badarinath's snowy[48]

Kirpal Singh, a captain in the Indian Medical Service discovered the shrine in Baghdad during the First World War, when the British-Indian army conquered Baghdad.[49] Subedar Fateh Singh, another Sikh soldier, announced the discovery in Baghdad.[50] The author Sewaram Singh, Kirpal Singh's brother located the gurdwara in 'the west of the town and between the old graveyard to the north and the present Baghdad. Samara railway line to the south.'[51] In his book 'The Divine Master', Sewaram Singh quotes Kirpal Singh's letter dated on the 15 October 1918, in which Kirpan Singh described the shrine as follows:

It is really a very humble looking building and known to very few people except the local Sikhs. To some Arabs it is known as well by the name of tomb of Bahlol. You enter the building by a small door, on which something is written in Arabic, not visible to a casual visitor. Even with attention it is difficult to read. I could not read it and hence could not copy it. I have taken a photograph of the outside which I shall forward to you in due course (sic!). Entering the building you come to a brick paved passage going to your right straight into the room (with a veranda) wherein you find the tomb and the Raised Platform. In the courtyard there are a few trees, mostly pomegranates. The room in which there are the platform and the tomb, has two doors, one of which is open whilst the other is barred. As you enter the room, you come face to face with the platform which roughly is about 2 to 2 ½ ft. high, and about 3' and 4' in dimensions. It is now covered with handkerchiefs

---

[48] Swami Anand Acharya 1919.
[49] Sewa Ram Sigh, *The Divine Master. Life and teachings of Guru Nanak*. Edited by Prithipal Singh Kapur. (Jalandhar: ABS Publications, 1988), 106.
[50] 'Sikh shrine in Baghdad lives on in memories.' *Dawn*, (published 27 January 2011). https://www.dawn.com/news/601882.
[51] Ibid., 105.

of various colours presented by the Sikhs. In the centre close to the wall you find a picture of Sri Guru Nanak, presented by some energetic Sikh, above which you find the slab with the writing which I reproduce in this letter for you. The name of the man in charge is Sayed Yusuf.[52]

In his article Manjeet Singh explores his correspondence with Sardar Kartar Singh Kartar, the late president of the Central Sikh Committee, Baghdad, regarding Guru Nanak's shrine in Baghdad. The caretaker of the shrine told him about an old Arabic manuscript mentioning Guru Nanak's visit, but it was stolen in 1920. The same year, another stone inscription was found in the wall to the east of Sheikh Abdul Qadir Jilani's shrine near Baghdad Railway Station East, but the wall collapsed, and the inscription has since been missing.[53]

Sardar Kartar Singh Kartar also wrote that the Central Sikh Committee, Baghdad, applied to the Auqaf Department for repair of the shrine, but received no answer thus sending their application to the High Commissioner in Iraq in the year 1931. The Sikhs received permission and the repairs of the shrine were completed in 1934.[54] During the Second World War, another Sikh-regiment was stationed in Iraq. They constructed a gurdwara named 'Gurdwara Baba Nanak'.[55]

From 1970 onwards, Sikhs started migrating to the Middle East countries, because of employment opportunities available under the unprecedented development of physical infrastructure due to the oil boom.[56] There is no reliable information about how many Sikhs left Punjab and settled in Iraq. It is estimated that 5000 to 7000 Sikhs were living in Iraq in the 1970s and 1980s.[57] Most worked on the railways and construction.[58]

In 2003, the Gurdwara was bombed and destroyed. Harmeet Shah Singh, a renowned journalist visiting Baghdad wrote that a 'living symbol of Islam's cross-cultural engagements was levelled'.[59]

According to a news report, Abu Yusef was the caretaker of the shrine in 2011. Prior to the Iraq War, the Gurdwara had seen a few Sikh pilgrims. Non-Sikhs visited the place. The pilgrims would stay one or two nights, sleep

---

[52] Ibid., 106.
[53] See:Manjeet Singh, 'Past and Present and Guru Nanak's Visit to Baghdad' *The Sikh Review* (1969).
[54] See:Ibid.
[55] See:Ibid.
[56] Ajaya Kumar Sahoo, *Transnational Indian Diaspora. The regional Dimension*. (Delhi: Abhijeet Publications, 2006), 38.
[57] Ibid., 38-40.
[58] See: 'Iraq keen to rebuild damaged Sikh shrine' *DNA India* (published 25 May 2007) https://www.dnaindia.com/world/report-iraq-keen-to-rebuild-damaged-sikh-shrine-1099078.
[59] Harmeet Shah Singh, 'How Islam undid itself by ignoring bombing of Guru Nanak's symbol in Iraq. Destruction of al-Nuri mosque caps off the crisis within' *Dailyo*, (published 23 July 2017). https://www.dailyo.in/voices/islam-al-nuri-mosque-guru-nanak-isis-bhai-gurdas-sikhism/story/1/18546.html

in the courtyard, cook food and share it with others.[60]

Current situation and Khalsa Aid

The gurdwara has been completely destroyed. Only parts of the outer walls can be seen today next to the shrine of Bahlol at a cemetery just behind Baghdad's railway station. Only a mihrab remains in one of the walls. Since 2018, a gate protects the space of the former gurdwara. For a long time, the Sikhs wanted to rebuild the gurdwara and the Iraqi government seemed to be keen to do so. In 2007, the Iraqi National Congress chief Ahmed Chalabi said that the fanatics destroyed the gurdwara and that he wants to rebuild it. Not only did the Sikhs leaders and Sikh-organisations want to see the gurdwara rebuilt in new glory, but also Indian spiritual leaders like Sri Sri Ravi Shankar.[61] The president of the Shiromani Gurdwara Parbandhak Committee, Avtar Singh Makkar, contacted the Indian government as well as the US Embassy in Indian regarding the rebuilding of the gurdwara.[62] Until now, no action has been taken to repair or rebuild the gurdwara due to the ongoing political crisis.

In 2014, ISIS took over the city of Mosul. 39 Indians, mostly labourers from Punjab, were captured by the ISIS. It was believed that they were held captive in a prison in Badush (Nineveh Governorate, Iraq). India's External Affairs Minister Sushma Swaraj promised the families of the missing Indians to bring them back to their homeland. In March 2018, the Indian government confirmed that all of them had been killed in Iraq by the IS. The remains were found near Badush and DNA tests confirmed the identities.[63] Since the political situation in some areas like the Kurdistan Region of Iraq is stable, workers from south-Asia (also Sikhs) came for labour. Therefore, many Sikhs are working at the airport in Erbil.

The current political events resulted in a change for Sikhs in Iraq and there is also a new form of Sikh 'migration'. The international NGO 'Khalsa Aid', which has the motto 'Recognise the whole human race as one', supports victims of disasters worldwide. They provide food, water, clothing, medical, and sanitation supplies. Everything began when Ravinder Singh saw the photos of the refugees in Kosovo in 1999. In that year the Sikh community also celebrated the 300th birth of the Khalsa Ravi Singh has been inspired by it:

---

[60] See: 'Sikh shrine in Baghdad lives on in memories.' *Dawn*, (published 27 January 2011) https://www.dawn.com/news/601882.

[61] See: 'Iraq keen to rebuild damaged Sikh shrine' *DNA India*, (published 25 May 2007) https://www.dnaindia.com/world/report-iraq-keen-to-rebuild-damaged-sikh-shrine-1099078.

[62] 'SGPC to honour scribe for reporting on gurdwara in Iraq' *One India*, (published 21 April 2008) https://www.oneindia.com/2008/04/21/sgpc-to-honour-scribe-for-reporting-on-gurdwara-in-iraq-1208772245.html.

[63] '4 years after they went missing, govt confirms 39 Indians killed in Iraq by IS' *Times of India*, (published 21 Mai 2018) http://timesofindia.indiatimes.com/articleshow/63389361.cms?utm_source=contentofinterest&utm_medium=text&utm_campaign=cppst.

At the time of the celebrations across the UK, and around the world, there were terrible images on the news of refugees struggling to cross the cold and mountainous border to reach a safer and peaceful Albania.

I read in the newspaper about a small group who were organising an aid convoy to Albania – the Sikhi teaching of 'Sarbhat da Bhalla' came rushing to my mind.

I phoned the group from the newspaper and asked to join them to help deliver aid donated by the Sikh community who had been extremely generous in giving food and money – within two weeks we were on our way with two trucks and a van load of aid to Albania. Khalsa Aid was born.[64]

Khalsa Aid also started many projects in Iraq providing humanitarian aid. One campaign 'Providing Bread to Syrian Refugees in Iraq' organised a camp with 16,000 people on the border between Iraq and Syria. This project was launched in June 2014. The Yazidi and Assyrian communities had to leave their homes because of the rise of the ISIS. Khalsa Aid and the local authorities and also the Swedish Doctors Association are working together to provide the people with food. Therefore, they also established a bakery to produce fresh bread, which is a staple in the traditional diet of the Yazidi.[65]

In July 2014, Khalsa Aid started to help economic migrants from Punjab to get back to their homelands because they were not secure following the rise of the ISIS. Many Punjabis worked as manual labourers in Iraq and had financial problems to leave the country. In the context of the campaign 'Displaced Sikhs in Iraq' Khalsa Aid organised the flights from Iraq to Punjab.[66]

Since 2016, they have also been providing Yazidi girls and women with essential clothing. The girls and women 'have returned from ISIS captivity, traumatised and with nothing but the clothes their captors had forced them to wear'.[67] In that 'Project Dignity' Yazidi girl and women get a budget and they can choose their own clothes as a symbol of freedom. Khalsa Aid buys the clothes from local Kurdish businesses that had also suffered losses due to the war. Khalsa Aid is working with local authorities at the Office of Kidnapped & Rescue Department in Dohuk.[68]

Khalsa Aid launched the campaign 'Restoring Electricity to Assyrian Orthodox Christians' in the town Bartella in Northern Iraq in August 2017. After the town had been under the control of IS for two years, Khalsa Aid is aiding its recovery. The church had been used as a training school by the ISIS

---

[64] 'About Us' *Khalsa Aid*, (no date) https://www.khalsaaid.org/about-us (accessed 23.09.2018).
[65] 'Providing bread to Syrian refugees in Iraq' *Khalsa Aid*, (published June 2014) https://www.khalsaaid.org/projects/providing-bread-to-syrian-refugees-in-iraq (accessed 23.09.2018)
[66]. 'Displaced Sikhs in Iraq.' *Khalsa Aid*, (published July 2014) https://www.khalsaaid.org/projects/displaced-sikhs-in-iraq (accessed 23.09.2018).
[67] 'Project Dignity: Essential Clothing for Yezidi women, ex-slaves of ISIS' *Khalsa Aid*, (published January 2017) https://www.khalsaaid.org/projects/project-dignity (accessed 23.09.2018).
[68] Ibid.

and it is necessary to restore the electricity[69]. 'The church is the hub of the community and restoring electric was a great morale boost for the community.'[70]

Another campaign is 'Langar Aid' with the slogan 'Feeding humanity'. The aim is to provide food and water in areas affected of disasters and wars. In the 'Middle East Project', Langar Aid has provided 864,000 meals and 500 litre clean water with an impact on 16,000 lives.[71]

Conclusion

Guru Nanak's visit to the Middle East, and Baghdad specifically, are a fact that can be supported by numerous historical sources. Discussions about religious topics with the custodian of the shrine Piran Pir Hazrat Dastgir Abdul Qadir Jilan and maybe also with the successors of the renowned Sufis Pir Bahlol were recorded. The guru spent at least 11 years travelling around the Middle East. Additional evidence can be found in the form of inscriptions on stones that were found during the First World War by Sikh soldiers of the British-Indian army. They also discovered Guru Nanak's shrine. With the permission of the Iraqi government, the shrine had been repaired and during the Second World War a Gurdwara had been built there.

Guru Nanak's visit and interfaith dialogues show not only that Baghdad had been an important multi-ethnic and multi-religious city at that time, but also that the Islam was open to a dialogue and open for debates about religion and the Quran as well; something easily forgotten or overlooked by so-called Islamic organisations, such as the Islamic State or Al-Qaida, which are not only destroying the symbols of other religious communities in their captured areas but also the pillars of humanity.

The place of the former Sikh Gurdware in Baghdad. (Picture: Thomas Schmidinger)

As Guru Nanak preached the humanity and the equality of all human-beings, his followers are helping the people in need and providing them with food and clean water. They started many projects and campaigns to help the people who have nothing and have lost everything regardless of religion, gender, and social background.

---

[69] 'Restoring electricity to Assyrian orthodox Christians' *Khalsa Aid*, (published August 2017) www.khalsaaid.org/projects/restoring-electricity-to-assyrian-orthodox-christians (accessed 23.09.2018).
[70] Ibid.
[71] See: 'Middle East Project.' *Langar Aid,* (no date) http://langaraid.org/projects/syria-project/ (accessed 23.09.2018).

CHAPTER 6

CHRISTIANS IN IRAQ

Thomas Schmidinger

Unlike Syria and Palestine, Iraq was never a predominantly Christian land. Nevertheless, Iraq has a long history of Christian presence and one of the oldest Christian communities in the world. Christians, like Muslims and Jews, always played an important role in Iraqi society and even politics. Although the number of Christians declined in recent years, the diversity of Christian denominations in Iraq is still remarkable.

The last Persian empire before the Islamic conquest, the Sasanian Empire (224-651 AD), had the official religion of Zoroastrianism but tolerated Christians of the Church of the East[1] and the Syrian Orthodox Church (Jacobite). The Sasanian Empire favoured the Church of the East and was particularly suspicious towards the mainstream church that later became the Orthodox Church because of its connection with the Roman and Byzantine Empire. Therefore, churches in the tradition of the Church of the East were the largest and most important stream of Christianity, although its Uniate wing – the Chaldean church – emerged as the largest Christian denomination today.

Oriental Orthodoxy and Eastern Catholics

The Islamic conquest of the Sasanian Empire in 651 also opened Mesopotamia for the Byzantine Orthodox tradition; however, the Church of the East and the Syrian Orthodox Church remained dominant in Mesopotamian Christianity. Roman Catholic missionaries created the Chaldean Church in 1552 as a splinter group of the Church of the East. This version of the Church of the East has full communion with the Roman Catholic Church and is today the largest Christian confession of Iraq. However, the Church of the East still exists and split in two churches in 1964, with the Ancient Church of the East under its present Catholicos-Patriarch Mar Addax II based in Baghdad and the Assyrian Church of the East under its present Catholicos-Patriarch Gewargis III, who has

---

[1] Often called Nestorian in Western texts, although the church members reject this terminology.

considering moving its patriarchal see from Chicago to Erbil.

Likewise, the Church of the East also has a Roman Catholic version of the Jacobite Syrian-Orthodox Church, the Syrian-Catholic Church created in the eighteenth century. Both the Syrian-Orthodox and the Syrian-Catholic Church are still present in Iraq. Besides the Roman Catholic offshoots, these churches also had Protestant offshoots, who also still have some communities in Iraq. While all these churches use forms of Aramaic as liturgical language and many of their believers also still speak Aramaic dialects as their native languages, they do not all identify as part of the same ethnic group.

Although mutually understandable, the Aramaic-speaking Christians of different denominations have different dialects and also different identity concepts. This resulted from the Ottoman Empire defining collective identities by religion and not by language or 'nation'. The relevantly new discussion about the common national identity of these Aramaic-speaking Christians brings up rival concepts of ethnic belonging. Nevertheless the region's Aramaic-speaking Christians are all interchangeably referred to as Assyrian, Chaldean, Chaldo-Assyrian, Syroyo, Syriac or Aramaic. Nevertheless, some political actors use these terminologies with sectarian undertone; some political parties only see adherents of their own denomination as part of their 'nation'. However, most of these parties are stronger in neighbouring Syria, where the Assyrian Democratic Party, founded by Adam Homeh in 1978 follows a strict sectarian line that sees only adherents of the Church of the East as 'real Assyrians'. In Iraq, these discussions are a bit easier, because most Aramaic-speaking Christians consider themselves as part of the same ethnic group. The name of this ethnic group is more heatedly debated than the issue of a common ethnicity. The debate about the name resulted in the 2003 adoption of the neologism Chaldo-Assyrians for official use.

These Aramaic-speaking Christians of Iraq and particularly the adherents of the Church of the East have a history full of tragedy. Survivors of Ottoman ruler's genocide of 1915 (Sayfo) from Hakkari (Kurdish: Colemêrg) and Urmia,[2] they found refuge in British Iraq.

A history of the complicated relationship between these Assyrians from Hakkari and the Kurds is far beyond the scope of this brief survey of Iraqi Christians. However, Kurds, like Simkoyê Şikak (Simko) participated in the slaughter of Assyrians in 1915 and Assyrians participated in a Russian massacre of Muslim Kurds in Rawanduz in 1916. Britain also used these surviving Assyrian fighters for their Iraq Levies to control Iraq[3] and did not

---

[2] Joseph Yacoub, *Year of the Sword. The Assyrian Christian Genocide. A history.* (New York: Oxford University Press, 2016).

[3] R.S. Stafford, *The Tragedy of the Assyrian Minority in Iraq.* (London/New York: Routledge, 2009), 63-73.

protect them after Iraq gained independence in 1932. Moreover, some scholars still debate whether Britain accepted the attacks against Assyrians following Iraq´s independence as a test for the new Iraqi army.

However, only one year after Iraqi independence, in August 1933, the Iraqi army commanded by the Kurdish officer Bakr Sidqi al-Askari massacred up to 3,000 Assyrians from more than 60 villages between Duhok and Mosul. The so-called Semele massacre – named after a village that recently became a suburb of the city of Duhok – became a turning point for the history of the Assyrians in Iraq: 'the Assyrians that had been most resistant to incorporation in Iraq found new homes in neighbouring Syria, the patriarch and his family were exiled to Cyprus and the remaining Assyrians in Iraq accepted their position as a religious rather than an ethnic minority, relinquishing their rights to any kind of "national home" in Iraq.'[4]

In the 1970s, national Assyrian parties were re-established in resistance to Arab nationalism. Only with the recent confessionalisation and ethnicisation of politics in Iraq did these parties seriously address the issue of an Assyrian homeland.

In contemporary Iraq, the political weakness of the shrinking minorities also created many political conflicts along party lines. Besides denominational and ideological conflicts, the political fragmentation of the Aramaic-speaking Christians in Iraq increased with the creation of Chaldo-Assyrian Parties by Kurdish political actors. Chaldo-Assyrians were always part of the secular political parties in Iraq. The Iraqi Communist Party had a legendary Aramaic-speaking Christian leader Yusuf Salman Yusuf, better known by his nom de guerre Comrade Fahd, who was publicly hanged in 1949. Others, such as Tariq Aziz (originally Tariq Mikhail Youhanna) played an important role in the regime of Saddam Hussein's Arab Socialist Ba'ath Party.

An important, explicitly Christian-Assyrian party, The Assyrian Democratic Movement (ADM), established in 1979 was established as a nationalist Assyrian Party in opposition to the regime of the Ba'ath Party. It still exists under the present leadership of Yonadam Yousip Kanna. The ADM and some other minor Chaldo-Assyrian parties strictly oppose the integration of predominantly Assyrian-Aramaic regions into the Kurdistan Autonomous region. They demand an autonomous region for the Assyrians. Other pro-Kurdish Chaldo-Assyrian Parties, such as the Chaldean Democratic Union, the Chaldean Syriac Assyrian Popular Council or the Bet-Nahrain Democratic Party ask for a Christian Aramaic region within the Autonomous Region of Kurdistan.

---

[4] Heleen Murre-Van den Berg, 'Light from the East (1948-1954) and the De-Territorialization of the Assyrian Church of the East' In *Religion beyond its Private Role in Modern Society*. Edited by Wim Hofstee / Arie Van der Koji. (Leiden/Boston: Brill, 2013), 115-134: 120.

The Aramaic-speaking Christians in Nineveh governorate are not only the largest group of Christians in Iraq, but they were also the most affected by the attacks of ISIS in 2014. Therefore, this article is followed by a long text about these Chaldo-Assyrian Christians written by Emanuel Youkhana.

The Iraqi Armenians are another group of Christians. Like the Assyrians/Chaldeans/Syriacs, the Armenian are both an ethno-linguistic and religious minority. Seta Ohanian from the Armenian Academy of Science gives an overview of adherents of the Armenian Apostolic, the Armenian Catholic and the Armenian Protestant Church in Iraq.

Eastern Orthodox Christians

Besides these Christians, Iraq has Christians of other denominations and languages. Most use Arabic both in their liturgy and their daily lives. However, Baghdad as an international metropole, also has a history of foreign Christian communities who used different languages. Kurdistan also has a small group of Kurdish converts who formed a Kurdish Church.

A large group of Christians outside the Assyrian-Aramaic group and the Armenians are the Eastern Orthodox Christians of Iraq, who belong to the family of churches united under the Ecumenical Patriarch of Constantinople. There was an early presence of Eastern Orthodoxy in Mesopotamia but the rivalry between the Sassanian Empire and the Byzantine Empire led to repression of the churches affiliated with the Byzantine Empire. Only after the Islamic conquest of Iraq could the Orthodox Church reorganise. Orthodox Christians in Iraq came under ecclesiastical jurisdiction of the Eastern Orthodox Patriarchate of Antioch.

Until today, the Metropolitan of Baghdad and Kuwait is under the jurisdiction of the Eastern Orthodox Patriarchate of Antioch and All the East. Constantine Papastephanou, who served as Metropolitan of Baghdad and Kuwait from 1969 until 2014, strongly shaped the Orthodox Church of Iraq during the period of Saddam Hussein and afterwards. Although the Metropolitan's seat still formally stays in Baghdad, his successor Ghattas Hazim moved the church administration to Kuwait that also belongs to his archdiocese.

The attacks of ISIS in 2014 also affected the members of the Eastern-Orthodox Church. In 2014, Metropolitan Ghattas Hazim expressed fear for the future of the Orthodox Christian presence in Iraq, Syria, and the whole Mesopotamia region. Hazim cited unspecified sources to claim that 90 percent of Iraqi Orthodox Christians have been displaced from their homes. Hazim added that only 30 of 600 Orthodox families remained in Baghdad.[5] After the recapture of the territories captured by ISIS in 2014, some of these

---

[5] Ghassan Rifi, 'Bishop: 90% of Orthodox Christians in Iraq displaced' *Al Monitor*, (published 21 October 2014). https://www.al-monitor.com/pulse/security/2014/10/christians-iraq-displaced-killed-war-conflict.html (accessed 9 April 2019).

families returned. Nevertheless, families only returned to Baghdad and not to Mosul, where none of the various Christian communities have re-established their former presence.

Like with the adherents of the Oriental Orthodox churches, Roman Catholic missionaries also targeted Eastern Orthodox Christians creating Uniate Eastern Catholic churches. Therefore, Baghdad has a Greek Catholic Church in addition to the Orthodox Church.[6]

Roman Catholic Christians

Besides the Chaldean Church, the Latin Roman Catholic Church became active in Iraq. The Roman Catholic Diocese of Baghdad was already established in 1632 and became an Archdiocese in 1848. Besides foreign nationals from Roman Catholic backgrounds, a small group of Iraqis also identify as Latin Christians. The seat of the Archdiocese is St. Joseph's Cathedral in Baghdad. However, most Roman Catholic religious orders who became active in Iraq mainly served the Chaldean Christians or even Christians and Muslims. Catholic orders were particularly active in the field of education. Dominican sisters and Carmelites opened schools and Jesuits were granted the permission to open a university in 1955. 'They were given one hundred and sixty-eight acres of land in Za´faranyia, an area fourteen miles south of Baghdad where they established a fine university. This university was very successful and its courses were recognised in Western countries.'[7] Christians and Muslims attended Roman Catholic schools and the Jesuit University because the institutions did not try to convert Muslims and had an excellent reputation. However, the Baathist regime nationalised most of the schools and the university.

Roman Catholics in Iraq always included Iraqis and non-Iraqis who lived in Iraq. Iraqi Roman Catholicism included British Catholics and Polish soldiers fighting alongside the Allies who were stationed in Baghdad. By the early twenty-first century, only 2,500 adherents of the Roman Catholic Church were left in Iraq and this has continued to shrink since 2003. Today the historic cathedral on Khulafa Street in Baghdad is in very bad condition. In recent years, the Coptic Church reused it and renamed it as St. Mary Maadi Church. However, the Coptic Church moved out and the extremely rundown building seemed to be unused in 2018.[8] Since the 1960s, the Saint Joseph's Cathedral in Alwiyah near Wathiq Square has been used as the main Roman Catholic Church in Baghdad.

The church 'Our Lady of the Hour Church' in Mosul with its significant

---

[6] Suha Rassam, *Christianity in Iraq*. (Leominster: Gracewing, 2005), 182.

[7] Ibid., 144.

[8] The adherents of the Coptic Church in Iraq are all workers from Egypt. With the political and economic crisis following the expansion of ISIS in 2014, most of them left Iraq. A Coptic church (St. Maria) in Silêmanî was never completed and was used as a shelter for displaced Christians in 2014. Only a very few Copts remained in 2018.

clock-tower, built by the Dominicans in 1893 was destroyed by ISIS in 2016. It is very unlikely to ever be rebuilt and reused as a church. Outside of Baghdad, the Roman Catholics have only one church (on the 14th of July Street in Basra).

Anglicans

As a former British colony, Iraq also has an Anglican church, the St George's Church in Baghdad. Closed during the regime of Saddam Hussein, it was re-opened after the fall of Saddam Hussein in 2003. As the only Anglican church in Iraq, it belongs to the Diocese of Cyprus and the Gulf that has its seat in Nicosia. It is outside the Green Zone, but heavily protected. In October 2009, two suicide bomb attacks against the church killed at least 150 people and injured more than 600 on the streets outside.[9] In 2014, the Archbishop of Canterbury ordered Andrew White, who had served as the vicar of St George's Church since 2005, back to Europe for security reasons. However, although former Vicar Andrew White was quoted by media that 'time has come where it is over, no Christians will be left'[10] White was not the last Anglican priest in Baghdad. After Andrew White left, Faiz Jerjees, the first Iraqi national ordained as an Anglican priest took over his responsibilities to the community.

With Faiz Jerjees, the community became more Iraqi; the mass is now celebrated in Arabic. The church's interior still has a memorial honouring the British troops who fell in World War I. However, the Bible on the lectern is now in Arabic and a new flag connects Arabic calligraphy with the English inscription 'Prince of Peace'. Faiz Jerjees serves a small community of about 300 Anglicans, most are Iraqis and it does not seem that these Iraqis would be willing to leave. A medical clinic and kindergarten have been opened. In fall 2018, an Anglican school was opened next to the church in Baghdad.[11] Like the kindergarten and the clinic, the school is open for adherents of all faiths and includes Christian and Muslim pupils as well as children from other religions of Iraq.

Adventists, Presbyterians, Pentecostals, and other Evangelical Churches

Already during the Ottoman period, Protestant missionaries reached present-day Iraq. In 1850, Presbyterians opened a mission in Mosul. The

---

[9] Episcopal Church News, 'IRAQ: St. George's Anglican Church damaged in deadly bomb attack' *The Episcopal Church*, (published 26 October 2009) https://www.episcopalchurch.org/library/article/iraq-st-georges-anglican-church-damaged-deadly-bomb-attack (accessed 9 April 2019).

[10] Hollie McKay, 'Christianity in Iraq is finished, says Andrew White, "vicar of Baghdad"' *FoxNews*, (published 21 March 2017) https://www.foxnews.com/world/christianity-in-iraq-is-finished-says-canon-andrew-white-vicar-of-baghdad (accessed 9 April 2019).

[11] ACNS, 'Celebrations as new Anglican school in Iraq opens next to St George's Church in Baghdad' *Anglican Communion Office*, (published 2 October 2018) https://www.episcopalnewsservice.org/2018/10/02/anglican-school-in-iraq-opens-next-to-st-georges-church-in-baghdad/(accessed 9 April 2019).

Reformed Church of America started a mission in Basra in 1889.

In 1923, Seventh Day Adventist missionaries started to convert Iraqis to their beliefs. After the opening of their first church at Nidhal Street in Bagdad in 1958, other churches followed. During the peak of the Adventists in Iraq, four churches in Mosul, Baghdad, Kirkuk and Basra had a total membership of nearly 200 people.[12] However, after 2003, one after the other had to close due to the lack of security. As a proselytising church, the Adventists had more problems with jihadist and other terrorist movements than the traditional churches of Iraq. An estimated 150 kilograms of dynamite was detonated outside their historic church in Baghdad on 10 September 2009. Since 2017, it is closed and 'under construction'. Most of the community has left Baghdad for the Kurdish region, where some had started to meet for worship already in 2011. In March 2018, a new Seventh Day Adventist Church was inaugurated in Erbil.[13]

Besides the Adventists, there are also other evangelical churches in Baghdad, Mosul and Basra. Some are old communities who split from mainstream churches, like the Armenian Evangelical Church and the Assyrian Evangelical Presbyterian Church in Baghdad. Others with origins in the United States started a relatively aggressive missionary work after the occupation of Iraq by the US in 2003. More than a dozen new evangelical churches started to operate since 2003. Besides the already existing Presbyterians and Adventists, missionaries from the Baptists, Methodists, the Church of the Nazarene, and Christian Alliance denominations started to operate in Baghdad and Erbil. Most members of these new evangelical churches came from other Christian churches and tried to convert Muslims, which created many tensions and was not seen favourably by Iraq's traditional churches.

In Kurdistan, the Kurdzman Church of Christ, that perceived itself as a national Kurdish evangelical Church, was already established in Erbil in 2000. It has only one church building in Erbil. However, they have also small groups of worshippers in Silêmanî, Duhok, Ranya and Kirkuk. The whole church has not more than 300 members, all made up by converted Muslim Kurds. They translated the Bible to the Soranî language and pray in both Soranî and in Duhok in Badhinî.

Ex-Amish brothers Steve and Jacob Lapp also started an 'emotionally healing' mission in Iraqi Kurdistan in 2007 through humanitarian work.[14] The predominantly Christian town of Ain Kawa hosts a church for Arabic-

---

[12] Allana Fereira, 'New Adventist Church building inaugurated in Erbil, Iraq' *Adventist News Network*, (published 12 March 2018) https://news.adventist.org/en/all-news/news/go/2018-03-12/new-adventist-church-building-inaugurated-in-erbil-iraq/ (accessed 9 April 2019).

[13] Ibid.

[14] Gerry Wagoner, 'Amish Ambassadors in Iraq' *Fulcrum 7*, (published 30 August 2016) http://www.fulcrum7.com/blog/2016/8/30/amish-ambassadors-in-iraq?fbclid=IwAR000LVC7tL-PN3rDTxRaXT2J3BOBy6JK8QvdfITYOD63V2LpNJ00bBAO9fs (accessed 9 April 2019).

speaking evangelicals, a Christian & Missionary Alliance Church. Another evangelical group called 'Faith Fellowship - International Church of Erbil' mainly serves Americans living in Erbil who are at least close to Pentecostalism.

The fastest-growing Christian denomination worldwide are the Pentecostal churches with about 280 million members. This current of Christianity developed from American evangelical Christianity in the early twentieth century, has become the most aggressive Christian missionary movement and tries to actively convert Muslims. The Pentecostal movement, born in the United States in a small church in a run-down section of Los Angeles and led by an African-American preacher 'erupted from among society's disenfranchised'[15] and expanded around the world. Most Pentecostals have a very positive attitude towards material wealth and capitalist accumulation; wealth and happiness is not just promised for the afterlife but also for the present life. This variety of Christianity goes very well with the neoliberal forms of capitalist economy advocated by the USA. Pentecostals have a growing influence in Latin America, Africa, and Asia.

Like some more traditional evangelical churches, Pentecostal churches came to Iraq via American missionary activities following the US occupation of Iraq in 2003. Baghdad has an Assemblies of God church and a New Life Church that both follow a Pentecostal form of Christianity. Converts in the Church of the East formed the Assyrian Pentecostal Church.

The fight against the so-called 'Islamic State' (ISIS) since 2014 has attracted more Christian missionaries. Once more, the ex-Amish Lapp brothers came to teach their nonviolent message of forgiveness and help local communities.[16] A radically different interpretation of the Christian message is delivered by the Free Burma Rangers (FBR), a militant evangelical group that started their work with Christian minorities in Myanmar (Burma) and supported their fight against the military regime in Myanmar. Their experienced medical teams were active in Sinjar and during the fight against the 'Islamic State' in Mosul in 2017. They continued their presence in Iraq during 2018. In spring 2018, they proudly presented new members who were baptised in the Tigris in Mosul, including an ex-Iraqi soldier, they called Ali on their website.[17]

Many of these missionary churches and groups have conflicts with Muslims as well as with traditional Iraqi churches. Many traditional Iraqi

---

[15] Harvey Cox, *Fire from Heaven. The Rise of Pentecostal Spirituality and the Reshaping of Religion in the Twenty-First Century*. (Cambridge: Da Capo Press, 2001), 24.
[16] Gerry Wagoner, 'Amish Ambassadors in Iraq' *Fulcrum 7*, (published 30 August 2016) http://www.fulcrum7.com/blog/2016/8/30/amish-ambassadors-in-iraq?fbclid=IwAR000LVC7tL-PN3rDTxRaXT2J3BOBy6JK8QvdfIYOD63V2LpNJ00bBAO9fs (accessed 9 April 2019).
[17] 'New Believers baptised in Mosul' *Free Burma Rangers* (published 29 March 2018) https://www.freeburmarangers.org/2018/03/29/new-believers-baptized-mosul/ (accessed 9 April 2019).

Christians, who would never try to convert a Muslim to Christianity, see the missionary work of some US-based evangelical denominations as a threat to the image of Christians.

More denominations and shrinking communities

Since the end of Saddam Hussein's regime, we face a contradictory development: While the number of Christian denominations and the number of converts in Iraq are growing, the overall number of Christians is shrinking. Especially in Baghdad, Mosul, and Basra, large groups of Christians have left Iraq since 2003 or moved from these cities to the Kurdish region, in particular to the Christian town of Ain Kawa near Erbil. The small town became a hub for Christians from all over Iraq. New churches of different denominations are erected there as Christians from central and southern Iraq migrate towards Kurdistan. Nevertheless, for some of these Christians, Ain Kawa is just a stopover on their way to Europe, America or Australia where many already have family members. Thus, in many parts of Iraq, Christianity has a very uncertain future.

Chaldean Church of Mother of Sorrows in Baghdad. (Picture: Thomas Schmidinger)

Orthodox Church of the Patriarchate of Antioch in Baghdad. (Picture: Thomas Schmidinger)

Former Roman Catholic Cathedral, later used by Coptic Christians under the name "Mary Maadi Church" in October 2018. (Picture: Thomas Schmidinger)

Adventist Church in Baghdad. (Picture: Thomas Schmidinger)

The Syrian-catholic Church of our Lady of Salvation in Baghdad's Karada District was attacked in 2004 by a car bomb and in 2010 by six terrorists of the "Islamic State of Iraq". Two priests, more than 40 worshippers, and several policemen and bystanders were killed. Since these jihadist attacks many Churches in Baghdad are fortified until today. (Picture: Thomas Schmidinger)

Holy Saturday 2019 in the Roman-catholic (Latin) Church of Basra. (Picture: Thomas Schmidinger)

The Old Syrian-Catholic Immaculate Church in Baghdeda (Qaraqosh or Hamdaniya) after the liberation from ISIS in spring 2017. (Picture: Thomas Schmidinger)

CHAPTER 7

FLEEING ISIS: ARAMAIC-SPEAKING CHRISTIANS IN THE NINIVEH PLAINS AFTER ISIS

Archimandrite Emanuel Youkhana

Excluding the Armenians[1] and some small groups of converts[2], the Iraqi Christians are the indigenous people of Iraq. Their roots go back thousands of years before Christianity in the lands of Mesopotamia.

In other words, I believe the Iraqi Christians are the *true* native people of Iraq, being descendants of the ancient Assyrians and Babylonians. The Aramaic-speaking Christians (Assyrians, Chaldeans, Chaldo-Assyrians) are not a new Christian community 'evangelised' by western missionaries, as is the case in many African and East Asian Christian communities.

Christian religion began to come to Iraq already in the first two centuries after Christ under the rule of the Parthians, 'who were open to the practice of different religions and seem to have tolerated the introduction of Christianity into their empire.'[3] Aramaic Christians in Iraq and their churches go back to the first generations who adopted Christianity through Jesus Christ's apostles. Their Christianity is older than European Christianity, and their existence in Iraq predates Islam in Iraq.

The ethnic and cultural identity of Iraqi Christians

The Iraqi Christians belong to various churches and denominations, but they share a common ethnicity and culture. They speak the eastern dialect of Syriac, which is the local language that descended from Aramaic, the language spoken by Jesus Christ.

However, many Iraqi Christians who lived in big cities such as Baghdad, Mosul and Basra long ago abandoned and forgot their mother language and began speaking Arabic, due to political pressure and persecution.

---

[1] For the Armenian Christians, see the article of Seda D. Ohanian in this book.
[2] For the converts, see the introduction on 'Christians in Iraq' of Thomas Schmidinger in this book.
[3] Suha Rassam, *Christianity in Iraq*. (Leominster: Gracewing, 2005), 29.

Nevertheless, they still believe they are not Arabs and have therefore kept their mother tongue, Syriac, as the mains language of their religious rituals.

Syriac, like other living languages, has different dialects. Each dialect has its particular character depending on the demography and surrounding circumstances. The map of Syriac dialects does not necessarily synchronise with the various churches of Iraqi Christians. This means that followers of different churches may speak the same dialect, while followers of *one* church might speak different dialects. However, speaking and understanding among these people is normal and easy because the minor linguistic differences of various dialects only involve pronunciation.

The Iraqi Christians share the same customs and social traditions which reflect their unified identity—Christian principles and values that have been in place since they embraced Christianity in its very early stages in Mesopotamia at the hands of Mar (Saint) Thomas (one of the Twelve Apostles), Mar Addai, and Mar Mary, two of the Seventy Apostles.[4]

Despite the accumulated historical diversity and schisms in their theological views and churches, the Iraqi Christians intermarry between their Christian denominations. And despite the multiple names ascribed to this cultural and ethnic entity in the past, they firmly believe in *the unity of their ethnicity, culture, and destiny*.

Demographic distribution of Iraqi Christians

Based on the historical claim that the Iraqi Assyrian-Chaldean-Syriac Christians are the indigenous people of Iraq, it is notable that their primary residences are the country plains around the historical capital of the Assyrian Empire of Nineveh (now Mosul).

Due to colonialism and the expansion of Islam (Arabs coming from the south and Kurds from the north and northeast), the whole region was eventually controlled by Muslims, forcing Christians to become a religious minority struggling to survive.

Many Christian towns in the region, such as Alqosh, Telkeif, Bartilla, Zakho, and Mangesh, still exist. Historical evidence indicate churches as well as Christian communities had a presence in big cities in Northern Iraq and Iraqi Kurdistan, such as Mosul and Erbil. Christians, however, also exist in other big cities such as Baghdad, Kirkuk and Basra. Their roots go back to earlier Assyrian and Christian communities; social and economic factors caused Christians to move to these cities to seek a better life. The Iraqi Christians have lived in Baghdad and Kirkuk since the times of the Abbasids,

---

[4] ميشيل شفالية, المسيحيون في حكاري وكوردستان الشمالية: الكلدان والسريان والاشوريون والارمن, ترجمة نافع توسا, مراجعة وتقديم الاب د. يوسف توما مرقص, بغداد, ٢٠١٠ ص ص ١٠-٢٥.

Mongolians, and Ottomans.[5]

Other political and security reasons played important roles in encouraging migration to large cities. From the 1960s to the 1980s, migration to the large Iraqi cities, especially Baghdad, has significantly increased because their historical places of habitation and villages in Iraqi Kurdistan, particularly in the regions of Duhok and Erbil, became sites of military battles between the Kurdish revolution and central government troops.

The pace of migration escalated, particularly after the Baath regime took power in Iraq in 1968 and began adopting a policy of burning the land. The policy of destroying the Assyrian and Kurdish villages in the north, lasted from 1974 to 1988 and resulted in the obliteration of 4,000 villages, among them some 120 Assyrian Christian villages and the destruction of more than 60 ancient churches. The regime also practiced ethnic cleansing by deporting thousands of Assyrians and Kurds to other places, replacing them with Arabs in the former Assyrian/Kurdish homes and villages. However, beginning in 1991 with the liberation of the Iraqi Kurdistan region, a significant movement began to return and rebuild the life in the destroyed villages. This movement increased Saddam's regime fell in 2003.

Therefore, we may describe the Christian demography in Iraq as follows:

I- The geopolitical demography, in terms of population and lands (towns, townships, villages) exists in two regions:

1- Iraqi Kurdistan region: particularly in the governorates of Dohuk and Erbil where around 120 Christian towns, townships and villages exist.

2- Nineveh Plains: where a substantial Christian population exists (to be introduced in detail in the sections that follow).

II- Christians in the big, mixed cities of Baghdad, Basra, Mosul, Kirkuk, and Sulaymaniyah have, has faced real threats, especially in Basra, Baghdad, and Mosul, because of a systematic anti-Christian terror campaign and ongoing religious cleansing in many parts of these cities.

This existence, which has survived over many centuries, might be extinguished if circumstances are not changed.

Iraqi Christian Demography

The current Iraqi administrative structure is composed of 18 governorates (or provinces), each composed of districts (the governorate centre is also always a district centre) which, in turn, are composed of a couple of sub-districts, to which the townships and villages belong.

The difference between the two aforementioned demographic types (i.e.

---

[5] Henry Field, *South Kurdistan: An Anthropological Study*. Translation of Zarzis Fathallah. (Erbil, 2001), 151-161.

in the Kurdish Region of Iraq and the Nineveh Plains, and other parts of Iraq) is that in both the Kurdish Region of Iraq (KRI) and the Nineveh Plains, people have a historical connection to the land.

This enables Christians to preserve, practice, and improve their collective identity and to have a political and administrative role in the planning and decision-making of these territories. In addition, social and cultural entities/services can operate and add value to the community. Whereas, in other parts of Iraq, Christians only represent a tiny part of the roughly seven million population of Baghdad or several thousand scattered amongst the millions of Basra, Mosul and Kirkuk.

The Christian presence in KRI has some important differences with the Nineveh Plains. The existence in KRI is mostly in rural villages (over 100) and in the big cities like Duhok, Ankawa (the sub-district in Erbil), Zakho and others; most of those villages are not mixed, i.e. all their people are Christian, while only a couple of them are mixed with Yazidis and/or Muslims, such as Sorka, Sorya, and others.

The size of the villages ranges from the small (up to 15 families) to the large (less than 100 families) and even to the largest of them, where the quantity reaches 250 families. The Christian villages in KRI are very exceptional in the region's history.

The Christians have never returned to the villages and regions from which they were forced to flee, e.g. Hakari, Tur Abdin (in modern Turkey), Urmia (in North Iran) and in Khabour (Syria). Only in Iraqi Kurdistan have the deported Christians gone back to their home villages and rebuilt their lives.

The Christians in the Nineveh Plains mainly exist in semi-large populated townships and towns. In many cases, Christian towns in the Nineveh Plains are district centres (e.g. Hamdaniya) or sub-districts (Bartilla, Alqosh).

There are no Christian towns or villages in Iraq south of the Nineveh Plains to the Saudi and Kuwaiti borders, nor to the eastern and western Iraqi borders. This illustrates important current and future concerns of Iraqi Christians amid geopolitical circumstances. It also poses new questions on the structure and future of Iraq and neighbouring countries.

Another important factor in considering the region's long-term borders is that the Christian Assyrian demography in KRI and Nineveh Plains has the same demography in Northeast Syria and Southeast Turkey (Tur Abdin), similar to the Kurdish demography in KRI which continues the Kurdish demography in Iran, Turkey and Syria.

The Census of 1977

Iraq, like all other Arab and Islamic states with many ethnic and religious minorities, lacks transparency regarding statistics and figures of minorities and their political, religious, social and cultural conditions. However, with the fall of the Saddam regime, many secret documents, statistics and reports were released and became available for researchers.

The Political Department in the General Security Directorate, the former regime's high office concerned with Iraqi religious minorities, noted in the Iraqi census of 1977:

> The results of the latest census of 1977 show Muslims in Iraq are the majority of the population. Their number is 11,474,293 persons; this is around 97% of the overall Iraqi population, which is 11,862,620. Therefore, the other four religious groups (Christians, Yazidis, Mandeans, and Jews) are religious minorities in Iraq. Their numbers are as follows: (Christians) 253,478 i.e., 2.14% of the Iraqi population; (Yazidis) 102,191 i.e., 0.86%, (Mandeans) 15, 937 i.e., 0.14% and (Jews) 381 i.e., 0.01%.

However, the study's most dangerous indicator is the continuous decrease in the annual population growth of Iraqi Christians. The paragraph titled 'Population growth indicators between religious groups in Iraq 1947–1977' notes:

> The population growth average between Christians was very close to that of Muslims for the period 1947–1957. The average was more than 3% per year. We notice the rapid decrease in growth to 1.6% between 1957 and 1965. Despite the fact that this is a very small average, it *continued to decrease rapidly* to reach 0.73% per year between 1965 and 1977. This is a very low average and is close to the population growth average in developed countries.

According to Operation World in the United Kingdom, the Christian population's annual growth in Iraq in 2002 was negative: -0.9%!

Table 7.1. Figures for Christian Demography in Iraq[6]:

Year	Total	Muslims	Christians	Jews	Yazidis	Mandeans
1947	4,562,000	4,256,000 = 93.34%	149,000 = 3.27%	117,000 = 2.56%	40,000 = 0.88%	
1957	6,339,960	6,057,493 = 95.54%	206,206 = 3.25%	4,906 = 0. 07%	55,885 = 0.88%	11,825 = 0.18%
1977	11,862,620	11,474,293 = 96.7%	253,478 = 2.14%	381 =0.003%	102,191 = 0.86%	15,937 = 0.14%

---

[6] For more details see: *Buratha News Agency*, (published 29 April 2012) http://burathanews.com/arabic/reports/155007.

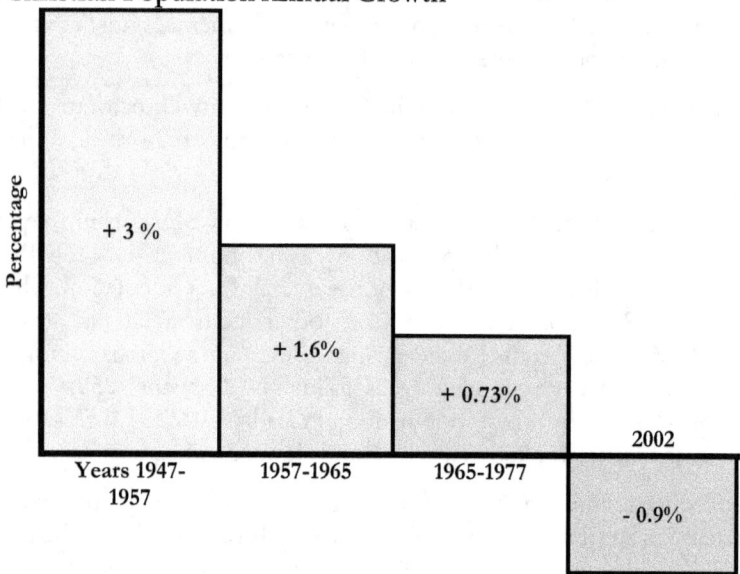

Iraqi Christian Population Annual Growth

Administrative and Geographic Origin of Nineveh Plains

The term 'Nineveh Plains' had never been used in administrative or geographical contexts the way it is used now in the Iraqi official documentation or administrative structures. After the Saddam regime was toppled in 2003, 'Nineveh Plains' emerged in the Iraqi political and media discussions and hence by the international media.

The term was created and developed because the plains became a sanctuary for Christians fleeing violence and organised terrorism which targeted them in the cities under Iraqi central government jurisdiction, such as Mosul, Baghdad, Basra, Anbar, and other areas in which Christians existed. In contrast, the Peshmerga forces and Asayesh security forces who receive their orders from Kurdistan region, had created on the Nineveh Plains, a stable atmosphere, except for some rare security breaches. Also, the Nineveh Plains had a historical Christian presence; for many IDPs, it had been their homeland before they migrated to bigger cities to seek better education and employment opportunities. Therefore, most IDPs in the Nineveh Plains after 2003 had simply returned to where they originally came from. The same applied to Yazidis— particularly those who living in Mosul and who sought security in the Yazidi towns and villages in the Nineveh Plains. Having the Plains transformed into a haven for Christians and Yazidis transformed the 'Nineveh Plains' into a term indicating an administrative area secured for minorities.

Despite the near universal acceptance of the term 'Nineveh Plains' and its constitutive administrative units—including Telkeif, Hamdaniya, Sheikhan districts along with their sub-districts and villages, and the Baashiqa sub-district that is under the jurisdiction of the central district of Mosul (Mosul city, the capital of the Nineveh governorate)—the geography and its administrative formation has been debated since 1991 because of changes in administration and security control over it, or some parts of it.

Nineveh Plains administrative composition[7]:

1. District of Telkeif, whose centre (capital) is the city of Telkeif, has two sub-districts, Alqosh, Fayda and Wana, and many villages.

2. District of Hamdaniya, whose centre is the city of Baghdeda (Qaraqosh or Hamdaniya), has two sub-districts, Bartilla and Nimrod, and many villages.

3. District of Sheikhan, whose centre is the city of Ain-Safni (Sheikhan), has the sub-districts Zelkan, Qasrok, Baadrah and Kalakji.

4. Sub-district of Baashiqa, which is under the district of Mosul city centre.

The cultural, religious and ethnic composition[8]:

Nineveh Plains, considered Iraq's most religiously, nationally, and culturally diverse area, contrasts with other, homogenous Iraqi cities. The Nineveh Plains contains Muslims, Christians, Yazidis and Kaka'aies, the latter of whom, despite being registered in the Iraqi identity directorate as Muslims, maintain their unique religious identity. Denominationally, the Nineveh Plains contains Sunni and Shia Muslims, as well as Catholic, Orthodox and Church of the East Christians. Arabs, Kurds, Chaldeans, Syriacs, and Assyrians live in the plains (the term 'Suryaye' is widely used to refer to Chaldeans, Syriacs, and Assyrians). The Shabaks, considered one of the mains ethnic/cultural groups of the Nineveh Plains, are mostly Shia Muslims with some Sunni Muslims, yet they dispute their national identity; some consider themselves to be Kurds, while others identify as Arabs. The third fraction presents themselves as being just Shabaks. The Arabic, Kurdish and Syriac languages are spoken on the Nineveh Plains, in addition to the language of the Shabak.

Economic Resources:

The 'Nineveh Plains' includes the area's basic economic resources of agriculture and animal husbandry, in addition to some food industries. Along with widespread cultivation of wheat and barley, Baghdeda (Qaraqosh) has the basic production of poultry and calves for Nineveh and neighbouring governorates. Baashiqa and its surroundings produce olive oil, Tahini, pickles

---

[7] For more details see: 'Ethnic Map of East Niveh Plains' *Umap*, https://umap.openstreetmap.fr/uk-ua/map/ethnic-map-of-east-nineveh-plains_80116#10/36.3909/43.1296.

[8] 'Iraq: Dreams of an autonomous Christian province in the Nineveh Plain are dashed' *Vatican Insider*, (22.07.2014) www.lastampa.it/2014/07/22/vaticaninsider/iraq-dreams-of-an-autonomous-christian-province-in-the-nineveh-plain-are-dashed-zb9qAzCWPrZezvH4fUaytN/pagina.html.

and related products.

Given the area's proximity to Mosul, the economic resources also include jobs related to small-scale industries as well as factories producing decorative stones. The Nineveh Plains is located between two mains roads, one of which connects Mosul, Iraq's second-largest city, and Erbil, the KRG capital. The second main road connects Mosul with Turkey through Duhok—hence the areas close to the borders of Mosul have now become important economic centres.

Religious Tourism:[9]

Despite the lack of infrastructure and weak support from the relevant federal and local governments, the Nineveh Plains have played a big role in religious tourism, with the potential to grow exponentially, since it includes many shrines and religious sites of all different religions.

The Plains' many important Christian monasteries include:

1. St. Hurmezd monastery in Alqosh, which is now run by the Chaldean Church (it was historically established and developed as one of the Church of the East's monasteries).
2. St. Matthew monastery in Mount Maqloub, which is one of the most ancient monasteries of the Orthodox Church.
3. St. Behnam Monastery in Namroud, which is the one and only monastery that belongs to the Syriac Catholic Church in Iraq.

Important religious shrines include the Prophet Nahum Shrine in Alqosh, which was formerly a synagogue and remains an important site for Jews. It is believed to be where the prophet Nahum is buried. Furthermore, the most sacred shrine in Yazidism, the Shrine of Sheikh Aadi in Lalish Valley, is located in the Nineveh Plains, in addition to other shrines in Yazidis towns also in the plains. For Shi'ite Muslims, the shrine of Imam Ridha, who was one of the twelve imams of Shi'ism, is located in the Nineveh Plains.

In addition to these religious sites, the Nineveh Plains has many archaeological sites such as Mesopotamia, Dour Sharokeen, and Nimrud (which are two Assyrian capitals), as well as being the location of Khanas, where the winged bulls ('Lamassus') were produced and shipped to Mosul via the Khousar river.

Let´s have a closer look to the Christian Demography in Nineveh Plain and its Administrative Geography.[10]

The Christian presence in the Nineveh Plains owes its strength to its historical roots, which go back to pre-Christian times, since the plains surrounds the city of Nineveh (modern-day Mosul)—one of the most

---

[9] 'Nineveh Plains' *Wikipedia* https://en.wikipedia.org/wiki/Nineveh_plains
[10] Otmar Oehring, *Christians and Yazidis in Iraq: Current Situation and Prospects*. (Berlin: Konrad-Adenauer-Stiftung, 2017), 13-15.

important capitals of the Assyrian Empire—as well as Dour Sharoukeen (modern-day Khorsobad), which was also one of the ancient Assyrian capitals. The Christian presence, therefore, is the most important demographic continuation for the Assyrian national existence.

A further strength of the Christian demography in Nineveh Plains is that they make up most of the key town and administrative centres that form the Nineveh Plains. Christians make up around 95% of Baghdeda (Qaraqosh, Capital of Hamdaniya district) and used to be the majority in Telkeif District just before the mass Chaldean migration to the United States of America because of an Arabisation policy; the city now has a majority of Sunni Arabs.

This also applies to the purely Christian city of Alqosh. The city of Bartilla once had a majority Christian population before the organised demographic change of the early 1980s. Now the surrounding Shabaks have increasing political and economic capabilities. The Christians in Baashiqa make up around 25% of the population with the Yazidis as the majority with 60%. The Christian demography in the Nineveh Plains suffers a key weakness of semi-detachment from neighbouring Christians with no connection on the ground among one another, in contrast to the Yazidis and Shabaks.

Christian Churches Diversity

The Nineveh Plains has a diversity of traditional Christian apostolic churches, except the Armenian Church. These include the Syriac Orthodox church, Syriac Catholic Church, Chaldean Catholic church, Assyrian Church of the East, and Ancient Church of the East. The density of these churches varies as they have different locations in the Plains' geography.

For instance: the Syriac Catholic Church, which some consider to be the largest church of the plains, is within the city of Baghdeda (Qaraqosh) while the Syriac Orthodox church has its followers in Bartilla, Baashiqa, Bahzani, Baghdeda, and the villages of Mergi, Lfaf and Maghara on the foot of Mount Maqlob and which are in the St. Matthew diocese.

However, the Chaldean church, which others claim as the largest church in the plains, is situated in the northern parts of the Nineveh Plains, in the cities of Telkeif, Alqosh through Batnaya, Baqofa, Telsquf, and in Jambour, Bandawaye, Sheikhan, Karmles (south of the plain). While the Assyrian Church of the East is present in small villages near Alqosh such as Sharafiya, or on the road connecting Alqosh to Sheikhan such as Ein Baqri, Dashqotan, Karanjo, Perozawa, Garmawa and Sheikhan; the inhabitants of these villages have roots from Hakari Assyrians (south of Turkey) who fled their country to Iraq during the Ottoman Genocide in WW1 against the Christians of the Ottoman Empire: Armenians, Assyrians Syriacs, and Greek. The Assyrians of Rekan area of Heesh, Estip and Maydan villages in Duhok governorate settled in Telkeif in the mid-1970s after being deported by the former Baath regime.[11]

The importance of the Nineveh Plains for Christians

The Nineveh Plains is important the Christians of Iraq for many reasons. The foremost include:

- It represents their deeply-rooted national and cultural identity going back to the centuries before Christ. They are the heirs of the Assyrians of the Assyrian empire whose mains capital was Nineveh (current Mosul). The plains encompasse other Assyrian capitals and cities such as Nimrud, Khorsabad, Khans, and others.

- With the great and continuous decline of Christian demography in Iraq, the Nineveh Plains is one of only two concentrated areas of Christians. (The other area is the governorate of Duhok in the Kurdistan region and some areas of Erbil, specifically Ankawa.) This important demographic presence in the Nineveh Plains has an additional important power component inextricably linked with Christian demography in Duhok governorate. This makes them vital, especially if the Nineveh Plains joins the Kurdistan region in the near or medium term, because this makes interaction between the Nineveh Plains and Duhok vital and influential in the long-term strategy of connecting with the presence of Assyrian Syriac Christians in northeast Syria and southeast Turkey (Tur Abdin).

- The Christian community in the Nineveh Plains has the economic resources of the vast land and the agricultural, industrial, and commercial establishments that have grown and developed cumulatively and have not been affected by the political unrest and conflict in Iraq (pre-ISIS). The Nineveh Plains, unlike the Christian villages and towns of Duhok, has not been subjected to displacement and destruction, which created an atmosphere of local stability sufficient for developing these resources.

- The Nineveh Plains, like the whole Christian presence, has many economic and academic capabilities. This makes investment in these resources for economic development in the Nineveh Plains possible and also makes them, especially in the parts of the plains that includes Yazidis and Christians (from Alqosh and Telsquf to Baashiqa and Bahzani), an environment suitable for economic activities that cannot be achieved in the rest of Iraqi denominated by Islamic environment, especially the Sunni and Shia Arabs.

- The Nineveh Plains, unlike all other Iraqi regions (except for the city of Kirkuk), is characterised by a diversity of religious, ethnic and cultural minorities without a specific identity holding a majority. This allows all its

---

[11] For more details, see: Walker, Frank: 'The Mission to Iraq' *Leben. A Journal of Reformed Life* 2/1 (2006). http://www.leben.us/volume-2-volume-2-issue-1/182-the-mission-to-iraq.

minority components, including Christians, to play a greater role in political, administrative, economic, and community activities in the plains. It is the right environment for Christians to play their role as a bridge between these different minorities.

• The Christian presence in the Nineveh Plains is characterised by its concentration and heavy weight in the centres of the administrative units, which enabled the Christians to assume important administrative positions in the administrative units of the Nineveh Plains (the mayor of Telkeif, Hamdaniyah districts, and mayor of Alqosh sub-district).

Nineveh Plains under Ba'ath regime

After the Ba'ath regime seized power by a military coup in June 1968, to some extent, it formed a secular regime with Arabian fascist policies imposed on non-Arab people such as the Kurds, Assyrians, and Turkmen. It later shifted to add an Islamic dimension to its rhetoric, practices, and policies, especially while the Iraqi-Iran war was still waging, then followed by the First Gulf War (Battle for Kuwait) led by the USA, and then the long economic siege imposed on Iraq.

The Nineveh Plains, the only area of Iraq without Muslims and Arabs as the majority of its inhabitants, became a target of the regime's Arabianisation and Islamisation policies. Since the 1970s, in parallel with forcibly displacing the Kurds and Assyrians from Iraqi Kurdistan followed by the collapse of the Kurdistan revolution in 1975 with the signing of the Algerian treaty and the Arabisation of large swaths of the Kurdish region (for example, the Slevani area in Duhok governorate), the regime adopted the policy of Arabising the Nineveh Plains and particularly its Christian territory. This policy expanded during the Iraqi-Iranian war by laws granting properties to Arab civil servants and military personnel in the Christian plains of Nineveh in Telkeif, Baghdeda (Qaraqosh), Bartilla, and other areas. Furthermore, these practices were followed by Islamising policies of building mosques in these areas and villages despite the light presence of Muslim families there. However, the regime intentionally neglected providing health, economy and education services to the the Nineveh Plains leaving it dependent on services provided in Mosul and hence under the Islamic Arabian influence. Also, the regime had tightened its grip on Nineveh Plains through its security agents despite the plains never any sort of demonstrations or opposition to the regime's policy even when the Iraqi revolution broke out in the aftermath of Kuwait war. Many Christian young people from the Nineveh Plains escaped the compulsory military service during the Iraqi-Iranian war by fleeing to Iranian territory through Kurdistan and then seeking asylum in the west. The same applied to many Christian families who fled their villages in the Nineveh Plains after the end of the Iraqi-Iranian war and as a result of the international sanctions imposed on Iraq; they sought asylum in neighbouring countries and then in the west.[12]

Pre-ISIS Nineveh Plains 2003-2014

The collapse of the Saddam regime in April 2003 was not just a regime change like other coups that took place in the Middle East and elsewhere. Saddam's totalitarian regime had held an iron grip on individuals and families of Iraqi community, and hence on all of the Iraqi state institutions; this resulted in the state itself collapsing, not just the regime. As a consequence, Iraq after 2003 was transformed into a territory of political parties with their loyal militias that imposed their own rule of law in particular areas.

The weak and scattered minorities without influential political and military establishments and the wealth of the Christians and Mandeans made them an easy, attractive target in the mid-south Iraq area by jihadist Sunni and Shia militias, as well as by organised crime gangs. The Shlomo Documentation Organization stated that 1,174 Christians including 14 clergymen have been killed between 2003 and 2014 (pre-ISIS) in territories under the Iraqi central government. In the terrorist assault on The Lady of Survival Church in Baghdad on 31 October 2010, 53 Christians were martyred while attending church service. There were 114 attacks on churches in Baghdad, Mosul, Kirkuk, Anbar, some of which have been targeted more than once. Christians were also kidnapped for ransom. [13]

All of these systematic assaults based on religious identity left the Christians with no choice but to flee to safer areas on the Nineveh Plains and Kurdistan region, or apply for resettlement visas to western countries. Some cities, such as Ramadi, Khalidiya and Habaniya, no longer have any Christians, whereas their presence has considerably decreased in the key cities of Baghdad, Basra and Mosul. Baghdad had an estimated 250,000 Christians before 2003, this number has decreased to approximately 40,000. Around 16 churches have been shut down in Baghdad. Therefore, Christians fled to Nineveh Plains as a safe territory for the following reasons:

- The stable security situation in the area which had been under the command of Peshmerga forces and Kurdistan Asayesh (security personnel).
- Almost all of the Christians had family roots in the Nineveh Plains, but left it years ago to seek better financial conditions in larger cities.
- The plains had a generally Christian-embracing atmosphere.
- The Arabic language taught in schools and spoken at official directorates and local markets made it easier for them to integrate.

---

[12] Veldkamp, Joel, 'The End of Christianity in Iraq, Part I: 1920-2003' *In All Things,* (published 6 March 2017) https://inallthings.org/the-end-of-christianity-in-iraq-part-i-1920-2003/.

[13] Veldkamp, Joel, 'The End of Christianity in Iraq, Part II: 2003-2017' *In All Things,* (published 7 March 2017). https://inallthings.org/the-end-of-christianity-in-iraq-part-ii-2003-2017/.

Whereas in Kurdistan, they would face difficulty with a Kurdish language they had never studied or spoken.

From the early days after April 2003, there had been multiple displacement waves to Nineveh Plain; for instance, in 2004, 2006, and 2010. The Yazidi community, like the Christians, also fled the larger cities, especially Mosul city in which no Yazidi person remained when ISIS took control. They went to Nineveh Plains and the Yazidi community complexes. This massive displacement to the plains created a huge pressure on the economic market as well as the infrastructure.

The table below from a survey conducted by Christian Aid Program – Nohadra – Iraq CAPNI, is a sample of the number and percentage of displaced Christian families who fled Iraqi cities to the Christian towns and villages in Nineveh Plains (See the table 7.1 below; the figures are from October 2006). For every three families, the fourth is a displaced one!!! The percentage is even more than in the governorate of Dohuk.

Some people incorrectly assumed that ISIS appeared, expanded, and controlled two-thirds of Iraqi territory including Nineveh Plains in summer 2014 as the result of 'cross-border terrorism' (as described by an Iraqi diplomat at a conference in the United Nation's sub-HQ on February 2018 in Vienna, Austria). However, ISIS had been present and growing with its jihadist ideology in the Sunni Arab community of Mosul city and surrounding territory. It resulted from the inflammatory rhetoric of the Baath regime's 'Faith Campaign' in 1996 that depicted the sanctions and its health and economic consequences on Iraqi living conditions as part of a western 'crusade' against Islamic countries.[14]

Table 7.1. Displaced families

Place	Residing families before exodus	Displaced families due to exodus	Place	Residing families before exodus	Displaced families due to exodus
Telkeif	1000	400	Ein Baqre	35	6
Batnaya	650	400	Karanjo	35	8
Baqofa	116	40	Dashqotan	20	0
Tellsquf	1100	400	Pirizawa	30	10
Sharafiya	90	21	Garmawa	5	1
Alqosh	1700	520	Sheikhan	200	150
Bartilla	2250	750	Baashiqa	750	315
Qaraqosh	5000	1050	Bahzany	155	50
Karmles	600	180	**Total**	13736	4301

---

[14] John L. Allen Jr., 'Trauma forms the invisible ruins ISIS left behind on the Nineveh Plains.' *Crux. Taking the Catholic Pulse*, (15 June 2018) https://cruxnow.com/crux-nineveh/2018/06/15/trauma-forms-the-invisible-ruins-isis-left-behind-on-the-nineveh-plains/.

Mosul city and the governorate of Nineveh have been an Arab Sunni stronghold with deeply political Islamic roots. Because of its Arabic ideology and its well-known stances against non-Arab components of Kurds and Assyrians, it formed, alongside the governorate of Anbar, a fertile environment for Sunni Jihadist organisations. The ISIS was publicly present in Mosul city for years until they controlled it completely and imposed their Sharia (laws) on the Mosul community and everyday life including the Christians.

Churches used to regularly pay money to the jihadi organisations in return for their own safety. These organisations pressured Christians to not show crosses or ring church bells. Christians also had to pay to protect their supermarkets and economic projects. The religious rhetoric along with education became jihadist rhetoric. The lifestyle, culture, and social environment in Mosul all came under the grip of Islamic Sharia.

These factors, along with the absence of the rule of law, created space to target the Christians, their churches, and their properties. More clergy were martyred in Mosul than all other Iraqi cities combined. These terrorist acts forced the Christians of Mosul to leave the city seeking security. Nineveh Plains was one of these areas where Christians from Mosul and the rest of Iraq headed to, something that created service and economic pressure on the host community in the plains.

The tense atmosphere of Mosul resulted in the Nineveh Plains communities fearing to connect with or seek services in Mosul and seeking alternatives. For example, the targeting of university buses that had been transporting students from Nineveh Plains to Mosul University on 2 May 2010 was perceived as an explicit threat. The jihadist ideology expanded to the Sunni Arabian community in Nineveh Plain; this could be explicitly witnessed through religious rhetoric on mosque podiums as well the lifestyle atmosphere. Once ISIS controlled Telkeif, many in the Sunni Arab community joined the insurgents and looted Christian, Yazidi, and Shia properties.

Nineveh Plains under ISIS

When ISIS gained control over the city of Mosul in June 2014, the Nineveh Plains, along with the governorates of Iraqi Kurdistan, turned into a safe haven for Mosul Christians and other non-Muslim, and non-Sunni communities fleeing from ISIS. Most observers and analysts believed that ISIS would, after Mosul, go to Baghdad through the governorates and Sunni territories.

However, for reasons that are still unclear, on 3 August, ISIS advanced to the Yazidi-dominated Sinjar region where it committed the terrible crimes of genocide, sexual slavery, and kidnapping, as well as destroying public and private properties. Sinjar was a warning for the Nineveh Plains, to which ISIS headed on 6 August, and so the Nineveh Plains gained a three-day advantage in which its inhabitants were able to escape to the governorates of Duhok and Erbil. When ISIS moved towards Erbil, the coalition air force intervened and stopped their advance so that the front lines were between the Peshmerga and ISIS. The lines remained unchanged until the retaking of the Nineveh Plains in the summer of 2016.

It is a painful coincidence that on the night of August 6, 81 years ago (1933), the Semile massacre began against the Christian Assyrians and its memory remains stuck in the collective memory of the people, and the wound is renewed again on 6 August 2014.

Thus, the Nineveh Plains, for the first time in its history, was completely emptied from its Christians, Yazidis, Shia Shabaks and, and groups of Sunni Shabaks. Most Arabs and Sunni Shabaks in Telkeif, Salamiya, Nimrod and Fadhiliya regions remained coexisting under and with ISIS. When front lines became stable, people returned to cities, towns, and villages such as Alqosh, Khatara, Jambur, Busan, Telsquf which had been abandoned out of fear of ISIS . In August 2014, Telsquf remained ten days under ISIS until it was liberated by the Peshmerga.

The occupation of the Nineveh Plains caused tremendous damage to personal and public properties, in addition to religious and archaeological sites and buildings, as well as infrastructure, shops, agricultural and industrial facilities, and others. The short and long-term effects of ISIS control of the Nineveh Plains have gone beyond the enormous physical and economic destruction that requires decades to rehabilitate. Physical destruction has moral and psychological effects and harms individual and collective human dignity. It also affected the links between the community components, especially among Christians and Yazidis, on the one hand, and Muslims, specifically the Sunnis, on the other. Restoring these damaged links, among other things, are the challenges of return to the Nineveh Plains after ISIS.

Post-ISIS Nineveh Plains 2016: Regaining Control on Nineveh Plain

I personally hesitate to use the term 'liberation' from ISIS for this term contains many meanings which remains incomplete. I would use the term 'retaking'; it refers to the reality on the ground. What has been achieved is no more than regaining security, military, and administrative control over the areas once under ISIS.

The Kurdistan Peshmerga forces had been on the thousand-kilometre frontline with ISIS stretched from the Syrian border in northwest to Diyala in the mid-east of Iraq. Therefore, retaking control over areas under ISIS from Sinjar to Kirkuk through Nineveh Plains should have been launched from Kurdistan territory, and Peshmerga forces should have participated in military operations. Despite the political conflict between Baghdad and Erbil along with their future ambitions some sort of agreement between Baghdad and Erbil concerning territory control after the retaking phase was necessary. This sort of agreement, some believed to have been American-sponsored, allowed the relaunching of military operations to defeat ISIS and regain control over the areas they once held.[15]

In Nineveh Plains, the Peshmerga forces would retake south of Mosul Dam then west to the south of Batnaya, Baashiqa to further west of Hamdaniya, while the Iraqi Army on the other side along with the Public Mobilisations Units (Alhashid) would retake the rest of the areas along with Mosul city till the Syrian border. Hence, the security and military control over Nineveh Plains shifted from being purely under Peshmerga and Asayesh control before ISIS to an area divided administratively between KRI and Iraqi federal government.

With the retaking of Nineveh Plains, the villages of Baqofa, Telsquf up to Alqosh, Baashiqa, and Bahzani up to St. Matthew were under Peshmerga jurisdiction. Whereas Telkeif, Bartilla, Karmless and Baghdeda (Qaraqosh) became under the control of the Iraqi Army and the Public Mobilisation Units (Alhashid). The Christians in Nineveh Plains had greatly feared this scattering and tearing apart between two security administrations and two constitutional administrations.

Taking back the Nineveh Plain, especially the east bank of Mosul city, revealed the enormous destruction resulting from ISIS control over these areas and resulting military operations. The people of the Nineveh Plains have been under great shock of the devastation to their own properties such as houses, trade businesses, and farmland. Also damaged were the infrastructure and service units of schools, health centres, water networks, electricity, and official directorates. The ISIS even intentionally demolished the churches and religious institutions of Christians, Yazidis, and Shia.

Nineveh Plains After Kurdistan referendum

In the summer of 2017, after regaining control of the ISIS military zones, the Iraqi political scene and KRI faced a new challenge of the Kurdistan Democratic Party KDP to call for a referendum on the right to self-determination and independence of Kurdistan from Iraq. The demand for self-determination is not new to Kurdish political parties. However, in Kurdistan, this demand cannot be isolated from its consequences on regional

---

[15] Michael Knights / Yousif Kalian, ' Confidence- and Security-Building Measures in the Nineveh Plains' *The Washington Institute,* (published14 July 2017) https://www.washingtoninstitute.org/policy-analysis/view/confidence-and-security-building-measures-in-the-nineveh-plains.

and international stability. Hence, the call for the referendum was unanimously rejected by all countries from the neighbouring countries, influential Middle Eastern countries and European and North American powers.

From the point of view of Christians, the referendum held in the Nineveh Plains reflected the big question about the administrative subordination between Iraqi federal government and KRI. The call for the referendum and its aftermath, followed by the expansion of the Iraqi army and the militias of the Popular Mobilisation and the decline of the Peshmerga caused confusion. Displaced people were less inclined to return to their homes in the Nineveh Plains. People identifying as Christian had been divided between the military and security administration of KRG (Baqofah, Telsquf, and the rest of the northern Nineveh Plains and the villages of Jabal Maqloub), and the region of the military and security administration of the central government administrative (Telkeif, Batnaya, Bahzani, Bartilla, Qaraqosh and Karmless).

The open question remains about reunifying the Nineveh Plains and restoring the natural, living, economic and social interaction between its regions. The complex and subjective answer is not limited to the wishes of the people of the plains, but includes interests and aspirations of Iraqi Shia, Kurdish and Sunni decisionmakers and the neighbouring countries. The Shia led by Iran and Sunni led by Saudi Arabia have turned Iraq and Syria into a conflicted arena that does not place a high priority on the interests of vulnerable minorities.

The de facto stability of Nineveh Plains encouraged more families to return home. Local and international humanitarian organisations, including United Nations organisations, helped fill the vacuum caused by the almost complete absence of the Iraqi government in reconstruction programs. (Appendix 5)

All returnees to the Plains faced significant challenges. The first and most basic challenge facing the displaced is the harm and destruction, partial or total, of their homes (see table in Appendix 4) and the looting and pillaging of all their household possessions. Families cannot deal with this challenge because their limited resources had already been exhausted during their displacement. International organisations could only partially rehabilitate the destroyed houses.[16]

The most important challenges are:

Plurality of security and military forces[17]: The Peshmerga and Asayish

---

[16] Yousif Kalian 'The Fate of Minorities in Post-ISIS Syria and Iraq' *Syria Deeply*, (published 10. January 2018) https://www.newsdeeply.com/syria/articles/2018/01/10/the-fate-of-minorities-in-post-isis-syria-and-iraq.

[17] Julie Ahn / Maeve Campbell / Pete Knoetgen, *The Politics of Security in Ninewa: Preventing an ISIS Resurgence in Northern Iraq*. Report. (Cambridge: Harvard Kennedy School / Office of Iraq Affairs, 2018).

forces in the Nineveh Plains areas under the control of KRG that offers a feeling of individual and collective safety, the Iraqi central government does not. For example, the military and security administration of the Christian-dominated areas under the control of the central government are shared with three politically affiliated militias: The Babylonian militia in Telkeif and Batnaya, the Shabaki popular mobilisation militia (Brigade 30) in Bartilla, Baashiqa, and Bahzani, and the Nineveh Plains Units in Qaraqosh and Karmless. The militias never provided stability and security for the people, and this is not expected in the Nineveh Plains.

Administrative Structure and Reference: Although the central government has officially recognised the administrative unit of the Nineveh Plains, many administrative units exist on the ground. For example, Sheikhan district, officially linked to the governorate of the Nineveh, and Alqosh sub-district, officially under Telkeif, both are practically under the authority of KRG. This duplication may not have much impact on the daily life of the Nineveh Plains people, where its impact is limited to several government departments and documents, but it is an effective challenge in any political process related to the normalisation of administrative and security conditions for the Nineveh Plains, or the application of the Iraqi Constitutional Article 140.

Political Intersections: All Iraqi political parties, with limited exceptions, have religious or sectarian affiliations. One reason might be the weak identification with the Iraqi state. The constitutional, legislative and administrative restructuring and political instability of post-2003 Iraq led to political forces using violence to achieve their demands. The plethora of political organisations active on the Nineveh Plains reflects its ethnic, religious, and sectarian diversity. These organisations seek to expand their popular base in various ways, including the misuse of security and administrative services. This puts additional strains on the daily lives of people of the area and threatens any practical programs to restore trust and peaceful coexistence among the communities.

Economic Challenges: The economic challenges of returning to the Nineveh Plains are not limited to the enormous destruction from ISIS or the accompanying military operations to regain control. Considerable medium- and long-term funding must transcend the complicated political, security and administrative situation in order to rehabilitate economic activity that ranges from small workshops to medium-sized activities (industrial and agricultural production plants) and large-scale livestock enterprises, e.g., area of Qaraqosh. This challenge is compounded by the total absence of the Iraqi state and the lack of financial resources. Funds are limited to the contributions of the already affected citizens and the humanitarian

---

https://www.hks.harvard.edu/sites/default/files/degree%20programs/MPP/files/Finalised%20PAE_Ahn_Campbell_Knoetgen.pdf

organisations operating in the region, whose limited resources cannot cover the needs.

Public-Service Challenges: the Iraqi state neglected for many decades the infrastructure and basic services on the Nineveh Plains. This neglect increased after 2003, especially with the conflict between the federal government in Baghdad and KRG. During the ISIS occupation, the deterioration of these structures and destruction increased. This has resulted in a lack of quantitative and qualitative minimum in basic sectors such as health, education, electricity, water, sanitation, and roads, which increases the burden of life for returnees.

This context shapes the challenges of rehabilitating places of worship, church-operated institutions, and service centres that include kindergartens, youth centres, welfare centres, sports and social centres. Rehabilitating worship places materially helps maintain identity and a sense of identity. Thus, the houses of worship are important in the process of return and stability. They send a message of future reassurance, which the central government has failed to do. This reconstruction has been left to the targeted communities with limited resources or international humanitarian organisations, which usually do not rehabilitate places of worship.

Challenges of Community Coexistence: Since the establishment of the modern Iraqi state, it has not had the strong cohesion that preserves society from dissonance and conflict between its components. During most stages of the history of contemporary Iraq, the state, its political system, and its military and security tools were part of this conflict; for example, the bloody conflict with Kurds and Shias.

The rapid expansion of ISIS control over nearly two-thirds of Iraq demonstrates the lack of community cohesion. The politicians of Iraq, as well as the people of the communities targeted by ISIS, did not know that many Sunni Arabs had aligned with the ISIS and joined and participated in the terrorist operations against components of their community that shared daily life in the cities and areas controlled by ISIS.

This makes it impossible in some places and difficult in other places to expect community peaceful coexistence based on trust and mutual respect. People remember bloody, painful events in their lives. The government does not have any real program to deal with this memory and offer victims of ISIS victims their legal, moral, and material rights such as transitional justice and accountability of those involved in crimes of ISIS. It does not compensate the victims and reassure victims that what happened will not be repeated again.

The official and institutional Iraq still has not dealt with what happened as an existential threat to the social structure. So far, no national debate has been held about what happened. Why did it happen? How did it happen?

How could its recurrence be prevented?

The constitution, Iraqi legislation, curricula of education, and political and religious discourse have not changed nor addressed the causes of the disaster. Hence, it is almost impossible for non-Muslim minorities victimised by ISIS to trust returning to predominantly Arab Sunni areas. For example, Christians and Yazidis find it almost too difficult to return to the city of Mosul or the city of Telkeif.

Peaceful coexistence among the communities of the Nineveh Plains is a big and growing challenge, especially with the recruitment of religious and sectarian political parties and their affiliated and influential militias in the Nineveh Plains. These political parties and militias existed even before ISIS with activities in the areas of Bartilla and Hamdaniyah by the Shia Shabak, and in Telkeif by the Sunni Arabs.[18] This reflected in the fact that the number of returnees to Bartilla is less than the rest of the areas; in Telkeif, returnees are almost non-existent.

Post ISIS Challenges in the Nineveh Plains

While these challenges affect all ethnic, religious and sectarian components in Nineveh Plains, the impact on the Christian community in the post-ISIS period relates to future Christian demography, which is threatened in many cities and areas of the Nineveh Plains.

Several factors affect Christian demography:

- The Christian population in the Nineveh Plains has been dispersed into isolated, unconnected islands and cities. Only some villages surrounding Alqos, and two villages near Telsquf and Batnaya are connected. The six Christian-majority cities in the Nineveh Plains are: Batnaya, Telsquf, Alqosh, Bartilla, Qaraqosh and Karmless). The other four Christian-inhabited cities are: Telkeif (majority Arabs), Sheikhan (majority Yazidis and Kurds), Baashiqa and Bahzani (65% Yazidis). The unknown number of Christian villages in Nineveh Plains are distributed according to administrative units as:

Telkeif: The centre (mixed with Arab majority now) and Batnaya.

Alqosh area: The area centre, Baqofah, Telsquf, Sharafiya, Bandwaye, Ein Baqre, Deshkotan, and Karango.

Sheikhan district: The centre (a small Christian population), Perozawa, and Garmawah.

Baashiqa district: The city centre and Bahzani (25%), the villages of Al-

---

[18] UNDP 'Social Cohesion Road Map for the Nineveh Plains launched in Bartela' UNDP Press Release, (published 14 March 2018) http://www.iq.undp.org/content/iraq/en/home/presscenter/pressreleases/2018/03/14/social-cohesion-road-map-for-the-nineveh-plains-launched-in-bert.html.

Faf. Mergy and Maghara.

Bartilla district: The Christian city centre (the percentage decreased from almost 100% in 1960s to 40% at present with Shabaks in the majority).

Al-Hamdaniya district: The city centre and Karmless.

This Christian demography is unlike the Yezidi, Shabaks, and Arabs, who are all located in urban and contiguous rural areas.

- Schemes of continuous demographic change began with the former regime and continued after 2003. In Telkeif, this was done by Sunni Arabs supported by Sunni political forces and with Gulf States funding. The Shia Shabaks supported by Shia parties and by Iranian funding also became demographic weapons. This has recently increased, post- ISIS, especially by the Shia Shabaks, with the political support of the central government and the military and security influence of Shia militias.

The weakness and fragmentation of Christian demography, on the one hand, and the weakness and fragmentation of effort and the political influence of Christian parties, on the other, means the Christians have a very weak and futile ability to face these demographic changes. In addition, the central government imposes difficulties and obstacles for obtaining documents such as identity papers. Citizens must visit the relevant departments in the centre of the city of Mosul. This is also the case when returning to official government work or to study at the university in Mosul. Many avoid this, which leads to not returning to Mosul or the Nineveh Plains but rather staying and integrating in the areas of displacement in the Kurdistan region or immigration.

- In parallel with the Christian demographic dispersion in the Nineveh Plains, Christians have a political dispersion and disagreement, albeit in a much more extreme manner, over the political vision of the Plains' future, its administrative structure and its dependence between the centre and the Kurdistan region.

This lack of agreement results from the delayed start of explicitly ethnic political activity of the Christians of the Nineveh Plains. Historically, and even today, they submitted to the influence of the non-Christians powerful parties or the majority parties. Furthermore, because the Nineveh Plains is a field of conflict between the federal government and KRI, the Christians' vision of the plains was/is divided between the influence of the centre (both Sunni and Shia) and KRG.

The Christian political forces could not even agree upon the demand to create a Nineveh Plains Province. The two members of Assyrian Democratic Movement, one of the largest Christian parties in the Iraqi parliament, voted on 26 September 2016 in favour of a decision not to change the administrative boundaries of the Nineveh governorate. Also, the Assyrian Chaldean political parties and Assyrian Democratic Movement did not agree to include the Nineveh Plains in the territories subjected to Article 140 of the Iraqi Constitution. This political dispersion and the lack of a unified vision has caused the Christian political and ecclesiastical authorities of the Nineveh Plains to miss the opportunity to have influential political forces in Iraq or the international community to support their causes.

Attractive international opportunities encourage continued migration from home. The large diaspora of Iraqi Christians offer more potential than the homeland, making it a magnet for those who remain in Iraq. This weakens the Christian presence and reduces the potential of the Christian community in the Nineveh Plains to face challenges; it becomes easier to escape the challenges and choose migration.

Requirements for sustainable Future

Action must be taken at the community, legislative and executive levels. Programs on the ground must be immediately launched, so as to reassure Christians in the Nineveh Plain that they are real participants in the region's administrative and political decision-making.

First: Self-Community:

- With the dispersed visions and efforts, contradiction and disagreement in many issues caused by the internal struggle within Christian community, it is necessary to launch and commit initiatives and organised frameworks to coordinate the political effort between the Christian political parties, on the one hand, and between them and the church references, on the other. They must agree on common issues and reduce differences and disagreements.

- Because current and future big political forces (Shia, Kurdish and Sunni) influence the future and structure of the political, administrative, and security administration of the Nineveh Plains, it is necessary to work on building political partnerships with these forces to serve a stable, participatory future among its components. With the demographic facts on the Nineveh Plains and its extensions in the Kurdistan region, partnerships with Kurdish forces are vital and positive. To achieve these alliances, especially the Kurdistan ones, the Christian political forces must change the populist, political discourse and Kurdish phobia.

- It is very important to apply Article 140 of the Constitution on the annexation and continuity of the Nineveh Plains with Kurdistan Iraq. The fragile Christian demography throughout Iraq cannot be divided into two separate demographics, each governed by a different constitution, legislations, administrative boundaries, and a different cultural and community atmosphere, especially as the administrative boundaries between KRI and the central Iraqi state will likely become a border between two states.

- It is very important to activate the economically and academically rich large Christian diaspora to invest its resources and potential in economic, educational and sustainable development program. Moreover, mechanisms and institutional frameworks must be developed to guarantee the professionalism and sustainability of these activities.
- While the declining Christian demography cannot be restored, the diaspora's resources and network of institutional relations with churches and international organisations can launch and operate Christian initiatives and institutions that serve the entire Nineveh Plains. This could strengthen the Christian's role in partnerships and social solidarity and compensate for the lost Christian demography.

Local community:

- A dialogue space should be launched to address issues of religious divisions and recommend positive religious discourse that avoids inciting hatred.
- Civil society should initiate programs of peaceful coexistence in which all community components, especially youth, participate in such activities as religious and national festivals, sports, artistic endeavours and media.
- Local administrative councils with secure financial resources could liberate communities from the control of both political parties and the central administration of the Nineveh governorate.
- The district or sub-district councils should determine programs and services in the centres of districts and sub-districts. This is greatly important for Christians throughout the Nineveh Plains, and the Yazidis in Baashiqa. While Christians constitute the absolute majority in Qaraqosh (the centre of Hamdaniyah) and Yazidis in the centre of Baaşhiqa, for example, the Christians in the district of Hamdaniyah and Yazidi in the sub-district of entire Baashiqa (centre and villages) are the minority. When Christians are a minority in the district council or the area, the majority ethnic group of the centre of the district or the sub-district can reject their programmes. For example, the district council of Hamdaniya rejected a request to build a convent for nuns in Qaraqosh. Similarly, the council in the sub-district of Bartilla, with a Muslim majority, rejected the allocation of land to build a church in

the centre of Bartilla, the Christian city. Administrative decisions can assist in the demographic change; for example, the council of the sub-district of Bartilla built a residential complex in Bartilla, despite the Bartilla Christian community disapproval because of concern over demographic change.

National Iraq:

- The Sunni Arabs must note the cumulative backgrounds and the context of the tragedy carried out by ISIS, addressing the roots of the tragedy and seek an atmosphere of acceptance, participation and coexistence.
- A serious national debate must be launched to study the tragedy, its causes, why and how it happened and preventative measures that prevent its recurrence. This is crucially important not only for justice for the victims, but also to reassure future generations that it will not recur. Laws must guarantee transitional justice and criminalise the discourse of hatred.
- All militias must be dismantled or pulled out of the Nineveh Plains. Public safety issues must be transferred to the security services and local police. In addition, in the short and medium-term, joint units between the Peshmerga and the Iraqi army, under control of the international coalition, will give a sense of demographic, social, and political security.
- A time limit must be set to implement the constitutional Article 140 under the supervision of the United Nations and the international community. In this context, adopt the 1957 census, because it is the only professional census conducted in stable political and security conditions without political agendas.
- When applying Article 140, the referendum must be held at level of the city and not the administrative unit. Christians are not a a majority in any administrative units of the Nineveh Plains (both at the level of the district or sub-district), while they form a good or absolute majority in most cities where they live.
- The Nineveh Plains Province Formation Project must be adopted. It gives the components of the Nineveh Plains the power of administrative decision, economic planning and security control over their regions, and gives them a feeling and confidence in their role in building the future of their generations. If the governorate cannot be formed due to the political conflicts of the influential forces, it is important to annex the Christian and Yezidi demographics in the Nineveh Plains with Dohuk Governorate in order to ensure and

strengthen the demographic connection.

- Because the central government is almost completely absent in the reconstruction programs of the Nineveh Plains, it must launch an adequately funded, special program to reconstruct, rehabilitate, and develop infrastructure and services in the Nineveh Plains.
- Reassuring messages must be sent from the central executive and administrative authorities, Nineveh governorate or from the various ministries and departments to the components of the Nineveh Plains. These message should include granting them priority in managing government departments (health, education, services) and avoid provoking any of the religious, sectarian, or national components.
- National-level initiatives should recognise religious, sectarian and national components and respect their role in the history and civilisation of Iraq. This will have a positive role in building the national identity through cross-affiliations. For example, naming residential neighbourhoods, streets, schools, institutions in different Iraqi cities with names of personalities of different components would build bridges between these components. Also, identifying a national holiday for each Iraqi components will have a significantly positive impact on the recognition, coexistence, and mutual respect between these components.

International:
- The international community should combat terrorism and dry up the sources of funding cross-border, systematic violence against religious minorities.
- International forces should recognise genocidal crimes and draw all legal, moral, and material consequences and implications.
- The international community and its institutions or influential countries must force the Iraqi federal government and KRI to commit to respecting human and minority rights in any political, economic, or military support programs.
- International, European or American office should be established to monitor the situation of minorities in the Nineveh Plains and submit periodic reports.
- A small Marshall Project should be launched for the reconstruction and economic development of the region.
- Institutional and community initiatives should support local civil society institutions and programs for peaceful coexistence.

We might be helpless, but never hopeless.

Christian Assyrians, regardless of their ethic nomenclature and church affiliation, are indigenous people of Mesopotamia, the Iraq of today, and they have had, throughout history, a distinguished role that surpassed the country's borders to serve various aspects of humanity. This role includes extending bridges, communication, and dialogue on ideology, culture, and science between East and West.

Their existence is threatened today because of what they were. They are still subjected to a well-planned campaign aimed to eradicate their existence from the Iraqi national memory and physically remove them from the land of their ancestors. This campaign utilises different means starting with the constitution and continuing with legislation, curricula, religious bigotry, and systematic physical removal of individuals and communities.

Today, the requirements to protect their existence in their homeland surpasses their capacity. Therefore, that protection becomes a collective responsibility of the Iraqi state and international actors. They suffer from a violation of international treaties set forth to protect human, social, and minority rights.

Today, the Assyrian Christians, after becoming a marginalised minority in their homeland, live on the hope of a future that will guarantee justice and dignity, for they, regardless of what they went through, still believe in that hope. We, Mesopotamians Assyrian Christians in Mesopotamia might be helpless but never hopeless. However, it is a conditional hope.

Let us keep our moral commitment in supporting and practicing the actions on the ground to keep the hope alive .

CHAPTER 8

ARMENIANS OF IRAQ

Seda D. Ohanian

Armenians have been living in Mesopotamia – modern Iraq – from times immemorial. According to Herodotus,[1] the Hellenic father of history, Armenians used to travel, long before the Christian era, from Armenia to Nineveh and Babylon over the Euphrates and Tigris rivers, importing, by means of round rafts, Armenian wines, dried fruits, fine horses, wheat, nuts and many other products. Historical accounts indicate that Tigranes the Great (king of Armenia during the Artaxiad dynasty from 190 BC to AD 12) defeated enemy armies of several countries, who endangered Armenia's security. Amongst these countries, he subdued Adiabene (Mosul) in 83 BC, which allowed Armenians to travel from the Armenian highlands to Mesopotamia, reaching as far as Basra and further down the Persian Gulf to the Far East.[2]

When Ctesiphon was the capital of the Sassanid Persia (AD 224-651),[3] historical accounts indicate that it had numerous Armenians of different professions and artisans of diverse trades such as merchants, goldsmiths, and scholars. However, a deadly epidemic reduced the number of inhabitants. The Armenians abandoned Ctesiphon in search of safer places. They gradually spread southwards, entered India, but lost their identity and integrated into the Indian society.[4]

During the Arab expansion in the seventh century, Armenia was also conquered, and numerous Armenians were brought to Iraq during the Abbasid caliphate in the eighth century.

---

[1] Herodotus, *History*, (Yerevan, 1986) 79-80.

[2] Arshak Alboyajian, *Armenians of Iraq*, (Yerewan:The Matenadarn Mashdotz Institute of Ancient Manuscripts, 200), 18.

[3] Ghazar Parbetzi, *History of the Armenians* (Yerevan) 320-321, 351-352. Ghazar Parbetzi, an Armenian chronicler and historian, lived from 442 to the beginning of the sixth century. Robert Bedrossian first translated this book from classical Armenian. Robert W. Thomson did a second translation entitled, *The History of Lazar P'Arpec'i* (Atlanta: Scholar Press/ Columbia University Program in Armenian Studies Suren D.Fesjian Academic Publications, 1991).

[4] Vartan Melkonian, *An Historical Glimpse of the Armenians in Iraq – From the Earliest Times to the Present Day* (Basra: The Times Press, 1957), 2.

However, the roots of the 'organised' modern Armenian community can be traced back to 1604 when Shah Abbas transferred the entire population of Arax and Ararat Vilayets, including the Armenian city of Julfa, (where Armenian merchants had connections with European and Far East merchants), to the new quarter of New Julfa[5] in Isfahan. This was a turning point in Armenians' history.[6] For various reasons, some of these people later moved on to Iraq and formed a very wealthy trade community competing with the financially and politically influential Jewish merchants, who had been in Iraq for centuries.[7]

The Armenian community has been established in Iraq well before the final occupation of Baghdad by the Ottoman Sultan Murad IV. Some attribute the Ottoman conquest of Baghdad to an Armenian artillery officer, Gog Nazar, in Sultan Murad's army.[8] Gog Nazar proposed to build a large cannon which could destroy the enemy's fortifications. Sultan Murad promised to reward him if his suggested plan was successful. Nazar's plan destroyed the strongholds and fortresses of the enemy and Baghdad surrendered on 25 December 1638. In appreciation, Sultan Murad fulfilled Gog Nazar's wish to construction of a church and cemetery for his fellow Armenians in Baghdad. The necessary *firman* was issued and the Armenian Church St. Mary was built in 1639 at the Meedan Square, which to this day is called *Gog Nazar Quarter (Mehallat Gog Nazar)*.[9] Another piece of land at Bab El-Mu'adhem was allocated for the Armenians to set up their cemetery, which does not exist anymore; a new one was built later beside St. Gregory the Illuminator Cathedral, the current centre of the Armenian Apostolic Church and its prelacy in Iraq.[10]

Due to several occurrences of the plague, the Armenian community dwindled. The church records show that in 1842 Basra had 33 Armenian families, while Baghdad had only 174 Armenian families.[11]

Currently, Armenians in Iraq consist primarily of western Armenians, who survived the Armenian Genocide. Their dispersion can be traced back to the late nineteenth century and the great massacres of 1894–1896 in some

---

[5] The relocated Armenians named this quarter New Julfa in remembrance of their native Julfa in Armenia.

[6] Thabet A.J.Abdullah, *Merchants, Mamluks, and Murder – The Political Economy of Trade in Eighteenth-Century Basra*, (New York: State University of New York Press, 2001), 95.

[7] Seda Ohanian, *Armenian Merchants' Activities in Iraq in the XVII-XIX centuries - The Problems of The History of Armenia – 2013 Yearbook* (Yerevan: National Academy of Sciences 2013), 90-105.

[8] Ibid.

[9] This church contains a small tomb-like structure in a niche on the inside of its left-hand wall, which has relics of the Karasoon Mangounk (Forty Children), who were massacred in Sebasdia (Svaz) because of their faith. Candles, sesame oil, incense, etc. are customary presents brought by pilgrims of all religions – Christians and Muslims alike – for use in the church. Gog Nazar may have been from Sebasdia and arranged to transfer the relics of the Forty Martyrs into Baghdad.

[10] Now the cemeteries of all Christians are situated on the old road Baghdad-Baquba.

[11] Seda Ohanian, 'The Iraqi Armenian Community in the 20th Century' *Arch. Mesrob Ashjian Book Series* 152/14 (2016).

regions of western Armenia. These massacres, the non-stop violence, and the continued unrest triggered the first major wave of Western Armenians emigration to nearby countries including Iraq, Syria, Lebanon, and Palestine.

The next and the most fateful emigration/exodus was of 1915–1922 that completely stripped Van and other western Armenian regions of its indigenous people, where they had lived for thousands of years. Although, Armenians defended themselves for several months, the sheer strength of the Turkish forces, the withdrawal of the Russian army from the Caucasus and shortage of food and ammunition eventually compelled the Armenians to flee. They sought to reach eastern Armenia through Berkri's Gorge, but had no alternative other than to change their route eastwards and enter Iran, where again they had to fight their way for five months until they met the British forces at Sayin Kala, near Hamadan in Persia, and were escorted into Iraq, which British forces had occupied since 1917.

The Armenians felt very grateful to the Hashimite Royal House for the 29 April 1918 letter from King Hussain Bin Ali, King of the Arab countries and Sharif of Mecca, addressed to King Faisal I and Emir Abdul Aziz Jerba, who were both then still princes and engaged in liberating the Arab countries. In this letter, King Hussain greatly sympathises with the Armenians' suffering. Here is the translation of this letter, long displayed in its original Arabic version at the entrance of each Armenian church in Iraq.[12]

THE HASHIMITE DIWAN (Headquarters)

In the name God, the Merciful, the Compassionate,

Praise be to God, alone.

From Hussain bin Ali, King of the Arab Countries, Sharif of Mecca and its Emir

To the grand and glorious Emir Faisal and Emir Abdul Aziz Jarba.

Greetings and God's peace and blessings be upon you.

These lines have been issued from Umm Al-Qura (Mecca) on the 18th Rajab 1336 (29.4.1918). We praise Allah, besides Whom there is no God, and sanctify and salute His prophet, the latter's progeny and companions. And we inform you that we are, thanks to Him, the Most High, in perfect Health enjoying His copious bounties and praying for the continuance thereof for ourselves and for. You. The object of this letter is the protection of the Jacobite[13] Armenian sect, who have stayed behind in your parts, areas and among your tribesmen, so that you should assist

---

[12] This letter was translated into English by Sayid Muhammed Ahmad, formerly named Khan Bahadur Mirza Muhammed, one of the leading advocates of Basra and it is included in Vartan Melkonian's book Ibid.16.

[13] Jacobite conveys here the meaning of Gregorian Orthodox.

them in all their affairs and protect them in the same way that you protect yourselves, your properties as your sons, and facilitate all what they need during their travels and sojourn because they are the proteges of the Muslims, about whom he, (the Prophet) – God's praise and peace upon him, – has said 'He who takes a camel's tether from them shall find me as his opponent on the Day of Judgement.' This is the most important matter to which I invite you to attend. And which I expect from your magnanimity and high-mindedness. May God lead us and you towards His success.

Peace be upon you and God's mercy and blessings.

(Sealed) Hussain Bin Ali

The number of the Armenians in Iraq swelled with the arrival of approximately 20–25,000 survivors of the Armenian Genocide together with about 50,000 Assyrian Christian who also fled the western Armenian provinces and some parts of Iranian Azerbaijan.[14]

Upon arrival in Baquba, the Armenians and their companions of misfortune, the Assyrian Christians, were sheltered and housed by the British forces in a tent city. This 'city' had three groups:[15]

A) The Armenians, chiefly from the region of Vasporagan (mainly from cities and villages around Lake Van), Bitlis and different parts of Asia Minor, who numbered approximately one-third of the camp population. These people were formerly Ottoman subjects.

B) The Assyrian Christians from the district of Hakkari, south of Van region, who also numbered approximately one-third of the camp population, formerly Ottoman subjects.

C) Assyrians and Armenians of Urumieh and Salmas Plains, who were formerly Persian subjects. These people comprised the remaining one-third of the camp population.[16]

When the refugees first arrived at Baqubah, the British authorities found it very hard to divide and separate them into their tribes and divisions. Therefore, for the first months the Armenians and the Assyrians were mixed. However, as they became more settled, a census was carried out, and the people were arranged throughout the sections according to their tribal divisions (regarding the Assyrians) and affiliations.

The whole camp, which covered roughly an area of one square mile,[17]

---

[14] Melkonian, Ibid. 30.
[15] H.H Austin, *The Baqubah Refugee Camp, An Account of Work on behalf of the Persecuted Assyrian Christians, 1920*, (London: The Faith Press, 1920), 3.
[16] Bt. Lieut. Col. Wilson A.T., Office of the Civil Commissioner –A report addressed to the Secretary of State for India, London, S. W. 1. Dated Baghdad, 4 December 1919.
[17] Ibid. 95.

was divided into three areas. Each area was subdivided into 11 to 13 sections. A British officer oversaw each area, and each section had another British officer looking after it, assisted by three or four British soldiers.[18] The British military personnel were responsible for assuring the cleanliness, welfare and discipline of their section. Later, the refugees themselves administered and looked after their sections and the British personnel was (except in few cases) exempt from these duties.

Table 8.1. Statistics of the Armenian Refugees at Baquba – 12 August 1919

Province	Region	Villages	Population	Notes
Bitlis	Sbargerd	20	384	
	Gargar	10	147	
	Bitlis	14	200	
	Khizan	16	209	
	Garjgan	13	209	140 Died
	Sghert	6	81	12 Left the Camp
	Total	79	1230	
Vasbouragan	Aghpag	22	1267	
	Ardjag	10	529	
	Timar	35	2753	
	Chadakh	26	970	
	HayotsTsor	33	870	
	Moks	24	456	
	Sara	1	79	
	Kavash	12	214	
	Van	24	2166	
	Nortouze	9	295	
	Kavar	5	166	
	Djoulamerg	4	96	
	Khoshap	3	135	786 Died
	Sadmantz	1	190	90 left the camp
	Total	209	10186	
Aderbadagan	Salmast	14	1002	90 Died
	Ourmia	29	1657	3 left the camp
	Total	43	2659	

Prepared by The Armenian Relief Committee of Mesopotamia

---

[18] Y. Vartanian. *From Desert to Desert*. (Venice: Mkhitarian Press House, 1923) 110-111.

Summary of Table 8.1

Province	Villages	Men	Women	Boys	Girls
Bitlis	79	510	463	205	203
Vasbouragan	200	3449	3559	214	1940
Aderbadagan	43	690	760	795	504
Total	331	4684	4782	1214	2647
Caucasian		35			

Actually present at Baquba	14109
Died since August 1918	1036
Left the camp in different directions	105

Signed by Mardiross Kouyumdjian

The refugees stayed here until the uprising of the Arab liberals in 1920 (known as The Great Iraqi Revolution of 1920), when the British forces had no alternative but to transfer the Armenians to another camp in Nahr Omar (north of Basra) and the Assyrians to Mosul and the surrounding villages.

The Armenians continued living at the Nahr Omar refugee camp, but at the same time, continued trying to find every possible way to return home. At first, they could not adapt to this totally strange country, where the language was incomprehensible, and the climate was completely different than the one they were used to in their Armenian highlands. This situation continued until June 1921, when the British authorities cut off the rations provided to the refugees and ordered, on short notice, the dispersal of the camp. The leaders of the Armenian Refugee Committee of Mesopotamia had to find other safe countries, where the refugees could, at least temporarily, be placed. After long and strenuous correspondence between all parties concerned (namely the Armenian Refugee Committee of Mesopotamia/Iraqi Government, which was then the British Protectorate, the Armenian National Delegation in Paris and the Soviet Armenia government) 8000 of the refugees were successfully repatriated in three ships to Armenia during October and November of 1921 and January of 1922. The third ship was reserved for the orphan children (850 including their teachers and caretakers) to be transferred to Jerusalem. However, to fill up the ship and bring it to an even keel, 2,000 refugees were taken on board for repatriation to Batum, Georgia, where they were transferred overland to Armenia. During the following years, until 1929, another 1000 refugees were transferred overland through Persia, by special arrangement with the Soviet authorities.[19] The remaining refugees had no alternative but to settle down in this hospitable country, where they found enough strength and courage to recover from their wounds, increase in number, prosper under the auspices of their

---

[19] The Independent Republic of Armenia was Sovietised on 2 December 1920.

Apostolic Mother-Church and the Armenian Catholic Church,[20] as well as the newly built Armenian private schools and public organizations.

But what was the situation of the Armenians in Iraq before the arrival of the refugees? During WWI, the small-sized,[21] but mostly wealthy, Armenian community members in Iraq,[22] like their compatriots in Armenia, lived in fear and panic. They, also, were subjected to arrest and deportation. Many of the community's elite were arrested and exiled to Der El-Zorand Ras El-Ayn in Syria, some of them never returned and perished in the deserts. One victim was the great teacher and headmaster Mihran Svajian, who had played a vital role in educating the Armenians, as well as the local youth of both genders and raised the level of the Armenian schools to the official El-Rushdiya schools.[23]

In north Iraq, a smaller wave of 3000 refugees arrived in Mosul from Der El-Zor and Ras El-Ayn slaughterhouses, through Sinjar, where they sheltered by the Yazidis and Zakho towns in October 1915. Dr. Krikor Astarjian, an Ottoman Army medical officer, sheltered some of these people. After the Mudros Armistice on 30 October 1918, more than 2000 of these refugees were transferred to Baquba camp, where living conditions were comparatively better and more bearable.[24]

In November 1918, an orphanage was opened in Baghdad besides the Holy Trinity Armenian church, as well as another one at Baquba refugee camp. A third orphanage was established in Mosul,[25] where more than 400 orphans of the genocide, were gathered from the streets and sheltered. Most of these orphans were transferred together with their teacher and caretaker to Baquba's orphanage and then relocated to Jerusalem.[26]

Schools were opened in Baquba and later on in Nahr Omar camps. Baquba had more than 2500 students (boys and girls), who were taught by 30 refugee teachers. However, in Nahr Omar, this number dwindled greatly due to the repatriation of up to 9000 refugees to Armenia and some refugees voluntarily leaving the camp. Both Armenians and Assyrians had tents

---

[20] The Armenian Catholic church in Baghdad was officially recognised as a separate church by the Ottoman central government in Istanbul according to a Royal Firman released on 3 February 1832, which was registered in the archives of the Ottoman Government in Baghdad on 12 April 1833. Father Sahag Stepanian went to Baghdad and granted the Armenian Catholic priest all the right to carry out baptism and blessing of marriages.

[21] Before the arrival of the refugees, the Armenian population in all cities of Iraq was barely 1000 persons.

[22] Stephen H Longrigg, *Iraq 1900 to 1950*. (Oxford: Oxford University Press, 1953) 11.

[23] J.M. Al-Najjar, *Education in Iraq during the last era of the Ottoman Rule 1869-1918*, (Baghdad: Al-Hurriya Press House, 200), 242.

[24] K.Astarjian, *A Backward Review upon Struggle for a life of 90 years*. (Beirut: Sevan Press, 1975).34. Also R. Kevorkian, *The Armenian Genocide*, (New York: I.B.Taurus&Co.Ltd., 2011), 652-653.

[25] Patriarch Zaven Der Yeghiayan, *My Patriarchal Memoirs*, (Cairo: NorAsdegh Printing House, 1947), 288.

[26] Seda Ohanian, *Armenian Merchants' Activities in Iraq in the XVII-XIX centuries - The Problems of The History of Armenia – 2013 Yearbook* (Yerevan: National Academy of Sciences 2013), 90-105, 41.

serving as churches, with priests from among the refugees.

When Iraq became an independent member of the League of Nations in 1932, the Armenians acquired citizenship and became fully entitled, loyal Iraqi citizens. They organised their lives according to the needs of their new 'homeland', integrated into the Iraqi society, but never forgot their Armenian national identity while playing a vital role in the development of the newly formed Iraqi government.

The Iraqi Armenian community is officially governed by its internal constitution, duly approved by the authorities. This constitution has been revised several times, according to the political and social situation in Iraq, the latest revision took place in 2005. This revision permitted the teaching of the Armenian language in private Armenian schools.

The main peculiarity of the migrants is that they embrace the idea of having two homelands. However, once a community is established, it becomes completely and closely shaped by the host country's political system, socioeconomic structure, cultural traditions and even local and foreign policies. Living in two cultures and identities – national and the host country's – takes great effort and skill, without condescending one to the other. For Armenians, these duties were fulfilled and strictly looked after by the church, (Apostolic and Catholic), the private Armenian schools and Armenian public organizations. The role of the church was particularly (and still is) invaluable to help the deportees (who afterwards became Iraqi citizens) – overcome their sufferings and start a new life. New churches were built and consecrated, the existing, centuries-old ones, were renovated. Armenian social and sports clubs were established. In 2019, Iraq has 14 Armenian Apostolic churches – (four in Iraqi Kurdistan, one under construction in Erbil).

In almost all cities and villages where Armenians settled, private schools were opened, often sharing the same grounds of the churches and charity and philanthropic organizations (Such as the Protectorate of the Needy Armenians in Iraq, which is The Armenian Relief Society or The Armenian Red Cross) – served the people in every way they could. Once the deportees were physically secured and felt the government's protection, they spared no effort to become good and loyal citizens of the host country. Despite the continuing political unrest in Iraq throughout the twentieth century, which continued through the first decades of the twenty-first century, the cultural and educational activities of the Iraqi Armenians community bloomed, especially during the second half of the twentieth century. Members of the Armenian community became renowned in diverse fields including theatre, music, literary, fine arts, printing, and press. These achievements represent the spiritual and mental support for the survival of people forced out of their homeland, cut off from their roots and anchored in a strange land.

After the revolution of 1958, the first Baathist takeover in 1963 which lasted only nine months, and the second in July 1968 resulted in continuous political unrest and substantial emigration of Christians including the Armenians. The emigration continued during the following decades and increased dramatically after the invasion led by the USA in 2003.

For the past three decades, Iraqis have faced continuous challenges. The eight-year Iraq-Iran war claimed the lives of hundreds of thousands of people from both sides; the Iraqi invasion of Kuwait – followed by international economic sanctions – led to the complete destruction of the country's infrastructure, including the deterioration or simply the absence of hygienic and sanitary conditions. Finally, the American-led invasion of Iraq by international troops in 2003 had catastrophic effects still felt today. These political disasters affected all the people of Iraq, especially the national and religious minorities. According to the Armenian church records, 45 Armenians have been killed since 2003 as a result of ethnic conflict or simply for criminal reasons, and 32 have been kidnapped for ransom. At the end of 2004, a newly built Armenian church in Mosul, still not consecrated, was attacked and burned down by insurgents.

Finally, the Armenian community in Mosul suffered immensely after the ISIS invasion. Survivors relocated to Iraqi Kurdistan or abroad. Some found refuge in several parts of Kurdistan including Duhok, where the first Armenian Apostolic church was consecrated in 2008.[27] Others returned to the recently established villages Havresk and Avzruk – both originally set up by survivors of the Armenian Genocide in 1929 and 1932 respectively in the Duhok governorate.[28]

A new community was established in Erbil, the capital of Iraqi Kurdistan, with its first church currently under construction. Today, Armenian Apostolic churches and communities exist in Zakho, Duhok, Erbil, Baghdad, Basra, and Kirkuk.

Besides the churches in Mosul, the Armenian Catholic church in Sinjar, St. George the Martyr, was also destroyed during the war with ISIS. The latter community has only two churches in Baghdad. Basra has always had a sizeable Armenian Catholic community, yet they have not been able to build their own church. Instead, they attend the Latin (roman-catholic) church in Basra.

The Armenian Evangelical community established its first church in 2003, which was partly destroyed in September 2008 during military actions in the area.

In 1947, an Armenian merchant and statesman, Iskendar Markarian, was

---

[27] Seda Ohanian, *Armenian Merchants' Activities in Iraq in the XVII-XIX centuries - The Problems of The History of Armenia – 2013 Yearbook* (Yerevan: National Academy of Sciences 2013), 90-105, 106.
[28] Ibid. 102-103.

elected to the Iraqi parliament representing all the Christians of Iraq, including the Armenians.[29]

Since 2013, the Iraqi Kurdistan parliament has a reserved seat for Armenians. During the elections of October 2018, Vahik Kemal was elected to the Kurdish parliament on behalf of the Armenian minority.

The political and economic insecurity in Iraq up to 2018 has compelled Armenians, along with other Iraqi citizens, to leave their homes. Armenians are migrating from a country, which at the beginning of the twentieth century, had welcomed them and offered the opportunity for a new and productive life which allowed them to benefit their own community as well as to the hospitable Iraqi state and people.

Memorial for the Genocide of 1915 in the Armenian village of Avzruk, Iraqi Kurdistan, 2014 (Picture: Thomas Schmidinger)

---

[29] Iskendar Markarian served on the Board of Directors of the Iraqi Chamber of Commerce, represented Iraq in The International Trade Conference in Italy in 1939 and a similar conference in New York in 1946.

3000 Tent-city of the refugees at Baquba, Iraq 1918-1920. (Picture: Ohanian collection)

Some of the Armenian children of Baghdad Orphanage in 1918. (Picture: Ohanian collection)

The Protectorate of the Needy Iraqi Armenians, Margil Chapter, 1952 (Picture: Ohanian collection)

St. Gregory the Illuminator Cathedral, the main Church of the Armenian-Apostolic Church in Baghdad. (Picture: Thomas Schmidinger)

St. Mary's Armenian-Apostolic Church in Basrah (Picture: Seda Ohanian)

St. Mary's Armenian-Apostolic Church in Basrah (Picture: Seda Ohanian)

St. Nerses Shnorhali (Graceful) Armenian-Apostolic Church in Duhok, Iraqi Kurdistan, 2008. (Picture: Seda Ohanian)

Easter 2015 in the St. Nerses Shnorhali Church in Dohuk (Picture: Thomas Schmidinger).

CHAPTER 9

THE YAZIDIS: RELIGION, SOCIETY AND RESENTMENTS

Thomas Schmidinger

No religious minorities in Iraq was more affected by the violence of the so-called 'Islamic State' (ISIS) than the Yazidis (sometimes spelled Yezidis or Êzîdî in Kurmancî) who suffered genocidal attacks by the jihadis in August 2014. However, the jihadist groups in August 2007 and in August 2014 were not the first to attack the Yazidis. For centuries they suffered under resentments and perennial violence by Muslims who accused them of 'devil worshipping'—a well-cultivated misunderstanding of their ancient religion.

Resentments against Yazidis are not only widespread within jihadi and extremist circles. They reach far into the mainstream of Kurdish and Arab Muslim societies. Many ordinary Muslims in Iraq would still not eat in a Yazidi home or buy foodstuff from a Yazidi because they think that Yazidis are dirty. Many ordinary Muslims who do not have any sympathies for the 'Islamic State', including people who actively combatted ISIS still consider Yazidis as 'devil worshippers'. Additionally, traditional Muslims considered them as infidels and not 'peoples of the book' worthy of protection like Christians or Jews.

Both accusations have been repeatedly used since the fifteenth century to justify persecutions against Yazidis. These persecutions have deeply affected how the Yazidi people view their own history. Yazidis describe the persecutions and genocidal acts against them with the Ottoman concept of the firman (decree). Up until the twentieth century, Yazidis claim to have been the targets of 72 firmans. Seventy-two represents the mythical number for 'very much'. In the twenty-first century, when the mythical dimension of this number was no longer known to most Yazidi people, many Yazidis began to count further and to describe the attack of 17 August 2007 on two villages in the Sinjar region as the 73rd, and the genocide of the ISIS in August 2014 as the 74th firman.

What are the religious traditions of the Yazidi and what are the misinterpretations used to justify centuries of persecution and resentment?

A specific form or monotheism

The Yazidi religion is a specific form of monotheism. Yazidis believe in God whom they call by the Kurdish name *Xwedê*. Many of their traditions go back to an age of the ancient Iranian religion, even before the reform of Zarathustra. It seems that some older pre-Zoroastrian forms of this religion survived in the western extensions of the Iranian world, that are now called Kurdistan. Although the ancient Iranian religion was polytheistic, it already had a chief god of their pantheon that could have developed into the *Xwedê* of Yazidis. Yazidi religion seems to have a common ancestor with Zoroastrianism; however, it is not a direct offspring of Zoroastrianism. Rather both have roots in an earlier form of Iranian religion and developed from Iranian polytheism into two different forms of monotheism.

Yazidis combine their monotheism with a belief in angels and a mixture of pre-Islamic Iranian religious traditions and Islamic traditions rooted in Sufism. The long history of persecution led to a clear dissociation of Yazidis from Islam; however, scholarly analyses of Yazidi religious traditions reveal that Yazidis have some traditions connected with Muslims.

Although the religion of the Yazidis has older roots, its present form resulted from a religious reform associated with 'Adī ibn Musāfir al-Umawī, a Sufi Sheikh from the Beqaa valley in present-day Lebanon, whose followers now call him Sheikh Adi (Kurdish: *Şêx Adî*). Sheikh Adi spent parts of his live in Baghdad before he retreated to Lalish, where his grave is located and today is the most holy place of the Yazidis. The Islamic followers of Sheikh Adi established an Islamic Sufi Order, the so-called Adawiyya. The Islamic scripts of Sheikh Adi do not indicate anything else other than that he understood himself as a Sunni Muslim. However, along with his his theological writing, 'his poetry is full of live, exultancy, and mystical inebriety with the wine of love'.[1]

This poetic side of Sheikh Adi fit very well with the local Kurdish tradition of poetry and the western Iranian religious traditions that must have been present in the region. In the thirteenth and fourteenth century, Islamic commentators still approved the Islamic scholarly work of Sheikh Adi.[2] Thus, earlier Islamic scholars, who were unaware of his poetry, did not perceive Sheikh Adi as a heretic. Nevertheless, his poetry connected with the local pre-Islamic traditions and helped to shape the religion of the Yazidis.

We do not know exactly how Sheikh Adis Sufism intermingled with these local religious traditions to emerge under today's name of Yazidism. The scholarly discussions about this process go far beyond this brief introduction to the religion; however, these traditions did become a fruitful new religious

---

[1] Garnik S. Astarian, / Victoria Arakelova, *The Religion of the Peacock Angel. The Yezidis and Their Spirit World.* (Abington/New York: Routledge, 2014), 38.

[2] John S Guest, *Survival among the Kurds. A history of the Yezidis.* (London/New York: Routledge, London, 2010) 18.

movement that became what we know today as the religion of the Yazidis. It is basically a monotheistic religion with many different influences by different mystical traditions of the Middle East including—but not limited to—Islamic Sufism, Christianity, Judaism, Manichaeism, Zoroastrianism, and, even possibly, the Mandaeans.

Peacock Angel is not the devil

The religion of the Yazidis draws from various Middle Eastern religions but has processed them into a unique religion that cannot be assigned or attributed to any other of the world religions. Despite similarities to Zoroastrianism, from which its essence originated, Yazidism has never undergone the development into dualism like the old Iranian religion.[3] Whilst Judaism, Christianity and Islam have adopted the idea of an evil antithesis of God from the Zoroastrian dualism, Yazidis know neither a devil nor a hell. Nevertheless, they have been repeatedly accused by Muslims—and partly also by Christians—of worshipping the devil.

On the one hand, the motives behind this false denunciation could be found in the mentalities of those who hate those who do not fear the devil. Thus, Yazidis belong to a monotheism purer than religions that integrated the Zoroastrian evil god Angra Mainyu as a devil into their own monotheism. On the other hand, the accusation of a 'devil worship' is also based on a misunderstanding resulting from an inability to understand the differences between Zoroastrianism and Yazidism.

Besides God (*Xwedê*), Yazidis also worship the Peacock Angel (Tawûsê Melek or Melek Taus), who is considered God's first and most faithful angel. Tawûsê Melek is not identical to Angra Mainyu but bears certain similarities to him. Both figures likely originated with the same figure of the ancient Iranian religion from which Yazidism and Zoroastrianism have emerged. Philip Kreyenbroek, a scholar who has spent decades researching Yazidism and Zoroastrianism, assumes that, at around 1000 BC, Zoroastrianism in eastern Iran had separated itself from the west Iranian religion because of Zoroaster's far-reaching reforms in that region. Whereas the old Iranian religion was still based on a God and a mediator between God and humans, in Zoroastrianism, the evil god Angra Mainyu originates with this mediator. In Mithraism, however, and with the Yazidis as well as the Ahl-e Haqq, the mediator remained good: Mithras in Mithraism and Tawûsê Melek in Yazidism. Kreyenbroek concludes that after Iran's dominant religion Zoroastrianism came into contact with this old western Iranian tradition during the pre-Islamic period, the good 'mediator' was identified as the evil Ahriman. This also explains why the good 'mediator' in Yazidism is wrongly

---

[3] Manfred Hutter, 'Zoroastrismus' In *Handbuch Religionswissenschaft*. Edited by Johann Figl.(Innsbruck/Wien: Vandenhoeck & Ruprecht, 2003)

associated with the Satan of other religions.⁴

Therefore, Tawûsê Melek is not the evil antithesis but God's mediator on earth who executes God's plan and mediates between humans and God. He is the manifestation of the Creator, but not the Creator himself, he is God's alter ego and inseparably linked to him.⁵

Yazidism has different traditional explanations about the origins of Tawûsê Melek and his role. A religious tradition, which is almost antiliteral and transmits its teachings not in timeless sacrosanct books but through orally conveyed religious chants, inherently has a pluralism of religious traditions which do not necessarily all have to coincide with each other. However, one of the traditions resembles the Islamic story of the devil even if it conveys a completely different essence. This resemblance might have contributed to the accusation of a 'devil worship'. In this tradition, Tawûsê Melek is considered to be one of the most important angels of God—similar to Satan or the Christian Lucifer before his fall. Because Tawûsê Melek was highly devoted to God, he kept God's first commandment not to worship anyone but God alone. Consequently, he refused to obey God's instruction to submit to humankind after Adam's creation. With this, God tested Tawûsê Melek; he then passed this test, distinctly different to the Christian and Islamic concept of hell, where this angel was punished and became the devil. In contrast to these two religions, Yazidis have no concept of hell as a place of eternal damnation. For the Yazidis, God is so omnipotent that there cannot be a second power of a personified evil beside him.⁶

However, the similarity of this story with that of the Islamic and Christian devils who arrogantly refused to submit to men, was used over centuries to accuse the Yazidis people of being 'devil worshippers'. One reason for this theological misunderstanding might also be that Sheikh Adi, who was himself an Islamic Sufi, but who played an important role in shaping present days Yazidism and whose grave in Lalish is revered by Yazidis, followed a Sufi tradition of exculpating Iblis, the devil. 'Re-voicing the mystics, who asserted that evil was also created by Allah, Sheikh Adi argued, that "If Evil exists without the will of Allah most high, then Allah would be powerless, and a powerless one cannot be God, since it is impossible for anything to exist in his house that he does not will, just as nothing can exist in that he does not know."'⁷

---

⁴ Philip G. Kreyenbroek, 'Die Eziden, die Ahl-e Haqq und die Religion des Zarathustra' In *Im Transformationsprozess: Die Eziden und das Ezidentum gestern, heute, morgen. Beiträge der zweiten internationalen GEA-Konferenz vom 04. bis 05.10.2014 in Bielefeld.* Gesellschaft Ezidischer AkademikerInnen (GEA), (Berlin: Vwb 2016), 32f.

⁵ Serhat Ortaç / Şefik Tagay, *Die Eziden und das Ezidentum. Geschichte und Gegenwart einer vom Untergang bedrohten Religion.* (Hamburg: Landeszentrale für politische Bildung, 2016), 57f.

⁶ Schmidinger, Thomas. *Kampf um den Berg der Kurden. Geschichte und Gegenwart der Region Afrin.* (Wien: Bahoe Books 2018) 19.

⁷ Garnik S. Astarian, / Victoria Arakelova, *The Religion of the Peacock Angel. The Yezidis and Their Spirit*

People of the book?

Muslims repeatedly use the fact that, unlike Jews, Christians and Zoroastrians, Yazidism is not a religion of the book, which means that protection by classical Islamic law would not apply. Indeed, it is an almost antiliteral religion whose religious contents and songs, the '*qewl*', were always passed down orally. Sheikh Adi did write some books; however, most were Islamic scholarly books who do not play any role in today's Yazidi religion—other than his orally transmitted poetry. Most Yazidis were illiterate until the middle of the twentieth century and even high-ranking religious officials were mostly illiterate. This does not mean that they were uneducated, but their religious education was not based on scripture, but on memorised hymns (*qewls*) and orally transmitted philosophies and stories.

This creates a problem between Yazidis and those Muslims who interpret the Islamic tradition as only tolerating religions with sacred books. As a consequence, the myth of a lost holy book of the Yazidis, the *Meshaf-ı Reş* (the Black Book) emerged among many Yazidis. During my field research in Syria, some Yazidi sheikhs told me that this book had been stolen by Austrians and that it was in a museum in Vienna. They asked me whether I could advocate for the return of the book to the Yazidis. However, this book neither exists in an Austrian museum nor in the Austrian National Library.

The background to this myth is that the Austrian Academy of Sciences published in 1913 a book by the Austrian orientalist Maximilian Bittner entitled 'The Holy Books of the Yazidi or Devil Worshippers'[8]. This relatively small book is based on scriptures of questionable authenticity obtained from Christian neighbours to the Yazidis. Nevertheless, it certainly could not have had the same significance for the Yazidis of the Middle East that the Quran has for Muslims, or the Bible for Jews and Christians, since no Yazidi copies of this 'Holy Scripture' have been preserved. The longing for such an authentic Holy Scripture derives from the desire that their Muslim neighbours recognise them as a 'religion of the book' and thus to be protected.

Another aspect of new attempts to create a written religious canon is that Yazidis have increasingly forced to leave their traditional homelands because of political oppression and massacres. Thus, political and social changes have caused a new kind of scripturalisation and canonisation of the Yazidi religious tradition[9] that will also change the religion.

Yazidi festive traditions

Yazidis have a rich religious tradition that goes far beyond the aspects

---

World. (Abington/New York: Routledge, 2014), 38.

[8] Maximilian Bittner, *Die heiligen Bücher der Jesiden oder Teufelsanbeter*. (Wien: Denkschriften der Kaiserlichen Akademie der Wissenschaften in Wien, 1913).

[9] Khanna Omarkhali, *The Yezidi Religious Textual Tradition: From Oral to Written Categories, Transmission, Scripturalisation and Canonisation of the Yezidi Oral Religious Texts*. (Wiesbaden: Harrassowitz, 2017).

that have been used against them in history. As a syncretistic religion with pre-Islamic roots and Islamic, Christian, Jewish, and other influences, they preserve a unique heritage of Middle Eastern religious traditions with different origins.

The Yazidis have many religious festivals and ceremonies. Some are oriented on the Muslim lunar calendar, others on the Iranian-Kurdish solar calendar. The year starts in April (2019 will be the Yazidi year 6769) with the New Year's festival called Serê Sal or Çarşemiya Sor (Red Wednesday) celebrated in all regions where Yazidis live. The Yazidi year starts with the first Wednesday in April, thus about two weeks after the Kurdish new year Newroz celebrated on the spring equinox. In Iraq, the festival also includes a Parade of the Sanjaqs. Iron or bronze peacock effigies are taken from their normal home, the residence of the Yazidi Prince (Mîr), and are paraded through the Yazidi villages of the Sheikhan region. In the past, this tradition might have also existed in other predominantly Yazidi regions, but today the Mîr of Sheikhan is the last Yazidi Prince, so the Sanjaqs tradition only continues in Iraq.

One of the most important festival of the year is Cejna Cemaiya, the 'Feast of the Assembly' at the most sacred place in Lališ that constitutes a seven-day pilgrimage to the tomb of Sheikh Adi ibn Musafir (Şêx Adî). Yazidis from all parts of Kurdistan and the diaspora gather every year for this festival in Lališ which also has other sacred landmarks such as two holy springs, called Zamzam (like the sacred well in the Great mosque in Mecca) and Kaniya Sipî ('The White Spring').

Other important festivals are Tawûs geran ('circulation of the peacock'), a festival for Sheikh Shems and the Ezî festival ('god´s festival') one week before the winter solstice. There are two periods of fasting for forty days, once in winter and once in summer; however, this fasting is sometimes reduced to three days. Yazidis in different parts of Kurdistan and Iraq also have several local saints and festivals of these local saints. Thus, some festivals differ from region to region.

Along with these general festivals, every Yazidi goes through different rites of passage. These rites start with the first haircut (*biska pora*) of boys, a kind of baptism (*mor kirin*) and the funeral at the end of life. Yazidis also know the tradition of an institutionalised relationship with a sister or a brother of 'the hereafter' that determines affinity of families without being related by blood. The selection of the brother or sister of 'the hereafter' is also an important rite of passage.

Society and religious hierarchy

Yazidis are strictly endogamous, which has caused many problems when Yazidis fell in love with non-Yazidis. Many Muslim groups denounced the Yazidis as especially cruel after her own family murdered Dua Khalil Aswad, a seventeen-year-old Yazidi girl from the town of Bashiqa, who fell in love with a Muslim man. Although the Yazidi religious leaders condemn such murders, such cases even happened in the Yazidi diaspora in Germany.

However, Yazidi endogamy goes far beyond the prohibition to marry non-Yazidis. The Yazidi society is based on three distinctive groups, who are most of the times called castes in literature, although this terminology is a bit misleading. Unlike Hindu castes in India, the Yazidi castes are not necessarily strictly hierarchal. Instead, they constitute different functions in society. Nevertheless, these three castes, the murids, sheikhs, and pirs, are only supposed to marry within their own group.

Besides these three groups, there are also subgroups and specific religious notables. The Prince (Mîr) is the traditional hereditary political/social leader of the community. Although the present Mîr, Tahsin Said Beg, has moved to Germany, the traditional residence of the Mîr and his family is in the village of Baʿdre in the Sheikhan region of Iraqi Kurdistan. Equally important is the Baba Sheikh (Bavê Şêx) who also has to be from a specific family, the Fakhr ad-Dīn-branch of the Shemsani-family. The Baba Sheikh is the community's spiritual leader and resides in Shekhan (in Arabic, *Ain Sifni*) between Baʿdre and Lalish. The Baba Sheikh has to live an ascetic live and is considered as the highest spiritual authority of the Yazidis. He is also the highest authority in Lalish. However, the daily affairs of Lalish are led by Baba Chawush, who is the highest religious notable permanently present in Lalish. Although subordinated to Baba Sheikh he is appointed by the Prince[10] and also has to live in piety and chastity. Other religious dignitaries include Baba Gavan, the Koceks who act as servants in Lalish, and different custodians of local shrines called Mijewir. Besides the castes, the tribes are still a constitutional element of Yazidi social system.

Iraq as the centre of the Yazidis

Iraq constitutes the religious centre of Yazidism and is its traditionally largest settlement area. Until the genocide of 2014, over 500,000 Yazidis lived in present-day Iraq.[11] The region of Shekhan (Şexan) has the most important religious sanctuary in Lalish (Lalis) with the offices and residences of both the Baba Sheikh (Bava Şex) and the Mîr, the two religious and traditional heads of the Yazidis. The heart of Iraq's Yazidi settlement area includes the region Shekhan, northeast of Mosul, the Sinjar mountain range (Kurdish: *Şingal*), which is located west of Mosul, and the adjacent plains. The Yazidis living there speak Kurdish, as do the Yazidis in Syria, Turkey, and the Caucasus. However, an enclave of the Yazidi people who speak Arabic as their native language live in the Nineveh Plains, east of Mosul in Bashiqa and

---

[10] Philip G Kreyenbroek / Khalil Jindi Rashow, *God and Sheikh Adi are Perfect. Sacred Poems and Religious Narratives from the Yezidi Tradition.*(Wiesbaden: Harrassowitz, 2005) 11.

[11] Birgül Açıkyıldız, *The Yezidis: The History of a Community, Culture and Religion.* (London/New York: I. B. Taurus 2010) 33.

Bahzani.

Under Saddam Hussein, the Kurdish-speaking Yazidis also faced the strong pressure of Arabisation. In the 1970s, the Baath Party regime forced Yazidi from Sinjar to leave their villages in the mountains and resettled them to easily controllable sites such as 'collective villages' and cities on the plains. Only a few settlements in the mountains survived the regime's confiscation of Yazidi land and transfer to Arab settlers. After Saddam Hussein's fall, this led to mass conflicts between Yazidis and these settlers.[12]

Both Arab and Kurdish Muslims have widespread prejudices against Yazidis. The allegation of devil worship is much more widespread than just within the extremist-jihadist milieu. Most Muslims and Christians often accuse Yazidis of being dirty and not washing themselves.[13] During many conversations with Muslims and Christians in the region, I was repeatedly told that the Yazidi religion forbids its followers to wash themselves. For this reason, it would also be harmful to eat with Yazidis or even at their homes and restaurants. Apart from the cities predominantly inhabited by Yazidis, they could never successfully operate a restaurant or a bakery simply because they would not have any customers.

The anti-Yazidi resentments among Iraq's Muslims and Christians and the crimes of the ISIS has a similar relationship to that between the anti-Semitic prejudices in nineteenth-century Europe and the crimes of National Socialism. Not each and every person was an anti-Semite, but most non-Jews carried some anti-Semitic resentments, which were hegemonic in society. Just like National Socialism only had to systematise, ideologise, and radicalise already existing anti-Semitic resentments, the ISIS was also able to build on widespread stereotypes and resentments against Yazidis when they attacked the largest settlement area of the Yazidis in Iraq in August 2014.

Thus, it is not enough to blame the so-called 'Islamic State' for the genocide committed against the Yazidis in Iraq. Instead, we need a broader debate about anti-Yazidi resentments and how Iraqi society historically related to religious minorities and marginalised groups.

---

[12] Eszter Spät, *The Yezidis*. (London: Saqi 2005), 81f.
[13] Christine Allison, *The Yezidi Oral Tradition in Iraqi Kurdistan*. (London/New York: Routledge 2001), 37.

Lalish, the most important holy place of the Yazidis in Northern Iraq. (Picture: Thomas Schmidinger)

Sherfeddin, the most important holy place in the Shingal/Sinjar-Region in Northern Iraq. (Picture: Thomas Schmidinger)

Yazidi men meeting in front of the Sherfeddin temple in the predominantly Yazidi region of Shingal. (Picture: Thomas Schmidinger)

Yazidi refugees from Shinal/Sinjar in the Kurdistan Region of Iraq. (Picture: Thomas Schmidinger)

CHAPTER 10

THE YAZIDI QUEST FOR PROTECTION IN SINJAR IN THE POST-ISIS IRAQ

Arzu Yılmaz and Bayar Mustafa Sevdeeen

This paper considers the future of Sinjar (Kurdish: *Shingal*) in the current context where local, regional, and international actors shape the political setting in Iraq after the so-called Islamic State (ISIS). It traces primarily the political and military dominance of the two prominent Kurdish political parties, namely the Kurdistan Democratic Party (KDP) and the Kurdistan Workers' Party (PKK) in Sinjar; and, in turn, it explores the newly emerging parameters of the Yazidis' self-understanding which reshapes their political identity and even their perceptions of ethnic belonging vis-a-vis the efforts for centralisation and decentralisation dictated from above. It argues that regardless of whether or not the geopolitical equilibrium in post-ISIS era would favour the Yazidi aspirations for self-rule in Sinjar, the vibrant Yazidi activism will not vanish soon and will add new dimensions to the Kurdish and Iraqi political landscape.

Yazidis: Torn Between Religious and Ethnic Identities

The Yazidis are an ancient ethnic/religious minority group of approximately one million people. Most Yazidis live in northern Iraq, but also reside in Syria, Turkey, Iran, Armenia, and Georgia as well as various European countries, especially in Germany. Yazidis speak Kurmanji, a dialect of Kurdish language and are mostly considered ethnically Kurdish, though their distinct religious identity is Yazidism.[1]

Yazidism, a monotheistic religions, combines several aspects of other religions such as Zoroastrianism, Islam, Christianity, and Judaism. The essentialist form of Yazidism, however, is basically driven by the narratives of massacres that took place throughout the history. The literature speaks of 72 *Ferman* (massacres) committed against Yazidis in the past. They have been targeted by violent campaigns mainly because Muslims regard them as

---

[1] Philip G. Kreyenbroek, *Yezidism in Europe: Different Generations Speak about their Religion*. (Wiesbaden: Harrassowitz, 2009).

heretical.²

Nonetheless, a significant part of this narrative also indicates that the Yazidis were targeted not only as a religious minority, but also as an ethnic Kurdish group. Arabisation of the Yazidis in Iraq during the 1970s, for instance, was an inseparable component of de-Kurdification of non-Arab regions.³

During those developments, the Yazidis were primarily aligned with the Kurdish national movements as the 'original/authentic Kurds' that survived despite centuries of assimilation efforts against the Kurds in the Middle East.⁴ Yet, the Yazidis mostly inhabited the mountainsides where the central authorities failed to reach out politically and militarily. In this context, the Yazidi experience with armed struggle and political mobilisation in the modern realm was basically shaped within different fractions of Kurdish national movements. Meanwhile, Yazidi Mirza, Dawood Dawood and Darwesh Avdi, who had been symbols of Yazidi defiance of oppression, remained as heroic stories.⁵ The social relations between Yazidi and Muslim-majority Kurdish communities, however, constantly rest on perceptions of each other's religious identities. Ultimately, the emphasis on Kurdishness always facilitated political interactions, but hardly hid the distinct Yazidi religious identity.

This state of affairs has changed radically when the Kurdistan Regional Government (KRG) military withdrew from Sinjar in the face of the ISIS attacks in 2014.⁶ In the eye of most Yazidis, the KRG was also responsible for the consequences of the ISIS attacks which, in the end, constituted another genocidal event in Yazidi history and became known as the 73rd Ferman.⁷ Nevertheless, despite the ongoing engagements with the PKK and the KDP, the Yazidis military and political goals in post-ISIS Iraq have centred around self-defence and self-rule in Sinjar. The motto of Yazidi survival has now become: 'Neither Arabisation nor Kurdification, but Yazidism'.⁸

---

² Ibid.
³ Eva Savelsberg / Siamend Hajo / Irene Dulz, 'Effectively Urbanized. Yezidis in the Collective Towns of Sheikhan and Sinjar' *Études rurales* 186 (2010), 101-116.
⁴ Ibid.
⁵ Elias Kasem, 'Hope Brings Unity as the Yezidis celebrate their New Year' *Ezidi Press,* (published 4 April 2015) http://www.ezidipress.com/en/hope-brings-unity-yezidis-new-year/.
⁶ 'Barzani slams Peshmerga leaders over Sinjar Withdrawal' *Middle East Eye,* (published 12 February 2015) https://www.middleeasteye.net/news/barzani-slams-peshmerga-leaders-over-sinjar-withdrawal-871892340.
⁷ Valeria Cetorelli / Isaac Sasson, Nazar Shabila / Gibert Burnham, 'ISIS' Yezidi Genocide' *Foreign Affairs* (published 8 June 2017) https://www.foreignaffairs.com/articles/syria/2017-06-08/isis-yazidi-genocide.
⁸ From a banner on Mount Sinjar, April 7, 2017, Sinjar.

Sinjar at a Crossroads

Sinjar, almost a forgotten Yazidi-populated district on Iraq's northwestern border with Syria, has suddenly become a crucial battle field for both internal and external powers after the ISIS attacked Sinjar on 3 August 2014. When the ISIS captured Mosul in June 2014, some thought that the ISIS would head towards Baghdad, but the ISIS surprisingly attacked Sinjar.[9] The ultimate goal of the ISIS was obviously to upset the status-quo in the Middle East by first connecting the territory of Iraq and Syria.[10] Therefore, Sinjar was an important target, in particular, because of Highway 47, which lies alongside Sinjar and linked the two biggest ISIS strongholds in Raqqa in Syria and Mosul in Iraq. Nevertheless, the ISIS had the opportunity to intensify its attacks in Syria after the fall of Sinjar,.[11] In addition, Sinjar was an easy target for the ISIS as it was inhabited mostly by Yazidis who have repeatedly been the victims of Muslim assaults without any significant cost to the aggressors. Throughout history, minority populated areas have always been easy to occupy for any external forces in the region.

From an international point of view, to safeguard political borders and the status quo in the Middle East, Sinjar had to be free of ISIS control. Therefore, the USA indifferent in the face of the ISIS expansion into Mosul in June 2014, reacted promptly with airstrikes against the ISIS in Sinjar on 7 August 2014.[12] The USA military attacks were, apparently, a necessary response to the genocidal killing and abduction of thousands of Yazidis in Sinjar. The international efforts to form the Global Coalition to Counter ISIL, however, also took place soon after the ISIS captured Sinjar.[13]

In November 2015, the US-backed Kurdish forces from both Iraq and Syria launched an operation to liberate Sinjar.[14] The PKK fighters, the PKK-linked Syrian Kurdish fighters called The People's Protection Units (YPG) and the KRG peshmerga forces fought side by side to defeat the ISIS in Sinjar. Meanwhile Sinjar has become a political and military hub for the Kurdish groups affiliated with the KDP and the PKK, in particular.[15] Despite

---

[9] Ned Parker / Isabel Coles, Raheem Salman, 'Special Report: How Mosul fell- An Iraqi general disputes Baghdad's story', *Reuters*, (published 14 October 2014) https://www.reuters.com/article/us-mideast-crisis-gharawi-special-report/special-report-how-mosul-fell-an-iraqi-general-disputes-baghdads-story-idUSKCN0I30Z820141014.

[10] Hannah Strange, 'Islamic State leader Abu Bakr al-Baghdadi Addresses Muslims in Mosul' *The Telegraph*, (published 5 July 2014) https://www.telegraph.co.uk/news/worldnews/middleeast/iraq/10948480/Islamic-State-leader-Abu-Bakr-al-Baghdadi-addresses-Muslims-in-Mosul.html.

[11] Harriet Alexander / Alastair Beach, 'How ISIL is funded, trained and operating in Iraq and Syria?' *The Telegraph*, (published 23 August 2014) https://www.telegraph.co.uk/news/worldnews/middleeast/iraq/11052919/How-Isil-is-funded-trained-and-operating-in-Iraq-and-Syria.html.

[12] Helene Cooper / Mark Landler / Alissa J. Rubin, ' Obama Allows Limited Airstrikes on ISIS' *The New York Times*, (published 7 August 2014) https://www.nytimes.com/2014/08/08/world/middleeast/obama-weighs-military-strikes-to-aid-trapped-iraqis-officials-say.html.

[13] 'The Global Coalition to Defeat ISIS' *U.S. Department of State*, (published 10 September 2014) https://www.state.gov/s/seci/.

[14] 'Battle for Sinjar: ISIS held town in Iraq liberated' *BBC News*, (published 13 November 2015) https://www.bbc.com/news/34806556.

[15] Denise Natali, 'Lessons from the Liberation of Sinjar' *War on the Rocks*, (published 25 November

the ongoing rivalry relations between the two parties, however, Sinjar soon turned into a symbol of Kurdish-Kurdish co-existence and a *de facto* connection between *Bashur* (South Kurdistan) and *Rojava (West Kurdistan)*. The Iraqi-Syrian political border has vanished once again after the ISIS, but this time in favour of the Kurds who pursue their own nation building. Nevertheless, just after the liberation of Sinjar, the KRG President Barzani called on global leaders to acknowledge the failure of the Sykes-Picot pact that had led to the boundaries of the modern Middle East and urged them to broker a new deal paving the way for a Kurdish state.[16]

The initial tally of such developments has demonstrated that Turkey and Iran would inevitably be active in Sinjar. Hence, Turkey, silent in the face of the ISIS attacks in both Mosul and Sinjar, vowed that it wouldn't allow Sinjar to turn into another Qandil. [17] Turkish airstrikes which constantly hit the PKK bases in northern Iraq, then also targeted Sinjar.[18] On the other hand, Iran leveraged its influence in Baghdad first to trigger the rivalry between the PKK and the KDP by backing the PKK-affiliated groups in Sinjar. The Shingal Resistance Units (YBŞ), for instance, joined Popular Mobilisation Units (Hasd Al-Shaabi) which consists of Iraqi Shiite militias under the control of Iran.[19]

In fact, both Turkey and Iran have strategic goals to expand their spheres of influence beyond their borders. In the last decade, Turkey has repeatedly voiced its neo-Ottoman desires,[20] while Iran has attempted to build a 'Shiite Crescent' via the Iraq-Syria border.[21] In this sense, the emergence of a *de facto* connection between Bashur and Rojava through Sinjar was not only a threat perceived in the context of Kurdish aspirations, but also to achieve those strategic goals. Whoever controls Sinjar would eventually have an upper hand in the region. In the end, however, Iran has obviously received such an opportunity when Hash Al-Shaabi took the control of first south of Sinjar in June 2017 and then Sinjar district as a whole in October 2017 after the

---

2015) https://warontherocks.com/2015/11/lessons-from-the-liberation-of-sinjar/.

[16] 'Iraqi Kurdistan President: Time has come to redraw Middle East boundaries' *The Guardian*, (published 22 January 2016) https://www.theguardian.com/world/2016/jan/22/kurdish-independence-closer-than-ever-says-massoud-barzani.

[17] 'Erdogan says Sinjar will not be 'new Qandil' for PKK' *Anadolu Agency*, (published 10 October 2016) https://www.aa.com.tr/en/politics/erdogan-says-sinjar-will-not-be-new-qandil-for-pkk/673511.

[18] Isabel Coles / John Davison, 'Turkish jets strike Kurdish fighters in Syira, Iraq's Sinjar' *Reuters*, (published 25 April 2017) https://www.reuters.com/article/us-mideast-crisis-turkey-iraq/turkish-jets-strike-kurdish-fighters-in-syria-iraqs-sinjar-idUSKBN17R0D2.

[19] Baxtiyar Goran, 'PKK military wing in Shingal, Hasd Al-Shaabi visited Tehran' *Kurdistan 24*, (published 25 January 2017) http://www.kurdistan24.net/en/news/46357dad-e6bb-4626-aad9-1f49b63cd926/PKK-military-wing-in-Shingal--Hashd-al-Shaabi-visit-Tehran-.

[20] Nick Danford, 'Turkey's New Maps Are Reclaiming the Ottoman Empire' *Foreign Policy*, (published 23 October 2016) https://foreignpolicy.com/2016/10/23/turkeys-religious-nationalists-want-ottoman-borders-iraq-erdogan/.

[21] Allison Fedirka, 'Iranian Expansion Spreads Beyond the Middle East' *Geopolitical Features*, (published 16 February 2018) https://geopoliticalfutures.com/iranian-expansion-spreads-beyond-middle-east/.

referendum in the KRG.[22]

One could argue that the territorial integrity and the political borders of the state of Iraq has been safeguarded once again after the defeat of the ISIS and the ill-fated referendum in the KRG. Nevertheless, reconstruction of Iraq is the new task on the political agenda for the next ten years. It is doubtful, however, whether the actual efforts to concentrate power and renationalise governance in Iraq could help Baghdad to control all of Iraq. The current political landscape, for instance, in Sinjar simply demonstrates that it is unlikely. Despite the statements about withdrawing their troops, both Hasd Al-Shaabi and the PKK are still operating in Sinjar while the central government is far from controlling the administrative units in the city.[23] It is also doubtful whether Baghdad could soon fill the power vacuum and secure civil life in Sinjar in the face of increasing Turkish and Iranian influence throughout Iraqi territory.

In view of such circumstances, Sinjar is likely to be a militarised zone on Iraq-Syria border and a no-man's land trapped in a regional power struggle. The Kurdish actors, however, still could change the course of developments in Sinjar. They failed to annex Sinjar to the KRG or to Rojava, but both the KDP and the PKK can upend domestic and regional balances in Sinjar.

Annexation of Sinjar by the KRG: Kurdification versus Arabisation

The strategic importance of Sinjar was recognised even at the beginning of the twentieth century when France and the United Kingdom agreed to draw the borders of Syria and Iraq. Despite all efforts, however, a full control over Sinjar has never been achieved. First, this cannot happen because of the geographical feature of the Sinjar mountains (up to 1469 metres high) stretching towards Syria. Second, the inhabitants of Sinjar have always been mostly Yazidis with a distinct religious identity and weak connections to the rest of the country. Nevertheless, in order to enhance Baghdad's military control, Sinjar was one of the primary goals of Arabisation policy in 1970s. In 1975, for instance, Saddam Hussein regime evacuated165 villages in Sinjar district and resettled the Yazidis in Arab populated areas of the Nineveh Plain. In addition, the Yazidis were forced to newly established mixed Yazidi Arab settlements, known as *Mucemma*, in order to melt into dominant Arab ethnic culture.[24]

This, however, changed in 2003 when the US invaded Iraq. The newly

---

[22] 'Winning the Post-ISISIS Battle for Iraq in Sinjar', *International Crisis Group* 183, (published 20 February 2018) https://www.crisisgroup.org/middle-east-north-africa/gulf-and-arabian-peninsula/iraq/183-winning-post-isis-battle-iraq-sinjar.

[23] Sangar Ali, 'Watch: PKK Affiliated Group, Shia Militia Block Shingal Administrations Return Despite Agreement' *Kurdistan 24*, (published 31 October 2018) http://www.kurdistan24.net/en/news/ac6eb96f-5ba7-4f9a-b07d-c76c6a96c6fc.

[24] Philip G. Kreyenbroek, *Yezidism in Europe: Different Generations Speak about their Religion*. (Wiesbaden: Harrassowitz, 2009).

emerging Kurdish entity KRG has succeeded to establish a relative dominance in Sinjar while the new Iraqi Constitution in 2005 designated the district of Sinjar a disputed area between Baghdad and Erbil. The importance of Sinjar for the KRG has relied on first and foremost the perception that Sinjar is an inseparable part of Kurdistan — likewise Kirkuk — while the Yazidis are primarily Kurdish despite their distinct religious identity.[25] In addition, military control over Sinjar assured the security of two major cities of Iraqi Kurdistan, Duhok and Zaxo, and the road that connects them.[26] Hence, soon after 2003, Kurdification of Sinjar replaced Arabisation as the KRG attempted to annex Sinjar within its territory.

According to local people, when the KRG peshmerga first arrived in Sinjar on 12 March 2003, the Yazidis received them with drums and flutes.[27] Such a warm welcome, however, relied on two days of hard negotiations between the KRG and Yazidi leaders. Yazidi leaders loyal to the Saddam Hussein regime were particularly reluctant to cooperate with the KRG in Sinjar as the KRG had strongly supported the American invasion in Iraq in 2003. In addition, before 2003, Sinjar was a sanctuary for the Yazidis who tried to escape from political oppressions and, in some cases, legal punishments that they face in Iraq including the KRG-governed region.[28]

The negotiations, however, resulted in the consent of prominent Yazidi religious and tribal leaders who were then the first Yazidi, in their history, appointed to administrative and political posts in Sinjar. In Sinjar Municipality, for instance, after 96 years, a Yazidi first became mayor in 2003.[29] Moreover, in 2004, the first Yazidi from Sinjar, since the founding of the Republic of Iraq, became an Iraqi National Parliament member.[30] After the 2005 Iraqi parliamentary elections, 7 out of 75 Iraqi Parliament members on Kurdistan list were Yazidis while one was from Sinjar[31]

Despite such a rapid increase of Yazidi representation in government, Sinjar was yet connected with the KRG. The relations between the KRG and Sinjar were mostly limited to patronage networks via the Yazidi elites who soon became members of the KDP and shaped the KDP dominance in all Yazidi populated areas. Between 2006-2010, six out of seven Yazidi members of Iraqi Parliament were from the KDP. This was mainly because most Yazidis in Iraq lived in Nineveh Plain, around the city of Duhok where the KDP has been the dominant party for decades.

---

[25] J.S. Guest, *Survival Among the Kurds: A History of the Yezidis*, (London: Routledge,1993).
[26] Interview with Serbest Lezgin, KRG Ministry of Peshmerga, April 4, 207, Duhok.
[27] Anonymous Interview with Yezidis in Sinjar, April 10, 2017, Sinjar.
[28] Interview with Sheikh Shamo, Lalesh Center, April 17, 2017, Duhok.
[29] Interview with Dakhil Qasim Hason, Lalesh Center, April 28, 2018, Duhok
[30] Interview with Hayder Shesho, Sharfadeen Temple, April 8, 2017, Sinjar.
[31] 'Council of Representatives Elections' *The Independent Electoral Commission of Iraq* (published 15 December 2005) https://web.archive.org/web/20070709172441/http://www.ieciraq.org:80/final%20 cand/IECI_Certified__CoR_Candidates_En_Ar.pdf

On the other hand, the two predominant Kurdish parties, the KDP and the Patriotic Union of Kurdistan (PUK) decided to split the disputed areas into two spheres of political and military influence in accordance with the power-sharing agreement brokered for the territory of the KRG itself. As a consequence, the PUK gained dominance in Kirkuk and southward toward Iran, while the KDP became almost unrivalled northward to the Syrian border including Sinjar.[32]

Under the KDP rule, the education system in Sinjar soon harmonised with the system in the KRG. Kurdish language gradually replaced Arabic in school curriculums while the Yazidi students were encouraged by scholarships to study at the universities in the KRG.[33] The annexation process of Sinjar peaked, however, when Al-Qaida affiliated groups killed 350 Yazidis in Mosul in 2007.[34] The Yazidi quest for protection, in the end, strengthened the KDP's dominance in Sinjar, while Baghdad was trapped in a sectarian war. Meanwhile, the KRG built the Siheyla bridge over the Khabur river in 2008 which connected Sinjar with the Kurdish cities Duhok and Zaxo where job opportunities as well as trade were about to boom.

The tide in Sinjar turned, however, when the peshmerga forces withdrew ahead the ISIS assaults in 2014.

The PKK in Sinjar

When the PKK first established its military bases in Iraq in the 1980s, its primary concern was to gain strength in areas close to the Iraq-Turkey border. On the other hand, unlike the Iraq-Turkey border, until the end of 1990s, the Saddam Hussein regime had a strong control over Sinjar to keep out any military and/or political interference. In such circumstances, the PKK could enter Sinjar once the Maxmur Refugee camp was established with the support of the Saddam regime near Mosul in 1998.[35] Via Mosul to Sinjar, then, the PKK found the opportunity to reach out Damascus; thereby, Sinjar soon became a strategic route to supply the PKK bases along the Haftanin-Zap line in Iraq.

Nonetheless the PKK could gain a foothold in Sinjar after the US invasion in 2003. Despite the KRG's prompt attempts to fill the power vacuum, lack of full military control over Sinjar paved the way for the PKK's access. The PKK's initial efforts were, however, not military but political. The PKK, for instance, organised the 'Democratic Freedom Congress of the Yazidis' in February 2004, and succeeded in recruiting 270 Yazidis from around the world as members of this newly formed organisation.[36] Contrary

---

[32] Interview with Haydar Shesho, April 8, 2017, Sinjar.
[33] Interview with Sheikh Shamo, Lalesh Center, April 17, 2017, Duhok.
[34] 'They won't stop until we are all wiped out' Among the Yezidi, people in mourning' *The Guardian*, (published 18 August 2007) https://www.theguardian.com/world/2007/aug/18/iraq.topstories3.
[35] Interview with Zeki Singali, PKK Commander, April 9, 2017, Sinjar.
[36] Ibid.

to the KDP, the PKK preferred to highlight the Yazidi identity instead of Kurdishness in its political discourse, which apparently attracted first the Yazidi youth. In this context, the PKK's primary goal was not to seize Sinjar at all. The PKK was mainly focused on recruiting more Yazidis into its armed-groups and to have free access to Syria via Sinjar.

The KDP's response to the PKK in Sinjar was to not react. Both parties had recently brokered a ceasefire after a long-lasting armed conflict in 1990s[37] Moreover, based upon their political and economic achievements in Iraq, the Iraqi Kurdish political parties finally won the power struggle for leading the Kurdish national cause. The KDP, then, did not push the PKK back from Sinjar as long as the PKK's presence in Sinjar was limited to political activities.

The power struggle between the KDP and the PKK in Sinjar, however, surfaced when the Syrian civil war erupted in 2012. The PKK-linked Kurdish groups seized a remarkable control over the Kurdish cities in Syria, which soon resulted in proclaiming three cantons under Kurdish rule.[38] The strategic importance of Sinjar was, therefore, not only a matter of logistical support for the PKK bases in Iraq, but also a matter of survival of the newly emerging Kurdish autonomous region in Syria. Furthermore, the PKK was finally able to interfere in the internal affairs of the KRG, which has been a goal since the 1990s.

The KDP-PKK Coexistence in Sinjar: Brothers, But Not Partners

After the ISIS captured the city of Mosul, it was assumed that the ISIS would head south to attack Baghdad. Nevertheless, the Iraqi troops soon withdrew from the Sunni-populated cities, including the disputed areas, and consolidated its defence to protect the Shia south and the capital city.[39] However, less than two months after the fall of Mosul, the ISIS moved north and attacked Sinjar on 3 August 2014.[40] The result was an all-out slaughter. In a few days, 10,000 Yazidis were killed, 6,255 were kidnapped while a hundred of thousands fled to Iraqi Kurdistan, Rojava, and Turkey.[41] Meanwhile the KRG forces lost the control of all the disputed areas. On 6

---

[37] Arzu Yılmaz, *Atruş'tan Maxmur'a: Kürt Mülteciler ve Kimliğin Yeniden İnşası*. (Istanbul: Iletisim, 2016), 152-163.

[38] Wladimir van Wildenburg, 'Syrian Kurdish party declares transitional government' *Al-Monitor*, (published 12 November 2013) https://www.al-monitor.com/pulse/originals/2013/11/syria-kurds-government-plan-wilgenburg.html.

[39] Suadad Al-Salhy / Tim Arango, 'Sunni Militants Drive Iraqi Army out of Mosul' *The New York Times*, (published 10 June 2014) https://www.nytimes.com/2014/06/11/world/middleeast/militants-in-mosul.html.

[40] 'UN alarm over fate of Iraqi Yezidi children', *BBC News*, (published 5 August 2014) https://www.bbc.com/news/world-middle-east-28663926.

[41] Lizzie Dierden, 'Almost 10000 Yazidis were killed or kidnapped in ISISIS genocide, but true scale of horror may never be known' *The Independent*, (published 9 May 2017) https://www.independent.co.uk/news/world/middle-east/isis-islamic-state-yazidi-sex-slaves-genocide-sinjar-death-toll-number-kidnapped-study-un-lse-a7726991.html.

August, 2014, the ISIS was just 30 kilometres far from Erbil, the capital city of the KRG.⁴²

With such developments, the KRG could hardly survive without the prompt US airstrikes against the ISIS while it lacked Turkish support despite the KRG asking for urgent help ahead the ISIS assaults.⁴³ Soon after, the KRG forces could succeed in pushing the ISIS back from some parts of disputed areas, for instance, from Kirkuk and Maxmur.⁴⁴ The KRG, however, cooperated with the PKK fighters in both Kirkuk and Maxmour to defeat the ISIS. In this regard, the Kurdish armed groups were for the first time in their history united and fought side by side against a common enemy. In the wake of this cooperation, Masoud Barzani, the President of the KRG, underlined the importance of such a historic moment by visiting the Maxmour Refugee Camp where the PKK-affiliated Kurds from Turkey had settled.⁴⁵

Due to the power-sharing agreement brokered in late 1990s, the PKK soon withdrew from the disputed areas where it cooperated with the KRG forces, but not from Sinjar. The PKK claimed that the rescue operation of the Yazidis was carried out by the YPG and the Peoples' Defence Force (HPG) fighters while 11,000 peshmerga already stationed in Sinjar abandoned the Yazidis. Therefore, the Yazidis in Sinjar have the right to claim for building up their own self-defence and self-rule which have the support of the PKK⁴⁶

Overall, the withdrawal of the peshmerga forces caused catastrophic consequences not only in Sinjar but also in relations between the KRG and the Yazidis. The Yazidis were frustrated with the KRG's failure in Sinjar while this badly harmed the ongoing annexation process. In fact, the KRG's military failure was not merely in Sinjar. But particularly the failure in Sinjar has caused destuctive political implication. Many Yazidis linked the peshmerga withdrawal with Sunni prejudice against Yazidis.⁴⁷ Such a perception weakened the newly built Kurdishness that the KRG has imposed from above to bind fragile relations between the the Sunni majority Kurds and their Yazidi brothers. Therefore, the PKK-promoted self-defence and

---

⁴² 'Ten days in Iraq: Aid drops, airstrikes and 200000 new refugees', *BBC News*, (published 19 August 2014) https://www.bbc.com/news/world-middle-east-28761383.

⁴³ Havdar Ahmed, 'Senior Kurdistan Official: ISIS was at Erbil's Gate, Turkey Did Not Help' *Rudaw*, (published 16 September 2014) http://www.rudaw.net/english/interview/16092014.

⁴⁴ Patrick Cockburn, 'ISIS: Iraqi Army Retakes Control of Oil Refinery Town as Kurds Stand firm Against Overstretched Islamic State' *The Independent*, (published 14 November 2014) https://www.independent.co.uk/news/world/middle-east/isis-the-kurds-strike-back-army-retakes-control-of-oil-refinery-town-as-kurds-stand-firm-against-9862538.html.

⁴⁵ Wladimir van Wilgenburg, 'Kurdish rivals unite to fight Islamic State' *Al Jazeera*, (published 16 August 2014) https://www.aljazeera.com/news/middleeast/2014/08/iraq-turkey-kurds-fight-islamic-state-201481581133776796.html.

⁴⁶ 'Shengal should be governed by Shengalis', *ANF News*, (published 14 May 2017) https://www.anfenglish.com/kurdistan/shengal-should-be-governed-by-shengalis.

⁴⁷ Interview with Haydar Shesho, April 8, 2017, Sinjar.

self-rule project for the Yazidis in Sinjar has quickly gained ground among all Yazidis.

Against this backdrop, however, the KRG has continued to affect the course of military and political developments in Sinjar. Nevertheless, most Yazidis who fled from Sinjar has found sanctuary mainly in the KRG governed cities, Duhok and Zaxo.[48] Also, the Yazidi were, in the end, rescued by a joint forces of the KDP and the PKK.

On 4 August 2014, for instance, when the ISIS seized the road that connects Sinjar with the rest of the KRG territory, tens of thousands of Yazidis were still encircled by the ISIS on Mount Sinjar.[49] In the absence of the peshmerga forces, no more than 20 PKK fighters were in Sinjar on 4 August. However, 50 YPG fighters promptly mobilised to open a corridor via Iraqi-Syria border to Rojava, which provided a vital opportunity for both the Yazidis in Mount Sinjar and the peshmerga forces who returned back to Sinjar.[50] Within two days, this corridor allowed 15,000 Yazidi families to flee from Sinjar to Rojava. Despite the mistrust to the KRG, only 5,000 of them stayed in a refugee camp set up and ruled by the YPG near Haseke, The rest of 10,000 families preferred to go back to the KRG territory via Rabia on 4 August, and then via Fish-Khabur on 5 August when Rabia fell in the hands of the ISIS.[51]

Meanwhile, 300 peshmerga could also reach Sinjar using the same corridor just three days after the ISIS attack, on 6 August.[52] The PKK presence in Sinjar became significant when 150 PKK fighters from Qandil arrived in Sinjar on 7 August 2014. The KRG president, Masud Barzani, authorised PKK fighters to take buses from the northeast of Iraqi Kurdistan to the southwest.[53] Therefore, the PKK and the KRG cooperated not only to rescue the Yazidis but to attack on the ISIS in Sinjar as well.

In fact, such a cooperation had resulted from negotiations held between the PKK and the KRG before the ISIS attacked Sinjar. As the PKK commander Zeki Sengali said, 'The representatives of the PKK and the KDP met several times to discuss a joint action in face of the ISIS attacks.'[54] The PKK even suggested to build a Yazidi military unit under the command of both the PKK and the KDP. The KDP, however, refused that suggestion and committed the peshmerga forces itself to securing all the Iraqi Kurdistan

---

[48] 'IDPs and Refugees in Duhok Governorate', *Duhok Governorate Board of Relief and Humanitarian Affairs, B.R.H.A.,* (published February 2016) http://www.brha-duhok.org/wp-content/uploads/Report%20of%202016.pdf.
[49] 'Yazidis still stranded on Mount Sinjar' *The Guardian,* (published 27 August 2014) https://www.theguardian.com/world/2014/aug/27/-sp-yazidis-mount-sinjar-isis-satellite-images.
[50] Interview with Zeki Singali, PKK Commander, April 9, 2017, Sinjar.
[51] Interview with Piroz, PKK fighter, April 8, 2017, Sinjar.
[52] Interview with Serbest Lezgin, KRG Ministry of Peshmerga, April 4, 2017, Duhok.
[53] Interview with Piroz, PKK fighter, April 8, 2017, Sinjar.
[54] Interview with Zeki Singali, PKK Commander, April 9, 2017, Sinjar.

region, including Sinjar.⁵⁵

In the end, the KDP could neither keep its promises nor explain why the peshmerga withdrew from Sinjar. The trial on peshmerga withdrawal from Sinjar didn't arrive at a conclusion.⁵⁶ Accordingly, the destructive political implications have continued to undermine the KRG's hold in Sinjar.

The PKK have also failed to achieve its goals in Sinjar. They succeeded in building some Yazidi military units commanded by the PKK and some self-ruled communities in Khanasor.⁵⁷ The PKK claims for Sinjar self-administration, however, has not gained a strong support among the Yazidis. Nevertheless the Yazidis were highly concerned with Turkey's assaults against the PKK in Sinjar, and with the uncertain fate of Kurdish autonomy in Rojava.⁵⁸ Ultimately, the Yazidi community in Sinjar was split mainly into two political and military spheres of influence between the PKK and the KDP while these two parties have to cooperate to preserve their foothold in Sinjar.

Liberation and Loss of Sinjar

Preparations for liberation of Sinjar took more than a year. Meanwhile, the KRG and the PKK each announced that they alone were about to free Sinjar.⁵⁹ The action began when the Anti-ISIS Coalition launched airstrikes in Sinjar on 3 November 2015.⁶⁰ On the ground, the KRG and PKK forces advanced separately against the ISIS. Sometimes, when they encountered with each other they consulted on how to move ahead; but, they did not fight under a joint command.⁶¹ A joint action between peshmerga and guerrilla forces took place only in the fight against the ISIS in the city of Sinjar.⁶² Nevertheless, the KRG flags with the PKK ones appeared side by side publicly once the city of Sinjar was freed from the ISIS.⁶³ By the end of the operation, each party claimed that the liberation of Sinjar was its own victory. However, the statements made by the US at the end of the military operation shaped the international narrative of the KRG forces success that liberated

---

⁵⁵ Cefer Eminke, KDP Politburo Member, May 27, 2017, Erbil.
⁵⁶ أسابيع المأساة الأيزيدية:طريق النجاة من المذبحة يشقّها حزب العمال الكردستاني، http://www.alhayat.com/article/592366/-أسابيع-المأساة-الأيزيدية-طريق-النجاة-من-المذبحة-يشقها-حزب-العمال-الكردستاني
⁵⁷ Tomas Kavalek, Competing Interests in Shingal District.
⁵⁸ Anonymous Interviews with Yezidis in Sinjar, April 10, 2017, Sinjar.
⁵⁹ Vera Mironova / Mohammed Hussein, 'The Struggle Over Sinjar' *Foreign Affairs* (published 5 June 2017) https://www.foreignaffairs.com/articles/middle-east/2017-06-05/struggle-over-sinjar.
⁶⁰ 'Department of Defense Press Briefing by Col. Warren via DVIDS from Baghdad, Iraq' *U.S. Department of Defense* (published 13 November 2015) https://dod.defense.gov/News/Transcripts/Transcript-View/Article/628932/department-of-defense-press-briefing-by-col-warren-via-dvids-from-baghdad-iraq/source/GovDelivery/.
⁶¹ Interview with Serbest Lezgin, KRG Ministry of Peshmerga, April 4, 2017, Duhok.
⁶² Interview with Zeki Singali, PKK Commander, April 9, 2017, Sinjar.
⁶³ 'President Barzani: Only Kurdistan flag will fly over Shingal, thanks US' *Rudaw*, (published 13 November 2015) http://www.rudaw.net/english/kurdistan/131120155.

Sinjar.⁶⁴

In the wake of liberation of Sinjar, efforts to annex Sinjar transformed into a new phase in the context of KRG's independence from Iraq. The KRG was, in fact, far from maintaining a full control over Sinjar. The PKK was also an actual military and political power in Sinjar.⁶⁵ Hence, the KDP has never facilitated the return of the Yazidi IDPs back to Sinjar after the liberation operation. True, neither the security nor the infrastructure in Sinjar were adequate for the return of the IDPs.⁶⁶ But the KDP has also been reluctant to support resettlement in Sinjar mainly because of the dual administration. The KDP has repeatedly called for the PKK to leave Sinjar. The KRG prime minister, Nechirvan Barzani even said that they might use force to push out the PKK from Sinjar.⁶⁷

In turn, the PKK had first a contradictory response. Murat Karayılan, a member of the Kurdistan Communities Union (KCK), said that, if necessary, they might consider withdrawing their troops.⁶⁸ However, Bese Hozat, another member of the KCK, refused to respond to such a call, and pointed out the right of Yazidis for self-administration.⁶⁹ The pro-PKK Kurdish media outlets, then, published different statements that Sinjar might be annexed as the fourth canton of Rojava Administration.⁷⁰

In the end, both the KRG and the PKK withdrew their troops from Sinjar. First, the KRG, on 17 October 2017, withdrew its forces after Iran-backed Iraqi militias called Hashd Al-Shaabi took control of Kirkuk and the disputed areas in Iraq.⁷¹ Then, in March 2018, the PKK announced that it would withdraw from Sinjar.⁷² Meanwhile, Hashd Al-Shaabi seized control over Sinjar for almost a year in the name of the central government in Baghdad; then, in August 2018, they also declared their departure from Sinjar.⁷³ As of January 2019, however, Baghdad has not successfully exercised

---

⁶⁴ Tim Arango, 'Sinjar Victory Bolsters Kurds, but could Further Alienate US from Iraq' *The New York Times*, (published 13 November 2015) https://www.nytimes.com/2015/11/14/world/middleeast/sinjar-iraq-kurds-isis.html.

⁶⁵ Tomas Kavalek, Competing Interests in Shingal District.

⁶⁶ Matthew Schweitzer 'Beyond Military Victory: Reconstructing Iraq After ISIS', *Global Observatory*, (published 17 January 2017) https://theglobalobservatory.org/2017/01/isis-iraq-united-nations-reconstruction/.

⁶⁷ Amberin Zaman, 'KRG PM: Talk of Iraqi Kurdish Independence red line for Iran, but not Turkey' *Al Monitor*, (published 23 December 2016) https://www.al-monitor.com/pulse/originals/2016/12/krg-iraq-kurdistan-region-nechirvan-barzani-iran-turkey.html.

⁶⁸ 'Teror Orgutu PKK Liderleinden Karayilan: Cekiliyoruz' *Sabah*, (published 30 December 2016) https://www.sabah.com.tr/gundem/2016/12/30/teror-orgutu-pkk-liderlerinde-karayilan-cekiliyoruz.

⁶⁹ 'PKK militants will not withdraw Sinjar' *Sol International*, (published 10 January 2017) https://news.sol.org.tr/pkk-militants-will-not-withdraw-sinjar-171391.

⁷⁰ 'Shengal should be governed by Shengalis' *ANF News*, (published 14 May 2017) https://www.anfenglish.com/kurdistan/shengal-should-be-governed-by-shengalis.

⁷¹ 'Iraqi Forces Drive Kurdish out of Town Sinjar' *The Guardian*, (published 17 October 2017) https://www.theguardian.com/world/2017/oct/17/iraqi-forces-drive-kurdish-fighters-out-of-sinjar.

⁷² 'PKK announces withdrawal from Sinjar' *Ahval News*, (published 23 March 2018) https://ahvalnews.com/sinjar/pkk-announces-withdrawal-sinjar-region.

⁷³ 'Official: Hashd Al-Shaabi Withdraws from Shingal' *Kurdistan 24*, (published 22 August 2018)

its authority in Sinjar. Seemingly, Sinjar is about to be trapped in a border zone between Iraq and Syria.

No Arabisation, No Kurdification, But Yazidizm

The third anniversary of the Yazidi genocide was held in front of a huge banner that read "Yesterday was genocide, today is the referendum, and tomorrow will be an independent state". It referred Saddam Hussein's anti-Kurdish campaign in the late 1980s that killed thousands of Kurdish civilians. At the event, Prime Minister Nechirwan Barzani said, "The voice of Sinjar in this referendum is very important because it is the voice of the Anfal genocide and the voice of the pains of our people". [74]

Nevertheless, most Yazidis voted for the independence of Kurdistan from Iraq.[75] Despite mistrust that derives from the frustration upon the KRG's military failure in Sinjar, the Yazidi IDPs have found safety in Kurdish-ruled region. Moreover, the recent parliamentary elections held in both Iraq and the KRG in 2018 showed that the KDP, in particular, have not lost its support in Yazidi-populated areas.[76]

Against this avidencr, however one can argue that there is a newly emerging Yazidi identity which places a higher priority on Yazidism instead of Kurdishness. In this regard, the Yazidis would likely shift towards Baghdad to make up for their losses within the context of the reconstruction of Iraq. Baghdad would obviously not support the Yazidi aspirations for self-rule while centralisation and re-nationalisation of the government has already taken place in Iraq. But under a fragile central authority rule, it is most probable that the Yazidi military units in Sinjar, for instance, could enhance their capacity and gain independence from both the KRG and the PKK forces' dominance. Indeed, such developments have already taken place by rapprochement between the Yazidi fighters and the Hashd Al-Shaabi forces.[77] But it is still questionable for many Iraqis and Yazidis whether this newly formed project for reconstruction of Iraq would succeed or result in another destruction as experienced before.[78]

On the other hand, the PKK may also side with Baghdad to preserve its foothold in Sinjar as long as Baghdad controls disputed areas. In fact, the PKK has always kept the doors open for cooperation with Baghdad against

---

http://www.kurdistan24.net/en/news/cd6c50f6-0f01-4feb-9be9-a402a194d590.

[74] 'PM Barzani: Kurds lost all hope with Baghdad, must protect themselves as a state' *Rudaw*, August 3, 2017,http://www.rudaw.net/english/kurdistan/030820172.

[75] أمير الايزيديين في العراق والعالم يطالب الايزيديين بالتصويت بـ(نعم)، http://www.basnews.com/index.php/ar/news/kurdistan/380023

[76] برلمان 2018 يخلو من ايزيدي سنجار ونائبة تلوم نظاماً 'سيء الصيت'، http://www.kurdistan24.net/ar/news/84d82dc7-fec7-4fdc-a88c-268d09b28566

[77] 'Yezidis Hashd leader: preparations Underway to Form Political Council in Shingal', *Rudaw*, July 10, 2017, http://www.rudaw.net/english/kurdistan/100720172.

[78] 'The Tricky Business of Rebuilding Iraq', Stratfor, February 2018, https://worldview.stratfor.com/article/iraq-war-rebuild-reconstruction.

the KRG's efforts to annex Sinjar. Nevertheless, the PKK's claim for self-administration in Sinjar has never challenged the unity of Iraq.[79] Even if the PKK withdraws all of its troops from Sinjar, the PKK will still have a control over Shingal Resistance Units (YBS) forces as it basically consists of the PKK-affiliated Yazidis in Sinjar even though 3000 YBS fighters have already joined as a local unit of Iraq's Hashd Al-Shaabi.[80] The PKK, however, could probably not survive in Sinjar under the Turkish threats which gradually undermine Yazidi support for the PKK.

Conclusion

For the Yazidis, the ISIS attack in 2014 constituted another tragic event in their history and a reminder that they could not rely on the protection of any other authority. This set inspired the irreversible development of local self-defence and self-rule in Sinjar. To this end, the Yazidis will keep shifting occasionally towards different political forces in Iraq considered better able to respond to their aspirations. An orientation towards the Iraqi central government, however, would likely strain the relations between the Yazidis and the Kurds. In this sense, the Yazidi case may be an Achilles heel of the Kurdish unity rather than the unity of Iraq.

---

[79] Sangar Ali, 'new PKK affiliate in Shingal says not right time for Kurdistan referendum' *Kurdistan 24*, (published 8 May2017) http://www.kurdistan24.net/en/news/2249375a-735c-490a-94e7-6208f589363e/new-pkk-affiliate-in-shingal-says-not-right-time-for-kurdistan-referendum.
[80] وحدات حماية سنجار تعلن إنضمام 3000 مقاتل من القضاء الى هيئة الحشد, https://www.alsumaria.tv/news/240048/ar/وحدات-حماية-سنجار-تعلن-إنضمام-3000-مقاتل-من-القضاء

CHAPTER 11

KAKAI INTERNAL DISPLACEMENT IN KIRKUK AND THE FEAR OF VIOLENCE FROM THE SO-CALLED ISLAMIC STATE IN IRAQ (ISIS)

Seyedehbehnaz Hosseini

The Kakai, also called Yārsan or Ahl-e Haqq, follow a religion that emerged thousands of years ago. Their monotheist religion has four principles: *Pāki, Rīsti, Nīsti,* and *Radā*.[1] Kakai speak a distinct language called 'Macho', a Gūrani Kurdish dialect, and are famous for agriculture and shepherding. They show a strong passion for playing music, because music is an essential part of their religion and rituals.[2] Originally, Kakai believe in *Doon-a-Doon* (life after death), where a soul passes 1,000 *Doon*[3] within 50,000 years, and continuously moves from one body to another until it reaches perfection.[4] They also believe that God manifested himself in different souls, such as Ali (the first Shia Imam) and Shah Khoshin, before embodying himself in the form of Sultan Sahak, the founder of the Kakai religion.[5] Kakai also believe that after 1001 transmigrations, the soul comes back to an everlasting home, and everything becomes part of God . In every period, someone had a sense of God, and each period was called the 'period of *Yār*'. The Kakai's belief has its roots in *Mithraism* and is similar to the *Yezidi*

---

[1] Translated as: purity and cleanliness of soul; truthfulness and justice; selflessness and humility; and content and satisfaction.
[2] For a complete description of *Tanboor*, see Partow Hooshmandrad 'Life as Ritual: Devotional Practices of the Kurdish Ahl-iḤaqq of Gurān' In *Religious Minorities in Kurdistan: Beyond the Mainstream. Studies in Oriental Religions* Edited by Khanna Omarkhali (Wiesbaden: Harrassowitz, 2014), 47-66.
[3] Jāme (clothe)
[4] Jean During, 'A Critical Survey on Ahl-e Haqq Studies in Europe and Iran' In *Alevi identity: Cultural, Religious and Social Perspectives.* Edited by Tord Olsson / Elisabeth Özdalga / Catharina Raudvere. (London: Routledge, 1998), 105-25, 143. Brahâm Elâhi, *La Voie de Perfection: L'enseignement d'un Maître Kurdeen Iran.* (Paris: Seghers, 1976), 17. Seyedehbehnaz Hosseini, 'Life after death in Manichean religion and Yārsān'in Fritillariakurdica' *International peer-reviewed Journal of Kurdish Studies* 13/14 (2016), 218. http://www.kurdishstudies.pl/?pl_fritillaria-kurdica-nr.-13-14, 218 (accessed 15 June 2018).
[5] Ziba Mir-Hosseini, 'Redefining the Truth: Ahl-i-Haqq and the Islamic Republic of Iran' *British Journal of Middle Eastern Studies* 21/2 (1994), 211-228.

189

religion.⁶ The Kakai religion does not believe in proselytising.

Methodology

This research uses primarily ethnographic data, including a secondary analysis of academic and scholarly literature. The study presents qualitative research undertaken from 2015 to 2018 after ISIS attacked Iraq. The main data collection technique was personal interviews. Answers could be open-ended and variable in length.

The interviews were conducted in Kirkuk, and its surrounding cities and villages, including Halabja, Hawar, Erbil, Suleymanieh, Daquq, and Alisaray villages. I used thematic analysis both to analyse material from the interviews, and to examine the relationship between the researcher and the participants. As part of the thematic analysis, I went through the text data and developed specific categories derived from key themes, words, and situations identified in the data. Due to the theoretical orientation and the purpose of this study, I constructed different categories around the general themes of social dominance, Arabisation, Islamisation and violence.

History of the Kakai in Iraq

Since the establishment of the Iraqi government in 1921, Kakai religious and collective rights have been neglected; they were never specifically protected in the Iraqi constitution like those of other religious faiths. Their religion was not officially recognised, and they were registered under Iraqi law as Muslims. They were exposed to further discrimination because they are Kurdish. Before the Second World War, Kakai were forced to change their official nationality to 'Arab' and they were deported and displaced from their original home-regions, which lie near the Arab-dominated areas. Such displacement with subsequent settlement by Arabs in the areas where Kakai used to live has been occurring since 1933.⁷

After 1963, under the Ba'athist regime, Kakais were exposed to attacks and deportations by the Iraqi National Guards, followed by further deportation campaigns in 1970-1971 and from 1975 to 1987. Kakai villages were destroyed and their people arrested, and some were executed because they were Kurds. The Kakai were deported from Baghdad and the Iraqi regions bordering Iran. In the beginning of the 1980-88 war between Iraq and Iran, their assets, houses, and belongings were confiscated, and they were persecuted in the same way as Feyli Kurds.⁸ In 1991, after Iraq was defeated in the Gulf War, the Kakai were displaced, and in 1991 they were

---

⁶ Philip G. Kreyenbroek, 'The Yāresān of Kurdistan' In *Religious Minorities in Kurdistan: Beyond the Mainstream.* Edited by Khanna Omarkhali. (Wiesbaden: Harrasowitz, 2014), 3-13.

⁷ Chaim Kaufmann, 'A security Dilemma: Ethnic partitioning in Iraq' *Harvard International Review* 28/4 (2007), 44-50.

⁸ Joost Hiltermann, *A Poisonous Affair: America, Iraq, and the Gassing of Halabja.* (Cambridge: Cambridge University Press, 2007), 133.

administratively forced to declare their official ethnicity as Arab.

The Kurdish people have existed in Iraq since the ancient Mesopotamian period. They have their own identity, language, and history. Kurds have largely been autonomous because of the rugged mountainous terrain where they live, their economic self-sufficiency, and their ability to defend their territory.[9] However, the Kurdish area in northern Iraq also has significant oil resources, and was therefore a target for Saddam Hussein's regime. Kirkuk, historically a cosmopolitan urban centre with sizeable Turkmen, Kurdish, Arab, Christian, and Jewish populations (listed in order of size), has long been a contested focus of demographic competition, since its development as an oil-drilling centre in the 1920s. The Kurds faced extreme persecution under the Ba'athist regime, with Saddam Hussein implementing a campaign of Arabisation of the Kurdish region from 1988. Saddam brought Arab people into the region in an attempt to lessen Kurdish control over their territory and contributed to a continuing distrust between Kurds and Arabs, which persists to this day. This operation, known as Operation Anfal was an ethnic cleansing campaign and 100,000 Kurds were killed with thousands of others rendered homeless.[10]

Following the Anfal Campaign, the Iraqi government forced the collectivisation and urbanisation of the Kurdish countryside and displaced the Kurdish population from what are today considered the disputed territories. Using resettlement incentives offered primarily to Shia peasants from southern Iraq, this policy sought to increase the Arab population of what were perceived to be 'sensitive areas' due to the disputed territories. These regions straddled the historical border between Arab and Kurdish rural populations.[11] The program of Arabisation continued in Kirkuk until the eve of toppling the Ba'ath regime. Throughout the 1990s, Kurds and other non-Arab residents continued to face harassment and pressure to change their ethnic identity and join the Ba'ath party.[12] During the 1990s, a further 120,000 persons were driven out of Kirkuk and other territories under Baghdad's control.[13]

Turkey also has a special interest in Kirkuk city, seeing it as the rightful home of the Turkmen minority, and strongly opposes its absorption into Iraqi Kurdistan. While the origins of the Turkmen are disputed, they are

---

[9] Aweed Dawisha, *Iraq – A Political History from Independence to Occupation.* (Princeton: Princeton University Press, 2013), 70.
[10] David Romano, 'The Future of Kirkuk' *Ethnopolitics* 6/2 (2007), 265-283.
[11] Nabil Al-Tikriti, 'There Go the Neighbourhoods: Policy Effects vis-à-vis Iraqi Forced Migration' In *Dispossession and Displacement. Forced Migration in the Middle East and North Africa.* Edited by Dawn Chatty / Bill Finlayson. (Oxford: Oxford University Press, 2010), 249-79. http://naltikriti.umwblogs.org/files/2010/11/British-Academy-Final-Proofs.pdf (accessed 10 June 2017).
[12] Human Rights Watch, 'Claims in Conflict: Reversing Ethnic Cleansing in Northern Iraq' *HWR*, (Published 2 August 2004) https://www.hrw.org/report/2004/08/02/claims-conflict/reversing-ethnic-cleansing-northern-iraq.
[13] David Romano, 'The Future of Kirkuk' *Ethnopolitics* 6/2 (2007), 265-283.

increasingly perceived in Turkey as an Iraqi Turkish minority deserving of support. Similarly, the Kurds also hold strong grievances and moral claims to Kirkuk, having faced extremely harsh treatment due to Saddam Hussein's Arabisation campaigns against the Kurdish region. The ethnic conflict overlaps with sectarian divides, in that Shia residents are seen as having ties and relations with Iran, even though most of Iraq's Shia are ethnically Arab. In an attempt to reverse Saddam Hussein's Arabisation campaign, the normalisation plan outlined in Iraq's constitution seeks to facilitate the return of Arab families to their places of origin; however, this has done little to restore goodwill among Iraqi Kurds.[14]

Kakai experiences during the ISIS attack in Iraq

ISIS invaded the area around Mosul, the second-largest city in Iraq, in the summer of 2014. This led to the displacement of Kakai from the regions surrounding the Nineveh Plains. The Kakai community's fear drove them to request the Kurdistan government to build up a special Kakai army to fight alongside the *Peshmerga* (the Kurdish Regional Government Army) against ISIS and to protect Kakai, because they could not trust other armies. Kakai were also driven by fear from what had happened to the Yezidi people at Sinjar; they did not want to face a similar fate.[15] ISIS destroyed the Kakai religious shrines in Iraq, the *Shah Hayas* and *Tekye Baba Heydari*. On 6 August 2014, when the plain around Mosul (Hamdanya) also came under attack by ISIS, the Kakai, Christians, Yezidi, and Shabak fled to safer areas. They settled in the Khabat district which belongs to the province of Erbil. They currently live in camps for internally displaced persons (IDP) in Erbil and other provinces. While all Iraqi citizens face daily insecurity due to terrorism, hostility against the Kakai by mainstream Muslims has intensified. Their Muslim neighbours often violently assault them. Present and past persecution is the primary reason for the community's reluctance to disclose their beliefs to outsiders.

Several reports indicate that some of the Kakai community had become Muslim to protect themselves from annihilation. Such conversions occurred in the distant past, but also recently due to ISIS, fear of their Arab neighbours, and extremist Islamic ideology. However, my interviews with the Kakai, who claimed to have become Muslim, revealed that they had never practiced Islam but had declared that they converted in order to avoid attacks from militant organisations like ISIS.

In 2014, the ISIS offensive in Iraq gained control of two villages, Albu Muhammad and Shukr Jayran. Mostly inhabited by Kakai. The ISIS forced

---

[14] Chaim Kaufmann, 'A security Dilemma: Ethnic partitioning in Iraq.' *Harvard International Review* 28/4 (2007), 44-50.

[15] After an attack by the Islamic State (IS or ISIS) in August 2014, under the name of Islam, ISIS militants took approximately 3,929 women and girls by force to the Tal Afar citadel in Iraq's Nineveh region.

them to flee their villages, leaving their houses, livestock, and agricultural lands behind. They survived that disaster, and now live in Daquq, a sub-district, in southern Kirkuk.[16] Kakais living in refugee camps comprise 2,128 families, which consists of 19,033 people from Mosul, Hamdanya district, and 35 families from the two previously mentioned villages Albu Muhammad and Shukr Jayran in the province of Kirkuk. After they gained control in these areas, ISIS fighters destroyed all the shrines and the temples belonging to Kakai.

Kakai face religious discrimination everywhere, starting from their Muslim neighbours. Many people discriminate against Kakai, because they practice different religious rituals. Kakai leaders in Kirkuk spoke to the media and claimed that the Kakai were Muslims and followed all the Islamic rites and rituals. However, some extreme Islamist scholars accused them of having double standards, and this led to other extremists verbally threatening the Kakai. Additionally, extremist teachers forced some Kakai students to perform certain Islamic religious rites.[17]

In interviews undertaken in Kirkuk and Daquq, Kakai people described their experiences of times when they felt that ISIS was close. One woman in Kirkuk said:

I prepare a bag and keep it near me at night; I am afraid of ISIS coming, my man was all night with a gun in the street, we are afraid of our Arab neighbours joining ISIS. The Peshmerga works for the Kurds and the Hashd al-Shabi militia works for the Iraqi Central Government, so I feel there will be a conflict later on. The Peshmerga control one side of Kirkuk province and the Hashd al-Shabi control the other side.

Throughout history, Kakai have kept silent due to hostile environments in all of Iraq. This situation dictates that Kakai must not disclose details of their faith, not only as a means of protection, but due to lack of democracy and the fact that, in this climate, they have no freedom of expression as a religious and social minority.

Forced Islamisation

The idea of religious diversity presents difficulties when most people claim formal allegiance to the state religion. However, a minority group without such state ties can find a solution through transforming a minor religion to resemble an accepted majority religion, or otherwise conceal the minority's religion.

Kakai have kept their beliefs hidden for many years. This secrecy has

---

[16] Seyedehbehnaz Hosseini, 'The Kakai - A Religious Minority in Iraq' *Journal of Contemporary Review of the Middle East* 5/2 (2018), 156-169.
[17] Ibid., 15.

prevented them from forming their own independent political parties or gaining representation in the parliaments of the central Iraqi government or Iraqi Kurdistan. Kakai associate themselves ethnically with Kurds, but a certain group of Kakai proclaims that Kakai are a distinct community that should have its own political representation. Although they are supposed to have holy places, Kakai places of worship may also be ordinary homes so as not to attract attention. They keep their religious book in *Jamkhane*[18] due to fear of persecution from their Muslim neighbours. *Jamkhane* is still a secret place for Kakai, and it is used for a special occasions or funerals. Kakai prefer to keep their places of worship hidden, because secrecy is part of their religion's philosophy.

In interviews, Kakai in Halabja and Kirkuk explained that they still practiced religious ceremonies in secret. Only other Kakai are permitted to attend. Even before ISIS, they had reason to be afraid of Islamist extremism and Kakai were sometimes kidnapped for ransom.

Only 100 Kakai live in the village of Alisaray, which lies midway between Tikrit (Saddam Hussein's hometown, and a stronghold of his supporters), and the Kurdish autonomous region in Iraq. This area is full of terrorists, and the Kakai are one of their easiest targets. Kakai farmers borrowed funds from the Iraqi Ministry for Agriculture to farm wheat and barley. When ISIS burned their crops, their situation worsened; they lost their jobs and moved to the city in search of schools and work. This illustrates the dire situation for Kakai in Iraq; the community is hungry, they do not have work, and some are forced to say they are Muslims for their own protection.

ISIS sought to conquer Kirkuk because of its strategic location, which would give them more power. People in Daquq and, especially in the village of Zankar, which is located close to ISIS territory, are in the worst situation. They were unable to leave their houses and farms as they did not have a place to go and had to stay in the conflict zone.[19]

The fear of ISIS forced many people to leave their homes. Those who did not want to leave their livestock behind tried to hide and go to another area, especially at night when they heard bombs.

The withdrawal of the Peshmerga forces who had prevented entry into the city and the Kakai district led to additional suffering for the Kakai: threatens, kidnapping civilians, and destruction of the shrine of Seyed Zibar.

---

[18] Apart from being a holy temple, *Jamkhane* is also a shelter for the poor and wanderers. The Kurdish regions have some cemeteries that have resting places for great religious leaders, which are called *Jamkhane*. Yārsāni gather there and observe their ceremonies. Whoever intends to take part in *Jamkhane* is required to obey some mandatory rules. The first and foremost is that the person who enters *Jamkhane* must wear a belt and a special hat. The other essential obligation in *Jamkhane* is that no one is allowed to broach personal and/or public affairs.

[19] Seyedehbehnaz Hosseini, 'The Kakai - A Religious Minority in Iraq' *Journal of Contemporary Review of the Middle East* 5/2 (2018), 156-169, 11.

For these reasons, the inhabitants of Shishakan, Alwa Pasha, Sid Abbas and Sid Hussein villages left the area. During the Iraqi election campaign, the Kakai were subjected to threatening phone calls, and roadside bombs were planted between the villages of West and East Daquq. Towards the end of 2017, a bomb explosion killed a Kakai citizen as he travelled from the village of Zanqar to the polling centre in the village of Tubazawa. Another bomb explosion on the road leading from the village of Ali Saray to Tubazawa killed a policeman and injured a civilian. On 1 October 2017, near the village of al-Zanqar, a group of armed men kidnapped Farhad Faiq Ould Agha, and all the people of al-Zanzar village were displaced to the district of Daquq. On 25 October 2017, a regiment of the Iraqi Federal Police arrived and announced that it would protect the villages of Zanqar, Ali Saray and Topazawa. Even so, police prevented Kakais entering into the city of Kirkuk from the main route leading from Daquq to Kirkuk and told them that they were forbidden to enter the city of Kirkuk, because they were Kurds. In the city of Khanaqin, the most famous symbol of the Kakai people, the shrine of Bawa Mahmoud, was subjected to a series of explosions.

Conclusion

Violence against Kakai by Arab Muslims is a structural feature of Iraqi society and the Kakai live with the threat of discrimination and violence. Furthermore, they are still not officially recognised as a minority. Some were forced to convert to Islam during the Arabisation campaigns by the Ba'athist regime and the subsequent violence, and in response lived in fear following ISIS attacks.

Kakai insecurity can also be traced to the early history of Iraq and the repeated claims of the incompatibility of Kakai and Muslim religions and cultures. The violence in Iraq has put the Kakai in an unbearable situation. Religious repression has seriously hurt their quality of life and increases incentives to leave the country. Discrimination against the Kakai minority, as well as Arab radical ideology that effectively erases their collective existence, thus strongly influences the total number of forced migrants who seek to leave the country.

The Kakai's religious identities are close to disappearing altogether because of the ongoing process of demolishing their cultural and religious heritage, which dates back centuries. There are many difficulties related to being a minority, and it is painful to belong to any stigmatised group. The Kakai community has still not been recognised as a religious minority either in Iran or Iraq. In both countries, governments instead officially classify them as a form of Muslims. Currently in Iraq, they are known as Kurdish, and their identity cards state that they are Muslim because their religious status is not accepted. The social dominance of Islamic radicalism also creates a danger that they will be assimilated to Islam. The future of Kakai in Iraq is thus unknown, since even today their religion is not mentioned in the Iraqi constitution and their personal identification documents. Kakai people's rights need to be defined correctly; they need protection and respect as a religious minority, and the liberation of Kakai villages and restitution of displaced people is also needed. Kirkuk is still not stable, since after the Kurdish military left the area, it came under the control of Hashd al-Shabi militia, which means that insecurity, violence, and kidnapping are constant elements of life in the city.

CHAPTER 12

THE SHABAK: BETWEEN SECULAR NATIONALISMS AND SECTARIAN VIOLENCE

Michiel Leezenberg

The Shabak are one of the less well-known ethnic groups of northern Iraq. The complexities of their recent history suggest that religious and ethnic minorities are not simply or merely victims, but also actors in their own right. Like neighbouring groups, they have been badly affected not only by the 2014 offensive of the so-called Islamic State (ISIS), but also by the earlier politics of the region. At present, their community is deeply divided, in a split exploited and exacerbated by other regional actors.

Traditionally, the Shabak were concentrated in a string of villages along the Mosul-Eski Kalak road in the Nineveh Plain. Apart from local religious leaders, the Shabak also had urban landlords, or *sâda*, in nearby Mosul, themselves belonging to orthodox Twelver Shiite families, for whom they worked as sharecroppers. Whenever rural Shabaks visited Mosul, they would come to stay at their sayyid's house, paying them all due respects.[1] The reverse side of this patronage (or *taba'iyya*) was the traditionally low status of the Shabak; one informant recalled he had once heard an ethnic Kurd derogatorily refer to them as 'settled Gypsies.'[2]

Theologically, the Shabak are – or were – close to the Alevis in Central and Eastern Anatolia, part of whom speak Zaza or Kurmanji Kurdish; but linguistically, they are closer to what is called 'Gorani' in the academic literature, their vernacular (called 'Shabakî') sharing many grammatical features with the Macho spoken by Kaka'îs in Kirkuk region and the Hawrami spoken in the Shahrizor area on the Iraq-Iran border. There are

---

[1] See in particular Amal Vinogradov 'Ethnicity, Cultural Discontinuity, and Power Brokers in Northern Iraq: The Case of the Shabak' *American Ethnologist* 1 (1974), 207-218.
  In a later paper Amal Rassam (= Amal Vinogradov), 'al-Taba 'iyya: Power, patronage, and marginal groups in northern Iraq' In *Patrons and Clients in Mediterranean Society*. Edited by E. Gellner / J. Waterbury. (London: Duckworth, 1977), 157-166. the same author specifically describes the relation between rural Shabak and urban sâda as one of patronage.
[2] Interview, Erbil, October 2018.

also some Sunni speakers of Shabakî; according to some, these should strictly be called *Bajalan* rather than *Shabak*; but terminology tends to be confused, confusing, and ambiguous. The theological and linguistic affinities of this group have not been satisfactorily explained. Most probably, the Shabak descend from Qizilbash troops associated with Shah Isma'il in the sixteenth-century confrontation between the Ottomans and the emerging Safawî empire in Eastern Anatolia; but in later centuries, when Ottoman rule had stabilised, these forces appear to have settled and lost whatever military prowess, or fighting reputation, they might have had before[3]. Thus, in the late Ottoman empire and in monarchical Iraq, the Shabak had the reputation for being unfit for any kind of military activity (Vinogradov 1974). This, however, may be due to other factors, like an initial reluctance in the face of Ottoman, and later Iraqi, attempts at conscription.

The Shabak have a sacred book of their own, the *Buyruq* or *Kitâb al-manâqib*. This book is written in Turkish, a language only a limited number of Shabak command, and plays a role only in some Shabak rituals. There are also a number of other texts written by Shabak religious specialists, like an Arabic-language refutation of the Yezidi faith and a *mawlûd*, or biography of the prophet, written in the Shabakî vernacular; but these do not appear to have had a wide circulation.[4] By and large, Shabakî is used only for purposes of private,spoken everyday communication.

The Shabak in Republican and Baathist Iraq

In republican Iraq, increasing numbers of Shabak joined the national army, giving the lie to the reputation they had enjoyed since late Ottoman times. More generally, they appear to have shared in the wider processes of transformation that promised, among other things, increasing access to education and health care, and state employment opportunities. For decades, there appear to have been pressures towards religious assimilation or conversion affecting the Shabak. Traditionally, each Shabak adult had a *pîr* or *dede* for a spiritual guide; their highest religious authority is known as the *bâbâ*.[5] The Shabak paid regular visits to local shrines, notably those of Ali Resh and Abbas; but al-Sarraf (ibid.) notes that already in the 1950s, Shabak were increasingly making pilgrimages to the Twelver Shiite shrines in the holy cities of southern Iraq, Kerbela and Najaf. These comments suggest that,

---

[3] See: Michiel Leezenberg, 'Between Assimilation and Deportation: History of the Shabak and the Kakais in Northern Iraq' In *Syncretistic Religious Communities in the Near East*. Edited by Barbara Kellner-Heinkele / K. Kehl-Bodrogi.(Leiden: Brill, 1997), 155-174.

[4] See: Mustafa Dehqan, 'A Shabak contemporary polemic against the Yezidi Religio'. *Oriente Moderno* LXXXVIII (2008), 1-5.

[5] A.H. al-Sarraf, *al-Shabak min firaq al-ghulât fi'l-'Irâq*. (Baghdad: Matba'at al-ma'ârif, 1954). Muhammad el-Shabak, 'The Shabaks: A Minority Identity Struggling Against Majority Identities' In *Minorities in Iraq: Memory, Identity and Challenges*. Edited by Saad Salloum (Baghdad: Masarat for Cultural and Media Development, 2013), 156-166 (Arabic version: 207-201 of the Arabic-language part), 101-103. See: Van Bruinessen 2000: 300.

with the increasing literacy and upward social mobility that became possible in the twentieth-century Iraqi state, Shabak laypeople tended to move towards, if not convert to, orthodox Twelver Shiism. Vinogradov, too, argues that in the 1960s, increasing numbers of Shabak were converting to Twelver Shiism.

But Shabak did not shift to Twelver Shiism alone. In the early 1990s, I conducted fieldwork among the so-called Sarlû or Sarlî, a *ghulât* community living in several villages near Eski Kalak just east of the Shabak-inhabited region. I quickly found out that these Sarlî were Ibrahimî Kaka'îs, whose sayyid lived in nearby Erbil. When I asked whether there were any Shabak living among them, my Sarlî hosts said that they, and a number of others, were Shabak themselves. Their ancestors had in recent times converted to the Kaka'î faith, apparently due primarily to the personal charisma of, or patronage offered by, an earlier Kaka'î leader, Fattah Agha.[6] Whatever the details of this conversion, it suggests that the Shabak's religious affiliation, or patronage, was already unstable or dynamic in late monarchical and early republican times.

In short, the rapid social development of Iraq during the 1950s and 1960s led not so much to a redefinition of the variety of the heterodox Shiite or *ghulât* faith specific to the Shabak, but rather to conversion to, or assimilation into, other groups. The experience of the Sarlî suggests that conversion to the Kaka'î faith, or assimilation into the Kaka'î community, was as easy for Shabak as conversion to Twelver Shi'ism.

Perhaps one should not overstate the scale of these conversions, however. The Shiite 'ulamâ themselves faced a severe lack of followers during this period, reflecting a widespread pattern of secularisation, and a widespread lack of interest in religious matters, let alone the development of politicised and revolutionary forms of religion, among the Iraqis coming of age in these years. During the 1950s and 1960s, when Communists and Arab and Kurdish nationalists could mobilise tens of thousands of people, the major centres of Shiite learning in Najaf and Kerbela could hardly attract more than a few dozens of pupils. Quite generally, in this period, loyalties and identities tended to be articulated in secular nationalist and/or ethnic, if not in Marxist vocabulary, rather than in religious terms, to some extent with the exception of the Da'wa party, which mobilised among Shiites in southern Iraq.

Far more momentous than any religious development, however, was the influence of the increasingly aggressive Arab nationalism that characterised the Baath party that ruled Iraq from 1968 to 2003. Between the 1960s and

---

[6] For more details see Michiel Leezenberg, 'Between Assimilation and Deportation: History of the Shabak and the Kakais in Northern Iraq' In *Syncretistic Religious Communities in the Near East*. Edited by Barbara Kellner-Heinkele / K. Kehl-Bodrogi.(Leiden: Brill, 1997), 155-174.

1980s, the most important question concerning, or facing, the Shabak was whether they were 'really' Kurds or Arabs, not whether they were 'really' Sunnis or Shiites. Increasingly, the Shabak found themselves under pressure from competing claims by the Iraqi regime, which claimed they were really Arabs, and the Kurdish movement, which argued they were really Kurds. These competing nationalisms came to a violent climax in 1975, but this period does not appear to have affected the Shabak directly. This was to change in the 1980s. The Iraqi regime's increasingly destructive and murderous suppression of the Kurdish insurgency in the 1980s culminated in the genocidal 1988 Anfal operations, in which an estimated 100,000 Iraqi civilians perished. These operations had been prepared for by the regime's 1987 census. According to Human Rights Watch, the areas outside of government control where no census could be held automatically became targets of the Anfal; these areas harboured Kurds, and to a lesser extent Yezidis and Assyrians.[7]

Although the Anfal did not specifically target the Shabak, they were also hit by the overflow of these operations. In the 1987 census, the regime only gave citizens the option of registering as either Arab or Kurd; this posed acute problems of loyalty for minorities like the Yezidis, the Shabak, and the Christians. The Shabak lived in an area under full government control, and had generally been loyal to the Iraqi regime, or at the very least tried to remain neutral in the confrontation between government and Kurdish movement. In the 1987 census, the Iraqi regime pre-emptively declared them to be Arabs rather than Kurds; when subsequently a number of Shabak leaders protested that they were Kurds, Saddam ordered their villages to be destroyed and their inhabitants to be resettled elsewhere in northern Iraq, mostly on the Desht Harîr plain North of Erbil.[8] Although not part of the Anfal proper, and realised only after the end of the final operation, these deportations appear to follow the same destructive logic that characterised the operations and, more generally, late 1980s Baathist policies in the north of the country.

The Post-Baath Constellation

The establishment of a region under de facto Kurdish control in 1991 announced an entirely new era for the Kurds in Iraq; but for the most part, the Nineveh Plain, and with it the Shabak and other inhabitants, largely remained outside this Kurdish-controlled zone; substantial numbers of deported Shabak, however, lived under Kurdish rule in the Harîr area. During the 1990s, an unknown number of these seem to have returned to

---

[7] See Human Rights Watch, *Iraq's Crime of Genocide: The Anfal Campaign Against the Kurds*. Report. (New Haven: Yale University Press, 1995). https://www.hrw.org/report/1993/07/01/genocide-iraq/anfal-campaign-against-kurds. In particular Chapter Ten, dealing with the 'final Anfâl' in Badinan region.

[8] For a photographic reproduction and a translation of the deportation order, see Human Rights Watch, *Bureaucracy of Repression: The Iraqi Government in its Own Words*. Report (New Haven: Yale University Press, 1994). https://www.hrw.org/report/1994/02/01/bureaucracy-repression/iraqi-government-its-own-words. 28-29) (accessed 15 September 2018).

their former homes. Also, during the 1990s, some Turkish actors attempted to claim the Shabak as 'really' Turkomans, or, as they called them, 'Iraqi Turks' (*Irak Türkleri*), supposedly in view of their Turkish-language sacred scripture. These efforts, however, were transparently motivated by a wish to counter Kurdish territorial claims, and do not appear to have had any lasting success.

The Kurdish-held region was different from the rest of Iraq in that, between 1991 and 2003, it witnessed the rise and subsequent demise, of political, and in part militant, (Sunni) Islam.[9] It also harboured relatively few Twelver Shiites. Thus, unlike the rest of Iraq, the Kurdistan Region did not become a theatre of chaos and instability, let alone increasingly violent sectarian conflict between Sunnis and Shiites, after the 2003 war. However, in the frontier zones between the Arab-dominated regions under central government control and Kurdish-held territory, the seeds for new troubles were sown.[10] In 2003, Kurdish Peshmerga had established a *de facto* military control over part of Kirkuk province, as well as in Sinjar and on the Nineveh Plain, even though these regions remained under *de jure* control by, respectively, the national government and the governorate in Mosul.

Article 140 of the 2005 provisional constitution called for these conflicts to be settled by referenda among the local population; but no such referendum was held in any of the disputed areas. All these regions had mixed and heterogeneous populations; and, as noted, the groups living on the Nineveh Plain could not unambiguously be called either Kurds or Arabs. KRG sources claimed that Yezidis and Shabak were 'really' Kurds, and that these areas should be attached to the Kurdistan region, since their population would be safer under Kurdish rule than as part of the Sunni Arab-dominated Mosul governorate, in which violent salafi-jihadî insurgent groups were on the rise. Despite the official Kurdish rhetoric, the KRG – and more specifically, the KDP, which until the ISIS offensive had an uncontested military dominance in the region, either treated the Shabak and other minority groups as second-class citizens or gave away all important posts in local government to party veterans. As a result, these groups were less than fully happy with Kurdish rule; repeated demonstrations against KDP behaviour in the region occurred, several of them ending with security forces

---

[9] For more details see Michiel Leezenberg, 'Religion in Kurdistan: Between Naqshbandi Sufism and IS Salafism' In *The Kurdish question revisited*. Edited by Gareth Stansfield. (London: OUP, 2017), 33-46.

[10] For an assessment of developments up to mid-2009, prior to the departure of American troops and prior to the outbreak of new forms of sectarian violence that would culminate in the IS offensive of summer 2014, see International Crisis Group, Iraq's New Battlefront: The Struggle over Ninewa. Report no. 90 (published 20.09.2009), https://www.crisisgroup.org/middle-east-north-africa/gulf-and-arabian-peninsula/iraq/iraq-s-new-battlefront-struggle-over-ninewa (accessed 15.09.2018). See: Human Rights Watch, On Vulnerable Ground: Violence against Minority Communities in Nineveh Province's Disputed Territories. Report (published 10.11.2009) https://www.hrw.org/report/ 2009/11/10/vulnerable-ground/violence-against-minority-communities-nineveh-provinces-disputed (accessed 15.09.2018). See also Le Michiel Leezenberg 'The End of Heterodoxy? The Shabak in Post-Saddam Iraq' In Religious Minorities in Kurdistan Edited by Khanna Omarkhali. (Wiesbaden: Harrassowitz, 2014), 247-267.

shooting at civilians. Already by 2007, a considerable part of the Shabak leadership appears to have had doubts about incorporation into the Kurdistan region.[11]

It proved impossible to reach a negotiated solution, not so much between the different population groups, but rather between the authorities in Erbil and Mosul, or Baghdad. Instead, the conflicting parties increasingly tried to co-opt or coerce these groups into siding with them; as a result, violence against these groups increased considerably in these years. Especially in the city of Mosul and its vicinity, robberies, kidnappings and even assassinations of minority members became increasingly frequent. In 2010, an Amnesty International report warned that the region's minorities were 'increasingly becoming pawns in a power struggle between an Arab-dominated central government and the Kurdistan Regional Government.'[12] The new – or renewed – confrontation between the secular nationalist Kurdish leaders and the Arab-dominated (and increasingly sectarian Shiite) central government in Baghdad led to new pressures on, and ruptures within, the Shabak and other minority communities.

After 2003, however, a new religious dynamic developed among the Shabak, who now no longer faced questions of whether they were Arab or Kurds (let alone Turkomans), but rather whether they were Sunni or Shiites. It was during this time that the slogan 'the Shabak are 65% Shiite, and 35% Sunni' became more widespread. Clearly, this shift reflects the rising sectarianism in national politics, in which a new and increasingly violent confrontation between Sunnis and Shiites developed; but it also reflected the new options for patronage relations on a national scale. As such, the new constellation caused a new rift in the Shabak community. Some Shabak believed that they were best off with Kurdish protection, and accepted the patronage of the KDP; others resented the latter's assimilationist claim that the Shabak were Kurds pure and simple, and hence decided to side with Shiite parties; yet others believed that the Shabak, together with the other minorities in the Nineveh Plain, should demand a distinct status for the region, but were unable to form a single front – or to resist the efforts by stronger regional actors to play off these groups against each other. Increasingly, Shabak and other minorities also became targeted by jihadi insurgents; over the years, kidnappings and assassinations of individual Shabak became depressingly frequent. Most dramatically perhaps, in August 2009, a dual truck bomb destroyed almost the entire Shabak village of al-Khazna, killing at least 28 people and wounding at least 130.[13] In August 2012, another suicide assault by a truck bomber in the Shabak village of

---

[11] See the confidential report, 'Shabak Reject Incorporation into KRZG,' published by Wikileaks: https://wikileaks.org/plusd/cables/07BAGHDAD276_a.html (accessed 4.11.2018).

[12] AI, report *Iraq: Civilians under fire*. (April 2010). *MDE* 14/002/2010, 16; quoted Hunter (2014: 331).

[13] 'Sectarian Bombings Pulverize a Village in Iraq,' *New York Times*, /published 10 August 2009). https://www.nytimes.com/2009/08/11/world/middleeast/11iraq.html (accessed 4.11.2018).

Muwafaqiya left 5 people dead and 50 injured.[14]

In the process, it seems, the distinct religious identity of the Shabak went through a deep, or accelerated, transformation. Although I have no concrete data on the matter, local informants have stated that the religious specialists of the Shabak, like the pîrs and dedes, have largely disappeared; instead, the Shabak increasingly appear to look towards the orthodox Twelver Shiite 'ulamâ in southern Iraq for spiritual guidance. This religious reorientation has been paralleled by several significant political shifts: various Shabak who are wary of Kurdish intentions have thrown in their lot with Shiite political parties in Baghdad rather than the KDP; the most well-known of these is Shabak leader Hunayn Qaddo, who is associated with al-Maliki's Shiite-leaning State of Law bloc in the Iraqi parliament. The pro-Kurdish faction was led by mulla Salim al-Juma'a, who occupied the Iraqi parliament seat reserved for Shabak until the 2018 national elections, when he was replaced by Qusay Abbas.

Increasingly, these political realignments seem to be reflected in Shabak religious self-definitions. One Shabak spokesman went so far as to deny any doctrinal differences between the Shabak faith and orthodox Twelver Shiism, claiming that the former was only an old-fashioned and outdated form of the latter.[15] Thus, the Shabak turned to new patrons in the wider political arena. As a result, the steadily rising Iranian influence in the region, both among Kurdish rulers and among the Shiite parties, became almost impossible to ignore by both heterodox and orthodox Shiite communities. Thus, there are reports of the Iranian consul Erbil paying repeated visits to Husayniyas in the Shabak-inhabited area.[16] Some Assyrian Christians have even claimed that Shabak, backed by Iran, have seized lands belonging to Assyrian villages in the Nineveh Plain, a claim denied by Shabak leaders.[17] Whatever the truth of the matter, this claim points to the unresolved land disputes underlying various local conflicts. Under Saddam, Shabak loyal to the regime had reportedly been rewarded with stretches of land; and undoubtedly, after 2003, new and competing claims to local lands emerged. Likewise, after 2003, Shabak appear to have migrated from their villages to nearby Christian (or majority Christian) towns in search of better health and education facilities; but the local Christians were wary of any change in the demographic balance.

ISIS and After

In a sense, the August 2014 assault by ISIS, the so-called Islamic State, was but the culmination of local sectarian tensions that had been simmering

---

[14] 'Deaths in Northern Iraq Attacks.' *Al-Jazeera*, (published 10.08.2012). https://www.aljazeera.com/news/middleeast/2012/08/2012810123417179160.html (accessed 15.09.2018).

[15] Interview, Shabak spokesman, Brussels, Belgium, July 2015.

[16] Interviews, local informants, Erbil and Duhok, Iraq, October 2018.

[17] Interview, Assyrian representatives, Brussels, Belgium, July 2015.

since around 2006, and had repeatedly escalated into deadly violence. One particularly dramatic aspect of this offensive was that ISIS warriors encouraged local Sunni Arabs to participate in evicting or even killing their non-Sunni neighbours, and in looting their possessions. In turning neighbours against each other, this move appears to have done serious, and long-term, damage to the social fabric of the region.

The ISIS offensive appears to have specifically targeted the region's ethnic and sectarian minorities; in the process, the Kurdistan Region's forces showed themselves unable to protect them. The genocidal ISIS operation against the Yezidis has been widely – and rightly – publicised. ISIS actions towards Christians and Shabak have been less visible, and less murderous, than those against the Yezidis; but they may end up being hardly less destructive. Christians and other minorities living in the Nineveh area were barely able to flee ahead of the lightning offensive, during which ISIS troops captured virtually all Christian and Shabak villages in Hamdaniya district Southeast of Mosul. Larger towns like Qaraqosh, Bartallah, and Bakhdida were also overrun; their entire Christian and other non-Sunni population fled. ISIS troops also came close to conquering al-Qosh, but were successfully held back by both Assyrian militias and the Kurdish Peshmerga. Eventually, these towns would be reconquered by the Kurdish Peshmerga as part of the joint Mosul offensive; but even after the ousting of ISIS, only part of the population returned.

An estimated 200,000 inhabitants of the Nineveh Plain are reported to have been displaced by the ISIS offensive. According to local sources, some Shabak villages were occupied and looted by ISIS fighters, with several hundred Shabak estimated to have been killed (Van Zoonen & WUriya 2017: 7). In this area, however, unlike in Sinjar, most of the civilian population was able to escape in time, and to seek refuge elsewhere, particularly in the regional capital Erbil. Most Shabak internally displaced persons (IDPs) were settled in camps like Hershem camp on the outskirts of Ain Kawa, and Baharka, the largest camp in the region, a few miles outside Erbil. Here, IDPs were living in tents with little heating for the winter and – initially at least – no cooling during summer, and with insufficient access to clean water and medical care. Hershem harboured relatively many Shiite or Shiite-leaning IDPs, including Shabak and Turkomans; Baharka sheltered IDPs from various backgrounds, also including Baghdadî Shiites as well as Sunni Palestinians ousted by Shiite militias. Although camp inhabitants were generally reluctant to speak openly about the political dimensions of what had happened, they gave the distinct impression of feeling let down, if not betrayed, by the Kurdish authorities, which had so singularly failed to protect them.[18]

---

[18] Personal observations and interviews in Baharka and Hershem refugee camps and in refugee settlements in Ain Kawa suburb, Erbil, Iraq, November 2014, August 2015.

The post-offensive fate of the Shabak IDPs appears almost as dramatic as that of displaced Yezidis and Christians. After initially being harboured in camps near Erbil, the Shabak IDPs were subsequently allowed – or, according to some sources, actively encouraged – to leave northern Iraq and to resettle in the Shiite south of the country; it is not clear whether it was primarily the KRG or the Baghdad government which had taken this initiative. An unknown number of Shabak remained in southern Iraq at the time of writing, either in refugee camps or in more permanent housing. Given the dispersal of Shabak refugees, and given the longer-term trends described above, there is at present a serious risk of the Shabak disappearing altogether as a distinct community. Not only is there a substantial pressure towards assimilation into the larger Kurdish and Shiite communities (without this necessarily leading to Shabak being fully accepted by either); but also, the apparent disappearance of a specifically Shabakî religious leadership will only accelerate existing tendencies. Thus, external pressures to assimilate are strengthened by internal divisions, primarily concerning which patron to choose in the wider political arena.

The 2014 ISIS offensive also led to a substantial militarisation of, or among, the Shabak community. In 2015, Shabak representative Salim Juma'a announced the establishment of a paramilitary force of some 1,500 Shabak, adding that 'a verbal approval was obtained by the Ministry of Defence to form a military force from the Shabak Community to fight the ISIS terrorists.'[19] Significantly, these forces were associated with Iraq's Shiite parties rather than with the Kurds: the new militia became subsequently known as the 30th Brigade of Hashd al-Sha'abi, the Shiite, or pro-Shiite, Iraqi militias that had been formed to counter IS.[20] The Shabak militia also came to be known as the Nineveh brigade. Although it claimed to be independent, it was widely seen as affiliated to the Badr forces, an outgrowth of the pro-Iranian Shiite Supreme Council of the Islamic Revolution in Iraq (SCIRI). Reportedly, it currently controls parts of northern Mosul as well.[21]

In 2017, the Shabak became an issue in the referendum concerning the independence of the Kurdistan Region. In June 2017, Iraqi MP Salim Juma'a reportedly called for the Shabak-inhabited region to be included in the referendum concerning the independence of the Kurdistan Region, encouraging all Shabak to support the referendum and to actively participate in it; but spokesmen like Qaddo were much more critical.[22] One of the

---

[19] Ahmed Hussein, 'Shabak community forms military force of 1500 fighters to fight ISIS in Nineveh' *Iraqi News*, (published 23.09.2014) https://www.iraqinews.com/baghdad-politics/shabak-community-forms-military-force-of-1-00-fighters-to-fight-isil-in-nineveh/ (accessed 15.09.2018).

[20] Phillip Smyth, 'Quwat Sahl Nīnawā: Iraq's Shia Shabak Get Their Own Militia' *Jihadology*, (published 12 January 2015) https://jihadology.net/2015/01/12/hizballah-cavalcade-quwat-sahl-ninawa-iraqs-shia-shabak-get-their-own-militia/ (accessed 15.09.2018).

[21] Interviews, local observers, Erbil and Duhok, Iraq, October 2018.

[22] Baxtiyar Goran, 'Shabaks support independence, call for their participation. Kurdistan24, (published 18.06.2017. http://www.kurdistan24.net/en/news/6eea8bfa-45b9-45db-998d-3177194d9998

referendum's fatal flaws was that the Kurdish authorities simply assumed support from the disputed territories under their control. Thus, the independence referendum was also held in disputed areas like Nineveh Plain, although the referenda required by the 2005 Iraqi constitution had not even been held yet. This provided the central government with a golden, and easily legitimised, opportunity: Iraqi government troops and Hasht al-sha'abi militiamen, including those of the Nineveh brigade, took over all disputed territories, including the Shabak-inhabited region, most of which had been under Kurdish control since 2003, with scarcely a fight. As of 2018, all disputed territories have reverted to the control of the central government forces, and in particular of (pro-) Shiite militias. Militarily, politically, and–last but not least–financially, they are once more directly dependent on Baghdad.

The consequences of this reversal are difficult to assess at present; but the already tense relations between and within the various groups of the area appear to have been further polarised. Outside forces have highly politicised the different population groups of the Nineveh Plains, in particular the remaining or returned Shabak. Although ISIS has been ousted, none of the underlying ethnic and sectarian problems, let alone land conflicts and other grievances, have been addressed. Since the 2017 referendum, the May 2018 national elections, and the September 2018 regional elections in the Kurdistan region, parliamentary politics appears to have stagnated both in Erbil and in Baghdad. Thus, the future of the Shabak is as unclear and as uncertain as ever; the recent militarisation of the Shabak seems to suggest a qualitative change in the question concerning their future, but also, unfortunately, the potential for new armed conflict.

It is to be hoped that, in the wake of the national and regional elections held in 2018, both the central government in Baghdad and the regional government in Erbil (the latter still being formed at the time of writing) will start placing the interests of the population above party politics. It will be a tough challenge, however, to revert the ongoing sectarianisation, and to restore a measure of mutual confidence among the population groups that have been torn apart, if not set up against each other, by the country's violent political conflicts. For the time being, the 2005 constitution, whatever its shortcomings, would seem the best basis for a peaceful resolution of outstanding conflicts. More important, however, is the creating, or reaffirming, of a spirit of compromise and accommodation among the main political actors. It is easy to be pessimistic or sceptical about the prospects for strengthening the rule of law, or for rehabilitating a sense of common and shared interests; but the Iraqis can afford neither scepticism nor pessimism.

(accessed 15.09.*2018*).

CHAPTER 13

THE HAQQA MOVEMENT: FROM HETERODOX SUFISM, TO SOCIO-POLITICAL STRUGGLE AND BACK

Lana Askari

One day I told my mother, I am going to join the *Mama Razayeti* [Haqqa movement under Sheikh Mama Raza]. She told me, your father is going to kill you. I said no, even if he would kill me I will go and convert anyway. I left and ran to the *takiye* (dervish lodge) and told them I wanted to convert. They quickly heated up some water and shaved my head, leaving only a little bit of hair on the top. This [taking off his cap and pointing to the small patch of long hair] has not been cut for over 50 years, it is still the same do you hear! During the time of the prophet, people had their hair like this. Our greeting '*ya karim, ya raza*', this is also from the time of the prophet. When I went back home I told my father I had joined Mama Raza and received a beating. However, after four nights, four brothers of the order came to our house and talked to my father. After a long discussion, they also converted my father. I was the first in my family in Sergalu village to convert. I came to the Haqqa with a clean conscious and therefore I am still part of it and still live in the *khanaqa* [rest- and guesthouse]. [1]

While growing up, I noticed some people who, when visiting my grandparents' house, would use a strange greeting, exclaiming '*ya karim, ya raza*' whilst slightly touching each other's palms, instead of a usual greeting of a handshake or kiss. Intrigued by this handshake, I decided to delve into the history of this movement that is part of my father's family and make a documentary film about the Haqqa.[2] In 2014, I filmed several interviews with

---
[1] Muhammed Aziz, filmed interview with author, 2014.
[2] I have an intricate relationship to this lineage. From my paternal grandmother side, I am the great-grand daughter of Mama Raza. Through my paternal grandfather, I am the great-great-grand daughter of Ali of Askar (not to be confused with shahid Ali Askari – son of Abdullah, another brother of Abdulkarim and Mama Raza), Abdulkarim and Mama Raza's cousin, and great grand-daughter of Hasan Mustafa, the brother of Abdulkarim and Mama Raza. The documentary film "The Haqqa Handshake" can be requested

the remaining followers and descendants of the Haqqa – a heterodox Sufi movement – established by Sheikh Abdulkarim in the village of Shadala, north of Sulaimaniya in Iraqi Kurdistan. Muhammed Aziz is one of the few *murid* (disciples) who has lived in the Kalkasmaq *khanaqa* for over 60 years. He converted when he was about seven years old.

In the early twentieth century, Sheikh Abdulkarim established the Haqqa as a religious-political movement following the Islamic Naqshbandi order. Establishing a different doctrine from mainstream Sufism, Sheikh Abdulkarim (1892/3-1942) taught practices that emphasised *yeksani* (equality). His successor, Sheikh Mama Raza (1905–61) took his teachings even further to include *xushek ew brayati* (sister- and brotherhood). Coming from the Arabic word *al-haq* (the truth), its followers were thought to have even screamed '*haqqa*' when being startled, as they would have been in such a continuous deep trance. This latter rumour is one of many that attempted to discredit the Haqqa and their progression in faith and social practise. As part of this wider publication on religious minorities in Iraqi Kurdistan, *bizudnaway Haqqa* (the Haqqa movement), who as a Sufi heterodoxy turned towards socio-political issues in the rural areas of Iraqi Kurdistan, provides an example of the region's peasant and nationalist struggles.

This essay will provide general overview of the movement's history and its current situation. While including other writings on this particular history, this paper is mainly based on filmed interviews with the Haqqa community, and visits to different sites of Kalkasmaq and Shadala. This film project also documents the community's knowledge and experiences. I argue that the religious-political character of the sheikhs and Haqqa, which saw its height around the early and mid-twentieth century, the decline of followers in the past decades, the push back into mainstream Islam, and the movement's split provide another example of power struggles in Iraqi Kurdistan. Other historical analyses of this area suggest similar rivalries lie at the forefront of Kurdish fragmentation[3] and the breakdown of the local political parties and the larger Kurdish Regional Government (KRG). Thus, rather than treating the Haqqa as merely an anomaly within the religious and political landscape in Iraqi Kurdistan (but perhaps indeed as an undervalued part of Kurdish history), it is very much part of existing socio-political structures and cannot be excluded from geopolitical developments of the past century.

The spread of the Naqshbandi order and start of Haqqa

The Haqqa can be seen as having two stages of development; firstly, founding by Sheikh Abdulkarim, and secondly, further development by Sheikh Mama Raza, also called *mama razayeti*. The Naqshbandi *tariqat* (Sufi

---

to be viewed by contacting the author through lana.askari@gmail.com

[3] Martin van Bruinessen, 'Kurds, states and tribes' In *Tribes and power: nationalism and ethnicity in the Middle East*. F. A. Jabar / H. Dawod (eds.). (London: Saqi books, 2002), 165–183. Wadie Jwaiweh, *Kurdish national movement: its origins and development* (Syracuse, NY: Syracuse University Press, 2006).

doctrine) originated in Central Asia and then expanded in Kurdistan through Mawlana Khalid in the early nineteenth century.[4] Based on Sufism, which adopts Islam's mystical experience of direct communication with God, Mawlana Khalid trained in India and successfully spread this order in Kurdistan due to Naqsbandi's autonomous growth, which was not based purely on succession through family lineage.[5] At the same time, disbanding the Kurdish emirates left a power vacuum replaced by Ottoman governors, who could not control conflicts and feuds. This environment led to a turn to the sheikhs standing outside of tribal structures, to resolve tribal conflicts. During this time, the Ottoman administration reformed land entitlement; *aghas* and sheikhs were able to register most land in their own names. In addition, sheikhs were granted *waqf* lands (land used to maintain mosques and shrines), which they treated as their personal lands. Van Bruinessen notes that the growing fear of imperial and Christian influence, and the lack of security following the collapse of the Kurdish emirates inspired people to turn back to religion and the sheikhs.[6] Thus, in this environment, the sheikhs gained power and many followers in the nineteenth century.

As Mawlana Khalid and the Naqsbandi order gained many followers, other Sufi orders such as the Qadari's, and the nobles and *aghas* of the Sulaimaniya area began to oppose him and plot his murder. One opponent Sheikh Ahmad-i Serdar lived near Shadala village so Mawlana Khalid went to talk to him and convinced him to join Mawlana and became a Naqshbandi. He became his *qadir*, and set his *khalifa* [person who has received permission from a sheikh to teach a *tariqat*] in Sargallu village. Another time, trying to escape the opposition in Sulaimaniya, Mawlana walked to Sargallu and was helped by Sheikh Ahmad of the area. Mawlana told him that if Sheikh Qadri had been older he would have made him *khalifa* instead of Ahmad. Sheikh Qadri went to Kirkuk and followed his father in becoming a *khalifa*. In Naqshbandi the *khalifa* is not inherited but goes to someone appointed because of their character and abilities. But this was an exception because Mawlana appointed Qadri-Sur himself.[7]

Mawlana Khalid told Qadri-Sur that, including himself, the order should have seven *khalifas*.[8] After Sheikh Mustafa's death in 1915, he was buried in Baghdad and his son Abdulkarim became the new *khalifa* and also sat in Shadala. While the Naqshbandi *tariqat* intended to not necessarily follow bloodlines, slowly the sheikh's position became hereditary and their tombs became a pilgrimage site, as both the Shadala and Khalkasmaq village shrines still are today.

---

[4] Martin van Bruinessen, *Agha, Sheikh and state: the social and political structures of Kurdistan*. (London: Zed books, 1992), 222-234.
[5] Ibid., 224 -226.
[6] Ibid., 232-233.
[7] Mustafa Askari, filmed interview 2014.
[8] See also the chart of the Barzanji family sheikh lineage (van Bruinessen 1992; 320).

Non-violence and equality

Sheikh Abdulkarim studied in Koya under Mullah Abdullah Jelli. He spoke and read Arabic, Turkish, Farsi, and Kurdish and made the hajj pilgrimage in 1922 and 1931. While his Ottoman identity card (*nasname*) says he was born in 1871/2, he had probably added about 20 years to his life to avoid being drafted by the Ottoman army because the card dates back to 1917 (time of WW1). The picture taken of him in 1936 by Cecil Edmonds[9] is unlikely to be of a man in his 60s, but more probably in his 40s.[10]

In 1920, Sheikh Abdulkarim's teachings developed into a separate form following Koranic ideas that sought *haqqiqat* (truth); he taught his *murids* peacefulness (*ashti*) and equality (*yeksani*). His followers discussed Sufism and some came to believe that the time of the Mahdi (redeemer of Islam – time of the Messiah) had come, mostly under the guidance of Hama Sur. Abdulkarim did not approve of such talk. Apparently, he also opposed his *murids* from seeing Shadala as another Mecca, somehow limiting the movement's messianic character. He disapproved of heretical behaviour, such as wearing jewellery or unclean clothes. However, while his followers considered ideas about the end of time and truth of Islam, he turned his *tariqat* into pure teachings removed from political and tribal affairs to lead his murids. *Zikr* (prayers reciting God's names) were not that distinct from other Islamic or Sufi rituals at this time but were not mandatory. He taught followers to improve their own situation in daily life, rather than looking to the sky for a saviour, and to find justice in creating an equal society. As Mustafa Askari points out, the messianic belief turned into a heterodoxy that tried to help rural people who had nothing.[11] Abdulkarim told people to stay away from bad people, to refute dictatorship through *agha* leadership and to do good beyond only taking prayers.

In their trance, the Haqqa would call out 'Allah' and 'Haqq'. Being different, other people named Sheikh Abdulkarim's community after his *tariqat* – Haqqa. The name was adopted, and from there on the Haqqa movement started. Most importantly, during this time, the state demanded taxes in the form of food; this resulted in widespread poverty and hunger. Abdulkarim's movement is thought to have relieved hunger and fought feudalism (to some extent) by distributing land from feudal landlords directly to the farmers.[12] Subsequently, he gained many followers in the Surdash area around Sulaimaniya.

Hadij Sheikh Abdulkarim addressed important problems resulting

---

[9] Cecil J. Edmonds, *Kurds, Turks and Arabs. Politics, travel and research in North Eastern Iraq, 1919-1925*. (London: Oxford University Press, 1957).
[10] Mustafa Askari, *Awardanawayek le bizudnaway Haqqa*. (Bagdhad: Alaa, 1983), 14-16.
[11] Ibid.
[12] Naqshibandi in: Thomas Schmidinger, 'The Haqqa Community: A Heterodox Movement with Sufi Origins' In *Religious Minorities in Kurdistan: Beyond the Mainstream*. Edited by Khanna Omarkhali. (Wiesbaden: Harrassowitz, 2014), 227–235.

from geopolitical shifts and the Kurds' powerlessness. WWI resulted in widespread hunger and poverty and need for a movement to increase hope for survival. Adulkarim named the movement equality, *yeksani*, but the British colonialists were afraid that Kurdistan would have the same revolt as in India with Gandhi or perhaps even as in Russia with the Bolsheviks. Out of fear that a regional movement could become national, the British colonialists arrested Abdulkarim in 1934. This was a turning point of the religion of Islam as it is was something different than Sufism.[13]

Many of Sheikh Abdulkarim's contemporaries were unsettled by his teachings. People spread bad propaganda against him because he did not interfere in tribal or Ottoman rulings. Subsequently, three mullahs (Islamic clergy) of the area wrote a letter to the mufti (expert in religious law) of Sulaimaniya asking for Abdulkarim to be imprisoned. In 1934, the Iraqi government, which had just been removed from the tight control of the British Mandate, imprisoned Sheikh Abdulkarim on the grounds of heresy. After the loss of their sheikh, thousands of his followers – the number is not exact – sold their belongings, burned their clothes and dressed in *guny* (cloth made of jute). They marched to Kirkuk and held protests for his release, much like the non-violent marches incited by Mahatma Gandhi in India around the same time. This event is remembered by the Haqqa community as *sali guny labar* (year of jute cloth). After interrogations, Said Ahmad Khanaqa, a sheikh of the Naqshbandi residing in Kirkuk and parliamentarian of the time, negotiated with the government for the release of Abdulkarim.

Rumours and stories about the Haqqa continued even after Abdulkarim's release. The British, protecting their interest and securing their position in Iraq, sent Cecil Edmunds, a political officer, to check these rumours of heresy and their threat to the administration. Edmonds visited Sheikh Abdulkarim in 1936 and describes in his writings the sheikh's appearance of wisdom and how his white clothing was set off by his freshly dyed black beard.[14] In his book, he also notes eccentric behaviour around the Haqqa: men and women bathing together, allowing dogs into the bathing water, passing around bowls of urine to drink from and even raiding a mosque in Sergalu village and burning the Koran.[15] As Schmidinger points out, many Western writers, such as Martin van Bruinessen or Michael Gunter, have mentioned Edmonds descriptions, but have not provided any critical analysis nor scepticism of these rumours around the Haqqa.[16] Some Haqqa descendants have described other stories about Edmonds visit to their

---

[13] Dr. Ali Askari, filmed interview with me, 2014.
[14] Cecil J. Edmonds, *Kurds, Turks and Arabs. Politics, travel and research in North Eastern Iraq, 1919-1925*. (London: Oxford University Press, 1957).
[15] Ibid., 204-206.
[16] Thomas Schmidinger, 'The Haqqa Community: A Heterodox Movement with Sufi Origins' In *Religious Minorities in Kurdistan: Beyond the Mainstream*. Edited by Khanna Omarkhali. (Wiesbaden: Harrassowitz, 2014), 227–235.

former sheikh.

> Edmonds, an Englishmen, went to Shadala and disguised himself as a *dervish* (member of mystical/Sufi order). Karim told him to sit down outside during prayer before praying with us. Upon seeing his face, Karim, in his sheikhly 'powers', recognised Edmonds face as not being a dervish and started talking to him.[17]
>
> Edmonds told him that they would give him money if he would stop taking about these Marxist things. Karim said that they didn't need money and they live in a self-sufficient community and lead simple lives. Edmonds went away and returned afterwards on an official visit and forbade him to continue. After this they captured Karim. His followers then dressed in jute and went to go get him.[18]

As van Bruinessen notes of the political aspect of heterodoxies in Kurdistan, 'I know of few prophetic or messianic movements in the strict sense in Kurdistan, but many political movements had a distinctly prophetic flavour to them. It is not an accident that most Kurdish nationalist revolts were led by sheikhs, who were also not the most orthodox ones'.[19] Earlier heterodoxies such as Alevi, Yezidism and the Ahl-e Haqq had become sustainable structures in their own right; however a few communities also developed in the nineteenth and twentieth century under the Naqshbandi order. Van Bruinessen[20] and Schmidinger[21] mention the most notable example of a messianic heterodoxy amongst the sheikhs of Barzan, Sheikh Abdulsalam I and his son, Mihemed, and under Sheikh Ahmad Barzani, who was deemed to be the God incarnate, leading to the blind obedience of his followers.[22] These sects returned in to mainstream Sunni Islam eventually in the twentieth century.[23] Throughout the twentieth century, the Haqqa movement continued to develop its teachings, the messianic character was subdued, and the social aspect of creating an equal society came to the forefront.

Turbulences in succession

In 1942, when walking back home from the mosque after an evening prayer, a rock (or some say a bullet) breaks Sheikh Abdulkarim's leg. After

---

[17] Faghri Mama Raza, filmed interview with me, 2014.
[18] Mustafa Askari, filmed interview with me, 2014.
[19] Martin van Bruinessen, *Agha, Sheikh and state: the social and political structures of Kurdistan*. (London: Zed books, 1992), 206.
[20] Ibid.
[21] Thomas Schmidinger, 'The Haqqa Community: A Heterodox Movement with Sufi Origins' In *Religious Minorities in Kurdistan: Beyond the Mainstream*. Edited by Khanna Omarkhali. (Wiesbaden: Harrassowitz, 2014), 227–235.
[22] Martin van Bruinessen, *Agha, Sheikh and state: the social and political structures of Kurdistan*. (London: Zed books, 1992), 244.
[23] Thomas Schmidinger, 'The Haqqa Community: A Heterodox Movement with Sufi Origins' In *Religious Minorities in Kurdistan: Beyond the Mainstream*. Edited by Khanna Omarkhali. (Wiesbaden: Harrassowitz, 2014), 227–235.

40 days, he died from what some believe to have been gangrene.[24] It is not known who attacked him, but what is known is that his succession became a point of conflict between Abdulkarim's older brother, Abdulkarim's younger brother Mama Raza, Abdulkarim's son Hama Agha Kani Tew, and Hama Sur who studied under Abdulkarim.

> Hama Sur looked European, but he was Kurdish from Shashokh village. He left the village to stay with his uncle to stay with Abdulkarim, he was a kid when he came to the *khanaqa* in Shadala. He was a small, but sturdily built with red hair. His uncle took him to Shadala and there he was brought up in the *Khanaqa* in Shadala. Here he stayed and worked for the KQ but he also sat with the Sufis and murids and became learned and was well spoken. As he grew older, he stopped his normal work and became a Sufi. After Karim's death, he also wanted to take over his place. He got the *mezer* (hat) and *jiba* (cloak) of Karim and put it on himself. Some brother and sisters got together and decided to follow Mama Raza, Karim's younger brother. After seeing people were following Mama Raza, Hama Sur got about 50 people together and went to Kirkuk and settled in the village of Klaw Qut in a commune. They had a good and equal life, but they didn't survive. They had couples, but no children, no coffee, tea or cigarettes. But they were really neat and well groomed, they always had a *mishki* (scarf used for the head), they were very well dressed and mixed together. They sold prayer beads and led simple lives.[25]

Hama Sur's commune was a collectively owned farm in a village later destroyed during the Anfal attacks in the 1980s. Hama Sur passed away in 1986 without a successor and this separate branch of Haqqa slowly died out.[26]

From *tariqat* to sister- and brotherhood

If we can think of Abdulkarim's time as the first wave in the Haqqa movement influenced by non-violent nationalist action, under Mama Raza, Abdulkarim's younger brother, the Haqqa experienced its second wave, shaped partly by the spread of socialism and communism as global ideologies. Mama Raza had lived in Shadala village to learn under Abdulkarim. After his brother's death, Mama Raza took the succession because many murids followed him because of his charism, but Abdulkarim's sons asked him to leave Shadala because of the power struggle for successor.

---

[24] Mustafa Askari, *Awardanawayek le bizudnaway Haqqa*. (Bagdhad: Alaa, 1983), 14-16.
[25] Mustafa Askari, filmed interview, 2014.
[26] As van Bruinessen notes, 'Hama Sur himself is apparently the only one who is more equal than the others in this "egalitarian" society: he disposes of much money, and he was said (in 1975) still to arrogate, in spite of his seventy years, the *ius primae noctis* of all the village girls' (1992: 326). However, the Haqqa community refutes these rumours.

Mama Raza first went to his oldest brother in Goptapa village, in the Chamchamal region towards Kirkuk, to ask for his support. When his older brother also asked him to leave, he went to the village of Askar to seek support from Raza of Askar, his cousin's son, where he was received well.[27] Here Mama Raza was able to develop his own teachings of Sufism intertwined with socialist ideas. He then chooses Kalkasmaq village to settle as the Sufis there, who had followed his father before, invited him to live with them.

Under Mama Raza, the Naqshbandi *tariqat* ended (as Abdulkarim was the seventh *khalifa*) and the Haqqa developed an even more social and communal character, which they called *xushek ew brayati* (sister- and brotherhood). The pillars of *Mama Razayeti*, are *hawghozi* (equality), *rastgoyi* (justice), and *brayati* (brotherhood). Not a focus on materialistic living, but rather an inner faith as in Sufism, as well as helping other people. Prayer and fasting were not compulsory, and equality for men and women, rich and poor were tantamount. They abandoned the custom of kissing hands, and a new handshake – '*ya karim, ya raza*' – was implemented when entering a room. The greeting was given to everyone in the room, upon which you would sit next to the last person who had arrived, making no distinction between class, age or gender. Women's rights were also introduced, forced and early marriage of women was stopped,[28] acts that were deemed immoral at the time by others.

Mama Raza erected a *khanaqa* in Kalkasmaq village, which became a communal living space, the brothers and sisters of the movement would live and work the lands together. The lands were divided amongst the farmers there. There were also instances where Mama Raza would receive farmers that would complain about *aghas* taking their lands. In this case he would buy the lands from certain *aghas* and give back the properties by registering the farmers as legal owners.[29]

> Food was served at the same time and equal for everyone. I once came there when I was little and you had to walk up the hill to the *khanaqa* yourself because there were no cars. When we arrived Mama Raza and all the brothers and sisters were sitting there. I had a big apple with me and brought it to Mama Raza, he told me to cut down the apple for all the people. I had to cut the apple into paper thin slices for people to merely taste the apple. Life was on equal terms.[30]

The Haqqa community grew further as a system of *bra sayara* (the moving brothers) was set up; these Haqqa followers acted as messengers, who would

---

[27] Son of Ali of Askar, who is the son of Abdulrahman – Hadji Sheikh Mustafa's brother.

[28] As were customs of *shirbaii* (bridewealth), *shilan* (dowry), and *tray surana* (tax paid to the *agha* for a marriage's first consummation).

[29] Mustafa Askari, *Awardanawayek le bizudnaway Haqqa*. (Bagdhad: Alaa, 1983).

[30] Mustafa Askari, filmed interview with me, 2014.

travel through villages to talk to people in the rural areas. In villages with many followers, a *takiye* was set up where people could meet or travellers could be helped or housed. These lodges had a wooden stick in front of the door (a sign of peace and non-violence), and women even headed some of them. People were asked to clean and groom themselves, men to shave their beards and people were asked to leave their shoes outside of the lodge. The villages collected money, the *takiye* and in the *khanaqa*, to be distributed amongst those in need in the community, supporting visitors, illness or marriages. The community's non-hierarchical and democratic decision-making process always involved a group of women and men.

The community undoubtedly grew as the poor would come to the lodges and the *khanaqa* to be fed or helped in another way. About 150 are estimated to have lived in the Kalkasmaq *khanaqa* up until the 1970s. Intellectuals and poets would also frequent the *khanaqa*; for example, Mama Raza had a close relationship with the poet Goran. The work in the communal farm was divided by age and knowledge, and food was served on serving trays to be shared by two people, an uncommon aspect as individual dishes were used on this tray, which as a luxury at the time.

> What Haqqa has done is very advanced and changed a movement in Islam that is completely different. I think myself that Haqqa is a great thing and a big thing of it is that it says in the rules of Naqshbandi is that you have to defend the poor. So, all Naqshbandi will never sit in front, all will sit on equal level... I'm a grandson of them and I never was treated differently than someone who wasn't of the family. I think myself that Haqqa is *piroza* (praiseworthy) and it is not for everyone, not everyone can do it because you have to be on equal terms and live together with everyone and share everything with them – equally, no difference in materiality, so that no one has more than another. All people can sit at the same level and eat the same food. This believe in equality is not something that everyone can do.[31]

Imprisonment and nationalist struggle

Mama Raza was imprisoned on three occasions, the first two were during Abdulkarim's time, the last one another important marker which the Haqqa call *yar whalli* (year of the stick). This latter event happed in 1944, when Mama Raza was captured in Dokan town, and sent to Imara prison, in the south of Iraq. Edmonds recalls this incident in his writings as an administrative error made by the *mutasarif* (district head) of Erbil (Hewler), and that upon meeting Mama Raza he did not deem him a threat to the administration. However, as van Bruinessen mentions,[32] and others of the Haqqa followers tell, they

---

[31] Amanj Askari, filmed interview, 2014.
[32] Martin van Bruinessen, *Agha, Sheikh and state: the social and political structures of Kurdistan*. (London: Zed books, 1992), 326.

believe that the Iraqi government imprisoned Mama Raza because he had helped Mullah Mustafa Barzani and the Kurdish resistance on several occasions. Earlier on, Sheikh Abdulkarim had received and helped Sheikh Mahmud Barzanji, who was leading the Kurdish uprisings against the British at the time. This time, Mama Raza had aided Mullah Mustafa by sending him troops when he had fled house arrest in Sulaimaniya and returned back to the Barzan region. On other occasions, the Haqqa had also aided in setting up of the Republic of Mahabad, and in negotiating the return of Barzani's troops from the Soviet Union into Iraqi Kurdistan.

Upon Mama Raza's imprisonment, thousands of his followers came together, sold their belongings and marched to Kirkuk by foot, where they surrounded the British office and asked for Mama Raza's release.[33] Promoting their peaceful demands, instead of any weapons they only carried an approximately one-meter-long stick of a *balaluk* (wild cherry trunk), called *dari ashti* (peacefull stick) or *dara qulla* (wooden stick).

> We went by foot all of us... Aisha the oldest daughter of Mama Raza died there. After that, in Kirkuk we stayed at Yar Whalli where we set up camp, an area in the north of Kirkuk to await Mama Raza for more than 2 months... we camped at an old military camp, we were poor... Mama Raza had an agreement with the government himself and that was when they released him.... We were kids at the time, when I went from Askar village to there, I remember that Mama Raza and the Haqqa where afraid of the government and also some other Kurdish groups because of he had so many followers from far away and the sheikhs there couldn't take this... We were 2,000 people there all from different villages.[34]

The first place to get together was in Goptapa village where all followers got together. From there a man, Hama Shutat, who sang 'first place is Goptapa, ohh brothers where is Mama Raza?' So, we went until we would find Mama Raza. In the Shwan area, the police captured thirteen men (one of them my father). They were brought to Kirkuk and we kept marching until Yar Whalli. The government wanted us to die because we had to stay under terrible conditions. Afterwards, we decided we would all stay in Kirkuk until he was released. In front of the house of Lion (the British), there was a park, we camped there a couple of nights. The government was scared and we were put in another neighbourhood, in some of the houses, but some of us had to sleep on the streets... So, the thirteen people who were captured were released and we were moved to another place. If Mama Raza negotiated for him to return to Sulaimaniya, then they

---

[33] Eyewitnesses claim that thousands of followers were there, Edmonds estimates the number at hundreds (1957).
[34] Muhammad Askari, filmed interview, 2014.

would release him.³⁵

The British allowed Mama Raza to go to the village of Byara, near the Iranian border, under the watch of Sheikh Alla'edin. After a year, he was allowed to go back to Kalkasmaq. In the decades to follow, the Haqqa sent troops to Qazi Muhammad in setting up the Republic of Mahabad in Iranian Kurdistan.³⁶ While Mama Raza promoted the idea of peaceful social change, he saw the Haqqa as part of the Kurdish struggle, but without a political affiliation to any parties. He received everyone that ran from the Iraqi regime, such as the Kurdistan Democratic Party and the Kurdish Communists. Many Communists were sent to Kalkasmaq to find shelter, thus the Haqqa became associated with the Communist movement, and shared socialist ideas. Although some people declared that Mama Raza became a Communist, he never joined any party and his teachings also forbade this because of their religious roots. After the coup d'état of 1958 overthrew the Iraqi king and *Mullah* Mustafa came back to Iraq, the Haqqa also became involved in the nationalist struggle.

In 1953, Mama Raza became partly paralysed from what may have been a stroke.³⁷ Too sick to travel he remained in Kalkasmaq for the rest of his life. For example, he could not travel to Baghdad to receive Mullah Mustafa when he returned to Iraq, but sent some Haqqa followers with a letter. In 1961, he passed away and his son, Sheikh Kaka Hama, took over the *khanaqa*. Mama Raza is buried next to his brother Sheikh Abdulkarim in the Shadala burial site. The collective farm in Kalkasmaq remained running in this capacity until the Ba'ath party turned to the Kurdish countryside.

> In the 1980s, the Iraqi army completed destroyed our village except for the concrete buildings so they could use it themselves... In 1986 when the Anfal campaign was happening, before everything the roads were blocked between the villages. We became homeless and we knew they wanted to erase the Kurds. So, we decided to fight in the peshmerga. My father, kaka Hama, then helped the *yeketi* (Patriotic Union of Kurdistan - PUK) under mam Jalal [Talabani] by putting together about 100 people to fight from his followers of which about 40 became martyrs. So, the Haqqa followers have fought along with the other groups in Kurdistan against dictatorship and colonialism. We kept on supporting our country and we are still ready for this support and help our fellow Kurds.³⁸

The Haqqa thus became part of the Kurdish struggle in these latter

---

³⁵ Mustafa Askari, filmed interview with me, 2014.
³⁶ The Republic of Mahabad was a short lived self-proclaimed Kurdish state within the region of Iranian Kurdistan (January – December 1946). Mustafa Barzani and his troops took part in establishing the republic but were exiled to the Soviet Union when it collapsed.
³⁷ Mustafa Askari, *Awardanawayek le bizudnaway Haqqa*. (Bagdhad: Alaa, 1983), 61.
³⁸ Sheikh Hawre, current sheikh in Kalkasmaq village, filmed interview with me, 2014.

decades and formed their own unit within the PUK. Both Shadala and Kalkasmaq village were destroyed by the Iraqi military under the Ba'ath regime, and had to rebuild their *khanaqa* in the 1990s. In 1994, kaka Hama died and his son, Sheikh Hawre, who also led the Haqqa unit of the peshmerga, became the new head of the community.

Present-day struggles

Currently, Sheikh Hawre and his family live in the communal house, with several (mostly elderly) murids still residing in their own quarters there. While numbers of residents and followers have gone down, they host visitors, especially during *Jazn* (Eid - Islamic holidays) when still about a thousand people visit the *khanaqa* and join in a communal meal. Visitors include current followers, the families of former followers, and guests from other sects or orders.[39] While helping others is still at the forefront of the Haqqa teachings, the once 'unorthodox' ideas that were introduced, such as equality and women's rights, have appeared elsewhere in society, leaving the *khanaqa* with a more mainstream Sunni character. As much of the urban and rural make-up of Kurdistan has changed, *zikr* is not performed communally anymore, and no Sufis are left in the *khanaqa*. The decline in followers can be attributed to political affiliation taking over former patron-client structures in the region, or as Sheikh Hawre puts it 'people are too busy in their lives now, but we serve the community in the way we can'. The movement's character has changed with the disappearance of the communal and religious factors.

The khanaqa in Kalkasmaq village around the mid-twentieth century. (Family archive, courtesy of Kirmanj Askari)

---

[39] For example, followers of the Baha'i religion frequent these areas as they believe their prophet had once resided in the mountains of this part of the Surdash region.

Askari

Screenshot from 'The Haqqa Handshake' (Dir. Lana Askari, 2014). *Murid* Hussein Hadji showing his room in the Kalkasmaq *khanaqa* with on the wall (f.l.t.r) a picture of Sheikh Kaka Hama, drawings of Mama Raza and Sheikh Abdulkarim, and two pictures of Hussein Hadji himself in his youth. (Lana Askari, Kalkasmaq, 2014).

Bomb left as a marker of history in Shadala village. Under the Ba'ath regime Kurdistan's rural areas were bombed and cleared to obstruct the guerrilla fighters in the mountains. (Lana Askari, Shadala, 2012).

The Haqqa Movement

Currently, the Kalkasmaq and Shadala *khanaqa* remain two separate branches with different leaders, Sheikh Hawre at Kalkasmaq and Sheikh Mahmood at Shadala, although they continue to share family ties. The sheikhs' families mainly own the lands, though the *khanaqa* continue to serve visitors and the Haqqa community. Political divisions within the branches have also created a split, as these affiliations come with funds and positions that secure the upkeep of the *khanaqa* estates—leading to inter-rivalry struggles about power over and the future of the Haqqa community. Both van Bruinessen[40] and Schmidinger[41] have raised the question of whether the Haqqa heterodoxy will remain intact or will develop in new ways. At present, the loss of followers, the halt in Sufi rituals and the decline of communal farming and living have led the Haqqa to resembling the more mainstream Islamic orders in Iraqi Kurdistan; the *khanaqa* now serves as a guesthouse for visitors who come during Islamic holidays or visit the pilgrimage sites.

In conclusion, while the Haqqa movement grew out of a messianic heterodoxy in the twentieth century, it went through different waves of change before it eventually returned to mainstream Islam in the twenty-first century. The Haqqa started under Sheikh Abdulkarim, whose teachings of equality and peacefulness were deemed unorthodox. Trying to create a better existence for people, the movement attracted thousands of followers in rural Iraqi Kurdistan. This first stage of the Haqqa lay the grounds for Abdulkarim's successor, Mama Raza, to develop the movement towards more socialist ideas of collective living and gender equality, which they called *xushek ew brayati*. Inevitably, these two stages cannot be separated with what was happening in the rest of the world, the spread of anti-colonial sentiments and non-violent protest, and the development of communism and socialism. With the Kurdish nationalist struggle intensifying from the 1960s onwards, the Haqqa joined the fight and thus this social-political movement was pulled back into larger Kurdish political structures. When the villages of Iraqi Kurdistan were bombed and cleared by the Iraqi military during the Ba'ath regime, the Haqqa also lost their villages. As rural areas were evacuated and Iraqi Kurdistan became urbanised in the past two decades, the political parties came to replace and incorporated tribal and religious affiliations into their patron-client structures. The Haqqa movement, as progressive as it was in its teachings, also became part of the larger political structures and lost its secular heritage, showing another example of fragmented Kurdishness in a once strong community that had sought to improve the lives of the rural poor.

---

[40] Martin van Bruinessen, *Agha, Sheikh and state: the social and political structures of Kurdistan*. (London: Zed books, 1992), 222-234.

[41] Thomas Schmidinger, 'The Haqqa Community: A Heterodox Movement with Sufi Origins' In *Religious Minorities in Kurdistan: Beyond the Mainstream*. Edited by Khanna Omarkhali. (Wiesbaden: Harrassowitz, 2014), 227–235.

CHAPTER 14

BAHAISM AND THE BAHAI COMMUNITY IN IRAQ: A FATEFUL PAST AND FRAGILE PRESENT

Maria Six-Hohenbalken

The Bahai community is one of the smallest religious communities in Iraq. As a transnational religion, Bahaism has its roots in Iran and neighbouring countries in the Middle East but today has seven million followers around the world with approximately 60 per cent living in Asia, 20 per cent in Africa, and 18 per cent in the Americas[1].

Although the Bahai have communities in several Middle Eastern states, they 'lack a strong regional base or close political connections with centres of power'[2]. Since the founding of the religion in the second half of the nineteenth century, Bahai have been living in various Iraqi towns and villages in which they could establish communities. In recent years, several have resettled in the Autonomous Region of Kurdistan Iraq, because of greater security and social stability[3].

In this chapter, I will briefly outline the shaping of the Bahai religion in Iran and its connections to today's Iraq and Kurdistan. Then I will briefly comment on the transnationalisation of Bahaism, before I stress the contemporary situation and political considerations in which a religious community can prosper in current Iraq and Kurdistan.

The formation of the Bahai religion between Iran and Iraq

Bahaism has its background in two earlier nineteenth-century movements, the Shia Shaikhism and Babism with its specific doctrines[4].

---

[1] Peter Smith, 'Bahaism: The Bahai Communities' *Encyclopedia Iranica* 3/5 (1988), 449-454. (published 15 December 1988) http://www.iranicaonline.org/articles/bahaism-iv.

[2] Juan R. I. Cole, 'The Baha'i Minority and Nationalism in Contemporary Iran' In *Nationalism and minority identities in Islamic societies*. Edited by Maya Shatzmiller. (Studies in nationalism and ethnic conflict. Montréal/Ithaca: McGill-Queen's University Press, 2005), 127-163: 130.

[3] Sa'ad Salloum, *Minorities in Iraq. Memory, Identity and Challenges*. (Baghdad/Beirut: Masarat for Cultural and Media development, 2013), 90f.

[4] For the emergence of Shaykhism and Babism, its doctrines, relatedness and history within Iranian Shi'ism see the dissertation of Denis Martin MacEoin, *From Shaykhism to Babism: A Study in Charismatic*

These movements developed during socioeconomic transformations and turmoil. Shaikhis[5] expected the return of the hidden Twelfth Imam in 1260/1844. In the 1840s, they joined the messianic Babi[6] movement rooted in Iran, when Sayyed ʿAlī-Moḥammad Šīrāzī announced himself as the 'gate' or the B*āb* of the Twelfth Imam. The Qajars reacted with extreme violence to this movement and sent troops to massacre the Babis and finally executed the Bāb.

Babism, a Shia movement preaching the coming of the Hidden Imam, also had adherents in the 1850s in the Kurdish regions. One of the earliest communities consisted of 5000 persons on the Ottoman Persian frontier, between Bâsh Qala and Qotur in Hakkari. This community did not spread in the following decades.

After the execution of the Bāb in 1850 and the pogrom following a Babi attempt to assassinate the Shah, the Babi movement suffered a leadership crisis. The titular leader was Mīrzā Yaḥyā, known as Ṣobḥ-e Azal, but from the mid-1860s the effective leader was Azal's elder brother, Bahāʾ-Allāh[7].

The Iranian notable and important Babi figure, Mīrzā Ḥosayn-ʿAlī Nūrī, 'Bahāʾ-Allāh' was imprisoned in Teheran and was later exiled to Iraq. In the 1850s, Bahāʾ-Allāh faced envy and hostility in Baghdad and decided to withdraw. In April 1854, he headed for the mountains around Silêmanî, where hardly anybody knew about his existence. There he lived two lunar years in disguise as a wandering dervish, but with connections to the local Naqshbandi Shaykhs. Due to the plight of the Babi community, he returned to Baghdad in May 1856. This retreat is today seen as a purification process[8], where he also wrote important poems and religious works. He spent two lunar years in retreat in the Kurdish mountains, mostly in the mountains of Sargalu close to Silêmanî. During his imprisonment in Teheran (1852) and his seclusion in Kurdistan, he had mystical experiences[9].

'None of Baháʾuʾlláh's followers shared his self-imposed exile and, consequently, no comprehensive history of those days is left to posterity'[10]. He and the Sunni Naqšbandī Shaikhs both belonged to nineteenth-century reformist tendencies. Both argued for the elimination of non-revelatory accretions to the pure Faith of Muhammad, e.g. the blind imitation (*taqlid*) or the doctrine of existential monism[11].

Renewal in Shīʿī Islam. (Cambridge: King's College, 1979).

[5] For the mystical cosmology, see Juan R. I Cole, 'The World as Text: Cosmologies of Shaykh Ahmad al-Ahsaʾi' *Studia Islamica* 80 (1994), 145-163.

[6] Within the Shīʿī communities, the Bâb is seen as the senior disciple of the Imâm. The last Imâm is assumed to be in Ghaybah (absence/ concealment), thus the Bâb is 'The Gate' to the Hidden Imam.

[7] John Walbridge 'Baha'i Faith' In *Encyclopedia of Islam and the Muslim world*. Edited by Richard C. Martin. (New York: Macmillan Reference 2004b), 100-101, 100.

[8] Bijan Maʾsumián, 'Baháʾuʾllá's Seclusion in Kurdistan' *Deepen Fall* (1993), 18-26, 21.

[9] In Kurdistan Bahāʾ-Allāh composed the poem 'Ode of the Dove' (Ar.: al-Qasida al-Waʾarqdʾi~ah) in which he referred to the mystical experiences during his retreat Peter Smith, *A Concise Encyclopedia* (Oxford: One World, 1999), 263.

[10] Bijan Maʾsumián, 'Baháʾuʾllá's Seclusion in Kurdistan' *Deepen Fall* (1993), 18-26, 18.

[11] Ibid., 24.

Back in Baghdad in the early 1860s, Bahā'-Allāh announced to a few adherents that he was the messianic figure promised by the Bab. The Bahai acknowledge the founding of their religion from Bahā'-Allāh in April 1863 with the private declaration in Baghdad.

'By the end of the 1870s those who had accepted the claim of Baha'allah were the large majority and came to be known as Bahais. A smaller number, the Azalis, stayed loyal to Subh-e Azal and vociferously opposed Baha'allah. A few accepted neither claim.'[12]

Bahá'u'llá was forced to move to Ottoman Turkey and went into exile in Edirne. There he 'publicly proclaimed his divine mission by sending letters to many of the world's leaders, thus formally renouncing Islam and launching the Bahai Faith'.[13] Due to these claims, the Ottoman representatives imprisoned him in Palestine, near Akka. He died in 1892 and Akka became one of the main religious centres. His writings and works include commentary on scripture, Baha'i law, comments on current affairs, prayers, and theological discussions of all sorts. (…) grounded in the esoteric Shia thought of the Bab (…)'[14].

Bahai today consider Bahā'-Allāh as a 'manifestation of God' and in line with the prophets Moses, Zoroaster, Jesus, and Muhammad.

Bahā'-Allāh had appointed his eldest son 'Abbās Effendi 'Abd-al-Bahā' as his successor, who established the institutional structure for the denomination (election of governing communities, thus spiritual assemblies). Already in the last decades of the nineteenth century, Bahaism spread from Iraq to Iran, Anatolia, Ottoman Syria, Egypt, Sudan, the Caucasus, Turkish Central Asia, India, and Burma. It is a very early example of a transnational religion fostered and spread by Iranian expatriates. The early Bahai community consisted almost entirely of former Muslims, who had belonged to the *ulamá*. Most of the perceptions were drawn from the Iranian Muslim milieu in which they lived.

In the decades up to the 1920s, Bahaism spread to Tunisia, Egypt, the Middle East, North America, Europe, East and Southeast Asia, South Africa, the Americas, and Australia[15]. The plans for a global expansion were realised in the first half of the twentieth century. In Iran, the Bahai continued to spread their religion, but faced several major persecutions (see below). 'Since its inception in 1979, the Islamic Republic of Iran has, despite denials and explanations, demonstrated every intention of destroying the Bahai community altogether. It has gradually and systematically confiscated all Bahai properties and investment companies, fired Bahai civil servants, dissolved all Bahai national and local

---

[12] John Walbridge 'Baha'allah (1817 – 1892)' In *Encyclopedia of Islam and the Muslim World*. Edited by Richard C. Martin. (New York: Macmillan Reference, 2004a), 99-100,100.

[13] Juan Campo, *Encyclopedia of Islam*. (New York: Facts on File, 2008), 85.

[14] John Walbridge 'Baha'allah (1817 – 1892)' In *Encyclopedia of Islam and the Muslim World*. Edited by Richard C. Martin. (New York: Macmillan Reference, 2004a), 99-100: 99f.

[15] Juan Cole, 'Bahaism. The Faith' *Encyclopaedia Iranica* 3/4 (1988), 438-446. (published 15.12.1988). http://www.iranicaonline.org/articles/bahaism-i (accessed on 30 December 2012). John Walbridge, 'Bha'allah (1817 – 1892)' In *Encyclopedia of Islam and the Muslim World*. Edited by Richard C. Martin. (New York: Macmillan Reference, 2004a), 99-100: 99f.

Spiritual Assemblies, and executed nearly two hundred of the country's most active and prominent Bahais.'[16] It is forbidden to practice rituals, to teach the religion to children, to donate money for the international organization and members face surveillance and control[17]. In more recent years, Bahai students were expelled from universities or barred from higher education[18]. In other states of the Near East where Islam influences state structures, Bahai are seen as heretics[19] and face persecution, or at least special control (e.g. Yemen).

Bahai beliefs developed in line with nineteenth century religious movements to simplify theology[20]. The Bahai elaborated a doctrine that enlarged the circle of ethics and transformed a religious ideology into human ethical principles. In the Bahai's creed, God is a totally transcendent, his existence cannot be recognised, so in this sense Bahais are against mystical traditions. Prophets are a form of a divine manifestation. Bahais acknowledge Jewish, Christian and Muslim prophets, Mohammad was followed by the prophet B*āb*, who was followed by Baha Allah.

Among the main sacred places of the Bahai are the places where Bahā'-Allāh lived; thus in Iraq it is the house in which he lived in Baghdad in al-Karkh[21] after being exiled from Iran and today of course the place of his last exile in Akka.

Bahaism introduces three closely interrelated types of unity: unity of the Creator; unity of religions in terms of origin, source and goals; and unity of the human race[22]. Bahais express that all religions share one truth, so the followers are encouraged to read the other divine books.

They also seriously promote international standards of human rights believing that human rights are an inseparable part of religious duties, they stress the necessity of cooperation among people, the need for comprehensive education and combating ignorance and illiteracy.

Bahais do not have any professional religious leaders, posts, or positions. The administration of the religion is managed by the Universal House of Justice, which is elected among the adherents. Bahais do not have public rituals or sacraments; adherents have the duty to join the community assembly every nineteenth day. The most important principles are moral and social education, gender equality, and the refusal of any kind of prejudice.

---

[16] Juan Cole, 'Bahaism. The Faith' *Encyclopaedia Iranica* 3/4 *(1988)*, 438-446.

[17] See Denis Martin MacEoin, 'Bahaism. Bahai persecutions' *Encyclopedia Iranica* 3/5 (1988), 461-464. (published 15.12.1988) http://www.iranicaonline.org/articles/bahaism-vii (accessed 15.08.2018).

[18] Human Rights Watch, 'Why They Left. Stories of Iranian Activists in Exile' *HWR* (published 13 December 2012) https://www.hrw.org/report/2012/12/13/why-they-left/stories-iranian-activists-exile (accessed 15 August 2018).

[19] Gordon D. Newby, *A Concise Encyclopedia of Islam*. (Oxford: One World, 2004 [2002]), 39.

[20] See Sa'ad Salloum, *Minorities in Iraq. Memory, Identity and Challenges*. (Baghdad/Beirut: Masarat for Cultural and Media development, 2013), 93 f.

[21] Ibid.

[22] Juan Cole, 'Bahaism. The Faith' *Encyclopaedia Iranica 3/4* (1988), 438-446. (published 15.12.1988) http://www.iranicaonline.org/articles/bahaism-i (accessed: 30.12.2012). Sa'ad Salloum, *Minorities in Iraq. Memory, Identity and Challenges*. (Baghdad, Beirut: Masarat for Cultural and Media development, 2013), 94.

Bahai in Iraqi history

One of the eldest Bahai community is in Iraq, which dates back since the 1850s. Bahai sources estimate that by the end of the nineteenth century, up to 5,000 Bahais had lived in Iraq, mainly in Baghdad. Restrictive policies caused that number to gradually decrease in the last century.

A community was founded in 1931 and a spiritual assembly was elected in 1934. During the times of the monarchy, Bahais managed to officially declare their identity. In the following years, they could establish the first central Bahai forum in the al-Sa'doun region[23]. Since the 1950s, the Bahai possessed a cemetery in the New Baghdad district, called the 'eternal garden.' Also, the Iraqi government registered the Bahai religion in the 1957 census. After the fall of the monarchy, restrictions and repressions gradually started. During the reign of the Baath regime, the Bahai experienced violent persecutions. Assemblies were closed, and laws were enacted to forbid Bahaism. In the late 1970s, everybody promoting the Bahai religion was sentenced to death[24].

Already in 1970, the Bahai religion was officially banned, the adherents were deprived of all their property and there was a legal prohibition to register the religion in civil records. Traces of the religion had to be extinguished from existing records and they were subsumed under the officially acknowledged religions, mainly under Islam. Members of the community faced imprisonment; political and religious representatives were sentenced to death at the end of the 1970s. 'In 1979, when Saddam Hussein assumed power, the law prohibiting Bahaism was amended and the punishment was increased to life imprisonment, and to execution in case of repeating the prohibited activities.' [25]

Law No. 105 of 1970 prohibits the Bahai faith, and the Regulation 358 of 1975 prohibited the issuance of a nationality identity card to those claiming the Bahai faith. Without this official citizenship card, people could not register their children for school or acquire passports.

The Minority Rights Group International, in its report in October 2014 refers to this rule 'Consequently, unless they made false statements about their religious beliefs and denied their identity, the Bahai could not acquire identity documents, passports, or birth, death and marriage certificates. In 2007, the Ministry of Interior repealed Rule No. 358. Thereafter, a number of Bahais managed to obtain ID cards stating 'Bahai' in the field of religion. However, Law No. 105 of 1970 was never revoked. Some Bahai were afraid to indicate their true religion on their identity cards as this could open them to discrimination in their dealings with government officials.'[26] In 2007, the Ministry of Interior again stopped the issue of Bahai identity cards, citing a law which prohibits conversion away from Islam, which hit those who had previously stated Islam as their religion when

---

[23] Sa'ad Salloum, *Minorities in Iraq. Memory, Identity and Challenges*. (Baghdad/Beirut: Masarat for Cultural and Media development, 2013), 96.
[24] Ibid., 97.
[25] Ibid., 98.
[26] Minority Rights Group International and Ceasefire Centre for Civilian Rights, *From Crisis to Catastrophe: The situation of minorities in Iraq*. (London: Minority Rights Group International, 2014), 23.

they obtained identity documents.

Concurrently with the tremendously difficult developments for the Bahai in Saddam Hussein's Iraq in the late 1970s, the situation in Iran deteriorated seriously, especially since the revolution of 1979. In the first years of the regime, 200 Bahais were executed, several imprisoned, their properties were destroyed, and the community was harassed as 'enemies of Islam' or agents of foreign powers, so many were forced to seek refuge.[27] This risky situation made Bahais either to hide themselves or try to emigrate from Iraq.

Bahai in Iraq after the fall of Saddam Hussein

Despite the openness that followed the fall of deposed president Saddam Hussein's regime in 2003, Bahais in Iraq were still hiding and fearing to publicly declare their religion. In the years after the Saddam regime, the Bahai religion was officially banned and Bahais were not allowed to list their religion on civil records. They had not regained their confiscated property and the decisions issued against them had not been revoked.

Only in April 2007 at the governmental level, 'the Nationality and Passports Department of the Ministry of Interior abolished (....) Decision No. 358 of 1975 which prohibited giving a national ID card to Bahais. In May 2007, ID cards were given to a few Bahais, but this was suspended under the pretext that Bahais have been registered as Muslims since 1975 and there is a government law that prevents Muslims to convert to another religion.'[28]

There are no official statistics on Bahais in Iraq, their exact number remains unknown. The Bahai community estimates they have about 2000 followers in Iraq[29], approximately 100 families in the community in Silêmanî [Sulaimaniya] and also in Duhok and in Erbil. In Iraq's Autonomous Region Kurdistan, Bahais seem to feel safer and more stable than Bahais in Baghdad, although they hardly dared to practice their faith publicly. In recent years, the situation seems to have improved slightly.

In 2011, the Iraqi Culture Ministry declared as a heritage site the house inhabited by Bahā'-Allāh when he was in Baghdad. The location previously had been a Shia ceremonial hall. Despite the violence and exclusion practiced against Bahais, a recent set of legal and religious developments serve the interests of Bahais and improve their social status, despite the slow legal progress.

Since 2014, the so-called Islamic State in Iraq has targeted those religious

---

[27] Juan Cole, *Sacred Space and Holy War. The Politics, Culture and History of Shi'ite Islam*. (London/New York: Tauris, 2002).

[28] Sa'ad Salloum, *Minorities in Iraq. Memory, Identity and Challenges*. (Baghdad/Beirut: Masarat for Cultural and Media Development, 2013), 99.

[29] see also US State Department, *International Religious Freedoms Report for 2014, Iraq, Section 1: Religious Demography*. Report. (published 14.10.2015) http://www.state.gov/j/drl/rls/irf/2014/nea/ 238456.htm (accessed 26.07.2016).

minorities seen as heretics in their extreme orthodox religious concepts. Therefore, Bahai and others such as Yazidis or Christians became one of the most vulnerable groups.

Bahai in the Kurdistan Region of Iraq

In 2015, the Kurdistan region recognised the Bahai as a religious minority. 'The Kurdistan Region's Ministry of Endowment and Religious Affairs has announced that Jews, Zoroastrians, Kakai and Bahais will have representatives in the Ministry to manage their religious activities in the future,'[30] following confirmation by the Kurdistan Regional Government (KRG) and according to the constitution. But concern was raised that not all the minority groups living in the KRI are specifically named by the law. Article 1 of the law has the overarching general clause, which does not name the groups but subsume it in the general category 'other groups'. A critique was raised that the law should mention each ethnic and religious minority group in order to grant effective protection for everyone.

Recently the Ministry of Endowment and Religious Affairs has installed, besides the two Directorates for Minority Affairs for Yezidi and Christians, an additional seven religious representatives, including one representing the Bahai community[31].

In 2017, after decades of suppression and invisibility the Bahai celebrated publicly the bicentennial of the birth of Bahā'-Allāh, the founder of the Bahai faith, in a ceremony in Baghdad. This ceremony was attended by state representatives, the Iraqi High Commission for Human Rights (IHCHR), United Nations representatives, and the civil society.[32] This ceremony has, of course, not only national importance, but overall importance for the transnational Bahai community because Baghdad has a special meaning in Bahai history. Bahā'-Allāh was exiled there from Tehran before he was exiled again in Istanbul and Edirne and sent to his last exile in Akka. The participants of the ceremony argued and explained the necessity to abolish all the laws prohibiting Bahai activities. Also, in 2017, during the Naw Rúz (Nowruz in traditional Persian cultures) festivities in Baghdad, the Bahai community could celebrate publicly after decades of covert commemorations. Naw Rúz is an important religious holiday because it ends the 19-day fast and marks the beginning of the Bahai year. The Bahai have launched a 'social dialogue initiative' that should establish a foundation for

---

[30] 'Kurdistan Region of Iraq recognizes Bahais as religious minority' *Bas News*, (published 24.08.2015) sensday.wordpress.com/2015/11/02/kurdistan-region-of-iraq-recognizes-bahais-as-religious-minority.

[31] Crispin M.I. Smith / Vartan Shadervian, *Wilting in the Kurdish Sun. The Hopes and Fears of Religious Minorities in Northern Iraq*. Report for the United States Commission on International Religious Freedom 2016. (Washington: United States Commission on International Religious Freedom, 2017).

[32] Sa'ad *Salloum*, 'After decades of suppression, Baha'is celebrate publicly in Baghdad' *Al Monitor*, (published 18.12.2017). http://www.iraq-businessnews.com/2017/12/18/after-decades-of-suppression-bahais-celebrate-publicly-in-baghdad/ (accessed 15.08.2018).

dialogue and coexistence in all components of Iraqi society.³³

In Kurdistan Iraq, the intermediary stay of Bahā'-Allāh³⁴ is not forgotten either in the Bahai community or in the Kurdish communities. In his book, *Iqân*, Bahā'-Allāh paints a vivid and interesting picture of his retreat in the Kurdish mountains. The adherents today see this retreat, like with Buddha, Moses, Jesus, and Muhammad before him, as a prelude to a mission to reform the human condition. Mehrdad R. Izadys explains that most important works of Bahai literature, such as J.E. Esslemont's *Bahâ'ullâh and the New Era*, have been translated into the dialects of Sorâni (by Husein Jawdat) and Gurâni. Izady stressed that there are several affinities with Kurdish religious and social values and tradition, such as the celebration of Naw Rúz, the practice of a mandatory ritual communal gathering at *Mahfels*, similar to the ceremony of the Cem of the Alevis, the transgression of the soul, a transcendent god, and an angelology (paralleled in the Yazidi belief).³⁵

A vulnerable minority

In general, the Bahai have a fragile situation in Iraq with legal issues only one concern. The minorities such as the Bahai are most vulnerable and people are affected by the developments and situations for their co-religionists in neighbouring countries, such as in Iran and other countries in the Middle East. Especially in Saddam Hussein's times, provocative writings against Bahais, which fuelled the public opinion against them. They were accused of undermining religion, of preaching atheism, of supporting colonialism and Zionism. Still today, the Bahai in Iraq, as well as in Silêmanî, fear consequences when receiving news from other Middle Eastern countries, such as in 2013 when a Bahai in Yemen was arrested, tortured, and accused of espionage for Israel.³⁶ Prejudice, strategies of exclusion, and public hate speech from extremist religious leaders in public still exist.³⁷

---

[33] Sa'ad *Salloum*, 'Nowruz becomes opportunity for dialogue in Iraq' *Bas News*, (published 21.03.2017). https://www.academia.edu/32941263/Nowruz_becomes_opportunity_for_dialogue _in_ Iraq (accessed 24.08.2018).

[34] Michael Curtotti, 'Bahá'u'lláh in Kurdistan: The Holy Man on the Mountain' *Beyond Forgiveness*, (published 17 April 2017) https://beyondforeignness.org/3473 (accessed 15.08.2018).

[35] Mehrdad R.Izady, *The Kurds: A Concise Handbook*. (Washington, D.C.: Crane Russak 1992).

[36] Lana Khalid, 'Baha'is in Kurdistan Region fear false allegations against their religion' *Kurdistan Tribune*, (published 13 February 2015) https://kurdistantribune.com/bahais-kurdistan-region-fear-false-allegations-against-their-religion/ (accessed 9.4.2019).

[37] see: Saad Salloum, 'Following controversial video leak, Iraq minorities seek to address hate speech' *Al Monitor*, (published 18.05.2017 with a reference to http://www.al-monitor.com/ pulse/originals/ 2017/05/iraq-minorities-hate-speech-shiite-endowment-jihad.html#ixzz4hvHNhN1N.

CHAPTER 15

KURDISH ZOROASTRIANS: AN EMERGING MINORITY IN IRAQ

Matthew Travis Barber

A significant movement of apostasy from Islam is underway in the Middle East, one that is simultaneously birthing a new religious minority. Kurdistan is experiencing a gradually intensifying revival of Zoroastrianism as increasing numbers of Kurds are converting to the tradition or affiliating with it at varying levels.

The following concise profile of that part of the movement that is emerging in Iraqi Kurdistan ("South Kurdistan" in Kurdish nationalist discourses) is based upon research involving a combination of textual sources that provide a historical contextualisation of the movement's origins and ethnographic data (procured in 2014 and subsequent years) that has made possible an analysis of the movement in the present. A longer forthcoming work will more fully present this research in order to elaborate on the themes surveyed briefly here.

Though no data exists regarding the number of converts, members of the movement believe that several thousand Kurds within Iraqi Kurdistan alone have already converted to Zoroastrianism. Many participate in official conversion ceremonies while others undergo conversion as a private shift of allegiances and/or spiritual orientation. Kurdish apostasy from Islam and identification with Zoroastrianism has been occurring inside of Iraq, Turkey, and Iran since at least the 1990s, often manifesting as individual responses to the nationalist writings of Kurdish intellectuals. These isolated conversions were often unconnected to any organized community of Kurdish Zoroastrians; in the 2000s, however, informal networks began to develop that brought these believers and affiliates together. Interest in Zoroastrianism among diaspora Kurds steadily increased over the same period and in 2012 a Kurdish Zoroastrian temple was opened in Sweden, which is home to a significant Kurdish diaspora. The movement in Iraq is now gaining increased momentum; in 2015, local Zoroastrian converts, empowered by Kurdish diaspora Zoroastrians, were able to secure legal recognition from the Kurdistan Regional Government (KRG) for the minority. This is a significant advancement in the public viability of the movement in that it provides, theoretically, a legal status for Kurdish affiliates with Zoroastrianism; however, this is not a straightforward matter because legal ambiguities regarding apostasy from Islam will continue to postpone any smooth resolution to questions regarding the emergence of a new religious community. Nevertheless, Kurds continue to join the movement and as this process persists, Islamic factions in the Kurdistan Region have been vocal in condemning the movement and have fomented opposition to it; consequently, converts to Zoroastrianism have been targeted with violence and persecution.

The phenomenon of Kurdish conversions to Zoroastrianism owes its intellectual foundation to nationalist discourses that evolved over the course of the twentieth century. The belief among Kurds that their ancestors were Zoroastrian or were connected to traditions related to Zoroastrianism precedes twentieth-century Kurdish nationalism, but it was in the twentieth century that the idea began to develop and become featured in nationalist discourses about Kurdish origins and heritage.

Most Kurdish nationalists who began to conceptualize a Kurdish Zoroastrian past were heavily influenced by Marxism and viewed the tradition as one of symbolic cultural value rather than as a religious tradition to be revived in practice. For them, Zoroastrianism was a historical vessel bearing (and in turn expressing) the core traits and values that define an essential character of the Kurdish people; in practice, Zoroastrianism was a largely blank canvas onto which they could project all noble attributes of the imagined Kurdish essence. However, a minority of these nationalists also saw potential in Zoroastrianism as a religious tradition that could be actively taken up and practiced and that could constitute a source of spirituality.

These two trends of Kurdish nationalist thought on Zoroastrianism have their respective counterparts within the current conversion movement, which contains, on the one hand, atheists and agnostics who adopt "Zoroastrian" as what they perceive to be a more authentic cultural identifier than "Muslim" and, on the other hand, believers who embrace Zoroastrianism as a theistic tradition. These two groups share a set of similar nationalist concerns and the desire to find an alternative to Islam, whether strictly for purposes of identity or as a faith tradition. The fact that nonbelievers and believers can be united under a single inclusive canopy speaks to the unique cohesiveness and flexibility of the conversion movement. Many converts inhabit an intermediary position between the atheist–theist poles, embracing Zoroastrianism as a kind of lived philosophical tradition that provides spiritual wisdom, awareness of the self, an enhanced connection to life and the universe, and a healthier relationship with nature and the planet. For those in this intermediary position, this philosophical approach can be presented as a purely moral or intellectual orientation, or in a more divine cast but which remains devoid of a personified god who makes arbitrary rules and demands of complex ritualistic behaviors.

The above description of the ethnonationalist underpinnings of the Zoroastrian conversion movement should not be construed as casting doubt on the potential legitimacy of the newly-adopted tradition for practitioners. People join religious traditions for a variety of reasons; their relationships with those traditions often evolve and develop after having embraced them. Kurdish nationalism may be the vehicle responsible for bringing converts to Zoroastrianism, but these converts are now engaging with the scriptural texts of a discursive tradition. Since Zoroastrianism is often thought of only in relation to the ancient world, there is a tendency to reflexively view a contemporary Zoroastrian revival movement as something based in pure nostalgia. But converts to Zoroastrianism are now interacting with and receiving religious instruction from the born-adherents of living Zoroastrian communities that comprise peoples of the present. On this basis, I opt not to use the term "neo-Zoroastrian,"[1] a label that might (unintentionally) convey a sense of reduced legitimacy or imply the existence of a barrier separating longer-established Zoroastrian communities from those who have more recently chosen to take up the faith. We need not call converts to Zoroastrianism "neo-Zoroastrians" any more than we would call converts to Christianity or Islam "neo-Christians" or "neo-Muslims," respectively.

Most converts have apostatized from Islam and harbor deep antipathy toward it, linking Islam to the legacy of oppression under Arab regimes. The dissociation from Islam that occurs through the conversion process is part of the forging of a new narrative of the self as more authentically Kurdish. However, the converts' adoption of Zoroastrianism is not solely about embracing an identity that affirms their nationalist sentiments but is often simultaneously characterized by spiritual motivations. Many converts are genuinely attracted to the spirituality of Zoroastrianism, which they find personally meaningful. This growing affinity for Zoroastrianism among Kurds seems to be propelled by a mixture of the influence of Kurdish nationalist thought and a personal search for spiritual growth.

Beyond an avenue for personal spiritual development, many converts also view Zoroastrianism as a tradition that can provide wisdom for life and new ethical resources for constructing a rejuvenated morality. In this way, they aspire to transform a society that they experience as corrupt, intolerant, prejudicial, and unequal for women. A theme of casting off intricate and purposeless ritual features prominently in the discourses of converts, but this should not be misinterpreted as a mere quest for permissiveness. Rather, the

---

[1] Used in Edith Szanto, "'Zoroaster Was a Kurd!': Neo-Zoroastrianism Among the Iraqi Kurds' *Iran and the Caucasus* 22 (2018).

converts conceptualize Zoroastrianism as an other-centered moral framework that can reorient practitioners toward humanity and the planet. Harmony with nature, care for the environment, and the cultivation of a compassionate consciousness are motifs that characterize the converts' interpretation of Zoroastrianism; converts speak enthusiastically about a central three-fold doctrine of Zoroastrianism—good thoughts, good words, good deeds—and often frame their new conception of divinity in terms of the practice of these three principles.

Another chief concern within the convert movement is the securing of a recognized legal status for a viable alternative to Islam. Some members of the movement who belong to its atheist "wing" have chosen to affiliate with Zoroastrianism because they wish to dissociate from Islam but are unable to profess atheism as a public identity in Iraq; they see Zoroastrianism, therefore, as the only alternative available to them. Legal recognition at the state level is also of paramount importance to the converts who approach Zoroastrianism in theistic or spiritual terms.

A step toward legal recognition was achieved by the Kurdish Zoroastrian community in the form of KRG "Law No. 5 of 2015, Protecting the Rights of Components [the term commonly used to refer to minorities] of Kurdistan, Iraq." This law is referred to less formally as the "Law of Minority Rights." It is the first law in Iraq to extend recognized status to Zoroastrians; however, the law is only effective in the Kurdistan Region and does not apply to the country as a whole.

The passing of the Law of Minority Rights enabled the Kurdish Zoroastrians to institutionalize their leadership through the creation of an official body and to secure governmental representation through the KRG's Ministry of Religious Endowments (*awqāf*) and Affairs, which is responsible for interfacing with the leadership of religious groups, including religious minorities, and managing their interactions with the government. Unsurprisingly, however, this young religious movement has already been targeted with governmental attempts at politicization and co-optation.

A common strategy employed by Kurdish political parties to maintain political hegemony is a system of financial patronage.[2] Through this system, "salaries" are provided to a community's important religious, tribal, and civic leaders, as well as to other figures among its educated elites. This tactic has particularly deleterious effects for vulnerable religious minorities who—rather than being able to mind their own affairs in a nonpartisan manner—are often forced into the patron-client dynamic and made to choose sides by affirming loyalty to a patron. Since most of northern Iraq's religious minorities live in areas that (after 2003) have been under the control of the

---

[2] See Reine Hanna / Matthew Barber, *Erasing Assyrians: How the KRG Abuses Human Rights, Undermines Democracy, and Conquers Minority Homelands*. (n.p.: Assyrian Confederation of Europe, 2017).

Kurdistan Democratic Party (PDK[3]), it is the PDK's approach to patronage that is particularly relevant. When a community leader accepts financial compensation from a political party that dominates—and therefore ultimately comprises—the government, this has the result of eliminating potential criticism of government policy that may be adversarial to the minority population that comprises the leader's constituency. The financial patronage system, therefore, constitutes the purchasing of loyalty and silence in regards to potential governmental abuses of political and human rights. This results in a sense of abandonment among many minority populations who experience the absence of political representation that will speak on their behalf and accurately articulate their interests. The PDK's clientelism has produced especially destructive consequences for the Yazidi and Assyrian minorities, most of whose bishops and other religious leaders have opted in to the patronage system and are therefore seen as politically illegitimate by much of their congregations.[4]

Beyond the problems of political representation that result from the patronage system, the policy also has an adverse impact on religion and spirituality because it obstructs the organic development of an authentic religious leadership that can be viewed by practitioners as genuinely committed to their well-being and spiritual care. The Ministry of Religious Endowments and Affairs is responsible for designating figures that represent the respective religious communities in the Ministry. These figures then carry the responsibility of securing governmental approval for a community's various religious activities, including the construction of places of religious worship. Through this official mechanism, the PDK (which currently controls this Ministry) is able to legitimize a faction within the particular minority community that is sympathetic to its policies, a sympathy that is usually procured through purchased loyalty, as described. This process can ultimately validate particular expressions of theology while sidelining others. This approach has already been implemented in regard to the Zoroastrian minority as the PDK (beginning in 2015 following the passage of the Law of Minority Rights) began to back a particular Zoroastrian entity at the expense of more organic expressions of the organized Zoroastrian community. The organization that the PDK has chosen to promote, known as Yasna, does not broadly represent the developing spirituality of the converts but approaches Zoroastrianism more in terms of cultural symbolism to the detriment of spirituality. Moreover, the leader of the Yasna organization (who maintains political relations with both PDK and PUK) was unilaterally appointed by PDK authorities in 2015—without consulting other leaders of

---

[3] To maintain consistency with this volume's usage, I here use the initialism derived from the Kurdish form of the party's title rather than the more common English initialism "KDP."

[4] For additional ways that minorities in northern Iraq and the Kurdistan Region have been deprived of political agency, see Reine Hanna / Max J. Joseph, *Iraq's Stolen Election: How Assyrian Representation Became Assyrian Repression*. (n.p.: Assyrian Policy Institute, 2018).

the Zoroastrian community—to represent Zoroastrians in the Ministry of Religious Endowments and Affairs. The appointment was made immediately after Kemal Muslim, the Minister of Religious Endowments and Affairs and a Gorran party member, was ejected from office during the mass expulsion of Gorran officials from the government. He was replaced as minister by PDK member Pishtiwan Sadiq.

Following the general approach to minorities described here, since that time the government has readily approved the opening of Zoroastrian centers run by Yasna while denying this approval to other centers, including those with larger constituencies that possess the capacity to open and manage temples. In 2016, the first Zoroastrian temple to function in Erbil was shut down by PDK *asāīsh* in November, four months after its opening. Its directors were given the reason that no Zoroastrian center would be allowed to operate in Erbil, but this justification was contradicted by the fact that the Yasna center was allowed to open without hindrance and continues to operate today. Such political favoritism contravenes the pretense of religious freedom enshrined in the Law of Minority Rights.

Despite these serious challenges posed by political meddling, the recognized legal status afforded to Zoroastrianism by the Law of Minority Rights has increased, to a degree, the public legitimacy of the movement which has in turn emboldened larger numbers of Kurds to affiliate with Zoroastrianism. Nevertheless, an additional challenge is presented by the absence of clear positions of Iraqi law regarding apostasy; this problem will likely continue to produce complications as the movement grows. The Iraqi Civil Status Law No. 65 of 1972 specifies that a non-Muslim can change his or her religion, implying by omission that *only* a non-Muslim can change their religion.[5] The Iraqi Law of Personal Status No. 188 of 1959 states that while a Muslim man may marry a non-Muslim woman of the people-of-the-book, a Muslim woman may not marry any non-Muslim man.[6] The same law states that shariʿa provisions will be followed regarding the validity of a marriage of two non-Muslims if one spouse converts to Islam; since it is not permissible for a Muslim woman to be married to a non-Muslim man, the law implies that the marriage would be annulled if the wife of a non-Muslim man converts to Islam.[7] Though these provisions do not directly refer to apostasy, they set a precedent for strict adherence to shariʿa jurisprudence in matters of religious status. This, in fact, is established in the first article of the Personal Status Law, stating that in the absence of a clear legislative position on an issue, the ruling will follow the applicable shariʿa provision. A similar position is expressed by the Iraqi Constitution itself, which could call into question the legitimacy of legal recognition for Kurdish Zoroastrians if

---

[5] Civil Status Law No. 65 of 1972, Article 20.2.
[6] Law of Personal Status no. 188 of 1959, Article 17.
[7] Law of Personal Status no. 188 of 1959, Article 18.

the bulk of those adherents became Zoroastrians through apostasy.

Legal dilemmas surrounding apostasy are compounded through issues related to the Iraqi national ID card system. Every Iraqi is issued a national ID that indicates their religion. The ability to change this religious designation follows Islamic law as articulated by Iraqi Civil Status Law No. 65 of 1972, which allows a non-Muslim to convert to Islam. The federal government will issue a new ID card reflecting this change of religion but as a rule will not issue ID cards reflecting a change of status from Islam to another religion. More than any written law, the actual practice of the government in its procedures for identity documents clarifies its position on apostasy. This creates a paradoxical conflict in the legal context of the Kurdistan Region: the KRG's 2015 Law of Minority Rights affords a recognized status to Zoroastrians, yet no convert to Zoroastrianism can officially qualify for that recognition as they will never receive an ID card reflecting their new affiliation.

Despite these legal ambiguities, the more immediate factor determining whether a convert can be open about his or her new tradition is the culture of the individual family, as the family remains the most important unit of social regulation in Kurdish society. A spectrum of family responses has characterized the experiences of converts, from supportive to indifferent to disapproving to hostile.

In contrast with the impediments to conversion that characterize the Iraqi and Kurdish contexts, it is evident that existing Zoroastrian communities have warmed to the Kurdish conversion movement, despite certain segments of established Zoroastrian communities (namely those in Iran and Parsis in India) having maintained long-held proscriptions against accepting converts. Other Zoroastrian communities, especially those in the West, have begun offering training and assistance to Kurdish converts, and even some Iranian and Indian Zoroastrians have begun to extend spiritual support.

The conversions of Kurds to Zoroastrianism involve at once an experience of becoming a more truly authentic member of a national community and, for those who also approach Zoroastrianism as a new religious tradition to be embraced, the adoption of a new system of ethics, values, perspectives, and even spiritual practices. The Kurdish Zoroastrian movement has made some surprising strides forward in its quest to achieve viability and secure legitimacy. It will certainly face serious challenges in the future but is also the beneficiary of supportive elements in the Kurdish diaspora as well as segments of the Zoroastrian establishment. Because this religious community has rapidly coalesced and remains at a formative stage in its development, it provides a unique case for the study of religious conversion as well as the early evolution of religious movements.

CHAPTER 16

MIGRANT RELIGIONS IN IRAQ: HINDUS AND BUDDHISTS

Ghazwan Yousif Baho

Religions are the primary source of human thought that explore ways to achieve integrity for human society. They are dominated by principles of peaceful coexistence amongst all people, regardless of sect, religion or nationality. They enable humans to live peacefully with God and with others. This cannot be achieved except through love, which cannot be achieved without knowing people, which, again, cannot be achieved without dialogue.

Migrants come to Iraq with different religious backgrounds. Especially Kurdistan has had an influx of migrants from South and Southeast Asia. Thus, not only Muslims and Christians came to Iraq, but also Hindus and Buddhists. Until recently, Buddhism and Hinduism were alien to Iraq and these belief systems are still not officially recognised religions. However, these religions are likely to become as present as in the states of the Arab peninsula such as Qatar, Bahrain, the United Arab Emirates, and Oman that host Hindu and Buddhist temples and organised religious activities. So far, in Iraq, both religions are practiced in privacy. Nevertheless, labour immigrants from countries like Nepal, India, or Sri Lanka bring these religions to Iraq, in particular to the Kurdistan Region of Iraq.

This chapter will first provide a historical introduction to Hinduism and Buddhism. Then, it will discuss how these religions differ from others in terms of spirituality and belief and also in their social construct. After that, a description of the geographic location and the number of their adherents will help us understand their future in Iraq.

The Hindu Religion

Some sources state that Hinduism began with totemism, a belief system where descendants worshipped their forefathers. They practiced their belief using the elements of nature and worshipped all living and non-living things. Today's Hinduism combines different local religious traditions that vary greatly between different regions. European and Muslim observers created the term 'Hinduism'; it was not a self-designation. 'Hind', the Arab word for

Migrant Religions in Iraq: Hindus and Buddhists

India, more or less means simply 'the religion of India'.

What we call today Hinduism has its roots in two different religious traditions and cultural complexes, the Indus valley civilisation that peaked between 2500 BC and 1500 BC and the later Aryan culture which developed in the 2nd millennia BC and migrated to India from the northwest.[1]

The first book of the Hindu holy scripture, the Veda, was compiled in the beginning of the first century BC. Hinduism began to develop and rise when Brahman seers started to compile the religion and create what is referred to as 'Brahminism'. This was during the eighth century BC and was accompanied with the organisation of religion and its rituals, especially the ritual of offering animal sacrifice for the forefathers. Between the eighth and seventh centuries BC, the Vedic religion saw further development in the form of Brahman priests, spiritual and liturgical practices, and a rising need for civil and religious organisation.

The holy scriptures emerged between the sixth and fourth centuries BC and became known as the Upanishads. The texts discussed spiritual reincarnation and karma; they led to the founding of Buddhism and Jainism as two religions growing out of the Hindu religion between the sixth and fifth centuries BC.

Siddhartha Gautama is considered to be the founder of Buddhism. He was born in the sixth century BC in a small city located near the Himalayas north of the Ganga river. His father was the chief of the Shakya clan in present-day Nepal and his mother was Queen Maya. During his days of luxury and youth, he began to seek answers about the meaning of life and the essence of human pain that a human suffers throughout life. He did not find any answer to these questions and neither did he find a solution around him. After several spiritual meetings with a hermit, Gautama Buddha, at the age of twenty-nine years, decided to follow the teachings of this hermit and left his wife to turn towards asceticism. For six years, he contemplated the universe in the company of five comrades. With the passage of time, Gautama realised that he was liberated from all physical desires and limitations. His mind had been cleansed from unclean thoughts. He had reached a condition of ecstasy and bliss i.e. 'nirvana' here on earth. Since then, he became the 'Buddha' i.e. 'the enlightened one'. In a short time, he gathered sixty of his companions and sent them as leaders of delegations to spread his call and preach his message to the entire world. Buddha's teachings found fertile ground in the Ganga basin throughout the two centuries after he passed away. The number of monks and followers began to grow. Several members of the ruling class also joined the ranks of the Buddhist religion. Narrations state that around five hundred monks came together after the death of Buddha to recall and create a written record of all teachings of

---

[1] Gavin Flood, *An Introduction to Hinduism.* (Cambridge: Cambridge University Press, 1996), 23.

Buddha. This scripture came to be known as the Tipitaka which contained principles of worship, sayings and teachings of Buddha, on the one hand, and beliefs and laws, on the other.

Eventually, Buddhism spread widely, thanks to Emperor Ashoka who ascended the throne of Magadh in 273 BC and ruled most of the territory in the current Indian state. Ashoka grew up under the tutelage of Buddhist teachers. However, Ashoka's greatest achievement was his view of Buddhism as a world religion. As such, he can be called the second founder of Buddhism because he gave it a global perspective by persuading its monks and missionaries to spread the word beyond the territories of India. Ashoka personally oversaw the sending of Buddhist missionaries and ambassadors to neighbouring, as well as distant, places. In the land of its birth, Buddhism declined after the seventh century AD.

As regards Hinduism, the growth of spiritual movements known as Puja (meaning worship) began from the early seventh century AD lasting until the seventeenth century AD; similarly, Hindu rituals affirming equality between worship and spiritual matters were also introduced during that period. Secret Hindu spiritual movements also came to grow in the seventh century AD lasting till the eleventh century AD. However, in the fifteenth and sixteenth centuries, Vasco da Gama encountered India and then Portuguese forces stormed the southern areas of the Asian continent, which also opened the path for Catholic evangelists to India.

In the nineteenth century, religions such as Zoroastrianism, Buddhism, Christianity, and Islam had an impact on modern Hinduism. This can be seen in 'Brahmanism', the new movement initiated by Ram Mohan in Kolkata, which sought to affirm the oneness of God.

Hindus and Buddhists began to migrate into Iraq in the early 2000s after Iraq and the Kurdistan Province were opened to the world towards the end of the 2003 Iraq war. The spread of social media in recent years has led to more knowledge about these religions.

Characteristics of the Hindu and Buddhist Religions: Beliefs, Spiritual Dimensions and Holy Scriptures

Hindus believe in the caste system and claim that it has been decided through divine justice and is therefore strictly unchangeable. The holy books are called 'Vedas' which mean wisdom or divine knowledge. They are among the oldest books in the history of religion and are a huge collection of texts about gods, creation, reincarnation, and holy and forbidden things. The Vedas were originally oral teachings written in the ancient Sanskrit language during different periods in time. Around 900 BC, Hindu monks began to write these books now classified into four types: Rig Veda, Yajur Veda, Sama Veda, and Atharva Veda. They contain local Indian philosophies, spiritual hymns, epics of war, thousands of songs praising gods and monks, prayers, and supplications. Furthermore, they contain ancient songs and early liturgies of humans, acts of worshipping nature. They mention how the eternal soul in religion and spirituality helps humans rise to the level of nirvana. Vedas wield a strong influence on Buddhism, Jainism and Sikhism, religions which were transmitted orally generation after generation until they were preserved in scriptures to become a holy treasure for their believers. The most popular and important books for the Hindus are the Bhagavad Gita and the Brahma Sutra.

Hindus believes in God, the Absolute Creator, and many male deities (Devas) and female deities (Devis), which represent the One Absolute God. They are considered as images of God and the incarnation of his works. Hindus believe in practicing their rituals in religious structures and temples, and by visiting the holy river Ganga where gods live. The pilgrimage to this river purifies and cleanses from sins and misdeeds and endears the pilgrim to the gods. The remaining ashes of dead bodies are mostly immersed in this river, as it is considered one of the holiest places in their religion. Hindus also regard celestial bodies such as the sun, the moon, the stars, and animals such as monkeys and snakes, which have special sanctity, as their gods. Hinduism believes in one absolute existential truth, with its numerous dual and triple forms and their many bifurcations and incarnations with ideal spiritual flexibility. Hinduism believes that animals hold special significance. They do not see a difference between humans and animals, because both have a spirit, and a soul can get transferred among them according to the principle of reincarnation. The cow, for example, is consecrated with unparalleled sanctity among all animals; therefore, it enjoys absolute freedom of movement on roads, and there are even statues of it in houses and temples. It cannot be slaughtered; eating its meat or benefiting from its skin in industries is prohibited. It must be buried with respect. Hinduism believes in an infinite number of incarnations and divine manifestations since incarnations and divine manifestations will continue till the last day of existence. Birth, marriage, death, pilgrimage, fasting, prayer, charity, yoga, and reincarnation are considered among the secrets of Hinduism. The Republic of India uses the Gregorian calendar of the Catholic Church for the state's civil purposes. However, when practicing ancient religious and cultural traditions, people use the ancient Indian calendar based on the lunar year. Hinduism is characterised by its many festivals and great religious celebrations, accompanied by religious hymns and traditional Indian music. Hindus all over the world celebrate Mahashivratri as the day of the birth of god Shiva.

Buddha's Teachings

It is not possible to understand the teachings of Buddhism without an understanding of Hinduism. Buddha himself grew up in Hinduism, but he rejected their method of knowledge based on theorizing and on abstract metaphysical matters.² Buddha did not pay much attention to merely metaphysical issues, believing that advocating the conduct of righteousness in life was more important than engaging in such theoretical questions. Buddhism, for example, has stripped the universe of the concept of the eternal creator who controls everything. Therefore, Buddhism is often called 'the atheist religion' or 'the religion without God.' This is not entirely true, but there is some truth in this assertion. Buddha did not deny the existence of the Brahmin gods, but he considered them incapable of providing any assistance to humans: It is possible for a person to save himself from the torment of existence through his personal capacities, that is by renouncing existence itself. All these teachings are found in the four noble truths that Buddha received under the Holy Tree, which represent the basic doctrine and the positive order upon which he built his religious thought:

a) The truth of pain or suffering: At the core of human life there is continuous suffering, from the first moments of birth until death. 'Birth is a pain, old age is a pain, sickness is a pain, death is a pain, coming close to those we hate is a pain, distancing ourselves from what we love is a pain, the inability to achieve what we desire is a pain. Youth, health, love and satisfying desires are good things for the human self, but the self is evanescent and when it is gone we suffer.'

b) The reality of the origin of human suffering: The drift towards appetites, and the desire to meet them, is the root of suffering.

c) The reality to stop suffering: Ignorance and attachment to material things can be overcome and eliminated. This can be achieved by curbing the desires originating from the three roots of the evil nature, and thus eliminating them altogether.

d) The reality of the road leads to the cessation of suffering: The road consists of eight stages, called the Octuple Noble Path: Right understanding, sound thinking, right speech, fair work, honest livelihood, persistent effort, mindful attention, and finally, appropriate focus.

Buddha did not leave behind any text or book expressing his beliefs and opinions. Most Buddha teachings left to his followers were oral. After his death, his followers compiled and wrote down these teachings. The Buddhist writings, written in the first period, were arranged in three groups, known as the Tripitaka or the Three Baskets: Sutra Pitaka, Vinaya Pitaka, and Abhidharma Pitaka. Buddhism was divided over time into three major groups: Hinayana, which means the small wheel; Mahayana, which means the big wheel, and Vajrayana, which means the diamond wheel.

---

[2] Father Amir Georgy al-Dominici, 'Budhists' *Bayn al-Nahrayn Magazine* 170 (2015), 70.

The Geography of Hinduism and Buddhism and the extent of its existence and followers

Today, Hinduism is the world's third largest religion, after Christianity and Islam, with a global share of about 13%. The 10 largest Hindu states with their many denominations: Nepal 89%, India 79%, Mauritius 52%, Guyana 40%, Suriname 30%, Bhutan 25%, Trinidad and Tobago 24%, Sri Lanka 15%, and Bangladesh 11%.

Hinduism is practiced by 80% of India's population of over one billion people. They account for 96% of the world's Hindus. Hinduism is not the official religion of its mother country, India, which is officially a secular country. However, Nepal has declared Hinduism as the official religion; most Nepalese people follow this religion, but freedom of worship is guaranteed to all while forbidding conversion to other religions (through proselytisation).

Buddhism, the fourth largest religion in the world after Christianity, Islam and Hinduism, has more than 500 million followers, or 8% of the world's population. Buddhism emerged in India in the fifth century BC as a refutation of the class system created by the Brahmin religion, which gave special privileges to the priests and regarded them as the highest class of the society because they alone could influence the gods and deal with them through rituals and offerings. This led to the emergence of religious and philosophical movements which rejected this system. The most important among them were Jainism and Buddhism. These two religions emerged simultaneously and for the same purpose. Buddhism today has spread to China, Japan, Sri Lanka, Thailand, Cambodia, Vietnam, Tibet, Mongolia, Korea, Taiwan, Germany, Pakistan, Nepal, and some regions of India.

Indians in Iraq

The history of people in Iraq from the current state of India goes back to the British protectorate. The British Army in Iraq had Indian soldiers of different religious backgrounds. Many were Sihks, but also Muslim and Hindu soldiers participated in the conquest of Iraq during World War I.

Some soldiers stayed but also merchants and workers from India came to Iraq between the 1920s and 1950s. An Iraqi Indian recalls this period of Iraq´s history: 'Indians worked everywhere, in offices, in factories, in retail, bank and some even owned their own businesses. The less qualified worked as administrators and clerks. The more qualified held higher positions in oil companies.'[3]

This early Indian migration to Iraq was mainly towards Baghdad and Basra. Some Indians married Iraqis and became Iraqi citizens. Some Hindus

---

[3] Margo Kirtikar, *Once Upon a Time in Baghdad. Two Golden Decades. The 1940s and 1950s.* (Bloomington: Xlibris Corporation, 2011), 186.

converted to Islam or Christianity, others practised Hinduism in their homes.

However, this early Hinduism in Iraq did not survive. With Saddam Hussein's war against Iran, the economic decline of Iraq and the international sanctions against the country, Iraq was no longer attractive for labour immigrants. People who had passports other than the Iraqi passport fled the country as hundreds of thousands of Iraqis also fled the country.

The future of Hinduism and Buddhism in Iraq

There are more Hindus and Buddhists in the Near East than in Europe, America and Australia. However, their proportion in Iraq and particularly in the Kurdistan region is close to 0.001 %.

Several Arab states in the region such as Bahrain, Qatar, the United Arab Emirates, and Oman, have living Hindu and Buddhist communities,. The most established Hindu religious community on the Arab peninsula is in Oman; it dates to 1507 when Indian merchants from the Sindh region settled in Muscat.[4] The oldest Hindu temple still existing in Oman is from the nineteenth century in Muscat. However, some well-established communities have their own temples in Salalah and Sohar. Buddhists came to Oman much later, after the 1970s. Their only place of worship is inside one of the Hindu temples in the capital region.

The migration of Hindus to other states of the Arab peninsula is much more recent and connected with the oil boom and the need of foreign labour in the Arab Gulf in the second half of the twentieth century. Nevertheless, today there are Hindu temples in the Arab Emirates (Abu Dhabi and Dubai), in Qatar (Doha) and in Bahrain, where several temples exist around Manamah. Only in Saudi-Arabia, where every religion other than Islam is forbidden, Hindu and Buddhist workers are completely banned from practising their religion.

Bahrain hosts several temples of Sri Lankan Buddhists. Also, most Buddhists in the United Arab Emirates come from Sri Lanka. They have a small temple in the Mahamevnawa Buddhist Monastery in Dubai. The labour immigrants from India, Sri Lanka and Nepal will probably also create their own temples. Like in the Arab Gulf, most of the Buddhists in Iraq are from Sri Lanka. Thus, the Buddhism practised in Iraq is mainly Theravada Buddhism. Immigrants from India and Nepal predominantly practise Hinduism.

These migrations to Iraq has been too recent and the people are not established enough to ask for the creation of such a public temple. If they worship their religion, they do that with small family altars in their homes. However, this can change within the next years. The experience of the Arab

---

[4] Rebecca L.Torstrick / Elisabeth Faier, *Culture and Customs in the Arab Gulf States*. (Westport/London: Greenwood Press, 2009), 36.

Gulf shows that the establishment of temples needs time; but does go together with establishing a community.

The Hindu and Buddhist presence in the Kurdistan region has been increasing continuously for many reasons; this include the region's freedom of religion and freedom of expression among various religions and communities and the facilities provided to foreign workers, including airports, schools, hotels, restaurants and other places In addition, there has been a continuous opening of new consulates in the region, especially for Far Eastern countries. The second, and the most important, reason is the peaceful coexistence promoted by the provincial government towards all the religious communities living in the province. The third reason is the integration of foreigners in various fields of Kurdish life as they lived side by side with their Kurdish neighbours during the difficult ISIS aggression, which was suffered by different parts of Iraq such as Mosul and the Nineveh Plain. Finally, Kurdistan was not only safer than other parts of Iraq, but also economically more attractive for foreign workers. While the rest of Iraq suffered under insecurity, Kurdistan had an economic boom until 2014, when the so-called 'Islamic State' (ISIS) did not only threaten the live of Iraqis of all parts of Iraq, but also the economic stability of the Kurdistan region.

Thus, the largest group of adherents to Hinduism and Buddhism lives in Kurdistan today. However, this does not mean that they only live in the Kurdistan Region of Iraq. A sizeable number of Hindus from India and Nepal live in Baghdad. They do not have a temple, but as in Kurdistan they meet for certain Hindu religious festivals to worship their Hindu gods.[5] Although there is not yet any official temple, Hindu workers meet for important religious festivals. On Internet, one can find videos of Hindu ceremonies in Erbil, held at the residential compounds of Indian workers of the Erbil steel company at Guwer Road.[6] The workers have erected a small altar in their rooms to worship at home. These private meetings in Erbil and Baghdad might be the nuclei of future communities that could also erect official temples for their adherents.

Summary, Conclusion, and Epilogue

Hinduism and Buddhism have a long history spanning more than thirty centuries and are intertwined with the history of the world's most ancient countries in the ancient Far East, providing a religious, spiritual and social colour to the people they embrace, even to this day. They were able to establish temples with diverse traditions, languages and civilisations, most of which still exist.

---

[5] See for example this video of Indians workers celebrating Ganesh festival in Baghdad in 2006: https://www.youtube.com/watch?v=JKUw_ZN447M

[6] See for example: https://www.youtube.com/watch?v=QVrQjO1JAdw

We conclude from this long history that these religions, despite the tyrannies that have been inflicted on them since their inception until today, have still been able to establish a culture of tolerance and peace and coexistence in the countries in which they were conceived and from which they spread. These basic principles, according to which their founders lived their lives and preached, have been transferred to the entire world. The history of migrants from India to Iraq in the early twentieth century was interrupted by war, sanctions, and economic decline. Today, these religions are spreading in the Kurdistan region to participate with their spiritual brethren: Muslims, Christians, Yezidis, Sabian Mandaeans, and all other sects, in spreading their message of tolerance and coexistence within a society that believes in a culture of peaceful coexistence in accordance with the freedom of religion, of thought, and of expression. This would be fertile ground to permanently establish these religions and create temples for their future followers.

www.ingramcontent.com/pod-product-compliance
Lightning Source LLC
Chambersburg PA
CBHW051539230426
43669CB00015B/2659